# Palgrave Studies in Maritime Economics

**Series Editors**
Hercules Haralambides
Erasmus School of Economics
Erasmus University Rotterdam
Rotterdam, The Netherlands

Elias Karakitsos
EN Aviation & Shipping Research Ltd
Athens, Greece

Stig Tenold
Department of Economics
NHH – Norwegian School of Economics
Bergen, Norway

Palgrave Studies in Maritime Economics is a new, original and timely interdisciplinary series that seeks to be pivotal in nature and improve our understanding of the role of the maritime sector within port economics and global supply chain management, shipping finance, and maritime business and economic history. The maritime industry plays an increasingly important role in the changing world economy, and this new series offers an outlet for reviewing trends and developments over time as well as analysing how such changes are affecting trade, transport, the environment and financial markets. Each title in the series will communicate key research findings, shaping new approaches to maritime economics. The core audience will be academic, as well as policymakers, regulators and international maritime authorities and organisations. Individual titles will often be theoretically informed but will always be firmly evidence-based, seeking to link theory to policy outcomes and changing practices.

More information about this series at
http://www.palgrave.com/gp/series/15187

Stig Tenold

# Norwegian Shipping in the 20th Century

## Norway's Successful Navigation of the World's Most Global Industry

Stig Tenold
Department of Economics
NHH – Norwegian School of Economics
Bergen, Norway

Palgrave Studies in Maritime Economics
ISBN 978-3-319-95638-1      ISBN 978-3-319-95639-8   (eBook)
https://doi.org/10.1007/978-3-319-95639-8

Library of Congress Control Number: 2018952928

© The Editor(s) (if applicable) and The Author(s) 2019. This book is an open access publication.
**Open Access** This book is licensed under the terms of the Creative Commons Attribution-NonCommercial-NoDerivatives 4.0 International License (http://creativecommons.org/licenses/by-nc-nd/4.0/), which permits any noncommercial use, sharing, distribution and reproduction in any medium or format, as long as you give appropriate credit to the original author(s) and the source, provide a link to the Creative Commons license and indicate if you modified the licensed material. You do not have permission under this license to share adapted material derived from this book or parts of it.
The images or other third party material in this book are included in the book's Creative Commons license, unless indicated otherwise in a credit line to the material. If material is not included in the book's Creative Commons license and your intended use is not permitted by statutory regulation or exceeds the permitted use, you will need to obtain permission directly from the copyright holder.
This work is subject to copyright. All commercial rights are reserved by the author(s), whether the whole or part of the material is concerned, specifically the rights of translation, reprinting, reuse of illustrations, recitation, broadcasting, reproduction on microfilms or in any other physical way, and transmission or information storage and retrieval, electronic adaptation, computer software, or by similar or dissimilar methodology now known or hereafter developed. Regarding these commercial rights a non-exclusive license has been granted to the publisher.
The use of general descriptive names, registered names, trademarks, service marks, etc. in this publication does not imply, even in the absence of a specific statement, that such names are exempt from the relevant protective laws and regulations and therefore free for general use.
The publisher, the authors and the editors are safe to assume that the advice and information in this book are believed to be true and accurate at the date of publication. Neither the publisher nor the authors or the editors give a warranty, express or implied, with respect to the material contained herein or for any errors or omissions that may have been made. The publisher remains neutral with regard to jurisdictional claims in published maps and institutional affiliations.

Cover illustration: Hans Berggren/GettyImages/Fatima Jamadar

This Palgrave Macmillan imprint is published by the registered company Springer Nature Switzerland AG
The registered company address is: Gewerbestrasse 11, 6330 Cham, Switzerland

*For havets folk – A la gent del mar*
*For those who sailed, for those who worked long days in the office,*
*and for those who waited at home.*

# Acknowledgements

This book is the result of more than two decades of research on Norwegian shipping. Along the way, I have benefitted greatly from the conferences and publications of an international community, centred around the International Maritime Economic History Association (now the International Maritime History Association). The most important pilot in these academic waters was Skip Fischer (1946–2018), and this book is dedicated to his memory.

Over this period I have had interesting discussions with many people, who have shaped my ideas on maritime history in general, and the Norwegian dimension, in particular. I am grateful to Yrjö Kaukiainen and Jari Ojala in Finland; Gelina Harlaftis and Ioannis Theotokas in Greece; Lars Chr. Bruno, Espen Ekberg, Even Lange, Eivind Merok and Lars Fredrik Øksendal in Norway; Jesús Maria Valdaliso in Spain; Martin Bellamy, Peter N. Davies, Roy Fenton, Maria Fusaro, Hugh Murphy, Sarah Palmer, David J. Starkey, David Williams and the late John Armstrong in the UK. In Copenhagen I have collaborated closely with CBS Maritime, in particular Martin Jes Iversen, René Taudal Poulsen and Henrik Sornn-Friese, and in London I have had the pleasure of sharing the vast shipping experience of Otto Norland and Martin Stopford. At home in Bergen I have learnt much from discussions with Dag Bakka jr., Bjørn Basberg, Geir Belsnes, Camilla Brautaset, Jan Tore Klovland, Victor D. Norman, Bjørn Sjaastad, Siri Pettersen Strandenes, Arnljot

Strømme Svendsen and Roar Ådland, as well as colleagues at the Bergen Maritime Museum and NHH – Norwegian School of Economics.

The majority of this book was written when I was on Sabbatical at the Department of Scandinavian Studies at the University of Washington in Seattle. I know that this stay has made the book different, and I believe that it has made it better. I am grateful for the warm welcome from Christine Ingebritsen, Lars Jenner, Andy Nestingen, Tina Swenson, Olivia Gunn and Terje Leiren; the last two have also been particularly useful in discussions about the contents.

Although this is not a textbook, I "tested the waters" with students in my Maritime History and Economics class, who commented upon the first two chapters. Their reward was getting their names in an academic book. Well done, Kristoffer Bringslid, Nils Petter Farstad, Thomas Rødahl Fossland, Sindre Gripsgård, Benjamin Hui, Ruth Søyset Jensen, Nekane Larrañaga Pesquera, Boudewijn Leereveld, Jørgen Fie Padøy Mathiesen, Herman Hjort Rabsch, Steven Orpheus Sacopayo Schmidt, Samme Snakkers and Ruben ten Berge. Bjørn Basberg and Sina Øilo Tenold have also read parts of the manuscript, and provided useful comments.

Four people have read and commented in detail on the manuscript, and deserve a special mention. Jan Tore Klovland, Hugh Murphy, Klaus Remme and Marit Øilo have been very helpful, and have uncovered mistakes and inconsistencies that slipped through my net. Any remaining are of course my own responsibility, but I am extremely grateful for their help and enthusiasm.

Academic publishing is rapidly changing, and new possibilities are opening. The costs of the Open Access-publication of this book have been paid for by *Norges Rederiforbunds Fond for NHH* [The Norwegian Shipowners' Association's Fund for NHH] and *Norges Handelshøyskoles Publiseringsfond* [The NHH Publication Fund]. I am lucky to have their help in disseminating my research. I would also like to thank Taiba Batool, who commissioned this book project, as well as Publisher Rachel Sangster and Editorial Assistant Joseph Johnson at Palgrave Macmillan for their patience and support during the writing process.

# Contents

1 A Brief Introduction to Norwegian Shipping   1

2 The Starting Point: A Small Country, but a Major Maritime Nation   21

3 The First World War: The Neutral Ally   63

4 Crisis? What Crisis? Norwegian Shipping in the Interwar Period   91

5 The Second World War   133

6 Bigger and Bigger: Shipping During the Golden Age, 1950–73   159

7 The Shipping Crisis   195

| 8 | Rebound: The Return of Norwegian Shipping | 231 |
| 9 | Onshore and Offshore: The New Maritime Norway | 259 |
| 10 | Epilogue: A Century of Norwegian Shipping | 275 |
| Index | | 311 |

# List of Figures

| | | |
|---|---|---|
| Fig. 1.1 | Norway's merchant marine (1000 grt) and share of the world fleet, per cent, 1900–2000 | 6 |
| Fig. 1.2 | The Norwegian foreign-going fleet, share of total by region, 1900, per cent | 13 |
| Fig. 2.1 | Norwegian foreign-going shipping 1900, by country and region, per cent | 26 |
| Fig. 2.2 | Shipping volumes (1000 grt, left axis) and freight revenues (million kroner, right axis) 1900 | 28 |
| Fig. 2.3 | Estimates of the Norwegian fleet, 1800–1900, 1000 net register tons | 41 |
| Fig. 2.4 | Average annual fleet increase and decrease by source, 1851–1900, 1000 net register tons | 43 |
| Fig. 3.1 | Norwegian losses during the First World War by year, 1914–1918, seafarers and 1000 grt | 79 |
| Fig. 3.2 | The shipping speculation boom, stock exchange indices (1913 = 100), 1914–1921 | 82 |
| Fig. 4.1 | Gross freight earnings, nominal and real, 1900–1939, NOK million | 98 |
| Fig. 4.2 | Steam and motorship shares, per cent, 1900 and 1938, based on gross tonnage | 111 |
| Fig. 4.3 | The number of tanker companies in various Norwegian regions, 1919–1939 | 114 |

## List of Figures

| | | |
|---|---|---|
| Fig. 4.4 | Norwegian lay-ups, quarterly estimates, 1920–1939, 1000 dead weight tons (dwt) | 122 |
| Fig. 5.1 | Losses during the Second World War, persons and 1000 grt, 1939–45 | 146 |
| Fig. 6.1 | GDP per capita, long-term trend and actual development (1000 1990 Int.$), 1900–2000 | 162 |
| Fig. 7.1 | Average economic growth, based on PPP-adjusted GDP, 1950–73 and 1973–2001 | 198 |
| Fig. 7.2 | Seaborne crude oil transport demand, trillion ton-miles, 1962–1973 and 1974–1985 | 202 |
| Fig. 7.3 | Supply and demand in the tanker market (1970 = 100), 1970–1987 | 203 |
| Fig. 7.4 | The crisis index. The Norwegian fleet and tankers, number of seafarers and shipping companies and net freight earnings (1970 = 100), 1970–1987 | 215 |
| Fig. 7.5 | Norwegian market shares, world fleet and major segments, 1973 | 219 |

# List of Tables

| | | |
|---|---|---|
| Table 2.1 | The world fleet and seaborne trade of leading countries, 1900 | 23 |
| Table 2.2 | The Norwegian fleet, transport and revenue, 1900 | 30 |
| Table 2.3 | Norwegian ships' most important port calls and voyages around the turn of the century | 31 |
| Table 4.1 | The 10 leading Norwegian shipping companies, 1 September 1939, fleet size and structure | 120 |
| Table 7.1 | The break in development; output growth, inflation and unemployment, 1965–1985 | 197 |
| Table 7.2 | From good to bad—a comparison of strategic indicators at the start of the shipping crisis | 206 |
| Table 7.3 | Leading Norwegian niches and niche companies | 222 |
| Table 8.1 | The development of important OECD fleets, 1973–1987 | 233 |
| Table 9.1 | The 15 most important maritime countries and territories, January 2001 | 267 |

# 1

# A Brief Introduction to Norwegian Shipping

For the past 15 years, Norway has topped the *Human Development Index*, a world ranking of the standard of life in different countries reported by the *United Nations Development Programme*.[1] The ranking takes into account factors such as health, education and income.

Norway's high Gross Domestic Product (GDP) *per capita* and a far-reaching—but expensive—welfare state, explain the pole position. Norwegians have practically free access to health provisions and education, financed through a high level of taxation. Although the *per capita* GDP is boosted by substantial revenues from petroleum exploration, the country was a high-income economy—with a standard of life that was above average in a European context—even before the discovery of oil. However, Norway had an economic structure that differed from practically all other "developed" economies.[2]

---

[1] In twelve of the fourteen reports published after 2001, the country was number one, toppled only by Iceland in 2007 and 2008; see UNDP (2014), Table 2, 164. Based on revised figures, following a 2010 reformulation of the equation used to calculate the Human Development Index, Norway ended up at the top in 2007 and 2008 as well.

[2] For a discussion of the atypical Norwegian development, see for instance Sejersted (2002) or Brox (2016). The best English-language presentation of its economic development is still the slightly

Given that Norway is a small economy, relations with other countries are particularly important for economic welfare. Unlike other wealthy nations, the Norwegian economy was not built on the production or exports of manufactured goods. The high living standards in the latter half of the 20th century were primarily the result of a combination of exports of staples—petroleum and fish—and services. As such, the development followed an already established pattern.

The modern Norwegian economy took shape in the second half of the 19th century. It was built on three export pillars; wood, fish and shipping services. These continued to be the major exports until the large-scale exploitation of offshore oil and gas reserves from the 1970s onwards. By far the most important of these three was the seaborne transport of goods—shipping—which typically made up between a third and half of the export revenues. Norwegian shipowners and seafarers sold their shipping services all over the world, ensuring revenues that were necessary to finance the imports of essential foodstuffs, raw materials and manufactured goods.

## An Important Maritime Nation

Seaborne transport is the lifeblood of the world economy. Shipping ties countries together in a system of production where raw materials, intermediate goods and finished products are efficiently moved between countries and continents. Reductions in transport costs have encouraged specialization and division of labour on a global scale, ensuring a massive growth in production and income. World welfare increased as economic relationships between nations tightened, and more and more countries became involved in the development of a truly international economy. Seafarers, shipping companies and shipbuilders have thus made our increased standards of living possible.

Throughout the 20th century, Norway was one of the world's leading maritime nations. This small country, situated in the north-western

---

outdated Hodne (1983), but see also Moses (2005). A new and convincing story, unfortunately only in Norwegian, is Sandvik (2018).

corner of Europe, at times carried more than 10 per cent of all cargoes that were transported by sea. When manufacturing production spread, first within Europe, then to North America and onwards to Japan and other countries in Asia, Norwegian ships and seafarers ensured safe and efficient transports of inputs and outputs within an increasingly complex system of production. Moreover, the merchant marine played a particularly important role during the two world wars, aiding the Allied cause and ensuring the supply of vital goods at high economic and personal costs.

Shipping is the most global of all industries. The main means of production—the ship—usually operates outside national boundaries. Therefore, the rules are different in shipping than in other types of business. The international character of the industry makes it possible to combine inputs from different countries to a much larger extent than in other types of production. The 20th century saw Norway develop into one of the world's wealthiest countries, with a high standard of living and matching wage levels. Still, Norwegian shipping companies remained competitive in the cutthroat international shipping industry. This position is testament to a favourable starting point, as well as skilful adaptation to new technologies, markets and conditions.

The country's important role in the maritime industry was a source of pride already at the start of the century. In the official Norwegian publication for the 1900 *Exposition Universelle* World Fair in Paris, the maritime heritage is explained in the long-winded flowery prose of the time: "The geographical position and physical condition of Norway and the natural disposition of the Norwegian people, have always caused their intercourse with other nations, through commerce and shipping, to be of the greatest importance to the country, both as regards the economic and industrial life of the people and the whole national and cultural development [...] The long coast-line, with its many well-protected harbours, renders shipping a livelihood especially adapted for our country; and the Norwegians have at all times excelled in their inclination and ability for this occupation."[3]

---

[3] Kiær (1900, 403). As the following discussion will show, the term "at all times" should be taken with a small shipload of salt.

Therefore, at the very beginning of the 20th century, Norway tried to project an image of a major maritime nation, where the close relationship to the sea was an inevitable, instinctive inclination. There is undoubtedly an element of truth in this; Norwegians—primarily men—were drawn to the sea in large numbers. However, this "destiny-based" explanation undermines an important aspect of the development: the pragmatic explanation. Seafarers took to the sea out of necessity, not because it was in their nature. Shipowners invested in shipping because it was profitable, not to facilitate their compatriots' desire to sail the world.

The aim of this book is to explain how Norway managed to maintain its position as a leading maritime nation throughout the 20th century, despite fierce international competition and a series of technological and institutional changes. It is a story about a small country and its increasingly close economic relations with the rest of the world—a country that has benefitted greatly from, but also been challenged by, economic "globalization."[4] We will follow the development in four different arenas—or, rather—one arena, where our focus varies between four interrelated perspectives; the international, the national, the regional and the company perspective.

## The International Shipping Industry

In order to see the complete picture, we have to start at the international stage. Here, Norwegian shipping companies found a demand for transport that they could satisfy, as well as significant competition from foreign shipowners. It is difficult to explain the development of Norwegian shipping without paying close attention to the underlying basis: the international economy, with its ebbs and flows and with the associated fluctuations in shipping demand and supply. Norwegian and international shipping went hand in hand, and it is impossible to understand one, without also taking into account the other.

---

[4] For extensive discussions of history and globalization, see Osterhammel and Petersson (2005) and O'Rourke and Williamson (1999). Starkey and Harlaftis (1998), contains a series of papers on various aspects of shipping and globalization.

The shipping industry has changed tremendously during the 20th century—technologically, commercially and institutionally. The first decades are typically associated with the emergence of the large luxurious ocean liners that steamed across the North Atlantic. Ships such as *Deutschland, Kronprinz Wilhelm, Vaterland, Lusitania* and the iconic *Titanic* represented Anglo-German rivalry in the quest for the *Blue Riband*—the speed record across the Atlantic—for size records and for market dominance. Still, this was the high-end of international shipping. For the Norwegians, the starting point was very different and much less glorious.

Norway—not even a fully independent nation until 1905—was a minor in world politics. Similarly, the country did not have the resources to participate in the bells and whistles race for the domination of the Atlantic liner trade. Instead, most of the ships plied the world's oceans, looking for business opportunities and using the skilful seamanship of their captains and crews as their main selling point. Norwegian ships handled transport needs all over the world. As the European dominance of international trade and world politics declined later in the century, this global approach turned out to be a fortunate strategy.

In 1900 Norway had a substantial, but increasingly uncompetitive, sail-dominated fleet, much of which had been bought second-hand from countries that had modernized their merchant marines. According to some, Norway was at the time known for its "excellent sailors and rotten ships."[5] Nevertheless, the country's shipowners had managed to establish a number of profitable niche markets, where ships and seafarers could be put to good use. These were usually not in the liner trades—the regular "bus services" of the sea—but in the so-called tramp trades, where the Norwegians would offer to "transport anything, anytime and anywhere."

This vast international arena will be the backdrop of our story, the stage on which the players perform. The international arena restricts the room to manoeuvre and influences development. However, a book about *Norwegian* shipping clearly has to have a national dimension. Within this national setting, we find the pre-conditions for the sector's growth; the entrepreneurs, the resources, the networks, the skills, the traditions, the

---

[5] Hovde (1948, 259).

values and the policies. Thus, with regard to the national level, we will have to answer two crucial questions:

- If we want to learn about the development of the shipping industry in the 20th century, why is Norwegian shipping more relevant than, say, Swedish, Italian, Nigerian or Argentinian shipping?
- Which factors—specific to Norway, either alone or in combination—can explain the country's leading role in international shipping throughout the 20th century?

Finding the answer to the first question is relatively easy: the Norwegian influence on world shipping was simply greater than that of most other nations, which makes the country's role more relevant. Figure 1.1 is an illustration of the size of the Norwegian merchant marine and its share of the world fleet. This is a far from straightforward measure, and over time both the sources and the manner in which the share is calculated has changed. Still, as a rough indication, the pattern in Fig. 1.1 is useful.

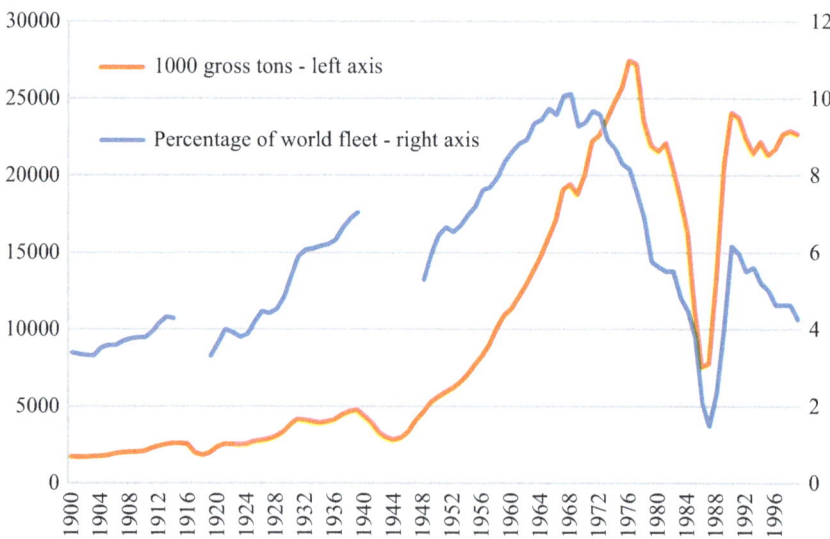

**Fig. 1.1** Norway's merchant marine (1000 grt) and share of the world fleet, per cent, 1900–2000. (Source: Statistics Norway (2000), Table 417, 348–350. See footnote)

On average, for all of the 20th century, almost 6 per cent of the world's fleet was in Norwegian hands. And—for comparison purposes—the Norwegian share of world population in the period declined from around 1.3 per cent to less than 0.8 per cent, illustrating the disproportionate Norwegian participation in world shipping.

Figure 1.1, shows the development of the Norwegian fleet, and the country's market share, throughout the 20th century.[6] The fleet grew slowly around the start of the century, though the ongoing transition from sail to steam provided a structural quality improvement that is obscured in the data, and thus also in the figure. The losses of the First World War led to a temporary decline in the fleet, before an interwar growth that was atypical in an international perspective and led to a growing share of the international market.

The Second World War led to massive losses, and the pre-war tonnage volume was not recovered until 1949. From then on, the Norwegian fleet increased at an enormous pace—doubling in the 1950s and doubling again in the 1960s—before the market crashed spectacularly during the great shipping crises of the 1970s and 1980s. The subsequent reduction of the fleet was unprecedented—by some measures, the decline amounted to more than 75 per cent from 1977 to 1987—but in the late 1980s, a policy shift gave the Norwegian merchant marine a new lease of life.

---

[6] Figure 1.1: Data on the Norwegian fleet from Statistics Norway (2000), Table 417, 348–350. Based on sailing ships larger than 50 gross register tons (grt) and steamships and motorships larger than 25 tons. In order to get a consistent series, the following conversions have been made for the period 1900–1909: Conversion from net to gross tonnage by adding 8.6 per cent for sailing vessels and 65 per cent for steamships and motorships. Reduction by 10.9 per cent for sailing vessels and 0.8 per cent for steamships and motorships in order to neutralize the inclusion of vessels smaller than 50 tons (sailing ships) and 25 tons (steamships and motorships). Conversion factors estimated on the basis of 1909 data. Data from 1987 onwards include the Norwegian Ordinary Register and the Norwegian International Ship Register. Share of world fleet estimated on the basis of data for steamships and motor vessels in *Lloyd's Register*, various issues; OECD, *Maritime Transport*, various issues; and UNCTAD, *Review of Maritime Transport*, various issues. Estimates before 1907 are based on data from Statistics Norway. Given the late transition from sail to steam in Norway, the share of the world fleet is more than one percentage point lower in 1900 than if sailing vessels were included, but the discrepancy decreased as sailing ships were phased out in Norway as well. Due to changes in definitions across time, the series should be seen as an approximation. For instance, if we include Norwegian ships flying foreign flags, and use deadweight tonnage as the basis for the comparison, the Norwegian share in the year 2000 would almost be double the 4 per cent shown in the figure.

The bounce-back was spectacular, with the fleet multiplying by a factor of three over a four-year period. The introduction of the Norwegian International Ship Register (NIS), which enabled the use of low-cost foreign seafarers on Norwegian-flagged vessels, was the most important reason for this strong influx of new tonnage. Even though the pre-crisis position was never regained, the country remained one of the most important players in the international shipping industry.

Norway's significant position in international shipping at the start of the 20th century reflected the prominent role that shipping played in the Norwegian economy. In an article published in the prestigious *Journal of Political Economy* in 1893, Anders Nikolai Kiær, Director of Statistics Norway and the leading international maritime statistician at the time, presented data on tonnage *per capita* in the leading maritime nations in 1890. Norway's 1100 tons per 1000 inhabitants was more than double that of the second-ranked "Great Britain and Ireland."[7]

The fact that the average Norwegian "controlled" more than a ton of shipping capacity is a good illustration of how much of the country's resources must have gone into this sector. Such *per capita* calculations are "statistical doping," though. Relative measures might be misleading, and they can give small countries an appearance of importance that is not necessarily warranted. However, in the case of shipping, the Norwegian position shines even without such trickery—the country established its position among the five leading maritime nations in the 1870s, and largely maintained such a rank over the subsequent century.

So, clearly a book about the Norwegian merchant marine can tell us a lot about the development of the international shipping industry in the 20th century. The crucial roles played by Norwegian ships, shipping companies and sailors make their experiences relevant. The answer to the second question above—about how Norway's leading role can be explained—is not as straightforward. It will take a book to answer.

---

[7] Kiær (1893, 361).

## What Is "Norwegian Shipping"?

There is one major challenge, however. As suggested in connection with Fig. 1.1, the national dimension is evasive, and even more so as we move closer towards today. At the start of our period, it was relatively evident and uncontroversial to define what "Norwegian shipping" implied and what a "Norwegian ship" was. The flag, the crew and the ownership all pointed in the same direction. Subsequently, and particularly in the past decades, this link between the industry, the nation, the workforce and the assets—or capital—became eroded. Consequently, one of the things to address in this book is the manner in which the concept of "Norwegianness" has changed. Gradually the ties between the home country and the ship have been transformed, or in some cases even severed.

A related question is whether it is possible to distinguish a "Norwegian way of doing shipping", what we could call a "typical" Norwegian business strategy. There are undoubtedly some strategic elements—for instance related to the organization of ownership and investments, the market orientation, the choice of technology, etc.—that have distinguished Norwegian shipping companies from those in other countries. At the same time, even these strategic elements have changed across time, influenced by technological possibilities, market developments, policies and domestic and international conditions.

Differences in strategy among shipowners in different countries led to a variation in the type and condition of ships, and these national preferences were even evident to outsiders. In his book *Fish Story*—"regularly described as a seminal work on the theme of globalization"—the American photographer and critic, Allan Sekula, refers to what he called "a biased national physiognomy of vessels." In his scheme, at a point in time that he imprecisely refers to as "in the past," Norwegian ships were "neat," while the ships that belonged to their Greek competitors were "grimy."[8]

However, neither the strategies nor the "national physiognomy" were static. Today, there is little reason to expect that there will be such

---

[8] Roberts (2012, 3) and Sekula (1995, 12). This phenomenon—why Norwegian ships were more modern and well-kept than Greek vessels—had a relatively simple economic explanation; see the analysis of the differing strategies of the two countries' shipping companies in Tenold and Theotokas (2013).

variations between Greek-owned and Norwegian-owned ships. Greek ships are no longer generally grimy, Norwegian ships are not necessarily neat. Vessels from these two nations might in fact be indistinguishable—identical down to the ensign flown at the stern of the ship, which could belong to Panama, Liberia or the Marshall Islands.

Shipping changed, ships changed and Norway changed. In broad terms, Norwegian shipowners entered the last century with a fleet that consisted of a high share of outdated sailing vessels, went through periods with investments in relatively modern and large ships, in particular oil tankers, before finishing the century with a fleet that was known for being expensive, technologically advanced and geared towards certain smaller niche segments. Yet, while this broad pattern represents the typical Norwegian development, it clouds the diversity of the country's shipping sector.

There have been substantial strategic differences among Norwegian shipping companies, and some of these differences also follow a geographical pattern. With regard to the level of activity and the international orientation, the sector has been much more important in the southern part of the country than in the northern part. Moreover, it is possible to identify a traditional East Coast/West Coast dichotomy—a tool favoured by everyone from marine biologists to poets and rappers. This difference between the east and the west has been evident when it comes to investments, networks and market orientation. It becomes clear by looking at the fleets and how the ships are employed, and anecdotal evidence and interviews with industry participants underscore the contrasting attitudes between the eastern and western parts of Norway.

## Regional Differences

Although their markets were found all over the world, the Norwegian shipping companies used to have strong links to their home base in a specific city or region. At the start of the 20th century, these companies were usually local businesses, with workers and funding often found in the neighbourhood—but used globally. Gradually labour and capital would be sourced from locations further away—even crossing international borders in the last quarter of the 20th century. Some of the older Norwegian shipping companies successfully managed this transition, from local ventures to multinationals, while others were unable to transform their business models and disappeared.

The aggregate company developments—the business histories—make up the whole. Here we find the reasons for the growth and demise of individual businesses and of maritime cities and regions; the latter often referred to in political parlance as "maritime clusters." There is a tendency for companies in the same environment to act in a similar manner—either because of identical stimuli or due to a common mind-set. Local fortunes depend upon the success or failure of individual companies, and when these act in the same manner, the whole region becomes affected by their development.

An example of such a regional paradigm is the Agder-region, on the south coast of Norway. In the late 1870s, Agder shipowners controlled around a third of the Norwegian fleet. Given that Norway at the time was the world's third largest shipping nation, with around 6 per cent of the world fleet, investors in the Agder-region owned around 2 per cent of the world's merchant marine. This was a spectacular share for a region with only 150,000 people. In the middle of the 1870s, Agder controlled more sailing ship tonnage than did Russia, Sweden, the Netherlands or Greece.[9]

The position was not sustainable. The shipping hegemony in Agder was based on a business and ownership structure that initially had been associated with the building of wooden ships at local yards. This implied that the investments were closely linked to the increasingly uncompetitive sailing ship technology, as was the region's subsequent demise. Shipping companies in Agder—many of them organized as part ownerships in possession of only one sailing ship—followed their vessels on the path to extinction. When the ships were demolished—or perished at sea—there were seldom sufficient funds to reinvest in new tonnage.[10]

---

[9] Computed on the basis of data in Jeula, 1875. If we count "a ton as a ton", and consider both sailing ships and steamships, the Agder fleet would be marginally larger than the fleets of Sweden and Russia.

[10] In this instance, "shipping company" refers to the part ownerships that were the formal owners of the ships; a corresponding owner might manage a larger fleet and have interests in more than one

By 1925, the Norwegian share of the world merchant marine had been reduced to 4.5 per cent, and Agder's share of the Norwegian fleet had plummeted to 5 per cent. Therefore, within the span of two generations, ownership in the Agder-region had gone from 2 per cent to 0.2 per cent of the world fleet.[11]

The Agder example is extreme, but it illustrates the fact that local distinctions are important. Based on the pattern of ownership in 1900, we can identify a set of broad geographical typologies that had developed over the previous decades. The capital, Kristiania (now Oslo), was big, but unsophisticated. Kristiania had the largest tonnage, measured in simple terms, but was surpassed by Bergen when we take into account the quality of the ships, specifically the fact that steam vessels were more advanced and could transport larger amounts of goods due to their higher efficiency.

Bergen had a distinct lead in the transition from sail to steam, with a diffusion that very much mimics the British experience. Steam tonnage surpassed sail tonnage in Bergen in 1884—an impressive 25 years before the same thing happened for the fleet registered in the rest of the country.[12] While Kristiania and the homeports around the Oslofjord held an intermediate position in the transition, the South Coast was clearly the home of the traditional sailing ships. As the subsequent development would show, by 1900 these sails represented a dying technology that lost out in one market segment after another.

Norway is a long country, stretching from the 57th parallel to the 71st parallel north. Most of the population, as well as the cultural, political and economic centres, are situated in the southernmost quarter of the country. This imbalance has characterized the shipping industry as well—in 1900 more than 95 per cent of the Norwegian fleet was owned in this part of the country.

---

ship. However, the part ownership functioned like today's project investments. After the end of the project, the remaining capital—the sales price, the demolition price or insurance money—was paid out to investors.

[11] See Johnsen (2001) for an analysis of the development. Agder shipping was subsequently rejuvenated, before another spectacular haemorrhage during the shipping crises of the 1970s and 1980s.

[12] Pettersen (1981, 45).

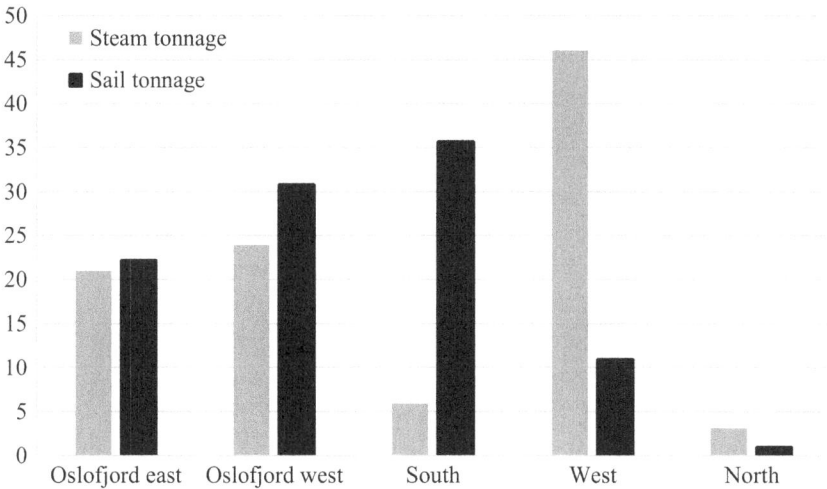

**Fig. 1.2** The Norwegian foreign-going fleet, share of total by region, 1900, per cent. (Source: Statistics Norway (1902), Table 1d, 9–10. See footnote)

Figure 1.2 illustrates the large geographical differences in the ownership of the Norwegian fleet at the start of the 20th century. The figure shows Norway divided into five regions, with their respective shares of the country's sail and steam tonnage.[13] The differences between the west of Norway, which includes Bergen, and the south, are striking. Data for the ships engaged in foreign trade show that South Coast shipowners owned more than a third of the country's sailing tonnage, but only slightly more than 5 per cent of the steamships. Shipowners in the western part of Norway owned almost half the foreign-going steam fleet, but only slightly more than 10 per cent of the sailing ship fleet.

---

[13] Figure 1.2: Statistics Norway (1902), Table 1d, 9–10. Based on ships of all sizes engaged in the foreign-going fleet. Vessels engaged in domestic coastal trade and sealing and whaling (including walrus hunting) are excluded. The categories include the home ports in the following regions:
  Oslofjord East: Smålenene, Akershus, Kristiania
  Oslofjord West: Buskerud, Jarlsberg and Larvik, Bratsberg
  South: Nedenes, Lister and Mandal
  West: Stavanger, Bergen, Søndre Bergenhus, Nordre Bergenhus
  North: Romsdal, Søndre Trondhjem, Nordre Trondhjem, Nordland, Tromsø, Finnmarken.

This geographical division becomes even more striking if we look at individual ports. By 1900, steamships made up almost 97 per cent of the Bergen fleet—even when we count "a ton as a ton" and disregard the fact that a ton of steam capacity was much more efficient than a sailing ship ton.[14] In southerly Arendal, on the other hand, the white sails still ruled—sailing ships made up around 90 per cent of the city's tonnage.[15] Other ports on the South Coast were clinging even harder to the old technology. The home port of Lillesand housed only one steamship—68 tons of modernity—but in excess of 40 sailing ships, amounting to more than 21,000 gross tons. Moreover, seven other towns, mainly on the South Coast, had substantial sailing ship fleets, but not a single steamship above 50 tons.

Shipping's important economic role was of course reflected at the local level—in investment and employment, naturally, but also in status and politics. In a country where nobility had been abolished by law at the start of the 19th century, wealthy shipowners came to play crucial roles in their communities. When the playwright Henrik Ibsen wrote about *The Pillars of Society*, the main character was an impatient businessman involved in shipping and shipbuilding.[16] This is a literary example of the privileged positions that shipowners had in towns and cities along the coast—and art imitated life. The maritime men were important at the national level as well—three of the first five Prime Ministers in "independent Norway" were shipowners. Egeland points out the remarkable fact that Michelsen, Mowinckel and Knudsen, "the three dominating Norwegian politicians – one should indeed use the word 'statesmen' – in the first four decades [of the 20th century] came from the shipowning profession."[17]

---

[14] This and subsequent calculations based on vessels above 50 tons in Statistics Norway (1902); see Fig. 1.2 for an explanation.

[15] Though, to be fair, the sails were far from as white as they are usually depicted, and they were also substantially more patched. Perhaps a better description would be "sails in 25 shades of white and another 25 shades of black."

[16] An alternative title, favoured by the Royal Shakespeare Company, is *The Pillars of the Community*, which perhaps better reflects the local dimension. The main character of the play, Karsten Bernick, was allegedly modelled by Henrik Ibsen on Morten Smith-Petersen, a Grimstad shipowner who was married to the author's second cousin.

[17] Egeland (1973, 73).

## Shipping Companies

The skilled and lucky ones could make a fortune from shipping, but it was also a risky undertaking. Compared with other countries and other Norwegian industries, the "turnover" of shipping companies was very high. Throughout the 20th century, in booms as well as crises, established companies went bankrupt or ceased operations for other reasons—broken partnerships, deaths, succession challenges, low profits or high competition. However, the businesses that disappeared were usually replaced by new companies—with the exception of one particularly violent period, during the crisis of the 1970s and 1980s.

This turbulence was not all negative. In fact, to a large extent the modernization of Norwegian shipping took place through the establishment of new companies—and removal of old ones—rather than as a result of transformation within existing organizations. Out with the old and in with the new. This does not mean that there are no shipping companies with long traditions in Norway. Among the largest shipping companies in Norway at the start of the 21st century, we find quite a number of "old timers"; of the 30 largest shipping companies in Norway in 2003, 18 were established before 1960, and another three had links—though not unbroken ones—to companies that existed in 1960. However, an international comparison reveals that the turnover was substantially higher than, for instance, in neighbouring Denmark.[18]

Just like the shipping sector itself was transformed, the shipping companies' business models changed dramatically during the 20th century. Shipping companies have faced major shifts in markets, technology, infrastructure, capital, competence and policies—shifts that have been so dramatic that, in current management consultancy lingo, they would be labelled "disruptions." To prosper and survive, the companies had to adapt their business models and long-term strategies to the new circumstances. Those that did not, lost out in the competition and ultimately failed, replaced by entrepreneurs that understood the new regimes.

The 20th century saw the shipping companies' business models develop from single vessel partnerships based on local factors of production, to

---

[18] Compare the developments in Tenold (2012) and Sornn-Friese, Poulsen and Iversen (2012).

stock exchange-listed multinational conglomerates that drew labour and investment funds from a global pool. This development took place against the backdrop of a series of technological "revolutions" that changed the manner in which shipping companies went about their business. The transformations that first spring to mind are the changes in shipping technology. New building materials and shifts in the means of propulsion—from wood and sail, to iron and steel, steam and diesel—changed the skill set necessary to build, operate and commercially manage ships. Moreover, as ships became more expensive, the need for financing and insurance changed, as did the competence necessary to manage a shipping company.

Likewise, innovations that were not directly related to shipping also played important roles. Knowledge—often determined by access to information—is essential to make good decisions in shipping, as in most other industries. However, shipping companies have to base many of their decisions on information from markets that are far away. In the 19th century, sailing vessels often had very little contact with the "headquarters" on land, making the ship's master particularly important for decision-making.

During the 20th century—with the exception of the two major wars—the access to and quality of information constantly improved. As a result, the fabric of the shipping industry changed. Innovations in communications technology—first from the telegram to the telephone, then from the telex to the telefax, finally to the internet and satellite links to ships at sea—muted the effect of distance. The technological improvements changed how decisions were made and who made them.

The changes in the business model also had ramifications for the spatial distribution of shipping companies—a process sometimes referred to as "a dislocation of the comparative advantages."[19] As the infrastructure changed and the need for capital and managerial competence increased, Norwegian shipping became increasingly centralized. Proximity to information sources—and to other shipping industry participants—became more important. The captains, far from home, were no longer the main decision-makers. Now the shipowners, with improved access to

---

[19] Fritz (1980, 148).

information, increasingly decided the business and instructed the captains by means of telegraph.

While the ownership of sailing vessels had been extremely dispersed at the start of the 20th century, now the large towns and cities gained a clear advantage. Most shipping company headquarters were located in the larger cities by the second half of the 20th century. Still, the industry continued to play an important economic role in more remote areas. With regard to employment, in particular, the shipping industry provided job opportunities for people based in rural districts and in sparsely populated parts of the country.

The number of Norwegian seafarers reached a post-war peak in 1960. That year, more than 53,000 seamen paid tax in *bygder* [non-urban municipalities]. In fact, the proportion of seamen in such rural areas was almost twice as high as the proportion of seamen in the cities.[20] Consequently, due to the employment opportunities in the merchant marine, Norway could maintain a relatively scattered population, partly neutralizing the trend towards urbanization. Country boys did not have to go to the city to find work—they could go to sea.

Another long-term effect is through family life and gender relations. Norway is known for being a country with gender equality in most areas, and the shipping industry might have influenced this. In many families, the male breadwinner would be at sea for long periods. As a result, many Norwegian women were given organizational and economic responsibilities that would be uncommon in other countries.[21] Moreover, towards the end of the 20th century, when seafarers' journeys home were more frequent, it was often expected that men would take care of the house and the children. Both of these factors might have contributed to the lauded Norwegian gender balance.

These two examples illustrate how activities in foreign waters have had profound implications for the development of Norwegian society on land. Shipping has influenced the nation and the population in ways that are neither intuitive nor obvious.

---

[20] Statistics Norway, Tax Statistics (1961, 74). Not all of these seafarers were engaged in foreign-going shipping.
[21] See Lønnå (2010), for a number of examples.

# Norwegian Maritime History: An Update

The standard work on Norwegian shipping, *Den norske sjøfarts historie* [The history of Norwegian shipping], was 40 years in the making. Originally intended to be one 560-page volume, in the end it counted more than 3000 pages across six large books.[22] One reviewer acerbically remarked that no detail was considered sufficiently insignificant to be left out, and "glimpses of genius" were marred by "free-hand drawing" where "the imagination was given free rein."[23]

The scope of this book is more modest, just like the period under investigation is more concise. The book is structured as a chronological voyage through Norwegian shipping in the 20th century. It is not an all-embracing or definitive history, and that has never been the intention. Rather, it is an attempt at describing the major long-term trends, while at the same time analysing how Norwegian actors—authorities, shipping companies and seafarers—have adapted to the challenges and opportunities in one of the world's most competitive industries.

# Bibliography

O. Brox (2016) 'En særnorsk vei til velstand?' *Nytt norsk tidsskrift*, 32:3, 219–228
J.O. Egeland (1973) *Kongeveien*, Volume II (Oslo: H. Aschehoug & Co.)
M. Fritz (1980) 'Shipping in Sweden, 1850–1913', *Scandinavian Economic History Review*, 28:2, 147–160
F. Hodne (1983) *The Norwegian Economy* (London: Croom Helm)
B.J. Hovde (1948) *The Scandinavian Countries 1720–1865*, 1948 reissue (Ithaca: Cornell University Press)

---

[22] The full title of the series can be translated as "The history of Norwegian shipping from the earliest age until our own time." With a timeline like that, and the interruption of two world wars, it is perhaps no surprise that the original three-year project period turned out to be too optimistic. For a presentation of the interesting process behind the book, see the editor's postscript in Worm-Müller (1951, 481–487). A separate supplement, Schreiner (1963), brought "our own time" up to 1920.
[23] Schreiner (1952, 267, 259 and 256). After the harsh review—which also called parts of the series "scientifically worthless"—the reviewer was asked to write the follow-up volume, covering the period 1914–1920.

B.E. Johnsen (2001) *Rederistrategi i endringstid: Sørlandsk skipsfart fra seil til damp og motor, fra tre til jern og stål 1875–1925* (Kristiansand: Høyskoleforlaget AS)

A.N. Kiær (1893) 'Historical Sketch of the Development of Scandinavian Shipping', *The Journal of Political Economy*, 1:3, 329–364

A.T. Kiær (1900) 'Commerce and shipping' in S. Konow & K. Fischer (eds) *Norway: Official publication of the Paris exhibition 1900* (Kristiania: Aktie-bogtrykkeriet)

E. Lønnå (2010) *Sjøens kvinner: ute og hjemme* (Oslo: Spartacus Forlag)

J. Moses (2005) *Norwegian Catch-up: Development and Globalization before World War II* (Aldershot: Ashgate)

K. O'Rourke & J Williamson (1999) *Globalization and history – The Evolution of a Nineteenth-Century Atlantic Economy* (Cambridge: MIT Press)

J. Osterhammel & N.P. Petersson (2005) *Globalization: A Short History* (Princeton: Princeton University Press)

L. Pettersen (1981) 'Fra kjøpmannsrederi til selvstendig næring, 1860–1914', *Bergen og Sjøfarten III* (Bergen: Bergens Rederiforening og Bergens Sjøfartsmuseum)

B. Roberts (2012) 'Production in View: Allan Sekula's Fish Story and the Thawing of Postmodernism', Tate Papers No. 18

P. Sandvik (2018) *Nasjonens velstand. Norges økonomiske historie 1800–1940* (Bergen: Vigmostad & Bjørke AS)

J. Schreiner (1952) 'Review of Den norske sjøfarts historie', *Historisk Tidsskrift*, 36, 255–295

J. Schreiner (1963) *Norsk skipsfart under krig og høykonjunktur, 1914–1920* (Oslo: Norges Rederforbund/Cappelen)

F. Sejersted (2002) *Demokratisk kapitalisme* (Oslo: Pax Forlag)

A. Sekula (1995) *Fish story* (Düsseldorf: Richter Verlag)

H. Sornn-Friese, R. Taudal Poulsen & M.J. Iversen (2012) '"Knowing the Ropes": Capability Reconfiguration and Restructuring of the Danish Shipping Industry', in S. Tenold, M.J. Iversen & E. Lange (eds) *Global Shipping in Small Nations: Nordic Experiences after 1960* (New York: Palgrave Macmillan) 61–99

D.J. Starkey & G. Harlaftis (1998) *Global Markets: The Internationalization of the Sea Transport Industries since 1850* (St. Johns: IMEHA)

Statistics Norway (1902) *Tabeller vedkommende Norges skibsfart i året 1900* (Kristiania: Det Statistiske Centralbureau/H. Aschehoug & Co.)

Statistics Norway (1961) *Skattestatistikk for inntektsåret 1960* (Oslo: Statistisk Sentralbyrå)
Statistics Norway (2000) *Statistisk Årbok 2000* (Oslo: Statistics Norway)
S. Tenold (2012) 'Boom, Crisis and Internationalized Revitalization' in S. Tenold, M.J. Iversen & E. Lange (eds) *Global Shipping in Small Nations: Nordic Experiences after 1960* (New York: Palgrave Macmillan) 26–60
S. Tenold & I. Theotokas (2013) 'Shipping innovations: The different paths of Greece and Norway', *International Journal of Decision Sciences, Risk and Management*, 5:2, 142–160
UNDP (2014) *Human Development Report 2014* (New York: United Nations Development Programme)
J.S. Worm-Müller (ed) (1951) *Den norske sjøfarts historie: Fra de ældste tider til vore dager*, 2:3 (Oslo: J.W. Cappelens Forlag)

**Open Access** This chapter is licensed under the terms of the Creative Commons Attribution-NonCommercial-NoDerivatives 4.0 International License (http://creativecommons.org/licenses/by-nc-nd/4.0/), which permits any noncommercial use, sharing, distribution and reproduction in any medium or format, as long as you give appropriate credit to the original author(s) and the source, provide a link to the Creative Commons license and indicate if you modified the licensed material. You do not have permission under this license to share adapted material derived from this chapter or parts of it.

The images or other third party material in this chapter are included in the chapter's Creative Commons license, unless indicated otherwise in a credit line to the material. If material is not included in the chapter's Creative Commons license and your intended use is not permitted by statutory regulation or exceeds the permitted use, you will need to obtain permission directly from the copyright holder.

# 2

# The Starting Point: A Small Country, but a Major Maritime Nation

> Norway is larger than anyone knows:
> Every ship, under the waving flag,
> On the endlessly empty sea
> Is a new part of Norway adrift[1]

At the start of the 20th century, the sentiment of the Nordahl Grieg poem quoted above undoubtedly rang true: Norway and its flag was everywhere. The country's ships were anchored in or voyaging between ports all over the world, facilitating the growth of commerce and enabling the formation of a truly international economy. Through ships, sailors and shipowners, this small country on the outskirts of Europe reached very far.

Norway had the world's fourth largest merchant marine, trailing only supremely dominant Great Britain—with around half of the world's seaborne transport capacity—Germany and The United States. Around 6.6 per cent of the sailing fleet and 3.6 per cent of the steamship fleet were flying the Norwegian flag.

---

[1] Grieg 1922, "The Flag" from *Rundt Kap det gode Haab*, author's translation.

Shipping had continued to increase in importance after Kiær made his international comparison a decade earlier. Norway's merchant marine amounted to 1227 tons per 1000 inhabitants—so the "average" Norwegian actually owned more than one ton of shipping tonnage. Consequently, the shipping capacity *per capita* was high—much higher than the UK in second place, more than three times higher than Denmark in third place and more than four times higher than fourth-placed Greece. In other words, no country had put such a large share of its investments in ships.[2] No country depended as much on shipping.

Table 2.1 provides an overview of the world's merchant marine and the seaborne trade volume of the most important participants in the international economy in 1900.[3] The left side of the table shows the size of the fleets; the sailing fleet, the steamship fleet and the total tonnage. The column "effective tonnage" is the best measure of the carrying capacity of the fleet; here the figures have been adjusted to account for the higher productivity of steam vessels. Britain clearly dominated the oceans, with more than half of the steamships and more than 48 per cent of the "effective" world fleet.

The column "seaborne trade" shows the seaborne exports and imports of the various countries. Great Britain was in the lead here as well, with a demand for transport that was higher than the sum of the next two countries, the United States and France. However, the country's hegemony within world trade was on the wane—slightly less than 24 per cent of the total shipping demand was accounted for by British trade.[4]

---

[2] See Table 2.1 for sources. There is a theoretical possibility that another country might have had a higher relative share of its investments in shipping (for instance if total investments were much lower than in Norway). However, based on what we know about the economic structure of the countries at the time, the claim that Norway had put the highest share of its investments in ships is undoubtedly true.

[3] Table 2.1: Statistics Norway (1902a), Tables I and K, 168–169. Based on vessels above 50 tons, 31 December 1900. Tonnage figures for Russia refer to 1895, and do not include ports on the Caspian Sea and the Pacific, while the tonnage figures for Italy refer to 1898. US tonnage figures refer to 30 June 1900. British American seaborne trade refers to Canada, and British Australian to Victoria and New South Wales. Tonnage *per capita* refers to estimated tonnage, where one steamship ton is equal to 3.6 sailing ship tons. For a more precise description of the data behind the shipping movements, which include vessels in ballast, see the original source, Table K.

[4] Refers to the countries included in the sample in Table 2.1. In 1874 the British share of the world fleet had been more or less identical to this, but the share of world trade was higher. On the relationship between merchant marines and trade, see Ojala and Tenold (2017).

### The Starting Point: A Small Country, but a Major Maritime Nation

**Table 2.1** The world fleet and seaborne trade of leading countries, 1900

| | Sail tons (1000) | Steam tons (1000) | Sum tons (1000) | Effective tonnage (1000) | Tonnage per 1000 inh. | Seaborne trade (1000 tons) | Shipping per 1000 inh. |
|---|---|---|---|---|---|---|---|
| GB and Ireland | 1923 | 7150 | 9073 | 27,663 | 667 | 98,524 | 2377 |
| Germany | 558 | 1347 | 1905 | 5407 | 96 | 30,208 | 536 |
| USA | 1405 | 938 | 2343 | 4782 | 63 | 45,312 | 595 |
| Norway | 930 | 499 | 1429 | 2725 | 1227 | 6159 | 2773 |
| France | 394 | 597 | 991 | 2543 | 66 | 40,097 | 1039 |
| Italy | 483 | 374 | 857 | 1830 | 56 | 17,005 | 547 |
| Spain | 91 | 435 | 526 | 1657 | 91 | 25,695 | 1408 |
| Japan | 148 | 330 | 478 | 1336 | 31 | 7386 | 168 |
| Sweden | 256 | 257 | 513 | 1181 | 230 | 14,984 | 2917 |
| Br. Australia | 164 | 234 | 398 | 1006 | 182 | 13,889 | 5390 |
| Denmark | 111 | 245 | 356 | 993 | 405 | 11,754 | 4798 |
| The Netherl. | 68 | 252 | 320 | 949 | 186 | 17,061 | 3343 |
| Br. America | 446 | 103 | 549 | 817 | 109 | 14,543 | 2708 |
| Russia | 152 | 173 | 325 | 774 | 7 | 14,451 | 124 |
| Greece | 176 | 165 | 341 | 770 | 298 | 5622 | 2176 |
| Austria | 14 | 184 | 198 | 676 | 26 | 4718 | 180 |
| Finland | 252 | 46 | 298 | 418 | 154 | 4058 | 1496 |
| British Asia | 73 | 92 | 165 | 404 | 1 | NA | NA |
| Brazil | 77 | 77 | 154 | 354 | 24 | NA | NA |
| Belgium | 0 | 96 | 96 | 346 | 52 | 14,526 | 2170 |
| Hungary | 10 | 63 | 73 | 237 | 12 | 1846 | 96 |
| Argentina | 41 | 38 | 79 | 178 | 36 | 14,543 | 2609 |
| Portugal | 56 | 24 | 80 | 142 | 26 | 15,341 | 2826 |
| Chile | 35 | 28 | 63 | 136 | 41 | NA | NA |
| Rumania | 4 | 11 | 15 | 45 | 8 | 1939 | 328 |

Source: Statistics Norway (1902a), Tables I and K, 168–169. See footnote

The fact that Great Britain had 48 per cent of the tonnage and 23 per cent of the seaborne trade movements suggests that Britain's fleet exceeded the country's shipping needs by a factor of more than two. In other words, more than half the shipping services it produced was "exported" and took place between other countries. This makes sense when we consider the manner in which British shipping lines served ports, particularly Empire ports, all over the world. The only country with a larger surplus of shipping capacity relative to its own trade was Norway, which was 16th of the countries with regard to the volume of seaborne imports and exports, but fourth with regard to the size of the fleet.[5]

To illustrate how the world had been divided into countries that performed shipping services for others, and countries whose trade was transported on foreign keels, we can consider a hypothetical world where shipping services were not traded internationally. If the ships only carried the countries' own seaborne trade, each Norwegian "ship ton" would transport 2.26 tons of cargo annually, while each British "ship ton" would carry 3.56 tons of cargo.[6] At the other end of the scale we find Portugal where, if the country's trade was transported solely on Portuguese ships, each "ship ton" would have to carry more than 100 tons of commodities on an annual basis.

By 1900 the Portuguese depended upon ships from other nations—for instance Norway—to carry their cargoes. That year, 187 Norwegian ships called on Portugal, and only one Portuguese ship came to Norway. Less than 10 per cent of the Norwegian ships that went to Portuguese ports came directly from Norway—more than 170 ships were involved in the trade between Portugal and other countries.[7]

---

[5] A caveat: the volume of seaborne trade in itself does not determine the need for shipping capacity. In order to fully find a country's actual "transport demand," the distance that the cargoes are transported must be taken into account as well. Thus, the almost 14 million tons of Australian exports and imports—much of it going to or coming from Europe and the Americas—led to a higher demand for tonnage than the around 17 million tons of Italian seaborne trade—much of it transported in vessels pottering about in the Mediterranean or on short voyages to other European countries.

[6] The "world average" would be 7.4 tons of cargo per ship ton, based on the countries where we have data for both fleet and shipping. Six countries—in addition to Norway and the UK, Japan, Germany, Austria and Greece—were below the world average, and can be considered "theoretical net exporters of shipping services." Of course, a lot of confounding factors imply that this calculation is imprecise. However, it can at least give us an indication of the countries that had large fleets relative to their trade, and vice versa.

[7] Statistics Norway (1902b, 54–55 and 25).

The Portuguese example illustrates that maritime hegemony is not permanent. The Iberian country that four centuries earlier had become famous for its first-class explorers, whose exploits were based on superior technology and outstanding nautical knowledge, had become insignificant in international shipping by the start of the 20th century. Indeed, four Norwegian cities—Bergen, Kristiania, Tønsberg and Stavanger—had larger fleets than Portugal. The Bergen fleet alone was more than four times larger than the Portuguese merchant marine. The descendants of Henry the Navigator had clearly lost their course.

The Norwegian ships, on the other hand, were all over the place, serving the needs of world trade. Although sailing ships had gradually been squeezed out of most short-distance trades by the more efficient steam vessels, Norwegian sailing ships remained competitive in certain market segments; copra from the Pacific, wheat from the Americas, coal from Australia and guano and nitrates from the western coast of South America. Here, voyages were long, and there was little reason to pay a premium for speedy transport of such cargoes, so the sailing ship technology was still viable. Moreover, ships make money when they are carrying cargo from A to B, not when they are lying still. In ports with inferior facilities, where loading and unloading was cumbersome and slow, it made economic sense to have an old, cheap sailing vessel lying idle for months, rather than a modern and expensive steamship.

While some owners had found niches that suited their old sailing ships, others operated at the diametrically opposite end of the market, focusing on modern vessels and shorter distances. Bergen-based steamship owners held such a strong position in the US fruit trade that questions had been asked in the US Congress about the Norwegian dominance.[8] In East and Southeast Asia Norwegian ships found favour with local customers, as they were seen as less intrusive and threatening than those of the leading colonial powers, the UK, Germany and France.[9]

To illustrate the manner in which the Norwegian fleet was utilized— where the Norwegian ships were engaged—we can look at two different

---

[8] *New York Times*, 08061894, 5. Of the 63 ships included in a survey of the fruit trade, 37 were Norwegian.
[9] See Brautaset and Tenold (2010).

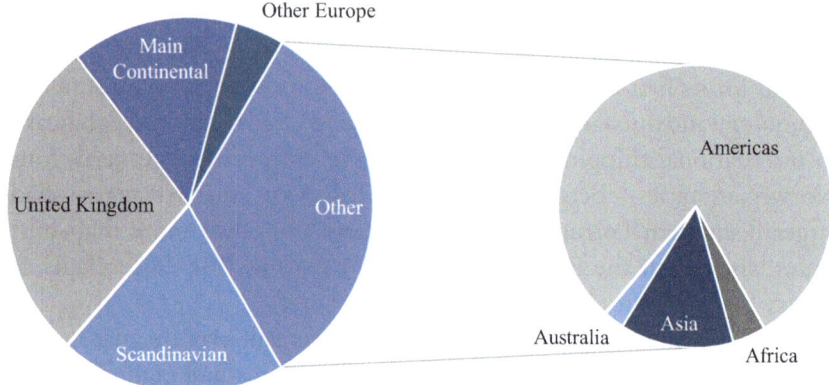

**Fig. 2.1** Norwegian foreign-going shipping 1900, by country and region, per cent. (Source: Statistics Norway (1902a), Table 55, 73. See footnote)

sources from the start of the century. The first is the official Norwegian statistics, while the second is the voyage information provided by *Lloyd's List*. The quality of the contemporary Norwegian statistics is considered particularly high in an international perspective, reflecting the fact that Anders Nicolai Kiær, the Director of the Central Bureau of Statistics, since 1869 had been given a "special responsibility" for the compilation, coordination and comparison of international shipping statistics.[10]

Norwegian ships had a market share of around two-thirds in the country's own imports and exports. The most important competitors were British ships—carrying slightly more than 10 per cent of Norway's foreign trade—followed by Danish, Swedish, German and Russian/Finnish ships.[11] The home trade—slightly more than 4 million tons—only made up around one-eighth of the volumes carried by Norwegian ships.[12] In other words, more than 87 per cent of "the production" took place between foreign ports.[13] Figure 2.1 gives an indication of the most impor-

---

[10] See Lie and Roll-Hansen (2001), Bjerkholt and Skoglund (2012, 22–27) and Kiær (1876–1892).

[11] Calculated on the basis of Statistics Norway (1902a, 70). Perhaps surprisingly, the share is more or less identical regardless of whether we include vessels arriving and leaving in ballast.

[12] See Fig. 2.1 for details. The figure differs from that in Table 2.1, where ballast movements were included.

[13] Statistics Norway (1902a, 73).

tant markets—though again, it is important to remember that the effect of sailing distance is not taken into account.

Figure 2.1 shows that around two-thirds of the cargoes that the ships carried came from or were bound for Europe.[14] With more than a quarter of the entries and exits, the UK was the single biggest market for Norwegian ships, reflecting the crucial role that the British Empire played in international trade around the turn of the century. Interestingly, Norwegian ships transported more cargoes to and from "the Americas"—North, Central and South America—than to and from Scandinavia.

Revenue-wise, Britain also appeared to be in the lead, with gross freight earnings of more than NOK73 million, as shown in Fig. 2.2.[15] Earnings from the American market were only marginally smaller, at NOK69 million, but were in fact more important. The reason for this is the manner in which the business was conducted: many of the ships trading on the Americas operated on time charters, where the Norwegian owners did not have to pay bunkers and port costs.[16] So, when it comes to the amount

---

[14] Figure 2.1: Data refer to total tonnage and are taken from Statistics Norway (1902a), Table 55, 73. The statistics are based on the tonnage of the ships cleared, rather than the weight of the cargo. While ships in ballast are reported separately, but included in these figures, the statistics are not adjusted to reflect ships that are not fully laden. There are some missing reports in the data, see Statistics Norway (1902b), Tables 18–20, 54–81. Given that vessels are registered both on their ingoing and outgoing voyage, their transported volumes are counted twice, but this has a minimal impact on relative shares.

The groups include the following categories from the statistics:

Scandinavia: Norway, Sweden and Denmark (including Iceland and the Faroe Islands).

UK: Great Britain and Ireland.

Main Continental: Germany, the Netherlands, Belgium, France, Portugal and Spain.

Other Europe: Russia/ Finland; Italy, Malta and Austria-Hungary; and Turkey, Rumania and Greece.

The Americas: North America; West Indies, Mexico and Central America; South America.

[15] Figure 2.2: Data refer to ingoing and outgoing laden tonnage, excluding vessels in ballast, and are taken from Statistics Norway (1902a), Table 55, 73. There are some missing reports in the data, see Statistics Norway (1902b), Tables 18–20, 54–81. Given that vessels and revenues are registered both for the ingoing and outgoing voyages, transported volumes and gross freight earnings are double-counted. The category "adjusted gross freight earnings" includes vessels operating on time charters, and are not included in the data presented in Statistics Norway (1902a), Table 55, 73.

Groups are the same as in Fig. 2.1.

[16] Almost 40 per cent of the earnings in the Americas were reported after coal and port costs had been deducted, compared with less than 10 per cent of the British earnings. In the trades on Japan and China, practically all of the earnings—more than 99 per cent—have been categorized as timecharter revenues in the statistics.

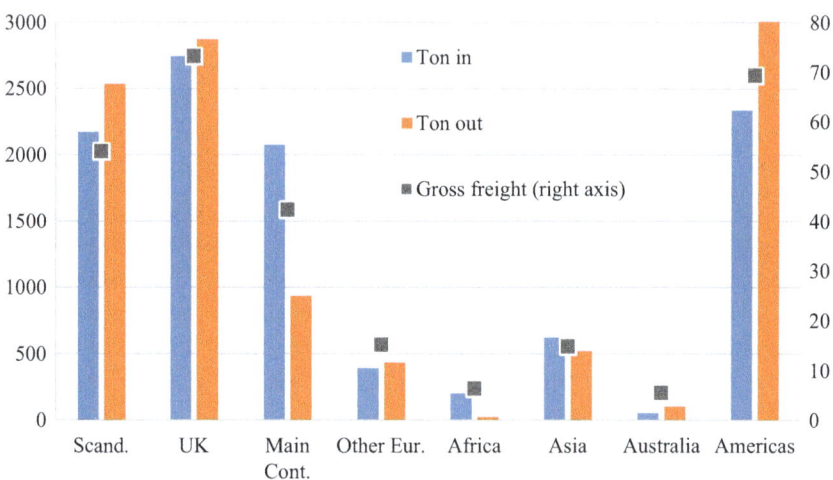

**Fig. 2.2** Shipping volumes (1000 grt, left axis) and freight revenues (million kroner, right axis) 1900. (Source: Statistics Norway (1902a), Table 55, 73. See footnote)

of money that was returned to Norwegian sailors and investors, the most important market at the start of the 20th century was the Americas, particularly the United States, which was responsible for two-thirds of the gross freight earnings from that region.

The gross freight earnings do not show profits, as they usually do not take into account the costs accrued abroad when "producing" the transport service. Operating costs were typically higher for steamships than for sailing ships, due to their appetite for coal. However, there were substantial variable costs for sailing ships as well—although the wind was free, sailors had to be paid and fed, and ropes and sails had to be maintained, and were changed with surprisingly high frequency.

The tonnage data in Fig. 2.2 do not include ships travelling "in ballast"—ships that were sailing from one port to another without revenue-generating cargoes. Differences between ingoing and outgoing volumes thus reveal the disequilibria in the trade of the various parts of the world. Continental Europe and Africa, in particular, had much larger volumes entering than going out, while there was an export surplus, volume-wise, from Australia and the Americas.

Thanks to A.N. Kiær's insatiable appetite for shipping statistics, we also have data that can illustrate the differences between various types of vessels. Table 2.2 provides a snapshot of the differences in efficiency and revenue between sailing ships and steamships at this point more or less midway through the transformation from sail to steam.[17]

It may seem surprising that the revenue per ton transported was more than NOK19 for the sailing ships, compared with NOK11 for the steamships. Two factors can explain this. First, we know that sailing ships transported their cargoes relatively far, which is not captured when a simple ton measure is used as the basis. Second, the difference in efficiency between the two ship types shines through; the average steamship transported more than 10 times as much cargo in a year as the average sailing ship. Even though the sailing fleet was almost twice as large as the steamship fleet, the latter transported more than three times as much. Gross freight earnings per ship were more than six times higher for steamships, and in 1900 each "steamship ton" earned 186 kroner, compared with 55 for each "sailing ship ton."[18]

The data above provide information about where the Norwegian ships were employed and suggest some differences between regions and vessel types. Although the Norwegian statistics inform us about the countries that were visited, they only include a single locational marker for each voyage—either country of departure or country of arrival. In order to understand both where ships came from and where they were going, as well as the importance of individual ports, we can turn to the British periodical *Lloyd's List*. With London still very much the centre of world transport and commerce, *Lloyd's List* provided producers, charterers, traders, brokers and others involved in the shipping industry with news and information.

---

[17] Table 2.2: Information on number and gross register tonnage (grt) from Statistics Norway, 1901, Table 35, 51. Based on vessels listed as part of the foreign-going fleet, 31 December 1900. Information on volumes and revenues from Statistics Norway (1902a), Table 55, 73. To avoid double counting, volumes and gross freight earnings are estimated as the average of inward and outward volumes and values.

[18] Higher variable costs would offset some of the steamship profits. The differences between estimates per ship and per ton are accounted for by the fact that the steamships in this part of the fleet were on average 85 per cent larger than the sailing ships: 670 versus 361 tons.

Table 2.2 The Norwegian fleet, transport and revenue, 1900

| | No. | Grt (1000) | Volume (1000 t.) | Transport total | Ballast (%) | Kroner/laden ton | Kroner/fleet ton | Kroner/ship |
|---|---|---|---|---|---|---|---|---|
| Steamships | 720 | 482.2 | 7877 | 24,257 | 35.1 | 11.4 | 186.4 | 124,813 |
| Sailing ships | 2562 | 923.7 | 2659 | 8606 | 38.2 | 19.1 | 54.8 | 19,773 |

Sources: Statistics Norway (1901), Table 35, 51 and Statistics Norway (1902a), Table 55, 73. See footnote

The Starting Point: A Small Country, but a Major Maritime Nation    31

**Table 2.3** Norwegian ships' most important port calls and voyages around the turn of the century

|    | Port | Per cent of calls | From—to | Per cent of voyages |
|----|------|------|---------|------|
| 1  | New York | 3.8 | Cardiff—Vera Cruz | 0.4 |
| 2  | Liverpool | 3.3 | Cardiff—Pernambuco | 0.4 |
| 3  | Cardiff | 3.0 | Cardiff—Bahia | 0.3 |
| 4  | London | 2.8 | Quebec—London | 0.3 |
| 5  | Hamburg | 2.1 | Laguna—Hamburg | 0.3 |
| 6  | Pensacola | 1.9 | London—Quebec | 0.3 |
| 7  | Buenos Aires | 1.7 | Trapani—Stavanger | 0.3 |
| 8  | Quebec | 1.6 | Hamburg—New York | 0.3 |
| 9  | Savannah | 1.5 | Pensacola—Buenos Aires | 0.3 |
| 10 | Rio Janeiro | 1.3 | New York—Stettin | 0.2 |
| 11 | Newport | 1.2 | Belize—Goole | 0.2 |
| 12 | Philadelphia | 1.2 | Cardiff—Maranham | 0.2 |
| 13 | Clyde | 1.1 | New York—Hamburg | 0.2 |
| 14 | Table Bay | 1.0 | Cadiz—Rio Grande | 0.2 |
| 15 | Marseilles | 1.0 | Liverpool—Halifax | 0.2 |

Source: *Lloyd's Weekly Shipping Index*, various issues, 1882, 1892 and 1902. See footnote

Ports all over the world were regularly visited by Norwegian ships, captains and crews, but Table 2.3 illustrates that some were more important than others.[19] The high concentration of world trade is evident—the 12 most important ports made up more than a quarter of all port calls in the data from *Lloyd's*. But Norwegian ships of course travelled to more exotic locations as well. In the decades around the turn of the century, they were registered in at least 1200 different foreign ports, according to

---

[19] Table 2.3: *Lloyd's Weekly Shipping Index*, various issues, 1882, 1892 and 1902. *Lloyd's Weekly Shipping Index* compiles listings from the *Lloyd's List* daily, and for simplicity, *Lloyd's List* is referred to in the text. Based on a purpose-built database of 9660 voyages by Norwegian vessels in 1882, 1892 and 1902. For each vessel listed in *Lloyd's Weekly Shipping Index*, two random voyages—one in the first half of the year and one in the second—have been selected. See Brautaset and Tenold (2010, 203–222) for more detailed information about the database. Due to the nature of the material included in *Lloyd's Weekly Shipping Index*—it records "all mercantile vessels on ocean voyages", but with some exceptions—ships trading locally in Europe are likely to be underreported. This refers primarily to sailing vessels "on voyages from one port to another in the Continent of Europe, between the White Sea and Cape Finisterre" and "between the UK and ports on the Continent as far south as Cape Finisterre", as well as steamships "trading between the UK and ports on the Continent, between the Scaw and Loire" and "trading between ports on the Continent between the North Cape and the Loire."

*Lloyd's List*.[20] Places such as Nash Creek in New Brunswick, Canada (population: 150), with a post office, a store and a factory specializing in the production of doors and doorframes, were clearly a contrast to the New York or London metropolises.[21]

The voyages listed above were the most frequent ones for Norwegian vessels. To some extent, they reveal the Norwegian specialization; transport of bulky cargoes from British coal ports and North American timber ports. The highways of the seas, where the infrastructure was good, the traffic density was high and the conditions were usually predictable, were less important for the Norwegians. Many of these passages were dominated by the large liner conferences, where the mighty British, American and Continental shipping companies colluded to reserve cargoes and ensure high freights. The voyage Paspébiac–Llanelly does not have the same ring as New York–Liverpool, but Norwegian ships could not afford to discriminate.[22] They travelled everywhere—from Aalborg to Zarate; from Wuhu to Ha Ha Bay.[23]

This snapshot of Norwegian shipping in 1900 shows a small country that is clearly "punching above its weight" in the international shipping industry. In the 1870s Norway had the third largest fleet in the world; by 1900 the country had been relegated to fourth place. But in no other country had local investors put so much of their resources into ocean-going ships. How can the strong position that shipping held in Norway, and the country's central role in the international shipping market, be explained?

---

[20] This figure is likely to be underreported. Information from smaller ports was less likely to get to London and the compilers of the *Lloyd's List* in time. Moreover, the publication did not report extensively about smaller ports on the European continent; see the note to Table 2.3. The economic historian Jan Tore Klovland, who has meticulously collected information on more than 200,000 voyages from the period 1835–1920, has more than 2400 different ports listed in his material. It is likely that the majority of these were visited by Norwegian ships.

[21] Information on Nash Creek from the Provincial Archives of New Brunswick.

[22] And it was a dangerous trip. Captain Hansen's barque *Pons Aelli*, the only Norwegian ship registered between these two ports in 1902, had to be abandoned in the middle of the ocean.

[23] Aalborg (Denmark) and Zarate (Argentina) were quite common destinations. However, the data set contains only one observation each for Wuhu (China) and Ha Ha Bay (Newfoundland).

## Why Norway? Geography, History and Culture

At the start of the 20th century, three fundamental features combined to explain how this small country had managed to become one of the world's leading maritime nations; geography, history and culture. The land and the sea shaped experiences, and experiences influenced values and attitude. The result was Norway, the maritime nation.

The first factor that can explain the Norwegian advantage in international shipping is geography. Without resorting to environmental determinism, it is evident that the sea and its firm grip on the coast and its inhabitants implied that Norway was destined to become a maritime nation. In fact, the name of the country—the Norðvegr—refers to a protected sailing route along the coast, it is "the way to the north." Thus, whereas the names of other countries usually refer to the territory on land and the people living there—Franc*ia*, Scot*land* and Den*mark*—even the name Nor*way* refers to the sea and to movement.[24]

The shape of the country implied that the sea was a much more important means of communication and transport than the land. The topographical conditions—the high mountains that separated the fjords and the modest settlements along the coast—forced Norwegians to take to water and undoubtedly played a decisive role in the development of maritime know-how and their orientation towards the sea. Water provided the most important means of transport and was a significant source of supplies. The geography in the coastal areas had created the archetypal Norwegian sailors—the Vikings. Their ability to build advanced ships, their navigational skills and seamanship, as well as their outward orientation—all were features that we can see traces of in Norway in the 19th and 20th centuries. We see these traces, not due to an unbroken line from Viking exploits to modern Norwegian shipping, but because the geography that promoted and honed these skills remained constant.

During the 20th century, telecommunications, airplanes, cars, trucks and high-speed trains have revolutionized human interaction. However, to understand the role of the sea, it is important to remember that these

---

[24] Skre, Dagfinn (2014, 34–44). This is of course the opposite of nominative determinism; the country got its name because it represented the way to the north.

are new phenomena. Well into the 20th century, water bound people together, while land separated them. Water transport was the least costly and most efficient way of carrying cargo and people, and maritime skills thus became a means for economic and cultural survival in a country such as Norway. The sea connected markets and districts, while dry land—mountains, in particular, but also forests—kept communities apart.

Norway was a relatively large country size-wise—it has the longest coastline in Europe—but had a fairly limited agricultural resource base and low population density.[25] This encouraged the people to trade with others in order to get vital supplies; a domestic surplus of fish and wood was exchanged for necessities such as grain and textiles from Continental Europe. Much of this trade had been performed by vessels from the German Hanse and subsequently from the economically and politically advanced Dutch Republic. By the middle of the 17th century, Bergen was the only Norwegian city that had been able to build up a substantial merchant fleet; in 1640 it amounted to 3500 *lasts* and locally owned ships transported 40 per cent of the city's trade.[26]

The country's position—in the northern part of the European continent and cut off from vibrant markets—stimulated trade in general, and medium-distance trade in particular. The central role played by the sea, both in local communications and in the harvesting of resources, gave Norwegians an advantage in seaborne transport. Subsequently, in the 19th century, when markets were opened and international trade

---

[25] At 25,000 kilometres (km), Norway's coastline is the seventh longest in the world and longer than the coastlines of for instance the United States, New Zealand and China. According to data from CIA's *World Factbook* it is almost twice as long as that of Greece, which is second in Europe (not counting Russia and Greenland). Data from the Norwegian Mapping Authority suggest that the length of the coastline increases to more than 100,000 km when fjords, bays and islands are included; Statistics Norway (2015, 6).

[26] Figenbaum et al. (2009, 7). A *læst* [last] was an old measure of the size of ships, in Norway usually measured in terms of barrels of grain (12) or coal (18). However, the "commercelæst" was defined in the statistics as a weight measure (equal to 5200 pounds) before 1846, and as a volume measure (equal to 165 cubic feet) after 1846; see Statistics Norway (1948, 238). With the transfer to the Moorsom measuring system in 1876, a common means of translation was to set one last equal to around 2.1 net register tons. Almost half of the Norwegian sailings to the Baltic in the period 1575–1654, as registered in the Sound tolls, were by Bergen vessels. Around 1730 the city's monopoly in the trade on Greenland and Iceland was transferred to Copenhagen, reducing the need for tonnage.

increased, this skill became a selling point in itself. Moreover, the fact that Norway was not a major power actually helped business abroad, securing market access due to the apparent lack of colonial pretensions.

There is another geographic factor worth noting: Norwegian shipping was a widely dispersed economic activity. The ownership of vessels engaged in international trade was not confined to a handful of industrious cities or trading towns, but spread all along the coast. There was the aforementioned concentration in the southern part of the country, as fishing was the favoured maritime activity further north. However, in the south, although sea transport primarily was an urban activity, numerous small communities along the coast and in the fjords invested in tonnage and supplied seafarers for the international market.

This wide geographic dispersion of Norwegian shipping declined slowly. There was clearly a technological and financial element to the decline—in the first decades of the 20th century the ownership of expensive steam tonnage was primarily a city phenomenon, and showed much higher concentration than ownership of the more affordable sailing ships. In 1900 the three leading cities, Bergen, Kristiania and Tønsberg, controlled almost two-thirds of the steamship tonnage, while the three leading sailing ship ports, Kristiania, Arendal and Stavanger, controlled less than a quarter of the sail tonnage. Moreover, around 16.5 per cent of the foreign-going sailing ship fleet was registered in *bygder* [villages] along the coast. This was more than twice as high as the corresponding figure for steamships.[27]

Geography is intimately intertwined with the second reason for the strong Norwegian position in the shipping industry; history. The maritime dimension put its mark on the lives of the Norwegians: "In the history of the Norwegian people, the sea provides an eternally fluctuating course. Our national character and our culture have been determined by it, just like our political, social and economic life."[28]

Within Norway, the legacy as a maritime nation has always been very visible, even on shore; "in Western Norway [almost everybody] is a sailor.

---

[27] Based on Statistics Norway (1902b), Table 1, 3–9. See also Schreiner (1963, 14–19), for a discussion of the development in the period up until 1914.
[28] Egeland (1930, 3).

The hotel porter has an anchor tattooed on both forearms; the taxi-driver and the waiter talk the uninhibited English that is the *lingua franca* of the sea."[29] Statues and memorial plaques have been dedicated to courageous sailors, while streets, buildings, museums and galleries carry the names of prominent and generous shipowners.

The shipping industry is more present in Norwegian society than in practically all other European nations.[30] Some shipowners have established wealthy foundations that donate money to art and research, while other foundations target social issues, providing support for seamen's widows, their surviving children or sailors "in economic difficulties."[31] Some shipowners are highly visible public figures, while others—ironically—are famous for their anonymity. Finally, a large number of people still work in the offices of shipping companies, maritime insurance and financing companies, in shipping banks, ship brokers and other related business, or are engaged in a variety of maritime activities. They are part of the maritime legacy, and continue to be an important economic reality.

But even history has to start somewhere, at some time. Norway's rise as a major maritime nation was a protracted and erratic journey, one that did not achieve sustained and rapid growth until the second half of the 19th century. After the Dutch lost their dominant position in the trade on Norway in the middle of the 17th century, a specific pattern developed with regard to the advance of Norwegian shipping. When the major European powers—the UK, France, the Netherlands, Spain—were involved in wars, the Norwegian fleet increased. During periods of peace, or—even worse—when Denmark-Norway was involved in wars with their Nordic neighbour, the market share fell.

---

[29] The Norwegian Joint Committee on International Social Policy (1959, 20).

[30] Again, the exception would be Greece, where the maritime legacy also has a dominant position, in particular in Piraeus and on the islands. For a good introduction to the regional and family dimensions of Greek shipping, see Harlaftis and Theotokas (2004).

[31] In the early 1970s, the book *Norske sjømannslegater og stiftelser* [Norwegian seamen's endowments and foundations] was around 250 pages long and contained information on more than 400 individual endowments by shipowners, consuls, captains and their wives. Fittingly, the book was published by a fund established by the Norwegian Shipowner's Association to honour the memory of Norwegian sailors during the First World War; see Norges Rederforbunds Sjømannsfond av 1918 (1973).

The first half of the 18th century was a difficult period, and from 1696 to 1745 the size of the Norwegian fleet declined by almost two-thirds.[32] Still, seaborne transport at this time was not the specialized activity that it is today. Rather, shipping was closely linked to local trading houses and most of the transport was related to Norwegian exports and imports. Luckily, from a shipping point of view, many of the commodities that were exported from Norway—forest products, fish and minerals, mainly copper and iron—were bulky cargoes that needed a lot of cargo space relative to their value.[33]

The extent of third-country shipping was limited in the first half of the 18th century. However, shipping activities increased immensely before Denmark-Norway was drawn into the Napoleonic Wars, with the number of ships and sailors almost trebling in the two decades after 1776; "the country's merchant marine saw a larger expansion within a few years than it had during a whole century."[34] The basis for the growth was a combination of political stimulus, high demand abroad—a well-known phenomenon also during subsequent wars—and low operating costs.[35] According to a contemporary British source, the lower operating costs were a result of the fact that Norwegian sailors were "being paid a certain stipend for the voyage out and home, and not by the month (as is the custom [in Great Britain])." The effect of this incentive was clear; it "becomes in the interest of these foreigners to use every exertion in their power to accomplish the voyage in the shortest time possible."[36] Even in the late 18th century it was not uncommon to blame workers in other countries for their high productivity…

---

[32] Denmark-Norway re-entered The Great Northern War in 1709. In the period 1710–1713, Bergen lost 55 ships, almost half of the pre-war fleet, to privateers (who were basically government-sponsored pirates); see Dyrvik (1979, 107). In order to avoid privateers, ships could take to the sea when the sailing conditions were bad. This of course increased the probability of wrecking. When Denmark-Norway was involved in wars, Norwegian ships were sailing between a rock and a hard place.

[33] In the 19th century, another bulky cargo, ice, was added, and in the peak years around 1900 more than a million tons of ice was exported annually. Technological advances onshore—improved refrigeration and production of plant ice—led to a market meltdown, and the Norwegian ice exports had more or less dried up by the outbreak of the First World War.

[34] Schweigaard (1840, 131).

[35] Johansen (1992, 488–489).

[36] Quote from merchant's testimonial to a 1786 Board of Trade inquiry; Johansen (1992, 487).

The majority of the new ships were built in Norway, particularly on the South Coast.[37] Given current controversies in shipping, it is worth noting that in the first years of the 19th century, some of the vessels on the Norwegian register were owned by "foreigners, who by means of *pro forma*-documents enjoyed the advantage of our country's neutrality."[38] Thus, according to contemporary sources, Norway appears to have been an early example of a *Flag of Convenience*, enticing foreign owners by providing beneficial conditions. This was not the first time Norway was used to create a false sense of neutrality, but subsequent research has suggested that though the assertion is correct, the scale of this practice was limited.[39]

Again, Norway did well as long as the country stayed away from the conflict, but when Denmark-Norway was dragged into the war, there was little consolation in the Norwegian flag. In 1807, following the pre-emptive British bombardment of Copenhagen and the Danish-Norwegian entry into the war, more than 550 ships, as much as a third of the fleet, was lost. The effect on Norwegian shipping was devastating. In the subsequent years, British authorities continued to confiscate Norwegian ships, and by the end of the war more than 5000 Norwegian sailors had been put in prison in the UK, some for as long as seven years.[40] Although Norwegian privateering partly balanced the picture, the British might at sea was too strong.

In the short term, the Danish-Norwegian participation on Napoleon's side in the conflict had dreadful effects; famine, un(der)employment, increasing mortality, economic decline, financial and monetary collapse—"one of the bleakest periods in modern history."[41] In the longer term, the fact that Denmark was on the losing side, meant Norwegian freedom.

---

[37] Dyrvik (1979, 177). According to a survey of the pre-war fleet in *Den Norske Rigstidende*, 1 February 1815, 1 the three main shipbuilding areas were Arendal (174 ships), Bergen (170 ships) and Øster-Riisøer (Risør, 115 ships).
[38] Schweigaard (1840, 183).
[39] See for instance Kiær (1893, 333), or more detailed discussions in Thue (1980, 150–151), Tveite (1965) or Schreiner (1952).
[40] See for instance Berit Eide Johnsen's fascinating book on the cultural exchange that this entailed; Johnsen (1993).
[41] Eitrheim et al. (2016, 84–85).

At end of the war, Norway's status as a Danish province ended after almost three centuries.[42] Despite the introduction of a Norwegian constitution, the country's independence was very short-lived. In November 1814 the recently established parliament was forced to accept a union with Sweden. The attempt at full independence thus ended in futility and political compromise, and Norway became the "little brother" in a personal union with Sweden. In addition to the parliament and the constitution, Norway retained executive and judiciary powers, but the two countries shared the monarch—from the Swedish house of Bernadotte—and the foreign policy was conducted by the Swedish Ministry of Foreign Affairs.

The change in union partner had a positive effect on the Norwegian foray into world shipping. In terms of international trade, Sweden-Norway was not a minion. The countries exported large amounts of timber and wood; one of the most traded, and also most volume-demanding, commodities. Up until the middle of the 1820s Swedish timber exports were reserved for Swedish keels. Subsequently, as a result of an extension of *Mellanrikslagen* [the Interstate Laws] and the abolition of *Produktplakatet* [the Commodity Ordinance aka "The Swedish Navigation Act"], Norwegian ships were from 1825 allowed to compete on even terms with local ships in the transport of Swedish cargoes, for instance timber.[43] With Swedish protectionism out of the way, the lower-cost Norwegian vessels became an attractive alternative for Swedish importers and exporters. The share of Norwegian ships in Sweden's trade increased from 4 per cent in 1819 to 34 per cent in 1849.[44]

This expansion of Norwegian shipping in the first half of the 19th century was not based on long-distance trades, but that soon changed. In a Parliamentary discussion on maritime skills in 1839 it was emphasized that "it is not common – but rather an exception – that our captains sail

---

[42] The Kalmar Union between Denmark, Sweden and Norway was formed at the end of the 14th century. Sweden finally withdrew at the start of the 16th century, and Denmark gradually strengthened its grip on its Norwegian partner.

[43] On the effects of the Navigation Acts in Scandinavia, see Ojala and Räihä (2017). A provisionary decree that abolished the restrictions was introduced in May 1825 and confirmed by a law in August 1827.

[44] Kiær (1893, 34).

the distant seas." Consequently, the politicians saw the need for formal nautical education as limited. The reason was that the ships primarily operated in the North Sea—"at most extending to the Baltic"—where "experience to some extent can neutralize the lack of navigational knowledge."[45] In the second half of the 19th century, this local, northern European focus became relatively less important. Again, the basis was primarily political, and again, the political decisions were not made within Norway.

The aggressive acquisition of market shares in Sweden in the 1830s and 1840s was a prelude to what happened in the second half of the 19th century—though by then the backdrop was not just advances at the expense of a neighbour, but the lifting of restrictions on a global scale. After 1850 practically the whole world was opened up to Norwegian shipping, and the competence that Norwegian shipowners and sailors had built up became much sought after. The liberalization paved the way for a massive expansion of Norway's shipping interests.

In June 1849 Queen Victoria signed the Act that repealed the protectionist Navigation Laws, which had limited the participation of foreign ships in British trade and transport. At this time Great Britain was the centre of global commerce, and now the country opened its trade to ships of all nations. For Norwegian shipowners, the prey suddenly got much, much bigger, and the combination of low costs and high efficiency was a formula that triumphed in the British market. From 1850 to 1860 the Norwegian tonnage cleared in British ports increased by 191 per cent, and only the United States had a larger absolute increase in the transport of British trade.[46] Freed from the limitations of Sweden-Norway's imports and exports, and no longer hampered by protectionist measures abroad, Norwegian shipping flourished.

---

[45] Norway, Parliament, *Odelsthinget*, 13071839, 679 and 685. The politicians' powers of prediction were no better in the 19th century than they are today. Less than 18 months after this discussion, the first Norwegian vessel rounded Cape Horn. Among the cargoes that the brig *Preciosa* carried was *aquavit*, a traditional Norwegian potato spirit. Even today, aquavit is transported on ships crossing the equator, where humidity, continuous movement and temperature changes affect the maturation and the final taste. *Preciosa* became so famous that the Norwegian poet Henrik Wergeland wrote a shanty specifically about the ship. See *Nordlyset*, 05071844, 3 and Blom (1977, 177–180).

[46] Glover (1863, 14).

# The Starting Point: A Small Country, but a Major Maritime Nation    41

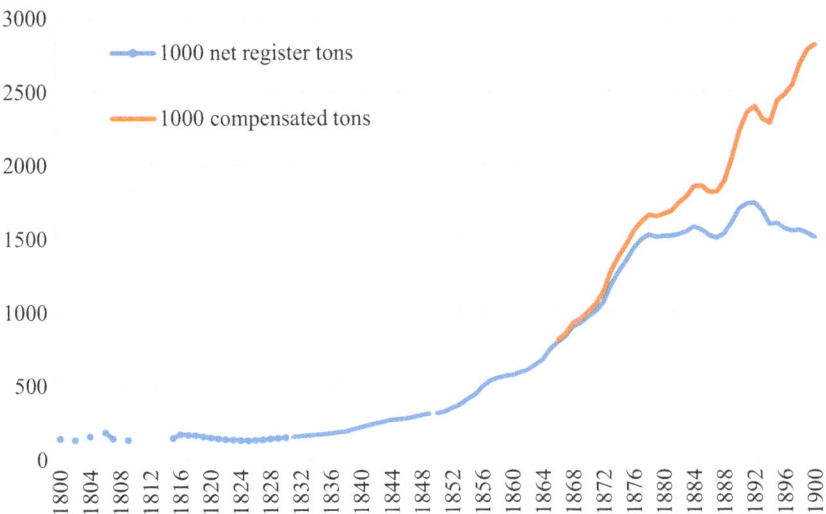

**Fig. 2.3** Estimates of the Norwegian fleet, 1800–1900, 1000 net register tons. (Source: Statistics Norway (1949), Table 126, 241–242. See footnote)

The liberalization of the international market was a necessary condition for the enormous expansion that took place in the second half of the 19th century. Figure 2.3 shows that the Norwegian fleet growth was characterized by strong fluctuations in the first decades of the 19th century, followed by a slowly upward-sloping trend from 1830 onwards.[47] However, the expansion in the period 1830–1850 was uneven, characterized by two steps forward and one step back.[48] From the middle of the

---

[47] Figure 2.3: For a good discussion of the problems of estimating the size of the Norwegian fleet in the 19th century, see Brautaset (2002, 118–128). Due to the considerations presented there, the data used here should be seen as a minimum, and are based on the following sources 1800–1809 from Dyrvik (1979, 177), 1815–1830 converted from the data in Commerselæster by the factor 2.1 from Kristiansen 1925; 1830–1865 based on Brautaset (2002, 258). Both of these sources have adjusted the official statistics, but refer to the full fleet, rather than the ships trading abroad; see also Broch (1876, 81). Data from the period after 1865 are taken from Statistics Norway (1948), Table 126, 241–242; the data on "compensated tonnage" imply that steamships have been multiplied by a factor of 3.6 to account for their higher efficiency.

[48] The data in Brautaset (2002, 261) suggest that the annual export of shipping services declined in 30 per cent of the years in the period 1830–1850, compared with 13.3 per cent in the period 1850–1865. The only years with decline after 1850 were 1857 and 1858, and are thus closely associated with what Hughes 1956, 194 refers to as "the first world-wide commercial crisis in the

century the development changed dramatically. In the period 1850–1875 the growth was both much stronger and more persistent than before.

The average annual growth rates increased from 0.18 per cent 1800–1830, a period with a see-saw pattern of growth and decline, to 3.85 per cent from 1830 to 1850. In the subsequent 15 years the Norwegian fleet grew at an astonishing 5.75 per cent annually, before falling back to 0.44 per cent in the years up to the turn of the century. The latter stagnation, however, was mitigated by the transformation from sail to steam. In fact, when we take into account the higher productivity of the steamships, the fleet continued to increase, with only a handful of hiccups, until the losses in connection with the First World War.[49] In terms of "compensated tonnage"—a measure of transport capacity that takes into account the superior efficiency of steam vessels—the average annual growth was 3.7 per cent from 1865 to 1900. This was a reduction compared to the previous 15 years, but still a relatively large increase and far higher than the growth in the economy in general.

After the removal of political restrictions had "opened up" the international market in the middle of the 20th century, there was a self-sustaining element to the Norwegian shipping industry. Regardless of whether we call this "path dependence" or "tradition," the fact of the matter is that Norway's fleet was very competitive in the international shipping market. It could offer reliable transport at a reasonable price. This was partly explained by the conditions at home: Norwegian shipping enterprises were very competitive in the quest for domestic capital and labour.

In the 1850s, the first decade of this expansive period for Norwegian shipping, additions to the fleet were to a large extent built domestically. The industry had access to "the raw materials and the builders needed to manufacture first-class ships"—particularly on the South Coast. Moreover, "shipbuilding geniuses such as for instance Annanias Dekke in Bergen" competed among the leading shipbuilders internationally.[50] The demand for ships outstripped the local supply and, from the 1860s

---

history of modern capitalism." For the Norwegian dimension of this crisis, see Eitrheim et al. (2016, 156–164).

[49] Estimates are average annual compound gross rates based on net registered tonnage; for information on the data, see Fig. 2.3.

[50] Egeland (1930, 31).

# The Starting Point: A Small Country, but a Major Maritime Nation 43

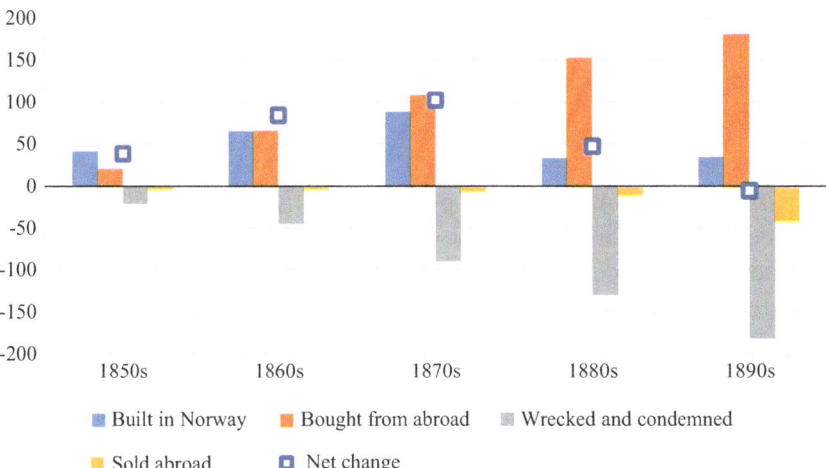

**Fig. 2.4** Average annual fleet increase and decrease by source, 1851–1900, 1000 net register tons. (Source: Statistics Norway (1968), Table 176, 364–365. See footnote)

onwards, a larger share of the new ships was imported.[51] One reason for the increasing imports was the fact that the authorities during the 1850s twice reduced, and then finally removed, the "naturalization levy," a tax on ships bought abroad.[52] This tax had been to the benefit of shipbuilders, but to the detriment of shipowners.[53] The other main reason for the growth was that shipowners in other countries—in particular the UK—modernized their fleets by investing in steam tonnage. Consequently, a large number of relatively inexpensive second-hand sailing ships were for sale in the international market in the last decades of the 19th century.

Figure 2.4 illustrates the sources of the Norwegian fleet growth.[54] The figure reveals that although more than half of the tonnage added in the

---

[51] Statistics Norway (1968, 364).

[52] Hodne (1980, 167).

[53] Though, at this time, there was a much larger overlap between these groups than today.

[54] Figure 2.4: Statistics Norway (1968), Table 176, 364–365. Net increase and decrease based on individual columns, which differ from the aggregate figures given in the original source. Supplemented by information from Statistics Norway 1949, Table 129. The original source points out that the figures for the early period are "incomplete, due especially to difficulties in securing exact data as to the great number of vessels not registered." The "unregistered" vessels are sailing

period 1850–1870 was bought from abroad, there was at the same time a strong increase in shipbuilding within Norway. The production peaked in 1875, when more than 264 ships, amounting to around 75,000 net register tons, were built.[55]

Fritz Hodne refers to shipping as "the leading sector" in Norwegian economic development in the period after the Navigation Acts were repealed. With its impressive growth rates, the shipping industry clearly outshone other large sectors. According to Hodne's calculations, shipping investments amounted to around 30 per cent of total gross investments in the quarter century after 1850.[56] As pointed out above, the main driver behind the demand increase was found abroad—more than three-quarters of the growth came from transport between foreign ports, and was thus totally independent of Norway's own transport demand.[57]

Still, conditions within Norway complemented its international development, facilitating the rapid growth of the fleet. There are two main reasons for the attractiveness of shipping employment and investments in Norway. First, the alternative employment and investment opportunities were limited. In the 19th century, Norway did not have large exploitable reserves of coal or other minerals. Moreover, the modest purchasing power among domestic consumers and the long distance to larger markets in Europe implied that the conditions for large-scale manufacturing production were relatively unfavourable. Nascent textile and mechanical engineering industries notwithstanding, Norway never went through industrial revolutions of the British or German kind.[58]

When life expectancy increased in the second half of the 19th century, migration became an important safety valve that checked population

---

ships smaller than 50 net register tons and steam and motor vessels smaller than 25 net register tons. This poses larger problems for the data on the number of ships, than for the tonnage figures, as the majority of the unregistered ships were small vessels.

[55] Based on the number of ships, production peaked in the second half of the 1860s. However, due to increasing average size, in tonnage terms the first half of the 1870s saw the largest production; see Fig. 2.4 for information on the statistics.

[56] Hodne (1981, 27). Based on slightly different data and methods from what we used above, Hodne calculates the annual growth rate of the fleet to be 6.8 per cent for the period 1850–1875.

[57] Calculated on the basis of ton-miles data in Brautaset (2002), 259.

[58] For a good overview of the discussion of Norway's industrial breakthrough, see Basberg (2006, 4–7).

growth. Around 800,000 Norwegians left for the new world in the period 1830–1920—in percentage terms, only Ireland had a higher outflow of emigrants.[59] The effect on Norwegian wages and living standards was strongly positive. The existing arable land would not have been able to sustain the increased numbers and the conditions were not favourable for a mass exodus into the secondary sector. With few domestic opportunities, employment at sea was another manner in which the surplus labour force could be utilized. Sometimes migration and seamanship was combined; Norwegian sailors had "gained such a reputation for ability and good conduct that they were eagerly sought by American captains."[60]

In a discussion of subsidies to shipping in the US Congress, it was pointed out that "[n]ecessity compels and tradition invites the Norwegians to become seamen." According to the Americans, "[Norwegian] capital and labor naturally turn to the sea, and laws which in the United States would be restrictive, in Norway are merely the affirmation of local customs. Thus the law requiring three-fourths of the crews of Norwegian ships to be Norwegian imposes no restraint on the growth of Norwegian shipping, while a similar law in the United States would virtually drive all our ships in foreign trade to foreign flags."[61]

The demographic development ensured an ample supply of seamen. A combination of local resources and institutions facilitated the investment in ships on which they could sail.[62] The early dominance of Norwegian-built ships was related to the type of organization—*partsrederiet* [the part ownership]—where local communities pooled their resources to invest in ships. The part ownerships were an ingenious way of raising investment capital for new shipping capacity, even though access to traditional equity and credit was limited. On the South Coast, "the forest, the wooden ship and the part ownership" were considered "the God-given foundation for shipping."[63] However, this organizational form also had its drawbacks, as it made long-term investment difficult.

---

[59] O'Rourke and Williamson (1999, 122).
[60] Gjerset (1933, 63).
[61] The original text says "compels." US Senate, 1922, *To amend Merchant marine act of 1920: Joint hearings before the Committee on Commerce*, Washington: Government Printing Office.
[62] Before the strong growth of the country's own fleet, many Norwegian sailors had found employment on, for instance, Dutch ships;
[63] Tønnesen (1951, 80).

In the early expansionary phase, in the 1850s, when the majority of the vessels were built in Norway, most new ships were constructed as "a cooperation between the builder, the timber merchant, the captain and the supplier. Farmers who delivered wood from their forests, craftsmen and ships chandlers thus participated with a smaller or larger part based on their deliveries and resources. The out-of-pocket expenses thus became very limited."[64] Shipping was a potluck business, where the owners contributed, often in kind, with what they had. The legal regime made the use of ships as collateral impossible. Although it was possible to borrow money on the basis of individual parts, it was also common to use dwellings, farms or friends and family as guarantee.

The part ownerships were "projects," where the investment horizon was the lifetime of the vessel. Profits were paid out at regular intervals or as and when they occurred—sometimes after every individual voyage. When the ship was sold, scrapped or lost, any remaining funds were paid out to the part owners according to their share of the investment. The project then ended—the business was over. Investors reduced their risks by diversifying and participating in several vessels, and it was easy to reinvest the funds in new ship parts.

A combination of tradition and agreements—within the boundaries of a very limited legal framework—served to regulate the part ownerships. According to *Sjøloven av 1860* [the Maritime Act] the vessel could only be insured if all part owners agreed. If the ship was not fully insured—or not insured at all—it was possible for individual owners to insure their parts.

In order to avoid costly foreign insurance arrangements, mutual associations were established along the coast. From a slow and late start in the second half of the 1830s, by the middle of the century around three-quarters of the merchant marine had been insured in mutual associations—"an astonishing breakthrough" for a type of organization that was new in a Norwegian setting.[65] It has been claimed that the efficient and low-cost insurance arrangements helped the Norwegian competitiveness.[66] The high market share remained well into the 1890s, when a larger

---

[64] Seland (1959, 143).
[65] Espeli (2010, 49).
[66] Espeli (2010).

share of the ships—in particular sailing vessels—began to sail without hull insurance.

As shipping played such an important role in local communities along the coast, "surprisingly large parts of the population became mobilized in the accumulation process."[67] Due to the in-kind nature of part of the investment, it would not have been possible to raise the same amount of capital for other purposes. The integration of shipping—and the other main export sectors, fish and forest products—in the domestic economy, implied that the export-led economic growth did not lead to an enclave-like structure of the kind seen in many developing economies, in particular those based on plantation crops and mining. Rather, the close integration created feedback-loops that strengthened the economic development. An analysis from the turn of the century concludes that slightly less than 6 per cent of the Norwegian population directly or indirectly depended upon shipping for their livelihoods, compared with 1.5 per cent in Denmark and 1.3 per cent in the case of Sweden.[68]

Shipping's role as a leading force with regard to employment and investment reflected the competitive advantages that the Norwegians had built up in international shipping—advantages that had become "unshackled" by the repeal of the Navigation Acts. Over the previous centuries, the Norwegians had developed skills that made them "formidable competitors" in the international shipping market; "The Norwegians are born shipowners and have developed the shipping industry for its own sake to a degree that is rare among Continental peoples," according to a British observer.[69]

The typical Norwegian ship in the second half of the 19th century was "the never-tiring tramp, which continually scours the Seven Seas in search of charters, loading from one port to another, and never knowing where she may have to sail for next, picking up cargo here and running light there, figuring frequently in the overdue list, and sometimes turning up after she has been posted missing, but always returning to her home port,

---

[67] Bergh et al. (1983, 113).
[68] Kiær (1900, 436).
[69] Fayle (1933 [2006], 272).

battered and weather-beaten, ready to sail again after an overhaul in dry dock and the renewal of her certificate of character."[70]

Shipping was hard work, and it was risky. In the last part of the 19th century, as the sailing ships got older, loss rates increased tremendously. Still, this dangerous, but profitable, activity lay the foundation for the Norwegian position as a major maritime nation. By the middle of the 19th century, shipping had become a crucial economic activity all along the coast in the southern part of Norway. Although the sector often had to share its key role—some places with forestry, other places with fishing or whaling—it was an integral part of the market economy, providing employment, investment opportunities and services. By the turn of the century, Norway had 10 ships for every factory.

## Norwegian Maritime Culture

So far, we have looked at the roles of geography and history—two relatively tangible concepts. The final reason that can explain how and why Norway managed to build up and maintain a dominant position in international shipping is more difficult to pin down; culture. Sometimes, "culture" is considered the refuge of the scoundrel; the trump card which historians and social scientists refer to when they have run out of arguments and facts. However, culture "remains our default term for covering the relation between forms and social processes."[71] It may be hard to define, but we usually know what it is…

In our context, the term "culture" contains two important dimensions. The first is what we can refer to as "maritime culture," which refers to the traditions, structures and practices that make Norwegians see themselves as a sea-going people and the sea as a natural extension of the land. When an 80-year-old captain explains that he did "his best" at sea, because he "wanted to assert Norway's honour as a sea-going nation with traditions back to the era of the sagas," that is the maritime culture talking—"the spirit of the sea."[72]

---

[70] An early 20th century presentation of tramp shipping quoted in Harlaftis and Theotokas (2004, 219).
[71] Halperin (2012, 133).
[72] Worm-Müller (1951, 487).

The second element is "Norwegian culture," which covers the manner in which society was organized, including the norms and values that gave Norwegian shipowners a competitive advantage internationally. Specifically, in most coastal communities in southern Norway, work on and investments in ships was an important activity.[73] As the legal infrastructure was limited, the concept of trust, regulated by and integrated in informal local networks, became important.

The cultural aspect, and here we are mainly talking about the maritime element, was clearly linked to the geographical and historical foundations. The influence from the surroundings, and in particular the visibility of shipping, enticed young males to see a career at sea as the embodiment of the ultimate dream. Norway was the land of the Vikings. Vikings went to sea. The sea began just outside the window. However, the culture also changed across time, hence "when the sailing ship era ended, a distinctive culture died out."[74] The transition to steam changed the life of most seamen both at sea and in port, but it did not change the perception of Norway as a maritime nation and Norwegian men as a seafaring tribe.

The mystery and attraction of the sea is a staple of seamen's memoirs: "I had my heart set on going to sea […] my greatest delight was to roam the waterfront and watch and listen to the sailors at their work in the ships' rigging, and their singing, hoisting and bending sails to the yards and spars, preparatory to the setting out for voyages to far places. Here was romance, here was life."[75] With a starting point such as this, it is perhaps not surprising that the boy in question ends up as a captain.

Another sailor rued "the sad day, when the fever of the sea no longer makes the pulse of the youth beat faster and no longer stirs their longing for new experiences and new, always new, horizons."[76] Of course, these

---

[73] In an international perspective, the largest Norwegian cities at the start of the 20th century, Kristiania and Bergen, clearly had small-city features; among the *bourgeoise*—the merchants and shipowners—everybody knew everybody. In 1900, the population of Inner London was three times as large as that of Norway.

[74] Tønnesen (1951, 165).

[75] Bratrud (1961, 8).

[76] Rasmussen (1952, 14); see also 36–40. Adolescents with romantic views of seamanship and the call of the sea are found, for instance, in Stamsø (1929), or the interview in Tranøy (1941, 41–43).

seamen's memoirs themselves—with their exoticism and tales of adventures in far-off places—ensnared new generations of sailors. The difference between domestic docility and adventures abroad was also emphasized by contemporary observers. "The wider horizon, the richer and more varied life abroad, the wonders of art and industry – contrasted with the monotony of life which often prevails in many small communities on the sea-coast – how all these must attract young lads," A.N. Kiær pointed out in his discussion of the "principal causes" behind Norway's standing as a maritime nation.[77]

Many of the seamen's memoirs tell stories of boys escaping impoverished circumstances in Norway, where the food, lodging and modest wages at sea become a means of survival.[78] For others, sea voyages were a part of the general education. "A custom that was quite common in seafaring towns, in particular in Bergen," was a period at sea, reminiscent of the apprentices' *Wanderjahre*. The bourgeoisie, businessmen and others that were involved in shipping, sent their "sons – with reassuring supervision – on a couple of months' voyage on a cargo ship, fostering maturity and giving experiences at an impressionable age." The voyages taught him (for it was invariably a boy) about "foreign places and peoples [...] and international trade and business."[79]

The allure of the sea around the turn of the century, when the sailing ships were still frequent guests in Norwegian ports, is self-evident. But "the call of the sea" kept its power well into the second half of the 20th century. For many of those growing up in the 1950s and 1960s, a period at sea became an important rite of passage, a gap year activity that marked the transition to adult life. For many young sailors there was "one common element: The dream of seeing and experiencing the wide world that one otherwise had only read or heard about."[80]

---

[77] Kiær (1893, 363). Kiær's reasoning, "How can these young Viking lads but long for the time when they, too, are permitted to cross the sea into the wide, wide world?", is almost poetic in its prose. The fact that the article was published in *The Journal of Political Economy*, a periodical that both then and now ranks among the most important in economics, illustrates the drastic transformation of economics as a branch of science. Today, authors in the journal argue by equation, not by interpretation; by positivism, not by prose.

[78] See for instance Tønnessen (1996), as an example of someone leaving for the sea out of necessity.

[79] Meidell (1968).

[80] Pettersen and Brundtland (2002, 72).

For the 19th and the first part of the 20th century, shipping was the most important lifeline to large parts of the world. Exotic cultures did not have many inroads into Norwegian society at this time; the country had a modest military and colonial presence abroad, and mobility was slow and limited for most people.[81] In the days before low-cost plane tickets, mass tourism and public broadcasting, information about distant places came primarily via seamen, missionaries, emigrants and a small number of merchants and adventurers.

The written seamen's memoirs were but a small part of the transmission of life at sea and abroad. More important were the gifts that the sailors brought home and the "taste of the sea" that they gave by means of stories, tall tales and songs. Shanties (work songs) and other seamen's songs were important culture bearers, anchored in the coastal communities, where young boys heard about Pensacola and Pernambuc—not Paris or Berlin.[82] Onboard the ships, the shanties had a function—they were used to coordinate the sailors' work. Ashore, their call-and-response could create a sense of community, bringing the sea back to the shore and stirring the adventurousness of those at home.

In seafarers' songs and shanties, sailors are portrayed as a strange combination of carefree and melancholic; without a care in the world, but longing for home. Strong drink and hard work are among the main themes, as well as love and loss. Rio de Janeiro, Hamburg, New York, the East Indies—foreign places filled with young girls whose main desire was to meet a "Norwegian sailor boy." The songs themselves reveal the global character of shipping; the chorus was often "imported"—sung in "a sailor-English that was almost as international as the melody."[83]

The transmission of seamen's culture through stories and songs was informal, but the country's sailors played a more formal role as cultural ambassadors as well. Several Norwegian museums built up their ethnographic

---

[81] This was an era of great contrasts. Many people never left their home town or village, those who did often went far—to the other side of the world.
[82] "Pernambuc'" refers to Pernambuco, in the north-eastern part of Brazil, the 18th most visited destination in the *Lloyd's List* data set with almost 1 per cent of the port calls. The contraction makes the word rhyme with the Norwegian *sukk* [sigh], which the sailor emits when he thinks of Norway. For the full lyrics to "Sing Sally Oh", a modern version based on Wergeland's poem about the Preciosa, see Brochman (1937, 28–32).
[83] Brochmann (1937, 39).

collection on the basis of what sailors brought home from abroad; they were instructed by the museums about which pictures and artefacts that would be interesting.[84] Foreign memorabilia—souvenirs, novelties, mementos and exotic objects—were common in the homes of sailors and their families. The sea was the path to the rest of the world; the seamen were the guides.

The "maritime culture" clearly made its mark on Norway. But how did "Norwegian culture" influence the country's foray into shipping?

In his analysis of Norwegian culture and society, the anthropologist Arne Martin Klausen identifies four features that characterize the country. Two of these, in particular, may have been important for the expansion of the country's shipping industry. The first is the fact that Norway can be characterized as a "small-scale society with a large degree of informal social control." This was particularly relevant for the many enterprises in towns and smaller cities along the coast, where the informal framework facilitated investment and partnerships. The second characteristic element of the Norwegian culture and society is the fact that the ideology of equality (egalitarianism) has a particularly strong position.[85]

The small transparent communities encouraged the dispersed type of ownership that characterized the Norwegian *partsrederier*. In the absence of a clearly-defined legal framework, the strong social control and the threat of social exclusion created a quasi-institutional legality. The shortcomings of the public legal system were thus neutralized. In this respect, the experience is not very different from that seen within some fringe religious movements, such as for instance Quakers. There was an awful lot of trust and good faith involved in the manner in which shipping investments were organized and business was conducted.

Joint investments and other interactions had the properties of a "repeated game"; you could not cheat your fellow shipowners, because you would have to look them in the eye when you met them in church or on the street. Moreover, you needed them to trust you with their resources in the future as well. Of course, not all business ventures followed this idealized model, but the "trust" aspect of Norwegian culture and society

---

[84] Austbø (2012). Missionaries made up the other significant group of collectors.

[85] Klausen (1999, 32–33) also emphasizes the strong Norwegian welfare state and the strong presence of the periphery in the political system, but these two features are not relevant in a 19th century setting.

clearly enabled and encouraged capital formation on a scale that would otherwise have been unthinkable.

When more modern types of incorporation, for instance limited liability companies, replaced the part ownership, the "old" mechanisms continued to play an important role. As we shall see, this cooperative spirit—between investors, but also between for instance shipowners, banks and insurance companies—continued to be relevant into the 20th century. The joint projects—sometimes with unlimited responsibility—were beneficial for all parties when the markets were going up and there was a need to pool resources to remain competitive, but they also meant that problems spread rapidly when the demand conditions deteriorated.

Trust between partners and other business relations—both before and after the existence of a more formal legal framework—was a Norwegian "character trait" that facilitated the country's shipping investment. Other results of this trust—for instance the low insurance premia in local associations—gave Norwegian owners a cost advantage that improved their competitiveness. So, the social control seen in the coastal communities, through its effect on investment and profits, undoubtedly helped build up Norway, the maritime nation.

The egalitarian nature of Norwegian society may also have boosted the maritime presence. Throughout the 19th century Norway was a society characterized by the absence of nobility, and with class differences that in an international perspective can be considered relatively low. For sure, Norway was far from an egalitarian paradise where paupers and princes went hand in hand. However, the fact that there were relatively weak class distinctions affected the development of a maritime Norway positively. For instance, the willingness to accept investments from all parts of the population—without discrimination—enabled capital formation.

"Practically all and sundry were a shipowner [in the 1860s]. Everyone that had saved some money usually did not give up until they had invested it in a part of a ship."[86] As ships became larger and more expensive, the number of parts per ship increased—from 4 or 16 to 64 or 100. After around 1890 the number of part owners increased, with many "new names," including "common people." Managing owners approached

---

[86] Vigeland (1943, 170).

"friends and enemies, the learned and the unlearned, the tailor and the shoemaker [...] until the sought-after 100/100 parts were safely anchored in larger and smaller portions of people's savings, from all of the city and from all walks of life."[87]

The pattern continued into the new century, when the organizational form gradually shifted from partnerships to limited liability companies. The shipowner Olav Ditlev-Simonsen, the *pater familias* of one of the most successful 20th century "shipping dynasties," had ordered a steamship; "it was not like now [1945] that the bank or the yard provided first priority [mortgage]. All of the capital had to be procured at once." For a couple of months Ditlev-Simonsen "travelled the country, like a sales agent for shipping shares." The shares cost NOK1000 each "and 90 per cent of the shareholders were small savers who at most could afford one or a couple of shares each, seldom more than five. They were tailors and shoemakers, bakers and wheelmakers."[88]

This notion that everyone—"the clergyman, the doctor, the district recorder, and in particular sailors, merchants, craftsmen, even servant girls"—had invested in shipping, is a generalization that should be modified.[89] Like investments in general, the majority of the funds came from the wealthiest. Although Olaf Ditlev-Simonsen claims that 90 per cent of the shareholders were small savers, his own company "signed up for a large part."[90] Still, there is little doubt about the fact that the shipping sector was a vehicle for social mobility.

The sailing ships offered careers for hard-working boys; the best and the brightest could rise in the ranks until they were masters themselves. Experience and skills were acquired on-board; along the way, if funds were put aside, the sailor could become investor. Towards the end of his career, when the experienced captain signed off, he would use his knowledge and take over as corresponding owner for one or more ships. Naturally, not everyone managed to reach that far—but the possibility *was* there. When Ordinary seamen had signed on a couple of times, they

---

[87] Pettersen (1980, 208 and 211).
[88] Ditlev-Simonsen (1945, 79–80).
[89] Due (1909), quoted in Sandvik (2018, 84).
[90] Ditlev-Simonsen (1945, 79).

became Able seamen, and could progress to Boatswains. Third mates could become Second mates and then First mates. And First mates could become Captains.

The two largest shipping companies in Bergen in 1890 had been established by former captains, and in the subsequent decade a large number of "captain shipowners" established new businesses, sometimes—but not always—in cooperation with clerks from existing shipping company offices.[91] When the Norwegian Shipowners' Association was established in 1909, the majority of the founding committee were former captains who had become "managing owners" or sons of captains who had gone ashore and continued their careers as investors and owners. "The captain who ventured his savings on his own vessel – that was once the very basis for the Norwegian merchant marine."[92] And they remembered where they came from. The previously mentioned Olaf Ditlev-Simonsen, who went to sea straight after his confirmation and by the outbreak of the Second World War controlled one of the largest fleets in Norway, called his autobiography *En sjøgutt ser tilbake* [A seaboy looks back].[93]

The main task of the managing owners was not unlike that of the captains; to navigate profitably and safely in conditions that were unpredictable and difficult to influence. During the great expansion of Norwegian shipping after 1850, the managing owner had often in practice been little more than the partners' book-keeper. Many—or most—of the short-term business decisions were made by a captain who was far away and difficult to instruct. As communication channels improved, commercial decisions about cargoes and trades could more easily be made at home. Former captains could combine their accumulated knowledge of ports and markets, with "ears on the ground" and information from other public and private sources, and then relay their instructions to the ships. Decision-making power moved from the sea to the home port.

---

[91] Pettersen (1980, 205).

[92] Aurmark et al. (1977, 79): the heading of the chapter, which deals with contemporary shipping in the 1970s, is called "There is still a room for sailors in the shipowning profession."

[93] Ditlev-Simonsen (1945). At the time of his death, the "seaboy's" group of companies owned 24 ships, amounting to 365,000 dead weight tons, slightly less than 3 per cent of the Norwegian fleet. Interestingly, his son, Halfdan—one of three sons that managed a shipping company—called his own autobiography, published 10 years after his father's, "A shipowner looks back." Here, he points out that "The landlubber-shipowners are in earnest entering Norwegian shipping with the generation to which I belong"; Ditlev-Simonsen (1954, 14).

## The First Decade of the New Century

When the 19th century became the 20th, Norway was not a fully independent nation; the monarch and the foreign policy were shared with Sweden. However, during the 19th century a distinct and separate Norwegian identity had continued to develop; a national-romantic cultural awakening and increasing knowledge and incomes stirred the flame of independence. The differences between Norway and Sweden—and in particular their diverging economic and political interests—became more pronounced. There is no doubt that the Norwegian emergence as a major maritime nation was an important part of the picture that led to the dissolution of the union and Norway's independence in 1905.

Due to the widespread activities of the country's shipping industry, Norwegians had economic interests and engagements all over the world. The country's shipowners thrived under the liberal economic trading regime that emerged in the second half of the 19th century. Sweden, on the other hand, had traditionally a European—rather than global—focus. Moreover, the country's burgeoning manufacturing industry sought protection, rather than liberalism. Thus, "Norwegians and Swedes were divided by basic economic and commercial differences."[94]

At this time, consuls—the national representatives abroad—were a crucial element of the mercantile and maritime infrastructure. These consuls were appointed by the Swedes, who were in control of the dual kingdoms' foreign policy. Naturally, they tended to have Swedish interests at heart. Norwegian politicians—led by the cunning Bergen shipowner Christian Michelsen, who was appointed Prime Minister in March 1905—consequently demanded separate Norwegian consuls. This controversy—followed by some clever political manoeuvring—led to the dissolution of the union and *proper* Norwegian independence in 1905.

Other things remained the same, however. Around the turn of the century, wars continued to create periods of exceptional revenues, while freight rates were depressed and following a long-term declining trend in more peaceful periods. The Second Boer War (1899–1902) enabled "every craft to obtain constant work and at highly remunerative freights,"

---

[94] Leiren (1975, 224).

while The Russo-Japanese War (1904–1905) created "an extensive trade in all merchandise, contraband and legal, with both belligerents, and a corresponding demand for tonnage."[95] Both conflicts had a favourable effect on Norwegian shipping revenues. In 1912 and 1913 freight rates improved again, not as a result of war, but due to a business cycle boom. The return from tramp shipping "which for several years had been around 5 per cent of the capital" increased to 25 per cent by 1913.[96] But the eternal problem with cycles is that after they have gone up, they are bound to go down.

Gunnar Knudsen, president of the Norwegian Shipowners' Association—who was also Prime Minister of Norway—was in a sombre mood when he opened the annual meeting of the association in early July 1914. Although the two previous years had been good, shipping supply was increasing faster than demand and the business cycles were not favourable. According to previous experience, he pointed out, freight rates would remain at a low level for at least three to four years.[97]

He was totally wrong.[98] Over the next four years, Norwegian shipping companies would see their most profitable period ever, and Norwegian sailors one of their most petrifying.

## Bibliography

E.A.V. Angier (1920) *Fifty Years' Freights* (London: Fairplay)
S. Aurmark, O-L. Skundberg & N. Schjander (1977) *Med verden som virkefelt: 18 norske shippingportretter* (Oslo: Hjemmet)
A.T. Austbø (2012) 'Sjøfolks medbrakte gjenstander – en problematisk museumskategori?' *Tidsskrift for kulturforskning*, 11:1, 25–39
B.L. Basberg (2006) 'Patenting and Early Industrialization in Norway, 1860–1914. Was there a Linkage?' *Scandinavian Economic History Review*, 44:1, 4–21

---

[95] Angier (1920, 101 and 115).
[96] Petersen (1949, 173).
[97] Thowsen (1983, 17).
[98] This was not the most faulty prediction that Gunnar Knudsen made that year. During the debate on the King's speech in February 1914, he pointed out that "At present, the political sky, globally, is in fact without clouds to an extent that has not been the case for many years." Norway, Parliament, *Stortingsforhandlingene* 1914, 17 February, 35.

T. Bergh, T.J. Hanisch, E. Lange & H.Ø. Pharo (1983) *Norge fra u-land til i-land: vekst og utviklingslinjer 1830–1980* (Oslo, Gyldendal)
Å.G. Blom (1977) *Folkeviser i arbeidslivet* (Oslo: Universitetsforlaget)
O. Bjerkholt & T. Skoglund (2012) *Anders Nicolai Kiær – en pioner i nasjonalinntektsberegninger* (Oslo: Statistisk Sentralbyrå)
O.M. Bratrud (1961) *Beating to Windward: Afloat and Ashore* (Seattle: published by the author)
C. Brautaset (2002) 'Norsk eksport 1830–1865 i perspektiv av historiske nasjonalregnskaper', *PhD-thesis* (Bergen: Norges Handelshøyskole)
C. Brautaset & S. Tenold (2008) 'Globalisation and Norwegian shipping policy, 1850–2000', *Business History*, 50:5, 565–582
C. Brautaset & S. Tenold (2010) 'Lost in Calculation? Norwegian Merchant Shipping in Asia, 1870–1914', in M. Fusaro & A. Polónia (eds) *Maritime History as Global History* (St. Johns: IMEHA) 203–222
O.J. Broch (1876) *Kongeriget Norge og det norske folk* (Kristiania: Steenske Bogtrykkeri)
D. Brochmann (1937) *Sjømannsviser* (Oslo: Tiden)
O. Ditlev-Simonsen (1945) *En sjøgutt ser tilbake* (Oslo: Cappelen)
O. Ditlev-Simonsen (1954) *En reder ser tilbake* (Oslo: Nationaltrykkeriet)
C. Due (1909) *Erindringer fra Henrik Ibsens ungdomsår* (Copenhagen: Græbes Bogtrykkeri)
S. Dyrvik (1979) *Norsk økonomisk historie 1500–1970*, Volume I: 1500–1850 (Bergen: Universitetsforlaget)
J.O. Egeland (1930) 'Norges sjøfart. Hvad den var og hvad den er', in G. Stenersen (ed) *Sjømannsboken; sjøfart, hvalfangst, marine: orientering i sjømannskap, veiledning til selvstudium* (Oslo: Norsk bibliotekforening) 3–37
Ø. Eitrheim, J.T. Klovland & L.F. Øksendal (2016) *A Monetary History of Norway, 1816–2016* (Cambridge: Cambridge University Press)
H. Espeli (2010) 'Fortropper for gjensidig skadeforsikring i Norge. Skipsforeningene og brannkassenes gjennombrudd på 1800-tallet: Likheter og forskjeller', *Årbok Norsk Maritimt Museum* 2010, 47–90
C.E. Fayle (1933) *A short history of the world's shipping industry*, reprint 2006 (London: Routledge)
P. Figenbaum, E.S. Koren, P. Norseng & T.L. Nilsen (2009) *Verdens fraktemenn* (Oslo: Arts Council Norway; The Norwegian Coastal Administration; The Directorate for Cultural Heritage and the Directorate of Fisheries)
J. Glover (1863) 'On the Statistics of Tonnage During the First Decade Under the Navigation Law of 1849', *Journal of the Royal Statistical Society of London*, XXVI, No. 1 (Mar. 1863)

K. Gjerset (1933) *Norwegian Sailors in American Waters – A Study in the History of Maritime Activity on the Eastern Seaboard* (Northfield, Minnesota: Norwegian-American Historical Association)
N. Grieg (1922) *Rundt Kap det gode haap: vers fra Sjøen* (Oslo: Gyldendal Norsk Forlag)
D.M. Halperin (2012) *How to be gay* (Cambridge: The Belknap Press of Harvard University Press)
G. Harlaftis & I. Theotokas (2004) 'European Family Firms in International Business: British and Greek Tramp-Shipping Firms', *Business History*, 46:2, 219–255
F. Hodne (1980) 'Stortingssalen som markedsplass. Analyse av statens grunnlagsinvesteringer 1840–1914', *PhD-thesis* (Bergen: Norges Handelshøyskole)
F. Hodne (1981) *Norges økonomisk historie 1815–1970* (Oslo: J.W. Cappelens Forlag)
J.R.T. Hughes, (1956) 'The Commercial Crisis of 1857', *Oxford Economic Papers*, new series, 8:2, 194–222
H.C. Johansen (1992) 'Scandinavian Shipping in the Late Eighteenth Century in a European Perspective', *The Economic History Review*, 45:3, 479–493
B.E. Johnsen (1993) *Han sad i prisonen – sjøfolk i engelsk fangenskap 1807–1814* (Oslo: Universitetsforlaget)
A.N. Kiær (1876–1892) *Statistique Internationale Navigation Maritime*, Volumes I–IV (Christiania: Le Bureau Central de Statistique du Royuame de Norvége)
A.N. Kiær (1893) 'Historical Sketch of the Development of Scandinavian Shipping', *The Journal of Political Economy*, 1:3, 329–364
A.T. Kiær (1900) "Commerce and shipping" in S. Konow & K. Fischer (eds) *Norway: Official publication of the Paris exhibition 1900* (Kristiania: Aktie-bogtrykkeriet)
A.M. Klausen (1999) *Olympic Games as Performance and Public Event: The Case of the XVII Winter Olympic Games in Norway* (New York: Berghahn Books)
T.I. Leiren (1975) 'American Press Opinion and Norwegian Independence, 1905', *Norwegian-American Studies*, 27, 224–242
E. Lie & H. Roll-Hansen (2001) *Faktisk talt – Statistikkens historie i Norge* (Oslo: Universitetsforlaget)
S.S. Meidell (1968) 'Sigurd Segelcke Meidell interviewed by Jakob Skarstein', *NRK Middagsstunden*, 26 August 1968 (Bergen: NRK)
Norges Rederforbunds Sjømannsfond av 1918 (1973) *Norske sjømannfond og stiftelser* (Oslo: Grøndahl & Søn)

K. O'Rourke & J. Williamson (1999) *Globalization and history – The Evolution of a Nineteenth-Century Atlantic Economy* (Cambridge: MIT Press)

J. Ojala & A. Räihä (2017) 'Navigation Acts and the integration of North Baltic shipping in the early nineteenth century', *International Journal of Maritime History*, 29:1, 26–43

J. Ojala & S. Tenold (2017) 'Maritime trade and merchant shipping: The shipping/trade-ratio from the 1870s until today', *International Journal of Maritime History*, 29:4, 838–854

K. Petersen (1949) *Norsk dampskipsfart blir en stormakt på verdenshavene* (Trondheim: E. Bruns Bokhandels Forlag)

E. Pettersen & H. Brundtland (2002) *Vi som dro til sjøs – Norske sjøfolks opplevelser fra etterkrigstiden* (Bergen: Edvard'en Forlag)

L. Pettersen (1980) 'Fra kjøpmannsrederi til selvstendig næring, 1860–1914', *Bergen og Sjøfarten III* (Bergen: Bergens Rederiforening og Bergens Sjøfartsmuseum)

A.H. Rasmussen (1952) *Tatt av havet* (Oslo: Cappelen). Published in English as *Sea Fever* (New York: Crowell, 1952) and (New York: Hastings House, 1960).

P. Sandvik (2018) *Nasjonens velstand. Norges økonomiske historie 1800–1940* (Bergen: Vigmostad & Bjørke AS)

J. Schreiner (1952) 'Review of *Den norske sjøfarts historie*', *Historisk Tidsskrift*, 36, 255–295

J. Schreiner (1963) *Norsk skipsfart under krig og høykonjunktur, 1914–1920* (Oslo: Norges Rederforbund/Cappelen)

A.M. Schweigaard (1840) *Norges Statistik* (Christiania: Johan Dahl)

J. Seland (1959) *Rederen og skipet. Kristiansand og Mandal fra seil til damp og diesel* (Kristiansand: Christiansands Rederforening)

D. Skre (2014) 'Norðvegr – Norway: From Sailing Route to Kingdom', *European Review*, 2:1, 34–44

T. Stamsø (1929) *Yngste jungmann ombord: Fra seilskibenes dager* (Oslo: Damm)

Statistics Norway (1902a) *Statistisk aarbog for kongeriget Norge 1902* (Kristiania: Det Statistiske Centralbureau/H. Aschehoug & Co.)

Statistics Norway (1902b) *Tabeller vedkommende Norges skibsfart i året 1900* (Kristiania: Det Statistiske Centralbureau/H. Aschehoug & Co.)

Statistics Norway (1948) *Statistiske oversikter 1948* (Oslo: Statistiske Sentralbyrå)

Statistics Norway (1968) *Historisk Statistikk 1968* (Oslo: Statistisk Sentralbyrå)

Statistics Norway (2015) *Minifacts about Norway* (Oslo: Statistics Norway for the Norwegian Minsitry of Foreign Affairs)

The Norwegian Joint Committee on International Social Policy (1959) *Norway and her sailors: A survey of social legislation* (Oslo: The Norwegian Joint Committee on International Social Policy)

A. Thowsen (1983) 'Vekst og strukturendringer i krisetider 1914–1939', *Bergen og Sjøfarten IV* (Bergen: Bergens Rederiforening og Bergens Sjøfartsmuseum)

J.B. Thue (1980) 'Skipsfart og kjøpmannskap, 1800–1860', *Bergen og Sjøfarten II* (Bergen: Bergens Rederiforening og Bergens Sjøfartsmuseum)

S. Tveite (1965) 'Framgangen for norsk skipsfart etter 1690', *Sjøfartshistorisk Årbok 1965* (Bergen: Bergens Rederiforening og Bergens Sjøfartsmuseum) 58–90

J.N. Tønnessen (1951) 'Fra klipperen til motorskipet', in J.S. Worm-Müller (ed) *Den norske sjøfarts historie: Fra de ældste tider til vore dager*, 2:3 (Oslo: J.W. Cappelens Forlag) 1–222

M. Tønnessen (1996) *Førstereisgutten* (Stavanger: published by the author)

N.P. Vigeland (1943) *Norsk seilskipsfart erobrer verdenshavene* (Trondheim: E. Bruns Bokhandels Forlag)

J.S. Worm-Müller (ed) (1951) *Den norske sjøfarts historie: Fra de ældste tider til vore dager*, 2:3 (Oslo: J.W. Cappelens Forlag)

**Open Access** This chapter is licensed under the terms of the Creative Commons Attribution-NonCommercial-NoDerivatives 4.0 International License (http://creativecommons.org/licenses/by-nc-nd/4.0/), which permits any noncommercial use, sharing, distribution and reproduction in any medium or format, as long as you give appropriate credit to the original author(s) and the source, provide a link to the Creative Commons license and indicate if you modified the licensed material. You do not have permission under this license to share adapted material derived from this chapter or parts of it.

The images or other third party material in this chapter are included in the chapter's Creative Commons license, unless indicated otherwise in a credit line to the material. If material is not included in the chapter's Creative Commons license and your intended use is not permitted by statutory regulation or exceeds the permitted use, you will need to obtain permission directly from the copyright holder.

# 3

# The First World War: The Neutral Ally

In the afternoon of Saturday 5 May 1917, the 19-year-old Fredrik W. Ilboe was feeding the engine of the Bergen-owned steamer *DS Nydal* with coal, as part of the black gang. He had 11 silk stockings on his left foot—luxury goods from the United States were valuable currency in a depraved Europe, and Fredrik had come across a box full of them. When the sight of an empty lifeboat a couple of hours earlier had suggested that there might be German submarines in the area, he had started to put on the stockings, the better to save them.[1]

Before Fredrik had managed to put the remaining 11 stockings on his right foot, there was a muffled bang that reminded him of a powder charge. Although the first German bombs were way off their target, the attacks got gradually closer, and Fredrik and his shipmates were told to abandon ship. He ran back to his quarters, picked up his best suit, the watch he had been given for his confirmation and a box of letters from home, before jumping into the lifeboat, where he landed awkwardly on the captain's lap.

---

[1] Based on the recollection in Ilboe (1970, 53–62) and the report from the maritime inquiry in *Sjøforklaringer over norske skibes krigsforlis, 1914–1918. B. 2: 1ste halvaar 1917*, 496–499. The U-boat in question was UC-72, under the command of *Oberleutnant zur See*, Ernst Voigt.

Fredrik's ship, *DS Nydal*, had been delivered to the company DS AS Vestlandet, managed by Frimann & Pedersen, in January 1917. The ship had a crew of 23 and was on her way from New York to Bordeaux with general cargo. *DS Nydal* had the Norwegian red, white and blue painted on the side of the hull, in order to signal neutrality. However, this was of little use after the Germans introduced unrestricted submarine warfare on 1 February 1917.

Four Norwegian ships—*DS Nydal* and another steamship, as well as two sailing vessels—were sunk by German forces on this Saturday in May 1917. All the seafarers—42 persons from the two steamships and 47 from the two sailing vessels—survived, but only after enduring arduous voyages in the lifeboats. Some of the crew from the frigate *Asra* were the most unfortunate. After two tough days in the lifeboats, they were taken on board the Danish ship *Hans Broge*. However, less than 12 hours after they had been saved, and before they had managed to reach land, the Danish ship was attacked. The sailors had to leave a sinking ship again.[2]

Being sunk twice in the span of 72 hours was not common, but the First World War undoubtedly took its toll on seafarers, ships and shipping companies. Norwegian neutrality had been challenged even before the Germans started their unrestricted submarine warfare. Interruption of Allied supply lines, by means of mines, raiders and the dreaded *U-Boote*, was a key element of the German strategy.

As the war progressed, the threats changed. In 1914, during the first months of the war, the majority of the lost vessels were victims of mines. The North Sea had quickly been turned into a veritable minefield, with only narrow corridors from the UK to The Netherlands and Scandinavia open to traffic.[3] In 1915 more than two-thirds of the lost Norwegian ships were sunk by torpedoes or grenades. The German cruisers were the main danger, but their efficiency was drastically curtailed by difficulties in obtaining sufficient coal. In the final years of the war, the dreaded submarines—invisible and deadly—took over.[4]

---

[2] Brochmann (1928, 114–115) and the report from the maritime inquiry in *Sjøforklaringer over norske skibes krigsforlis, 1914–1918. B. 2: 1ste halvaar 1917*, 501–502.

[3] For a captain's account of the difficulties of navigation in such waters—and in wartime in general—see Øvreseth (1932), which also includes maps detailing the extent of the mine operation.

[4] Petersen (1949, 203–204).

By the end of the 1914–18 war, around half the Norwegian fleet had been sunk or had disappeared, and more than 2100 seafarers had lost their lives. These substantial losses occurred despite the fact that the Norwegian government on 4 August 1914 declared neutrality. The country had less than ten years' experience of managing their own foreign affairs, and had no interest in the blocs, rivalries and political power play that had become an increasingly important part of foreign affairs on the Continent. Norway had perfected a policy of sitting still and hoping not to be noticed. When the main European powers started fighting, this stance was futile.

However, even before the outbreak of the war, the isolationist policy had peculiar effects. In Berlin in April 1908, six countries signed the North Sea Declaration, which confirmed territorial divisions and sovereign rights in the North Sea. Norway, with the longest coastline to the sea, was not among the signatories. Instead, the country relied on its integrity treaty from November 1907, where the main powers had assured Norwegian independence, territorial integrity and "the benefits of the peace."[5] The Norwegian desire to have its neutrality formally secured by the agreement, had been lost in negotiation. This "preserved Britain's freedom of manoeuvre in and around Norway in time of war."[6]

The fact that Norwegian neutrality was neither recognized nor guaranteed did not matter much. Shortly after the outbreak of the war, it became evident that the meaning of neutrality had become very flexible in the European political context. Germany invaded two neutral countries—Belgium and Luxembourg.[7] Subsequently, the Germans initiated all-out attacks on neutral ships. However, they were not the only ones redefining and challenging the concept of neutrality. The Allied powers, with the UK in the lead, "requested the right to regulate the trade of neutral countries to a degree that was unique in the history of the world."[8]

---

[5] Berg (1995, 71–98). The four major powers signing the integrity treaty were France, Germany, Great Britain and Russia. For the text of the North Sea Declaration, see Scott (1908, 200).

[6] Salmon (1993, 32).

[7] In fact, Belgium—sharing the Norwegian naivety and referring to its policy of perpetual neutrality—was the only other North Sea country that had not signed the 1908 agreement.

[8] Vogt (1938, 57).

Norway, on her side, stretched the limits of what neutral countries could and should do. The country started out with a modest pro-British bias, and gradually moved closer and closer to the Allies. This lopsidedness can be explained by ideological, economic and security considerations. In 1917 Gunnar Knudsen, Prime Minister and shipowner, ensured the Americans that "Under no circumstances would we go with Germany."[9] However, there had been no animosity between Norway and Germany before the war. In fact, the links between the two countries had been strong, both at the commercial and at the personal level. Germany was Norway's most important trading partner before the war broke out.[10] Moreover, Kaiser Wilhelm II had a particularly close relationship to the Norwegian coast and the Norwegian people, to the extent that the Norwegian fjords had been his preferred summer vacation destination for more than 20 years.[11]

Slightly more than a week before the invasion of Belgium and Luxembourg, Kaiser Wilhelm II returned prematurely from Balholm in the Sognefjord, north-east of Bergen, in his yacht *Hohenzollern*. According to his memoirs, he had learnt from Norwegian newspapers about the worsening relationship between Austria and Serbia, but the very same newspapers report that he received a dépêche when he was taking his afternoon walk on Saturday 25th July 1914. After reading the telegram, he abruptly returned to the ship, and left Balholm without warning at half past six in the evening.[12] At the same time, 38 German naval vessels

---

[9] Berg (1995, 255).

[10] With regard to Norwegian goods exports, Germany was the second most important country—the 1913 share of 21 per cent was only toppled by the 24 per cent going to Great Britain and Ireland. However, almost 30 per cent of Norwegian imports came from Germany—while the British share was 25 per cent; Statistics Norway (1914, 55). Still, these figures disregard the trade in services—including shipping—where Great Britain played the key role. The commodity trade with Germany exceeded the British trade by 6 percentage points. If we include the gross freight earnings from shipping services, Norway's trade with Great Britain exceeded the trade with Germany by approximately 7.5 percentage points.

[11] It has been claimed that Wilhelm II had a particular interest not only in Norway, but also in Norwegians. Based on the belief that their grandfather was the illegitimate son of *Der Kaiser*, a family on the west coast in 2012 changed their name to Hohenzollern; *Aftenposten*, 15 February 2014, 34–37.

[12] *Bergens Tidende*, 260714, 1. This story clashes with the Kaiser's memoirs, where he emphasizes that his returned started when he learned "from Norwegian newspapers—not Berlin—about the […] Serbian note to Austria"; http://www.firstworldwar.com/source/julycrisis.htm

that were in Norwegian waters were told to mobilize and return to their homeland.

When *Hohenzollern* travelled from the Norwegian coast to Wilhelmshafen in Germany, these waters were relatively safe. Just a few weeks later, the North Sea had become a strategically important part of the playing field and a crucial stage for the war theatre. Given the vital role that supplies and resources play during wars, the British attempt at isolating the German fleet and cutting off German supply became a lynchpin of their war campaign.

## The Crucial Role of Shipping During Wars

As the US maritime historian Michael Miller has pointed out, the 1914–18 war at sea was not primarily about naval ships fighting for local and global hegemony and control. Rather, "the real sea battle in the First World War pitched German surface raiders, mines, and especially submarines against merchant shipping in an effort to interdict and destroy Allied overseas supply lines."[13] This was not soldiers against soldiers on land or marines against marines at sea—this was military might against civilian seafarers.

The outbreak of wars usually leads to an increase in the need for seaborne transport. The belligerents need to move troops and supplies. Moreover, with normal trade relations interrupted, even neutral countries are forced to rely on more distant sources of supply, and often ships have to resort to inconvenient lengthy detours.[14] As a result, the demand for transport capacity increases. Parallel with this, the amount of tonnage available in the open market falls. Ships are requisitioned by the authorities and ship losses increase as a result of enemy action. Bottlenecks,

---

[13] Miller (2017, 1).
[14] For instance, rather than sourcing grain from Europe, Norway had to turn to the Americas. In 1913 Norway imported 50 tons of barley from the United States; by 1916 this had increased to almost 50,000 tons. Over the same period wheat imports from the United States increased from 2400 tons to 74,000 tons; Statistics Norway, *Norges Handel 1913*, 1914, 97–98 and *Norges Handel 1916*, 1918, 105. Imports of rye from Russia and Germany had amounted to more than 176,000 tons in 1913—by 1916 the imports were zero.

restrictions and time-consuming inspections in ports reduce the efficiency of the available vessels, and material and labour shortages make it difficult to keep up newbuilding activity in the shipyards. Shipping is no different from other markets. Increased demand and reduced supply usually have one immediate effect: higher prices.

Norwegian shipowners had previously benefitted from the freight rate booms associated with conflicts in both near and distant waters. This time, the situation was even more favourable. The strong increase in international trade in the second half of the 19th century—often referred to as the first era of globalization—had already laid the foundation for the growth of the Norwegian merchant marine. However, the expanding trade also implied that Europe had become much more dependent upon foreign supplies to meet everyday needs. When the war broke out, Great Britain imported almost two thirds of the calories that were consumed, as well as much of the raw materials that kept the country's industry going; cotton, wool, petroleum, various ores and rubber.[15] Shipping was more important than ever.

In the autumn of 1914, the German fleet was the second largest in the world, but British naval superiority rapidly neutralized the majority of the ships as the Allies took control of the sea lanes; "almost overnight, the German merchant flag disappeared from the high seas, not to reappear for more than four years."[16] Around 14 per cent of the world fleet, the share that the Central Powers held, was forced to remain in domestic and foreign ports. However, the blockade of Germany and Austria-Hungary also led to a decline in international trade, and a corresponding reduction in the demand for shipping.[17]

For the UK, superiority at sea was one of their main strengths—their policy had been "rule of thumb"-like: to have a navy that was at least as strong as the next two navies. The naval ships could be supplemented by vessels from the world's largest merchant marine. Relatively soon after the war had broken out, British merchant ships were put under Government control, and the authorities also introduced official maximum rates and

---

[15] Miller (2017, 1).
[16] Albion and Pope (1968, 233).
[17] Schreiner (1963, 89).

standardized contract terms. By the end of 1915, around 30 per cent of the British fleet had been requisitioned to contribute directly in the war campaign, transporting soldiers and other personnel, weapons and ammunition, provisions, etc.

Suddenly, two of Norway's most important competitors among the world's maritime nations were out of the picture. Some optimistic—and opportunistic—voices suggested that Norway had to take advantage of the situation. General Consul Storm, Chairman of *Den oversjøiske eksportforening* [The Overseas Exports Association] pointed out that Norway had an "opportunity to gain market shares in the world market that we will probably never see again" and should buy as many of the seized German ships as possible.[18]

This opportunistic business attitude was echoed in the press, where *Norges Handels og Sjøfartstidende*, the leading newspaper for merchants and shipowners, presented the dilemma as a choice between the "poverty line" [*fattigkasselinje*] and the "line of action" [*handlingens linje*]. The latter alternative "would lead to wealth, just as surely as the former would lead to ruin." Neutral Norway "should take advantage of the situation [...] and increase our exports. Our ships shall continue to sail and earn the high freights that are offered. [...] Right now, when the competition is weaker, it is time to assert ourselves, both internally and externally."[19]

The war years did see a spectacular increase in personal wealth in Norway, though the distribution was uneven. Speculators made rapid fortunes, and showed their windfall gains in obscene ways. For the majority of the population, however, the increased cost of living and the difficulties of obtaining crucial provisions were the main preoccupations. From 1914 to 1920, prices multiplied by a factor of three, and rationing

---

[18] The article, originally in *Norges Handels og Sjøfartstidende*, 090814, was reprinted in full in *Bergens Tidende*, 120814, 1 and by 21 August it had also reached the newspaper *Nordkap*. This offensive—in both meanings of the word—attitude was typical of the general consul. After the war, Storm offered his services to the Ministry of Foreign Affairs. When they declined his offer to act as "Envoyé Extraordinaire and Ministre Plénipotentiairie" in South America, his response was to publish an 80-page pamphlet about the politicians' "obstruction" and "tepidity"; Storm (1920). Based on the tone of this and other of his writings, it is evident that Storm today would have felt very at home in the comment section of online newspapers.

[19] *Norges Handels og Sjøfartstidende*, reprinted in *Tromsø Stiftstidende*, 190814, 1.

and black market premiums aggravated the situation. In other words, Norway managed to follow both the "poverty line" and the "line of action". A similar balancing act was seen in international politics. Norway stayed neutral throughout the conflict, but was in reality strongly involved, and ultimately played an important role for the outcome of the war.

## Hands Across the North Sea

Cut off from many of their normal sources by the British blockade, the German appetite for food and raw materials increased markedly. Norwegian exports to Germany more than doubled from 1914 to 1915, and in 1916 export revenues amounted to almost 300 million kroner, more than four times as much as in 1913.[20] Part of this was a result of increasing prices, but even when we correct for inflation, the Norwegian exports to Germany multiplied by a factor of more than three. Two types of commodities were particularly important during the first years of the war; minerals from Norwegian mines—in particular pyrite, copper ore and iron ore—and fish that could feed a German population on the brink of starvation.[21]

However, in 1916 Norway's westwards-leaning stance became more pronounced. This was not surprising—the British pressure for support intensified. Norway's position as a major cross-trader implied that politicians and shipowners had always tried to avoid challenging the UK, who through its navy and its network of bunkering stations was the ultimate maritime power. *Britannia* really ruled the waves, as guarantor of security, as energy provider and—most important for Norwegian shipowners—as market. The UK was still the centre of world trade, and an important entrepôt. Before the outbreak of the war, the number of Norwegian port

---

[20] Statistics Norway (1948, 223).
[21] Germany was the most important recipient of 24 of the 30 different types of fish and shellfish listed in Norwegian statistics in 1916; Denmark received more lobster, and the UK more salmon. With regard to canned fish, Germany was the leading importer in all categories, receiving marginally more than 50 per cent of all canned fish exports; Statistics Norway, *Norges Handel 1916*, 1918, 131–135.

calls in the UK was more than four times higher than the corresponding number for Germany.[22]

This bias was not only linked to shipping, but more generally to the leading British position in the provision of coal and many other crucial products. As a result, several Norwegian branch organizations entered into agreements to ensure supply. In August 1915, The Association of Cotton Factories *[Bomuldsvarefabrikkenes forening]*, fearing that cotton would be defined as "contraband", signed an agreement with the British Government.[23] This is one example of how neutral Norway's allegiance would become more and more determined by the question of supplies; "our foreign policy [...] became a petty, mercenary, self-serving policy – a 'trade policy' in every aspect, practical and materialistic."[24]

A similar situation occurred in connection with fish exports. In 1915, foreign buyers of fish were extremely active in Norway, and it has been suggested that the Germans tried to corner the market.[25] The Norwegian fishing industry was in a difficult situation. Although Germany and the Continent were the main targets for their exports, they needed "coal, petroleum, salt, tin, olive oil, hemp and cotton for ships and fishing gear", and it was estimated that the British had a market share of around 85 per cent in the supply of these goods.[26] For Norwegian fishermen, this was the worst catch of them all; Catch 22. They were in danger of losing the German market where they sold their fish, or in danger of losing the British inputs needed to satisfy this market.

An agreement on the sale of fish to Britain signed in the beginning of August 1916 was followed by an agreement on the export of copper ore

---

[22] More than 8000 Norwegian ships entered ports in Great Britain and Ireland in 1913, compared with less than 1800 ships entering German ports; Statistics Norway (1916, 48). The proportion of third-country trade was also higher for the British than for the German trade. Although Germany, as previously mentioned, actually supplied a higher share of Norwegian imports, the essential nature of the British products—in particular coal—gave them an advantage there as well.

[23] See Keilhau (1927, 97–104).

[24] Vogt (1938, 54).

[25] Hjort (1927, 18).

[26] Hjort (1927, 14); on the agreement between the UK and Norway regarding the sale of fish, see Hjort (1927, 9–193).

and pyrite, signed at the end of the month.[27] The fish agreement escalated tensions between Norway and Germany, and the latter responded by targeting shipping along the Norwegian coast. In the last week of September, ten Norwegian ships were sunk in the Arctic Ocean, and the ruthless manner in which the German submarines acted created a public outcry.[28]

With regard to the merchant marine, two considerations had to be taken into account. On the one hand, transporting cargoes for other countries had been its main employment, and was an important source of revenue. On the other hand, the ships played a crucial role in ensuring that Norway had fuel, food and other necessities. The transport to and from Norway thus became particularly important during the war, and the shipowners found that the authorities increasingly restricted their room to manoeuvre.

In December 1915 the government had introduced a provisional decree banning the sale of ships abroad, and this restriction was made into law in July 1916.[29] However, the export ban was largely unnecessary. Norwegian shipping investors were in a buying—not in a selling—mood. In both 1915 and 1916 the imports of second-hand tonnage were three times higher than they had been in the years just before the war, and from the autumn of 1915 Norwegian owners "occupied practically all the capacity on shipyards in countries that were still neutral, primarily Norway, Denmark, the Netherlands and the United States."[30] By the end of 1916, Norwegian newbuilding orders at US shipyards amounted to around 90 per cent of the country's annual production capacity.[31]

The Norwegian fleet reached a peak in August 1916, before the increased German aggression began to fully take its toll. More than 300,000 deadweight tons were lost in the last four months of 1916,

---

[27] As a result of the British dependence on imported foodstuffs, the entire exports of meat from Australia and New Zealand, and most of the Argentinian exports, had been bought up by the Board of Trade.

[28] As early as in November 1915 Sweden had denied submarines use of its territorial waters, except in a surface position in times of distress. A similar Norwegian resolution came 11 months later, and had only one exception from the total ban—submarines could enter Norwegian waters to save human lives.

[29] Keilhau (1927, 186).
[30] Haaland (1940, 18).
[31] Schreiner (1963, 363).

compared with around 265,000 deadweight tons in the first two years of the war.[32] The combination of a more violent German policy and a strong increase in the submarine fleet—which more than doubled during 1916—can explain the higher losses.

The UK had by far the largest merchant marine at the start of the war, but had similar preoccupations as the Norwegians; at home, people and machines needed foreign inputs to be able to keep going. The authorities introduced a plethora of regulations, including compulsory voyage permissions, maximum freights and requisitioning, but even that was insufficient to cover their transport needs. They consequently cast their eyes on the neutral fleets, and had the means to persuade them: foreign steam shipping depended on British coal. By restricting access to this vital factor of production, British authorities could influence the manner in which the vessels were paid and used. In the first half of 1916 they introduced maximum freights for foreign ships on certain routes, and refused to deliver coal to neutral ships unless they had secured a return cargo that would bring them back to the UK.[33]

For a while, the cooperation with the British was organized along the "one in—one out" principle followed by nightclub bouncers on a busy Saturday night. Norwegian vessels that were ready to sail to Scandinavia or The Netherlands with coal cargoes were not allowed to leave until they were replaced by another Norwegian ship.[34] These restrictions were relaxed when it turned out that the Norwegians reacted differently to owners from other neutral nations; "the dauntless Norwegians stuck to the dangerous work, but most others dared not risk their ships."[35]

A dispute about Norwegian exports of low quality pyrite to Germany led to a cessation of British coal exports to Norway from the end of 1916. However, "it was evident that the dependence of Norway on British coal" and the Norwegian shipowners' large fleet made them "genuinely anxious to employ their vessels in the service of the Allies," with whom they were already "on friendly terms."[36] In February 1917, shortly after the Germans

---

[32] Schreiner (1963, 134 and 304); refers to ships lost as a result of war hostilities.
[33] Hodne (1981, 448–449) and Klovland (2017, 10–12).
[34] Schreiner (1963, 165).
[35] Schreiner (1963, 166) and Albion and Pope (1968, 241).
[36] Fayle (1923b, 47).

introduced unrestricted submarine warfare, the Norwegian authorities accepted the demands, and the British stopped twisting the Norwegian arms.

Around the same time, the British Minister of Blockade, Lord Robert Cecil, approached the Norwegian authorities with the view of purchasing tonnage.[37] The basis for the approach was that "Norway had a greater amount of tramp tonnage to place on the freight markets than any other country except Great Britain herself."[38] The German escalation of the naval warfare—with a large number of much more efficient submarines—implied that the Norwegian fleet had become increasingly valuable. This paved the way for the tonnage agreement with the UK, negotiated in the spring and entering into force in the summer of 1917.

The tonnage agreement was a strange beast; it was negotiated by the Norwegian Shipowners' Association and the British legation in Oslo, but with both countries' authorities—the British Government and the Norwegian *Provianteringsdirektorate*t [Ministry of Provisioning]—looming insistently in the background.[39] The idea was that "all Norwegian shipping not required for the trade of Norway herself should, so far as possible, be employed in Allied interests, in return for a guarantee of the Norwegian coal supply."[40] As a result of this agreement, neutral Norway devoted its most important asset—the merchant marine—clearly to one side in the conflict. By this time, there was no doubt about where Norwegian allegiance lay.

According to the agreement, a substantial share of the Norwegian fleet was time chartered through Furness Withy & Co., as agents for the British authorities. Moreover, in the dangerous North Sea trade, Norwegian ships—which due to neutrality could not be armed—were replaced by British vessels.[41] Consequently, coal to Norway was "carried

---

[37] The fact that the British had their own Minister of Blockade illustrates the crucial role of this aspect of the war. Ironically, the Rt Hon Lord Robert Gascoyne-Cecil, First Viscount Cecil of Chelwood, CH, PC, QC, was in reality a keen supporter of free trade, and in 1937 won the Nobel Peace Prize for his work with the League of Nations.

[38] Fayle (1923a, 274).

[39] The nature of the agreement implies that there was no signed contract. Instead, the previous correspondence was used as the basis for the arrangement; Schreiner (1963, 176–177).

[40] Fayle (1923b, 48).

[41] Norges Rederforbund (1960, 17).

by armed British ships, among whom losses were likely to be smaller" while "the Norwegian steamers should be available for Allied service elsewhere."[42] The red-white-and-blue on the ships' side, which had previously functioned well when neutrality was an advantage, had to be substituted by war paint and camouflage, because it would otherwise signal to the submarines that the ship was unarmed.[43]

In late 1917, around 900,000 dead weight tons of Norwegian shipping, in addition to the requisitioned ships, served the Allies on time charters to the Executive, or on a trip-by-trip basis in the coal and ore trades. However, the important thing was not only the number of ships, but also the willingness to engage them in the most dangerous waters. A survey from January 1918 shows that 547,000 gross tons of Norwegian ships were performing Allied service in the war zone, compared with a total of 141,000 tons of Dutch, Swedish and Danish ships. The difference is remarkable: although Norway only owned slightly more than a third of the "neutral" Dutch-Scandinavian fleet, they had almost 80 per cent of the crucial tonnage servicing the war zone.[44]

Norway's novel definition of neutrality was exemplary from a British point of view: "In striking contrast to the friction which had arisen with so many neutrals, British relations with Norway were on a friendly footing."[45] When the United States entered the war in April 1917, the pressure on Norway intensified. The Americans demanded a complete termination of Norwegian exports to Germany, in order to secure food supply to Norway. While the Americans and the Norwegians played diplomatic ping pong, daily life became characterized by rationing, inflation and civil unrest. The famous explorer and scientist Fridtjof Nansen represented Norway in the discussions with the United States.[46] Initially, he suggested limiting food exports from Norway to Germany to 40,000 tons of fish and fish products, but only when Norway introduced bans

---

[42] Fayle (1923b, 218).
[43] Kloster (1935, 76).
[44] Estimated on the basis of Fayle (1923b, 261); ships in national trade with the UK are excluded.
[45] Fayle (1923b, 47); see also Hurd (1924, Vol. II, 244).
[46] Among the tasks he faced, was securing supplies to Roald Amundsen's expedition through the North East Passage, which led to "large and totally unexpected difficulties"; letter dated 040118; https://urn.nb.no/URN:NBN:no-nb_digimanus_17502

and restrictions on the exports of minerals and other military articles to the Central Powers was it possible to conclude a Norwegian-American agreement. The agreement, with severe limits on Norwegian exports to Germany, came into force in May 1918, after nine months of negotiations. Norway had truly become "the neutral ally."[47]

One of the main reasons for Norway's westward stance was the deteriorating view of Germany in public opinion, which made it easier for the authorities to align their policies with the Allies. The manner in which submarine warfare destroyed human lives and merchant ships—*neutral* lives and *neutral* ships—changed public opinion and inflamed anti-German sentiments. For the majority of Norwegian citizens, Germany and the Central Powers became "the enemy" during the course of the war.

Domestic incidents contributed to the changing attitude. In Bergen, *Den store spionsaken* [The great espionage affair] caused public outrage in the spring of 1917. Members of a spy ring had sold information about Norwegian ship departures to the Germans, betraying their compatriots.[48] The court case led to riots and demonstrations outside the courthouse, where the accused were harassed by a large mob.[49] In Kristiania, in an unprecedented break of diplomatic courtesy, the German diplomat and spy "Baron von Rautenfels"—actually the Finnish-born civil servant Walter Harald von Gerich—was arrested in June 1917. He had more than 200 bombs in his possession, some hidden in trunks that had been sealed by *Auswärtiges Amt, Berlin* [The Foreign Office, Berlin]. Among the explosives, which totalled almost a ton, were nine bombs concealed as lumps of coal, to be hidden in the bunkers depots of ships. Norwegian newspapers linked the case to previous "suspicious accidents at sea."[50]

---

[47] Berg (1995, 228–244); in the end, the fish exports were capped at 48,000 tons. The term "the neutral ally" is linked to Riste (1965).

[48] Four of the 14 spies that were arrested worked for *Det Bergenske Dampskipsselskap*, Bergen's leading shipping company. Due to the company's relatively limited losses at sea, the British authorities insinuated that "the owners may not have been completely ignorant of the malpractices"; see Keilhau (1951, 331–334).

[49] *Bergens Tidende*, 301117, 5 and 7–9. In addition to animosity against the accused, the basis for the "riots" was the relatively low number of police officers controlling the long queue of curious onlookers.

[50] *Dagbladet*, 230617, 1; Søhr (1938, 76) and Hambro (1958, 168–185).

The accomplices of "the bomber baron" were given relatively long jail sentences in Norway. "Baron von Rautenfels" himself was expelled from the country, but was given an amnesty in Germany and escaped prosecution.[51] This is characteristic of the international political situation during the war: the Norwegians pretended that they were neutral, and the Germans pretended that they respected the neutrality.[52] During the First World War, political, economic, strategic and military considerations overlapped and clashed, creating uncertainty and complexity for individuals and for businesses.

## War Risk and War Losses

Wars greatly increase the risk associated with shipping, and risk is sometimes difficult to deal with from a commercial perspective. Some weeks after the start of the war, Norwegian shipping companies, in cooperation with the government, established a compulsory and mutual war insurance arrangement.[53] This was an important step—crippling insurance premiums and lack of access to war insurance immobilized the fleet. Norwegian ships were already in or on their way to the lay-up buoys. Insurance premiums of 25–30 per cent of the value of the vessel had been quoted for some voyages across the North Sea, and the reduced shipping activity threatened both Norwegian imports of necessities and the freight revenues that financed them.[54]

In the UK, Denmark and Sweden the authorities had established insurance arrangements, but the value of the Norwegian merchant marine, relatively to the size of the public coffers, made such a solution difficult in Norway. Moreover, it was claimed that "Norwegian shipowners were known for chartering their ships on risky voyages, almost like a predilection, if the profits encouraged it"—not a strategy that will

---

[51] Søhr (1938, 72–98).
[52] The German Embassy had been invited to the opening of the sealed trunks, but did not turn up. When it was proven that they had broken the diplomatic rulebook, an obscure military agency was blamed.
[53] Nilsen & Thowsen (1990, 10).
[54] Petersen (1949, 177).

convince insurers.⁵⁵ Regardless of whether or not this claim was correct, if this was the general opinion, it would negatively affect shipowners' ability to obtain affordable insurance terms.

A committee was established on 11 August 1914, headed by Joh. Ludwig Mowinckel, Bergen shipowner and President of the *Odelsting*, one of the Parliamentary chambers. The committee worked rapidly, and the day after it had been appointed suggested the establishment of a compulsory and mutual insurance arrangement, where the authorities granted a temporary guarantee. Consequently, the costs of every individual loss would be shared by everyone. This solution was supported by both the politicians, who wanted to limit their own risk, and the shipowners, who wanted to limit the authorities' influence.

The increasing insurance costs were warranted. Neutral Norway suffered heavily during the First World War. More than 2100 seafarers lost their lives. Almost 950 ships, with a tonnage of more than 1.3 million gross register tons (grt)—corresponding to around half the 1914 fleet—were lost.⁵⁶ Given that they were sailing for a neutral nation, the Norwegian ships were unable to retaliate when they were attacked.

Figure 3.1 shows the official Norwegian loss figures during the war. With the introduction of unrestricted submarine warfare in February 1917, and subsequently with the US entry into the war, developments changed dramatically. The new German policy—targeting all ships around the British Isles, outside France and Italy and in the Eastern Mediterranean—implied that the target became the ships, not their cargoes. The introduction of convoys in the North Atlantic in the spring of 1917 managed to drastically reduce the losses in that region, and the decline was strengthened by the deployment of Norwegian ships to less-dangerous waters after the tonnage agreement.

---

⁵⁵ Keilhau (1927, 32).
⁵⁶ See Fig. 3.1, which is based on Statistics Norway (2000), Table 115, 115 and Statistics Norway (1948), Table 131a, 248. In addition to the data presented there, 943 seafarers and 69 ships with an aggregate tonnage of slightly more than 60,000 gross tons disappeared during the war, most likely as a result of mines or torpedoes; Statistics Norway (1919, 63). While these vessels are mentioned in the footnotes of subsequent statistics, the seafarers have disappeared there as well. Moreover, one sailing ship and three other ships sunk by mines in 1919, which left 24 sailors dead, are not included in the data. Figures for 1914 refer to the period after 1 August, while 1918 refers to the full year.

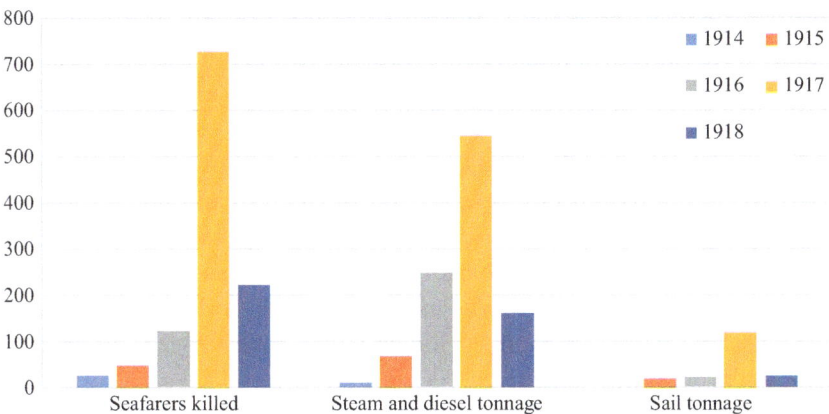

**Fig. 3.1** Norwegian losses during the First World War by year, 1914–1918, seafarers and 1000 grt. (Sources: Statistics Norway (1948, 2000). See footnote)

The acceleration of the German war at sea is evident from the statistics—as is the efficiency of the convoys at the later stages of the war. Regardless of the high losses, "posts at ships that were sailing in the danger zone were always in high demand," according to the economist Wilhelm Keilhau. With a lack of reality orientation that can often be found behind a large oak desk, he claimed that "For many [seamen] the spirit of adventure must have played an important role."[57]

The loss of a ship was not necessarily bad for the company's business. In the summer of 1917 it was claimed that a share in DS AS Vestlandet, the company that owned the recently torpedoed *Nydal*, was "a good paper," partly as a result of the income associated with the sinking.[58] The ship's insurance had amounted to more than NOK2.1 million, and the company had a book profit of NOK1.4 million as a result of the

---

[57] Keilhau (1927, 319–320). Wilhelm Christian Keilhau was Professor of Economics at the University of Oslo. He gradually reoriented his writings towards economic and business history, and his prolific authorship includes several books that were written because he had an axe to grind. Keilhau's uncle had been Minister of Defense in Norway in 1914, but was replaced two days after the country had declared its neutrality.

[58] *Bergens Tidende*, 260917, 7. A misprinted telegram about a torpedoed ship plays a central role in the Norwegian rags-to-riches "yuppie comedy classic" *Bør Børson jr.*; Falkberget (1920, 182–188).

insurance payout after the Germans had sunk the ship.[59] While such profits were subject to income tax and war gains tax in the first years of the war, from July 1917 insurance profits became tax exempt if they were reinvested in new shipping capacity.

For the seafarers on board the ships, the case was of course different. They received a hazard bonus as a result of the war, and half a month's extra pay if the ship was captured or sunk by the Germans.[60] This sounds ruthless, but was in fact not too bad: Danish and British seafarers actually had their wages stopped from the moment the ship was sunk. There was also compensation for personal belongings, and here we see the class system at play: captains were given 1000 *kroner*, mates were given 600 *kroner* and compensation for the rest of the crew was 400 *kroner* to cover clothes and other personal items that were lost.[61]

## *Jobbetid*: The Financial Boom

While the seafarers were counting their blessings, speculators were counting their money. The war led to an enormous increase in freight rates, and in revenues. In 1916, gross freight earnings—what foreigners paid for Norwegian transport services—were more than four times higher than they had been five years earlier, even when we take inflation into account. This massive inflow of money fostered optimism—shipowners reinvested their earnings, and shipping investments became attractive even to those outside the sector.

The war led to an enormous "investment" activity, where some shipping company shares doubled in value, then doubled again, and where the volume of transactions bordered on the ludicrous. High risk led to high potential profits: "Yesterday I bought a Tønsberg-boat at eleven in the morning for three and a half million, and sold it again at one o'clock for four," boasts one of the shipowners in Nordahl Grieg's classic play *Vår*

---

[59] *Bergens Tidende*, 180418, 5.
[60] Pedersen (1952, 170). In April 1918 this was increased to three months. Some shipowners were more generous than others; Fred. Olsen offered torpedoed sailors wages for the rest of the year, even if their ship had been sunk in January.
[61] Tønnessen (1960, 116).

*ære og vår makt.*⁶² The freight rate boom led to "an almost insatiable appetite for shipping shares and ship parts."⁶³

Still, economic success was primarily a question of good or fortunate timing. "The shipowners that had bought ships in the first half of 1914 [...] were winners in life's peculiar lottery" and for the first years of the war values increased steadily.⁶⁴ During 1915 the price of a relatively large ship multiplied by a factor of five, and the second-hand price exceeded the newbuilding price for a similar vessel by 80 per cent due to its prompt availability.⁶⁵ The price of the shares of shipping companies that owned such tonnage naturally soared.

From the end of 1914 to the peak in 1918 the value of shipping shares multiplied by a factor of almost six. Because freight rates showed particularly pronounced boom movements, shipping shares became the favoured speculative object among those looking for a quick boost of their personal wealth. There was a real economic fundament for the boom in the beginning; the high freight rates led to record profits—even after the increases in coal prices, wages and insurance costs were taken into account. However, as the war progressed, the development acquired all the properties of a "bubble." Investors ventured their money based on the expectation of continuing share price increases, rather than on the basis of future revenues.

The important factor was not the company's revenue stream, but the ability to sell the shares at a higher price at a later stage. The aim was to find an even greater fool in a game of musical chairs. Norway "had never seen a gold fever like that, and probably not a similarly vulgar and provocative exhibition of money."⁶⁶ Figure 3.2 illustrates how the shipping industry, more than other sectors, was affected by the boom and bust during the war.⁶⁷

---

⁶² Grieg (1935, 84).
⁶³ Thowsen (1983, 199).
⁶⁴ Keilhau (1927, 10).
⁶⁵ Kloster (1935, 40). In one case, the sale price of a ship increased by more than 300 per cent from May to December; Kloster (1935, 41).
⁶⁶ Egeland (1963, 9).
⁶⁷ Figure 3.2: Based on Keilhau (1927, 344–346). Data refer to end of month. The total index consists of the following indices (weighting in parentheses): Manufacturing (1/3); Shipping (1/3); Banking (1/6); Insurance (1/15); Whaling (1/15); Transport, etc. (1/30).

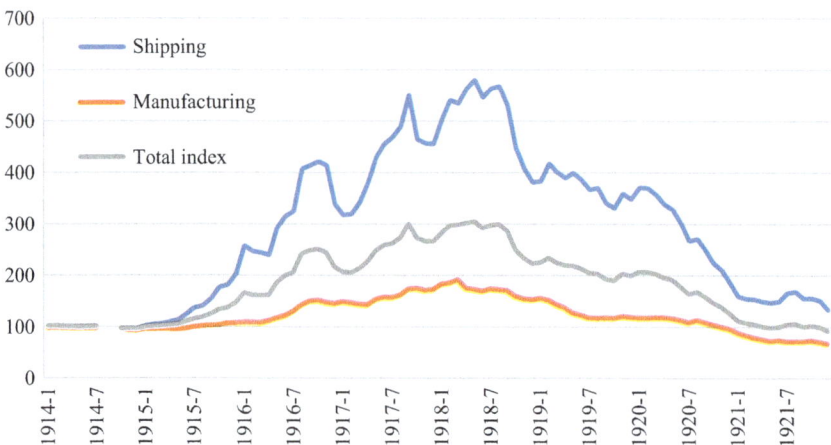

**Fig. 3.2** The shipping speculation boom, stock exchange indices (1913 = 100), 1914–1921

From a societal point of view, the development was unfortunate. The war, inflation and rationing accentuated the difference between the haves and the have-nots. Shipping investors undoubtedly belonged to the first group. In 1917 inequality in Norway was at its highest point in modern history.[68] Quite a lot of people became wealthy from speculation, but most major maritime cities typically had one or two entrepreneurs that stood out. This development was most pronounced in Kristiania and Bergen, where we find the most liquid stock exchanges.

In 1915 the shipbroker Christoffer Hannevig jr. in Kristiania invited investors to buy four old sailing ships that would be fitted with engines, and promised that one voyage would give a return of "more than 50 per cent of the purchase price."[69] At this point Hannevig was an outsider—and even frowned upon by established shipowners—but he still became the archetypal example of the new-found wealth during this early yuppie period.[70] By 1917 his fortune was allegedly NOK150 million—around

---

[68] Aaberge et al. (2016, 22).
[69] See the advertisement in *Morgenbladet*, 140215, 11.
[70] The Norwegian term for the period is *jobbetid*, referring to the *jobbing* of stocks—short-term investments looking for rapid profits, often associated with the British South Sea Bubble in the 18th century.

NOK5 billion in today's money: "Every child in Norway knows Hannevig. He has already become a mythical character, a Norwegian version of King Midas or brewer Jacobsen, a young Alladin or a new, shining *Askeladd*. Even before he started to splash millions about, it was established that he was the incarnation of the wonderful fairy-tale called *Norwegian shipping during the World War*."[71]

Hannevig owned shipyards in the United States and a bank with offices in Old Broad Street in London, in New York and in Aasgaardstrand—a Norwegian village of around 300 souls: "incredible fortunes have been made in a couple of years; shipowners have had to establish their own banks in order to accommodate the money."[72] In 1921 Hannevig, who by then was in his late thirties, and several of his companies went bankrupt. He subsequently spent a lot of energy on litigation against the US authorities, claiming compensation for yards that had been confiscated when the United States entered the war. The First World War's Norwegian King Midas died broke in New York in 1950.[73]

Tryggve Sagen, one of Hannevig's partners, is another rags-to-riches– to-rags story in Kristiania, while in Bergen the boom was associated with Erik Grant Lea.[74] He was a serial entrepreneur, who was also the victim of comparisons with King Midas and Aladdin.[75] Like many "jobbers," Lea had managed to get a large share of outside capital in his companies; in the first one he owned only 16 of the 750 shares.[76] This made him vulnerable for shareholder revolts, and in 1917 six of his companies were taken over by another "typical speculative partnership"—a dog-eat-dog world. The new managers were Bjørnstad and Brækhus, who also took

---

[71] *Dagbladet*, 281017, 6. King Midas should be well-known, and "Alladin" is a mis-spelt "Aladdin." "Brewer Jacobsen" refers to Carl Jacobsen, founder of the Danish brewery Carlsberg and regarded as one of the most successful businessmen in Scandinavia. *Askeladden* is one of the main characters in Norwegian folk tales, typically succeeding where others fail.

[72] *Dagbladet*, 030319, 4.

[73] Hannevig died, but the court cases lived on. In March 1960, the Norwegian Parliament discussed the aftermath of the case for the ninth time, as a response to a decision in the US Court of Claims the previous year; Norway, Parliament, Stortingsmelding 60 (1959–1960).

[74] On Sagen, see Haugstad (2017).

[75] See Tveit (1972) for a biography of Lea and reference to the comparison, and Imset (2009) on Hannevig.

[76] Thowsen (1983, 204).

over DS AS Vestlandet, to benefit from the insurance payout after *Nydal* had been torpedoed.[77] In the period 1917–1920 Bjørnstad and Brækhus "raided" 15 different companies to gain control of valuable tonnage.

Ships and ship shares changed hands at high frequency—and usually at higher and higher prices. Before the war there had been eight stockbrokers in Kristiania—during the war the number grew to several hundred, and informal transactions took place in restaurants and cafes. The boom and bust in the equity market cast long shadows. Several decades after the war, the image of the stock exchange was negative to many people, linked with speculation, unrestrained risk-taking, uninhibited spending and a gambling mentality that was alien to Norwegian values. Moreover, shipping was seen as the archetypal gambling activity; "old, peaceful Kristiania [had] succumbed to a deluge of papers, of shares, of warrants and of contract notes."[78]

The speculative fever was fuelled by an abundance of money so large that even crooks from abroad were attracted to it. The Australian Mister Angus, who promoted the idea of a self-stopping locomotive, left the country after having deprived investors of their funds. "There were invitations to subscribe [to new shares] that even the most ignorant must have understood were meaningless."[79] In the absence of good investment objects, the wealthy—and in particular the newly wealthy—chose risky investments and conspicuous consumption.

The abundance of money among the successful speculators was partly channelled into new investments, fanning the flames of the boom. Still, there were also funds for other purposes. The phenomenal profits were channelled into luxurious houses, expensive food and wine, horses and yachts. Enormous houses of exquisite materials were built, and the newspapers carried a large amount of advertisements for castles in Sweden and estates in Denmark. Christoffer Hannevig bought a 154-foot-long racing sailboat that had previously belonged to Count Gustav Krupp, but had been taken as prize of war in Germany in 1914. Sailboats were status symbols, and one investor owned a 12-metre, a 10-metre and an 8-metre,

---

[77] Thowsen (1983, 313).
[78] Keilhau (1923, 44). The book was published anonymously, with no reference to the author.
[79] Vogt (1938, 143).

in addition to a large motorboat and an inland estate equipped with telephones made of silver.[80]

Another favoured investment object was fine art. For investors like Hannevig and Lea, the boom and the wealth were temporary. However, for Norway, the abundance of funds had long-term cultural effects.[81] In 1917 large sums were donated to establish a trustee association for the Norwegian National Gallery. Tryggve Sagen, who was among the founders, had the previous year donated 60,000 kroner to the gallery earmarked for the purchase of foreign art—50 per cent more than the gallery's annual budget and almost four times as much as the gallery's public funding for art purchases. Works of art by famous and soon-to-be-famous artists were bought inexpensively on the Continent, helped by a strong Norwegian *krone* and the desperate circumstances in war-torn Europe; "the international art market had a broken back, and a group of trustees in Kristiania had a honeypot bursting with money."[82]

Fine art was hardly a concern for the population in general. For most Norwegians, the abundance of money was seen mainly in rising prices, and their bitter experience was that wages did not keep up. In 1916 and 1917 demonstrations and strikes were frequent in Kristiania and the other major cities. "Sailors are drowning, people are starving, capital is reaping the benefits," was the disillusioned message on a poster in a rally against the high cost of living.

As a result of the increasing inequality, social tensions grew—particularly in the cities and other places with manufacturing industry, where food was bought, rather than grown. Ordinary workers—and even more so the unemployed—struggled with rationing and the rapid increase in the cost of living. The lavishness and luxury that characterized the lifestyle of the most successful speculators were provocative. The result was a feeling of contempt and a growing class consciousness—syndicalists, communists and anarchists gained support. The revolution in Russia had created hope. Norwegian politics became polarized and was permanently changed.

---

[80] Vogt (1938, 158).

[81] In recent years, two fascinating books that deal with the link between the war profits and the arts have been published; Haugstad (2015, 2017). The latter book is a biography of Tryggve Sagen.

[82] Haugstad (2015).

The authorities increased their influence on the Norwegian economy during the war. Rationing and maximum prices became the order of the day. Monopolies were established and public expenses increased rapidly. The tax burden increased. Johan Schreiner, who has written the most extensive work on Norwegian shipping during the war, emphasizes that "the relationship to the authorities was radically changed [as] the traditional freedom of action was drastically restrained by commands from domestic and foreign branches of government. [...] A similar transformation occurred in the relationship between shipping company and seafarers."[83]

The Norwegian authorities and shipowners managed the difficult balancing act that the First World War represented *relatively* well. At the same time, it is evident that in public opinion, shipowners lost some of their sheen—they were now more closely associated with speculators than with society builders. There were still shipowners who played an important political role—Joh. Ludwig Mowinckel, for instance, would go on to become Prime Minister on three occasions in the interwar period. However, the boom had been particularly pronounced in shipping, and although fly-by-night "newcomers"—who saw casino-like opportunities in shipping—had been responsible for the worst excesses, many long-term, responsible shipowners were also tainted in the public's perception.

The 1920s would bring economic challenges as well. In the words of one shipowner, "The transition from the golden boom years was difficult, prices fell vertically, and many of those who at the beginning of 1920 were millionaires – at least on paper and according to tax reports and share values – were suddenly stony broke. Every day new bankruptcies and new misery, frauds and hair-raising stupidity were revealed."[84]

When peace returned in November 1918, many things had changed, both in Norway and at the international stage. As shipowners prepared for the post-war boom, the "first era of globalization" was still an ideal. Unfortunately, the 1920s and the 1930s never lived up to the expectations.

---

[83] Schreiner (1963, ii). In 1915 it was decided that the Norwegian Shipowners' Association would function as an employers' organization for the seafarers, and while this was initially of limited importance, it became an important role when peace returned.
[84] Ditlev-Simonsen (1945, 157–158).

# Bibliography

R.G. Albion & J.B. Pope (1968) *Sea Lanes in Wartime – The American Experience, 1775–1945*, second enlarged edition (Hamden: Archon Books)
R. Berg (1995) 'Norge på egen hånd 1905–1920', *Norsk utenrikspolitikks historie*, Vol. 2 (Oslo: Universitetsforlaget)
D. Brochmann (1928) *Med norsk skib i verdenskrigen* (Oslo: Norges Handels & Sjøfartstidende)
O. Ditlev-Simonsen (1945) *En sjøgutt ser tilbake* (Oslo: Cappelen)
K. Egeland (1963) *Vår ære og vår makt (introduction)* (Oslo: Gyldendal Norsk Forlag AS)
J. Falkberget (1920) *Bør Børson jr.* (Kristiania: H. Aschehoug & Co.)
C.E. Fayle (1923a) 'Seaborne Trade', Vol. II, *Official History of the Great War* (London: John Murray)
C.E. Fayle (1923b) 'Seaborne Trade', Vol. III, *Official History of the Great War* (London: John Murray)
N. Grieg (1935) *Vår ære og vår makt* (Kristiania: Gyldendalske Bokhandel)
C.J. Hambro (1958) *Under den første verdenskrig* (Oslo: Gyldendal)
B. Haugstad (2015) *Krig, kunst og kollaps – Reder-kapitalen og Nasjonalgalleriet* (Oslo: Schreibtisch Forlag)
B. Haugstad (2017) *Tryggve Sagen – Gutten Norge glemte* (Oslo: Schreibtisch Forlag)
J. Hjort (1927) *Utenrikspolitiske opplevelser under verdenskrigen* (Oslo: Gyldendal Norsk Forlag)
F. Hodne (1981) *Norges økonomisk historie 1815–1970* (Oslo: J.W. Cappelens Forlag)
A. Hurd (1924) 'The Merchant Navy', Vol. II, *History of The Great War* (New York: Longmans, Green & Co.)
C. Haaland (1940) *Norges skipsfart – hva den var og hva den er* (Oslo: Blix Forlag AS)
F.W. Ilboe (1970) *Fare Fare Sjømann* (Oslo: H. Aschehoug & Co.)
G. Imset (2009) *Christoffer Hannevig: gull, krig og krakk* (Oslo: Pax)
W. Keilhau (1923) *Tore Tank* (Oslo: H. Aschehoug & Co.) The book was published without the author being identified.
W. Keilhau (1927) *Norge og verdenskrigen* (Oslo: H. Aschehoug & Co.)
W. Keilhau (1951) *Norges eldste linjerederi* (Bergen: BDS)
K.U. Kloster (1935) *Krigsår og gullflom – Skibsfarten under verdenskrigen* (Oslo: Gyldendal)

J.T. Klovland (2017) 'Navigating through torpedo attacks and enemy raiders: Merchant shipping and freight rates during World War I', *Discussion paper SAM 07/2017* (Bergen: NHH – Norwegian School of Economics)

Miller, M. (2017) 'Sea Transport and Supply', in U. Daniel, P. Gatrell, O. Janz, H. Jones, J. Keene, A. Kramer & B. Nasson, *1914–1918-online. International Encyclopedia of the First World War*, issued by Freie Universität Berlin, Berlin 2014-10-08

Nilsen, Tore L. & Atle Thowsen (1990) *Handelsflåten i krig 1939–45* (Bergen: Bergens Sjøfartsmuseum)

Norges Rederforbund (1960) *Norsk skipsfart i vårt århundre: Hovedlinjer i utviklingen* (Oslo: Norges Rederforbund)

K. Petersen (1949) *Norsk dampskipsfart blir en stormakt på verdenshavene* (Trondheim: E. Bruns Bokhandels Forlag)

O. Riste (1965) *The Neutral Ally: Norway's Relations with Belligerent Powers in the First World War* (Oslo: Universitetsforlaget)

P. Salmon (1993) '"Between the Sea Power and the Land Power": Scandinavia and the Coming of the First World War', *Transactions of the Royal Historical Society*, 3, 23–49

J. Schreiner (1963) *Norsk skipsfart under krig og høykonjunktur, 1914–1920* (Oslo: Norges Rederforbund/Cappelen)

J.B. Scott, (1908) 'The North Sea and Baltic Agreements', *The Advocate of Peace*, 70:8, 200

Statistics Norway (1914) *Norges Handel 1913* (Kristiania: Det Statistiske Centralbyraa/H. Aschehoug & Co.)

Statistics Norway (1916) *Norges Skibsfart 1913* (Kristiania: Det Statistiske Centralbyraa/H. Aschehoug & Co.)

Statistics Norway (1918) *Norges Handel 1916* (Kristiania: Det Statistiske Centralbyraa/H. Aschehoug & Co.)

Statistics Norway (1919) *Statistisk aarbok for kongeriket Norge 1919* (Kristiania: Det Statistiske Centralbyrå/H. Aschehoug & Co.)

Statistics Norway (1948) *Statistiske oversikter 1948* (Oslo: Statistiske Sentralbyrå)

Statistics Norway (2000) *Statistisk Årbok 2000* (Oslo: Statistics Norway)

J. Søhr (1938) *Spioner og bomber: fra opdagelsespolitiets arbeide under verdenskrigen* (Oslo: Tanum)

O.J. Storm, (1920) *Utenriksreformen og Funktionærstyret i Utenriksdepartementet* (Kristiania: AS Sverre Mortensen, Ltd.)

A. Thowsen (1983) 'Vekst og strukturendringer i krisetider 1914–1939', *Bergen og Sjøfarten IV* (Bergen: Bergens Rederiforening og Bergens Sjøfartsmuseum)

N. Tveit (1972) *Fra gull til grønne skoger* (Oslo: Gyldendal Norsk Forlag)
J.N. Tønnessen (1960) *Norske Styrmandsforening i femti år, 1910–1960* (Oslo: Norsk Styrmandsforening)
P. Vogt (1938) *Jerntid og jobbetid: En skildring av Norge under verdenskrigen* (Oslo: Tanum)
I. Øvreseth, (1932) *Vi som var våbenløse – en skibsførers erindringer fra krigstiden 1914–18* (Oslo: H. Aschehoug & Co.)
R. Aaberge, A.B. Atkinson & J. Modalsli (2016) 'On the measurement of long-run income inequality: Empirical evidence from Norway, 1875–2013', *Discussion Paper 847* (Oslo: Statistics Norway)

**Open Access** This chapter is licensed under the terms of the Creative Commons Attribution-NonCommercial-NoDerivatives 4.0 International License (http://creativecommons.org/licenses/by-nc-nd/4.0/), which permits any noncommercial use, sharing, distribution and reproduction in any medium or format, as long as you give appropriate credit to the original author(s) and the source, provide a link to the Creative Commons license and indicate if you modified the licensed material. You do not have permission under this license to share adapted material derived from this chapter or parts of it.

The images or other third party material in this chapter are included in the chapter's Creative Commons license, unless indicated otherwise in a credit line to the material. If material is not included in the chapter's Creative Commons license and your intended use is not permitted by statutory regulation or exceeds the permitted use, you will need to obtain permission directly from the copyright holder.

# 4

# Crisis? What Crisis? Norwegian Shipping in the Interwar Period

On 14 October 1924, the reputable US newspaper, *The Washington Post*, featured an article on the Norwegian ship *Sagatind*, where the crew allegedly had ended up in a free-for-all fight after a "wild orgy on contraband cargo." The ship had been floating "aimlessly 40 miles off New York without a helmsman" two days earlier, when 22 representatives from the US Coast Guard vessel *Seneca* boarded. The Americans found "two sailors asleep in the wheelhouse. Below decks they found the rest of the crew. Some were asleep, some were in their bunks nursing broken bones, and some were staggering about in a stupor. Nearly all were nursing black eyes."[1] According to the newspaper report, the Coast Guard put the crew of 32 in irons, and confiscated the cargo, which consisted of more than 40,000 cases of liquor.

The crew received a heavy-handed welcome by the US authorities, and one mate was beaten so heavily that he lost three teeth and had to be hospitalized after he had tried to stop one of the customs officers from stealing a bottle of whiskey. Following the seizure, *Sagatind* was anchored off the Statue of Liberty. The illegal cargo was discharged to a Brooklyn

---

[1] *The Washington Post*, 141024, 10.

army base—with around 1000 cases of liquor mysteriously disappearing during the transfer.[2] It is evident that all the hard work during Prohibition made US officials thirsty.

The owner of *Sagatind* was AS Reidar, a company controlled by Finn Friis and Carl Otto Lund—the latter a High Court attorney who had served as mayor of Drammen in two periods and as a Member of Parliament from 1916 to 1921. The vessel had been chartered to an American smuggling syndicate through a French front man, and the ship had also spent large parts of June 1924 on "Rum Row"—the line of smuggling ships anchored just beyond the US maritime limit. Although the *Sagatind*-debacle received a lot of attention on both sides of the Atlantic, it turned out that the premise for the arrest of the ship had been wrong. The authorities wanted to use the *Sagatind* as a test case, but the necessary regulation against foreign smuggling ships had not yet been ratified by the Senate.

The missing legal basis created problems for the authorities, as a legal technicality implied that the US Coast Guard had no right to enter the ship 22 miles off the coast. The shipowners considered demanding compensation from the Americans, but after some gentle persuasion the claims were silently shelved. The seamen, on the other hand, entered into a drawn-out battle for damages. While the press reports of the contraband orgy turned out to be an early example of "fake news," the violence was real. However, the perpetrators were the US officials, rather than the seafarers themselves. Indeed, in some Norwegian newspaper articles the innocence—and sobriety—of the Norwegian sailors, and the heavy treatment that they had been given, were emphasized.[3] The seafarers were adamant that they deserved compensation for the detention and for the manner in which they were treated. Even 10 years after the event, they tried to convince the Norwegian authorities that reparations were justified.

The *Sagatind* incidence was one of the first examples of Norwegian presence in the less-salubrious part of the shipping sector—and

---

[2] *The New York Times*, 050225, 5 and *Nordisk Tidende*, 120225, 4.
[3] For a detailed account of the *Sagatind* story, see Johansen (1994, 13–23) and for a presentation that is favourable to the crew, see *1ste Mai*, 250628, 6. A more sober account—where the crews are neither angels nor devils—can be found in *Arbeiderbladet*, 150125, 9. Another good account of the smuggling business in general in this period is Chapters 1–3 of Lawson (2013).

undoubtedly the most publicized. Of course, *Sagatind* was not the only Norwegian ship engaged in smuggling during the Prohibition era, and it could be tempting to use the smuggling ships as an example of the increasing desperation of Norwegian shipping companies during a period of low activity in the shipping market. However, such an interpretation would be terribly wrong.

Although it has been claimed that the Norwegians had an exceptionally bad reputation with regard to smuggling, there are absolutely no indications that they were overrepresented among smugglers.[4] In fact, while the interwar period generally is considered a bad period for international trade and shipping, Norwegian shipowners stood out favourably, orchestrated an impressive resurgence and increased their share of the world fleet. More importantly, while they had controlled a fleet of relatively old and outdated ships before 1914, by the end of the interwar period Norway had succeeded in modernizing the fleet and had the world's youngest and technologically most advanced merchant marine.

In some ways, the interwar period saw Norwegian shipping culture at its best. Shipping companies were forced to look for new market opportunities, and when a viable course had been found, they managed to exploit the desperation of idle Swedish and Danish yards to secure cheap tonnage. Based on a combination of experience, knowledge and willingness to take risk—and helped by the requisite portion of luck—Norwegian shipowners managed to come strengthened out of a difficult period for world shipping.

## Between the Wars

The Great Depression is often the starting point for discussions about the low economic growth of the interwar period, but the Great Depression was both a symptom and a cause of more far-reaching problems in the international economy.

---

[4] For the claim about Norwegian reputation, see for instance Behr (1996). There is limited evidence to support the claim. In 1925, only 10 of the more than 330 smuggling ships in US waters were Norwegian; this 3 per cent share was lower than the Norwegian share of the world fleet; *Nordisk Tidende*, 050525, 1.

The First World War—at the time referred to as the Great War—brought an abrupt end to the liberal world economy that had developed in the decades before 1914. Although there had been signs of increased protectionism at the start of the 20th century, the benefits of specialization and division of labour were so large that international trade continued to grow, spurred by a dramatic reduction of transport and other transaction costs. Intercontinental migration flows of more than a million people annually also created substantial demand for shipping before the war.

The breakdown of the world economy during the war, the financial turmoil of the 1920s, the depression of the early 1930s and the sluggish recovery came as a surprise to most of those involved. When the First World War ended, there had been considerable optimism about the demand for transport as individual nations and the world economy itself embarked on the road to recovery. Although the main merchant marines had suffered substantial losses during the war, the enormous expansion of shipbuilding activity, particularly in the United States, meant that the fleet had actually increased marginally relative to its size before the war.

However, neutral Norway had suffered more than most.[5] The courageous—or foolhardy—employment of the fleet during the hostilities had led to substantial losses. At the end of 1918 the carrying capacity of the Norwegian fleet was around a quarter lower than it had been at the end of 1914. At the same time, there had been a structural shift in the fleet; the sailing ship tonnage had been more than halved, while the steamship fleet lost around 25 per cent. There was a strong increase in the proportion and tonnage of motorships, but from a relatively low starting point.[6]

During the war, the Norwegian merchant marine had developed unfavourably—both in terms of quality and quantity. Many of the additions

---

[5] According to data on the period August 1914–October 1918, in Statistics Norway (1919, 191), three countries had a higher net reduction than Norway (30%); Germany (44%), Belgium (48%) and Greece (47%). With the exception of Argentina, the fleets increased in all non-European countries for which we have statistics. The US fleet, increasing by more than 2.8 million compensated tons (154%), had the highest absolute and relative growth. However, a commonly published overview puts the Norwegian losses (49.6%) at the top, followed by Italy and Greece; see Egeland (1930, 18); Brækhus (1934, 106) or Haaland (1940, 18). This is based on gross losses—not taking acquisitions into account.

[6] Calculated on the basis of Statistics Norway (1919, 62).

from the war years were relatively old, inefficient ships. Although all capacity was useful during the war boom, Norway's competitive position had deteriorated severely, with the share of the world fleet falling by approximately a quarter—from around 4 per cent to around 3 per cent.

Throughout the war, materials and shipbuilding capacity had been in short supply, and ships that would under other circumstances have been considered inferior, easily found employment. There were also some novel solutions. One innovation was ships made of concrete. When the first large Norwegian-built ship made of concrete was launched in 1917, it was heralded as the ship of the future. The advantage of the concrete ships was that they did not rust and were easy to maintain—the disadvantage was that they for all practical purposes were quite useless outside the harbour, extremely slow and difficult to handle. Less than two years after the launch, the Norwegian Shipowners' Association referred to this "ship of the future" as a "totally unsuccessful vessel" and suggested that it would benefit the fleet if such "surrogate vessels" were removed.[7]

The desperate demand for tonnage also spurred a revival of shipbuilding on the South Coast of Norway. When activity peaked in the spring of 1918, some 80 yards that had been dormant for decades or engaged only in repair, had commenced the building of new ships. Norwegian owners also ordered almost 150 wooden ships—usually with auxiliary engines—in the United States and Canada. Some of the US contacts turned out to be "frauds," while others used the Norwegian instalments to build up non-existing yards, with little funds left to construct the ships. As the war spread, it became increasingly difficult to acquire new tonnage. In the United States, more than 40 newbuildings for Norwegian account had been confiscated by the authorities after the Americans entered the war—these were all steelships, as even the American authorities had limited interest in the wooden vessels that Norwegians had ordered there.[8]

Although those who fell victim to the confiscation were promised "just compensation" the case dragged on after the war. In 1919 most of the owners saw the return of their paid-in instalments—in total USD34

---

[7] Schreiner (1963, 404–405). For a detailed history of the loss-bringing operation of one concrete-built ships, see Langfeldt (1980, 76–79).
[8] Schreiner (1963, 396–405).

million plus interest—though with no reimbursement for the fact that the value of the contracts was around three times higher.[9] However, a break-out group owning 15 contracts, initially led by Christoffer Hannevig jr., refused to enter into an agreement with the US authorities. When their case was brought to arbitration in the Hague they received a smaller amount per contract than the less-aggressive owners. However, the interwar period was characterized by unpredictable fluctuations in most economic variables, and the recent depreciation of the Norwegian *krone* more or less neutralized the negative effect.[10]

For most shipping companies the Armistice of 11 November 1918 signalled the start of an optimistic period. Many companies had large funds available from a number of sources; insurance claims from vessels that had been lost, capital that they had raised from new investors eager to get a piece of the bullish market, and reserves built up as a result of the high profits during the war. In tune with this optimism, and encouraged by the possibility of avoiding excess tax, many companies had entered into newbuilding agreements. The ships were intended to go straight from the shipyards and into the prosperous post-war market, and the main problem was finding vacant building berths, not financing the investment. However, due to the high demand for yard capacity, there was a substantial delay in delivery; some shipowners had ordered vessels that could not be delivered until 1922. By then, the market had crashed.

Just like shipping had facilitated "the first era of globalization," the rebuilding of the world economy after the war would depend on shipping. Investors acted according to this belief, and in the slightly more than two years from the end of the war in November 1918 to December 1920, the world fleet increased by 39 per cent.[11] The post-war market was indeed prosperous, but for less than 18 months.[12] Shipping cycles peaked in February and March 1920. Then, abruptly, the market collapsed,

---

[9] Kloster (1935, 126).
[10] See Egeland (1973, 146–148); Egeland was present in the United States as representative for the Norwegian Shipowners' Association.
[11] Klovland (2017, 8).
[12] Furthermore, for parts of the prosperous period, regulations from the war, including maximum freights, were still in force.

reaching a trough around a year later.[13] The post-war adjustments were over more rapidly than anticipated, stocks were high and the international economy never really recovered. Shipping was hard hit, as employment for the ships became extremely difficult to find, even at very low rates.

During 1920 freight rates dropped by around three-quarters—one Norwegian shipowner compared the situation to "when the bottom falls off a barrel."[14] Ship prices followed suit, as lay-ups increased to a level that had not been seen before—and has never been seen since. The figure usually quoted is that half of the world fleet was idle at the worst point around the middle of 1921. The aforementioned *Sagatind* had made good money during the boom in 1920, with the owners paying a 10 per cent dividend, but the ship was laid up from early December 1920 to the beginning of August 1921.[15]

Still, this unsurpassed overcapacity was a short-lived shock, and had limited long-term effects. Although the severity was extreme, the post-war crisis was brief and more normal conditions returned quite rapidly. Thus, due to the brevity of the crisis, the overcapacity and high lay-up rates did not have the kind of detrimental effect on shipping company revenues and equity that we see during the longer, but less-violent, crises in the 1930s and 1970s.

In 1920 Norwegian gross freight earnings—shipping income from abroad—amounted to almost NOK 1.3 billion, a record that would remain until the Second World War. Figure 4.1 shows the development of the gross freight earnings in the first four decades of the 20th century, and the data illustrate the dramatic boom-and-bust that the First World War and the brief post-war boom represented.[16]

---

[13] Klovland (2016, 19).
[14] See Castelein (2015) or Klovland (2016); quote from shipowner Thoresen in Christensen (1933, 14).
[15] When *Sagatind* started trading again, one of its first cargoes was forest products that were transported on behalf of the Soviet authorities. This voyage also created quite a stir in the Norwegian press, as the timber originated with a previously Norwegian-owned sawmill that the "Bolsheviks" had "nationalized"; *Aftenposten,* 270722, 3. The Drammen shipowners Friis & Lund really knew how to pick the right customers.
[16] Figure 4.1: Gross freight earnings from Statistics Norway (1948, 277), with real figures deflated by means of the data in Grytten (2004).

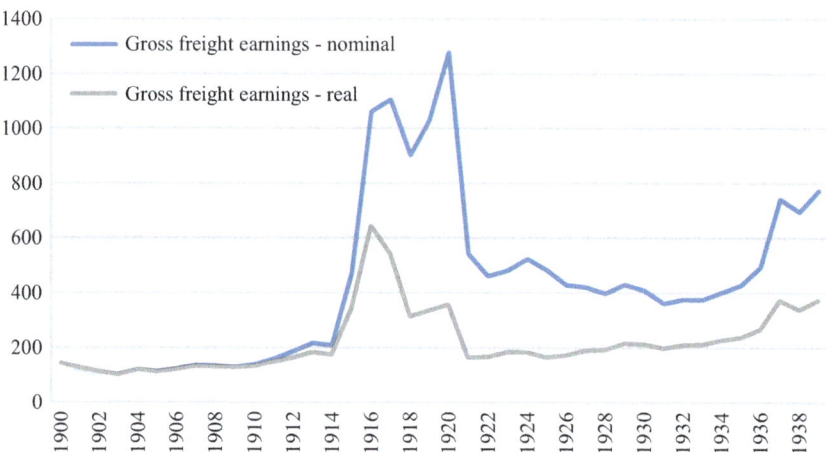

**Fig. 4.1** Gross freight earnings, nominal and real, 1900–1939, NOK million. (Source: Statistics Norway (1948, 277). See footnote)

The period 1900–1939 was characterized by violent price movements, both strong inflation and periods of deflation, which obscure the actual development. In real terms, revenues from abroad during the prosperous years (1915–1920) were typically around three times higher than in the period 1900–1914, and twice as high as in the subsequent period of peace (1921–1938). Consequently, even with the collapse of the 1920s and the crisis of the 1930s, Norwegian shipping revenues followed a gently upwards-sloping trend, and the level during the interwar period was on average around 50 per cent higher than before the war.

This positive development was atypical in an international perspective. For world shipping in general, the interwar period was characterized by structural changes, overcapacity and low profits. Freight rates saw a steep decline in the first half of the 1920s, while the 1930s were another "dismal period for the shipping industry."[17] The negative development of the shipping market reflected more fundamental problems in the world economy.

The attempts at rebuilding the international economy after the war were botched. Although the 1920s were prosperous and "swinging" in

[17] Klovland (2016, 17).

the United States, the world economy never rediscovered its pre-war rhythm. One problem was monetary conditions. The Germans paid war reparations to France and the UK, that used the money to service their war debts to the United States. How could the war-torn Germans finance this? Well, they borrowed money from the Americans. In monetary terms, the interwar period was a merry-go-round let loose, with mercurial exchange rate fluctuations, hyperinflation and extreme instability in the world economy.

A second problem was the lack of a hegemonial power; a sunset Europe that was unable to take responsibility for the functioning of the international economy. Before the war, European imports had been financed by a combination of "invisible earnings" from shipping, return on investments abroad and export revenues. Following the war, the decline of the European fleet reduced shipping earnings. Liquidation of investments, partly to finance the war, partly due to the "disappearance" of large debtors such as Tsarist Russia, implied that Europe had gone from being net creditor to becoming net debtor. Finally, the reduced advantage in manufacturing production—neutral countries had built up their own capacity—aggravated the adverse balance within merchandise trade. The limited scope for manufacturing exports was made even more difficult as a result of increasingly protectionist policies in important markets.

For shipping, the most important problem was international trade, where the First World War and the interwar depression had a negative effect. The liberal world order, characterized by relatively free trade, did not recover after peace had returned. Tariffs, quotas and other restrictions introduced during the war were difficult to remove, and well-organized interest groups fought to maintain their privileges. Protectionism had spread to new countries and new industries. For the shipping industry—whose basis is international exchange of goods and commodities—the breakdown of the liberal trading regime was particularly problematic.

When international trade sneezes, shipping catches a cold. When international trade catches a cold, shipping gets pneumonia. The interwar period never saw the kind of strong trade growth that had been characteristic for the decades before the war, and with the onset of the Great Depression international trade collapsed. However, uncritical use of trade data gives an overly negative picture of the development of shipping demand. For instance, although the value of world trade decreased by around 60 per cent from 1930 to 1932, this was primarily driven by a strong reduction of prices. Ships move cargoes, not money. In actual terms, the volume reduction—and the effect on shipping—was much lower.

Despite all the rhetoric about the slow growth of trade and the interwar collapse of the international economy, shipping demand in 1937 was in fact around 75 per cent higher than it had been in 1913, despite the fact that data on the development of world trade volumes only present a growth of 25 per cent. Three factors explain the fact that the demand for seaborne transport grew faster than trade in general. First, trade in raw materials—relatively heavy commodities that take up a lot of shipping capacity—increased faster than trade in less shipping-intensive cargoes such as foodstuffs and finished goods. Second, an increase in average distances pushed up transport demand. Finally, due to the increased specialization and changes in the international trading pattern, ships spent a larger share of their time in ballast.[18]

## International Shipping in Transition

The best example of the increased specialization is probably the interwar growth segment *par excellence*—oil tanker shipping. The main shift in seaborne energy transport was a relative reduction in the role of coal, and the concomitant upsurge of oil transports. Consequently, demand development was very conducive to oil tankers—and the tanker fleet increased tremendously. At the beginning of the 1920s, the tanker fleet made up less than 6 per cent of the world fleet and amounted to slightly more than 3 million gross registered tons. Almost 90 per cent of this was controlled by owners, mainly oil companies, in the United States and the UK. By 1937 the proportion of tankers had increased to more than 15 per cent, and American and British interests now controlled around half of this tonnage. The third largest fleet—slightly less than 20 per cent of all tanker tonnage—was owned by Norwegian shipping companies.

---

[18] Seland (1953, 11, 46–49).

The growth in the demand for oil transport is only one half of the story about Norwegian tanker expansion. The other half of the story is something that most of us tend to think of as a modern phenomenon: outsourcing. Starting before the war, but accelerating in the second half of the 1920s, there was an important shift in ownership of oil tanker tonnage. A substantial portion of tanker transport was outsourced from oil companies to independent shipping companies. In 1900 independent shipping companies owned around 10 per cent of the tanker fleet, compared with 80 per cent owned by oil companies and 10 per cent by governments. By 1923 the independent fleet had increased to 25 per cent of the tanker fleet, and by 1939 to almost 40 per cent.[19] This share increased amidst a tremendous fleet growth; the amount of independent tanker tonnage ballooned from 36,000 gross registered tons in 1900 to almost 4.3 million tons four decades later—an average annual growth of 13 per cent.

By leaving part of the transport to external service providers, the oil companies freed up resources to do what they did best—look for and exploit oil resources. However, a considerable share of the independent tanker tonnage was tied to the oil companies on charters of relatively long duration. The most famous outsourcing case concerned tankers sold from Anglo-Saxon Petroleum Co.—the transport arm of Royal Dutch/Shell—with 10-year charters back to the sellers. An impressive 26 of the 28 ships that were outsourced in the period 1927–1930 ended up in Norway, many of them on the South Coast.

Through a combination of purchases of second-hand oil company tonnage and an ambitious newbuilding programme, Norwegian shipping companies built up the world's largest independent tanker fleet. The oil tankers—with their highly specialized technology—supplemented liners and tramp vessels, and also encouraged another technological shift: the replacement of steam engines by diesel engines. This transformation also had implications for work on board—coaling jobs were removed and "the soot angels" were left on the ash heap of history. The character of life at sea changed dramatically in the decades either side of the turn of the century. First, the old shanties from the sailing ships were no longer

---

[19] Data from British Petroleum, cited in Middlemiss (1996, 14).

heard, as steam replaced sails and work in the masts was replaced by hauling of coal. Now that new type of labour-intensive activity has gradually disappeared as well.

The interwar period also saw a major shift in market shares in international shipping. There was a strong decline in the supremacy of the two major maritime powers—the United States and the UK. The United States had been oriented inwards—the way to the west was more enticing than the sea—through much of the second half of the 19th century. Indeed, the shipping and shipbuilding expansion during the First World War was a break from the norm. After the hostilities had ended, the United States established a large reserve fleet, to show readiness for another war situation. However, within commercial shipping, there was hardly any new investment. In the period from 1923 to 1939, the average age of the US fleet increased by 11 months annually.[20] The United States was better off leaving shipping to foreigners.

The basis for the British decline was different. In the 19th century, Britain had large advantages in manufacturing production, and also oversaw a political and commercial empire that spanned the world.[21] The history of the UK in the 20th century is the story of decline. Step by step the British advantages disappeared. The knowledge of how to build efficient machines, including steamships and their engines, was transferred to other countries. British coal was replaced as the main source of motive power. Finally, Britain's commercial and political empire was falling apart.

When the two leading maritime nations faltered, other countries were ready to take over. Four countries, in particular, managed to grab large market shares in the interwar period. Germany, starting from a low point with a practically non-existent merchant marine after the First World War, regained its former position as one of the world's leading maritime nations. In Japan, where the fear of colonization had gradually become replaced by imperial ambitions, the merchant marine played an important

---

[20] See Tenold (2006, 123).
[21] The song "Rule, Britannia!" was written in the 18th century, as a response to the infamous War of Jenkins' Ear. The shift from the imperative "Britannia, rule the waves" to the "vulgarly misquoted" statement "Britannia rules the waves" took place in the 19th century; Livingstone (2016, 186–187) and *The Windsor Magazine*, 1915, 73.

political role.[22] The growth of the German and Japanese fleets of course reflected the countries' role in the world economy.

The final challengers were less obvious; Norway had already been established among the Top Five of the world's maritime nations, but in the interwar period the Norwegian shipowners really solidified their position, increasing their share of the world fleet. While the world fleet practically "stood still," in tonnage terms, from 1923 to 1939, the Norwegian fleet more than doubled.[23] The expansion was to a large extent based on oil tankers with diesel engines, so by the end of the interwar period, the Norwegian fleet was both bigger and better. However, an increasing focus on the liner trade and a consistently strong position in old specialties such as the Caribbean fruit trade also helped the Norwegian fleet's expansion.[24]

The strongest growth in relative terms took place in Greece.[25] The country had been independent since the first half of the 19th century, but gained important territorial advances, primarily at the expense of the Ottoman Empire. Today, Norway is the only European country with a longer coastline than Greece, and the local basis for international shipping is not too different in the two countries.

The Greek expansion partly had the same foundations as the Norwegian, based on family and local connections. It had a decentralized pattern, with strong ownership interests on a number of islands. Many of the shipping companies did not have an administrative structure onshore, as "the technical and operational management of the ship took place at sea."[26] The country did not see a movement of shipping to the leading

---

[22] See Chida and Davies (1990), for the best English-language introduction to Japanese shipping.
[23] Calculated on the basis of *Lloyd's Register Statistical Tables*, various years. Figures do not include the US reserve fleet; see Tenold (2006, 246).
[24] In the middle of the 1920s, Norwegians accounted for around 60 per cent of the ships that were employed in the US fruit trade. They also had a large share of the transport of fruit from Spain in the summer—ships that in the winter often carried forest products; Egeland (1930, 43–44).
[25] The Greek fleet increased on average by almost 6 per cent annually from 1923 to 1939. For the basis of the expansion, see Harlaftis (1996, 181–206). For the other main nations, the Norwegian increase of 4.6 per cent came second, Germany with 2.5 per cent came third, and Japan's 1.62 per cent came fourth. The biggest decline was in the United States (minus 2.2 per cent), while the British fleet's increase during 1923–1930 was more than neutralized by its decline during 1930–1939, leading to an annual net decline of 0.8 per cent; see Tenold (2006, 117).
[26] Harlaftis (1996, 87) and Harlaftis and Theotokas (2004, 30–33).

urban centres, like in Norway. Indeed, when such a shift occurred in Greek shipping after 1945, it was not only to Athens and Piraeus, but also to the metropolises of London and New York.

The increase in the merchant marines of Germany and Japan can be explained by their large and growing economies. The ships aided and abetted expansive imperial ambitions that would subsequently come to have disastrous effects. Norway and Greece, on the other hand, had limited imperial ambitions and were relatively unimportant in international trade. However, they shared certain characteristics; limited domestic resources, long coastlines and an even longer maritime heritage. A crucial point for both countries is that their rise to the top of the shipping market has been centred on foreign, rather than home, demand.[27]

This latter element was even more notable in the case of Panama, the first of an unlikely group of maritime nations that entered the shipping market in the interwar period and would go on to dominate it in the last part of the 20th century. Panama was a small, poor country, but with an important role in international shipping after the opening of the Panama Canal in 1914. Five years later, *Belen Quezada*, a former US navy ship, became the first foreign vessel to fly the Panamanian flag.

The expansion of the Panamanian fleet is a reflection of the footloose nature of shipping. Part of the basis for the use of the registry was US policy—a reaction to the introduction of the labour-friendly Seamen's Act in 1915, which increased the cost level substantially for American ships. Interestingly, the man responsible for the "emancipation of [American] seamen" was a Norwegian immigrant, "Andrew Furuseth, the head of the International Seamen's Union (ISU) and a man of such implacable determination and virtue that he was frequently compared to Lincoln and Jesus."[28]

The Seamen's Act included minimum levels of crew size, as well as requirements for specific skills and payments. These regulations made ships registered in the United States particularly expensive and uncom-

---

[27] While Norwegian shipping companies had relied on intercontinental trade since the last part of the 19th century, Greek companies initially had more of a "home waters" bias. In 1938 almost half of the port entries of Greek ships were in the Mediterranean and the Black Sea, but after the Second World War Greek owners became more international and more "exiled" than anyone else.
[28] Gibson and Donovan (2001, 116).

petitive in many markets, and could be alleviated by the transfer to the Panamanian flag. Another impetus came from the Prohibition. *Belen Quezada* was a smuggling ship, which was followed on the Panamanian register by two "dry" US cruise ships that feared losing their market if they were unable to ply passengers with alcohol.

The final consideration that made Panama attractive was tax. The desire to avoid "double taxation" of profits in the UK and the investors' home countries was important when the whale ship *Vikingen* was transferred to the Panamanian flag in 1931. Subsequently, Honduras became the second "Flag of Convenience," primarily promoted by the United Fruit Company's desire to transport bananas cheaply.[29]

Although the first Flags of Convenience were introduced in the first half of the 20th century, the scale was limited, and the majority of those that used the new opportunities had specific purposes—they were to some extent "Flags of Refuge." The Flags of Convenience did not create any major controversy until after the Second World War. However, it was already evident that the special character of the shipping industry—its operation in unclear jurisdictions—created a need for special, and internationally coordinated, solutions. In 1920, the second conference of the International Labour Organization (ILO), held in Genoa, dealt specifically with shipping. According to the contemporary edition of *Encyclopedia Britannica;* "Of all industries, the shipping industry is the most essentially international, and of all callings the seaman's has perhaps received the least attention from the legislator."[30] This omission was what the ILO wanted to rectify, and the global character of shipping meant that it was a good test case for how the new organization could influence working practices.

In the early 1920s, ILO introduced a number of conventions regulating issues such as the minimum age for seafarers (14 years), unemployment indemnity for shipwrecked sailors, compulsory medical examination of seafarers under the age of 18, and so on. Another major issue was the suppression of the system of "crimps"—employment agencies that

---

[29] Carlisle (2009, 2017). Carlisle (2017), Chapter 7 also counts Danzig as the very first Flag of Convenience, but the juridical basis for this is so specialized that it is not usually taken into account.
[30] Entry "International Labour Organization", *Encyclopedia Britannica*, 1922 edition.

operated in a "dark, dark grey area," sometimes with shady tactics to ensure income from sailors looking for a ship to sign on.[31] Still, although a framework was in place to protect seafarers, the manner in which this was followed up in practice was far from impressive, and often the legislation was simply ignored. In an interwar period with substantial unemployment, workers—even the unionized ones—had been dealt a bad hand.

## The Hare and the Tortoise: From Laggards to Leaders

In Norway, regional seafarers' organizations dated back to the second half of the 19th century, primarily for captains.[32] However, from the beginning of the 20th century, the various groups of ratings also formed their own organizations; *Bergens Stuertforening* organized chief stewards from 1902, while able seamen and stokers started organizing around 1910.

The new organizations and legislation did improve the seafarers' lot. However, the main impetus for a safer and healthier life at sea did not come from unions or authorities. Rather, it was a result of technological improvements and the modernization of the Norwegian fleet. Although the conditions were far from luxurious, both the quality of board and lodging and the overall safety improved appreciably. Food regulations—partly as a response to scurvy, beriberi and other diseases—became based on nutritional science, and were helped by improved storage and shorter voyages.[33] Refrigeration improved food storage, and electricity improved

---

[31] See Bruijn (2005, 15–16), Bolle (2006) and Fink (2016), for an introduction to the maritime work of the ILO.

[32] Captains had been organized in guilds, with specific rights and obligations, centuries before this, but the first Captains' Associations [*Skipperforeninger*] were established in the middle of the 19th century.

[33] There were no requirements with regard to the quantity or quality of onboard food before the late 19th century. See Kloster (1942, 64–87) for an overview of the regulation of onboard provisions, with an emphasis on food. Based on contemporary sources, Kloster characterizes the victualling before 1840 as "meagre," although with ample servings of spirits, to "wake up" the crew in the morning when the ship was in port, and several times daily if work was particularly hard. From 1840 to 1870 spirits had usually been replaced by coffee, but the food was "much better, but still

sanitation. Still, the main technological advance was not related to welfare: "Comfort may be overestimated, but the technology that creates safety, cleanliness and convenience for passengers, at least deserves respect."[34]

Better food and cleaner surroundings helped seafarers in the long term; improvements in communications reduced the short-term dangers. The interwar period is known as the Golden Age of Radio, where the new technology had a massive cultural influence, in particular in the United States. At sea, the cultural impact was limited, but the overall effects even more important. In 1931 the first international radio code was published; still organized in a manner similar to the old flag signals, though vastly more useful over longer distances and when visibility was limited.

The frequently used *Lombard* code book contains more than 1200 pages of five-letter codes, and the amount of detail is staggering. It contains, for instance, around 22,500 codes denoting ports and places, more than 17,000 codes covering particular ships and at least 14,000 company addresses. The largest portion of the book—general codes—covers in excess of 830 pages. Among the more than 187,000 codes can be found, for instance, CLRKK (absinthe), GMRDA (drunkenness) and FPBDU (accidental death).[35] Another recent invention was radio navigation; "undoubtedly the best aid for safe navigation both on the ocean and along the coast."[36]

The improved communication became particularly important when it was combined with progress in other areas. Advances in the science of meteorology—to a large extent originating in Bergen—made the improved access to information particularly useful. Similarly, a service providing medicinal advice was established, implying that even small ships could benefit from access to qualified doctors. By the late 1930s, more than 400 Norwegian ships had shortwave radios installed, and were

---

simple." To illustrate the basic character of the equipment: in the middle of the 19th century, Norwegian sailors on US vessels were impressed by the fact that there was a medicine chest onboard.
[34] Kent (1925, 4).
[35] See Lombard (1934).
[36] Mohn (1942, 104).

able to stay in direct and frequent contact with the home country from practically anywhere in the world.[37]

Many shipowners began to take the welfare of sailors more seriously, and new vessels—in addition to some old ones—were equipped with book collections, both prose and educational literature. Indeed, seafarers were encouraged to use their spare time to study, in order to rise in the ranks. Norwegian owners and officers were also praised for their "admirable interest in and consideration for the crew's well-being and satisfaction."[38] In particular, the quality of the cabins and mess rooms was praised; the mess rooms for engine personnel on Norwegian tankers, were claimed to be of the same quality as the officers' mess rooms on British ships.

The most important improvement, however, was probably in the quality of the ship's structure—its seaworthiness, manoeuvrability and materials. In the 1890s, more than four Norwegian vessels were lost at sea every week. In the 1920s the corresponding figure was just above one, while in the 1930s "only" 37 ships were lost in an average year.[39] One reason for the decline was that the old, leaking and accident-prone sailing vessels died out and were replaced by state-of-the-art modern vessels. The average age of the Norwegian tonnage fell from around 19 years in 1914 to less than 13 years in 1939.[40]

From the early 1920s to the outbreak of the Second World War, the average age of the Norwegian fleet remained more or less the same, around 12–13 years. This had two implications. First, although the average age was the same, the fleet each year became one year "more modern"; it is the year the ship is built, not the age, which determines the level of its qualities. Second, although the Norwegian average age was static, the international fleet aged substantially in this period, as a result of lacking investment. In 1923 the average age was more or less the same as in

---

[37] Not everyone was happy about the development; a Bergen captain allegedly said that "We are indeed flooded with telegrams when we are in port; why should we be bothered by them at sea as well"; Albretsen (1942, 119).

[38] An anonymous British newspaper article quoted in Egeland (1930, 32).

[39] Calculated on the basis of Statistisk Sentralbyrå (1968, 177).

[40] The figure for 1913 is estimated on the basis of data in Einarsen (1938, 110). Apparently, the average age around 1880 was more or less the same; rough calculations based on Tønnessen (1951, 141).

Norway, by 1939 it had increased to almost 17 years. Consequently, compared with other countries, the Norwegian fleet became more modern, more competitive and more attractive.

The technology historian Håkon With Andersen has referred to the dramatic interwar transformation of the Norwegian fleet as a development from laggards to leaders.[41] As previously mentioned, Norway was no pioneer in the transformation from sail to steam. On the South Coast, in particular, sailing ships dominated well into the new century, and in 1916 Kristiansand was the sailing ship capital of the world, with almost 70 iron and steel sailing vessels.[42]

The pre-war tonnage level for steamships was regained in 1921, and the steamship fleet continued to increase until peaking in 1931. From then on, the reduction in steamship tonnage was offset by an increase in motor-driven vessels. By the beginning of 1939, Norway's share of the world fleet was around 7 per cent—more than double what it had been when the war ended, and for tankers the market share was an impressive 18 per cent.

The sailing ship fleet, on the other hand, silently disappeared during and shortly after the war. Counting around 1000 ships, and more than 600,000 gross tons, when the war broke out, only around a quarter of the ships were left by 1925. These were primarily the smaller, local vessels—in tonnage terms, the reduction from 1914 to 1925 amounted more than 90 per cent.[43] Around 180 ships, totalling almost 190,000 tons, were lost during the war.[44] In percentage terms the direct war losses amounted to slightly more than 30 per cent, compared with more than 50 per cent for the steam and motor ships. However, lack of reinvestment and natural scrapping of obsolete tonnage meant that the sailing ship fleet declined by more than half from 1914 to 1918, compared with a net reduction of roughly a quarter for the steamships. Nevertheless, as late as in 1920 there were still almost 80 sailing vessels larger than 1500 tons in the Norwegian fleet.

---

[41] Andersen (1992).
[42] Seland (1959, 258).
[43] Estimated on the basis of Statistics Norway (1948, 242).
[44] Vigeland (1949, 256).

The sailing ships had remained competitive in certain trades—in particular the transport of potassium nitrate from Chile—and on long distances. However, they were clearly a dying breed—and a large proportion of them died from "natural causes." One example is *Skaregrøm*, one of Norway's last commercially operated square-riggers, built in Port Glasgow on the Clyde in 1903. When the vessel was bought second-hand by the Grimstad-based shipowner Johan Bang in 1924, it was renamed after an old wooden barque that the owner's grandfather had built at his own yard in Grimstad in 1877. The first Norwegian-built *Skaregrøm* was lost on a trip from Marseille to New York in 1891. The name *Skaregrøm* is thus a good example of both the changing strategies (and the unchanging fates) of ships and shipowners on the South Coast.

In November 1926 the Scottish-built *Skaregrøm* finished loading timber in Fredrikshald (Halden), on the east side of the Oslofjord, and set sail for Australia. The captain, Peder Johannessen, had brought his wife and two of their children on the voyage. A week before Christmas, a major storm destroyed the rigging, leaving only the foremast and "a stump of the mizzen-mast." Johannessen managed to take the ship to the Azores, where *Skaregrøm* was condemned. The ship was subsequently towed to London, where the valuable cargo was sold. Captain Johannessen received a gold medal, and also a gold watch from the cargo's insurer.[45]

The sailing ship era was undoubtedly over in the interwar period, and in its final years the decline went rapidly. The shipping company S.O. Stray in Kristiansand, which owned 20 sailing ships in 1920, had disposed of all by 1925.[46] The city's sailing ship fleet declined from almost 50 ships in 1920 to 34 in 1922 and only four in 1925. Many of the Norwegian sailing ships were scrapped, others were lost and some were sold to foreign shipowners, for instance Åland's Gustaf Erikson, who operated windjammers in the South Australian grain trade.[47] Some had

---

[45] Based on Bakka (1998, 14–15), Vigeland (1949, 257–258), Drevdal (1994, 137–140).

[46] With wonderful irony, the main reason that S.O. Stray was liquidated some years after the last sailing ship was sold, was its badly timed investment in three modern motor ships, not the fact that the majority of the company's fleet had been sailing ships in the era of steam and diesel; Seland (1959, 226–229).

[47] See Newby (1956). Although the *Skaregrøm* had an unfortunate fate, *Pommern*, a former Eriksson-ship and a close, slightly larger cousin—also built in Port Glasgow in 1903—has survived and is today a museum ship in Mariehamn, Åland. See also Kåhre (1977, 1980).

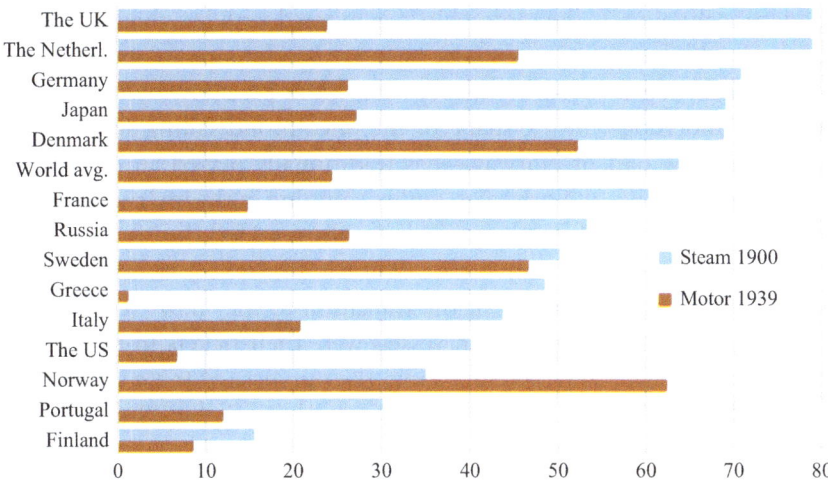

**Fig. 4.2** Steam and motorship shares, per cent, 1900 and 1938, based on gross tonnage. (Source: Statistics Norway (1902, 168; 1939, 324). See footnote)

more unconventional fates. The Stray-vessel *Alastor*, after a stint in Finnish ownership, ended up as the restaurant ship *Bounty* in the harbour of Margate in Kent after the Second World War.[48]

Figure 4.2 clearly illustrates the transformation of the Norwegian fleet from a technological laggard at the start of the century to a technological leader at the end of the interwar period.[49] Only relatively poor and technologically backward countries such as Portugal and Finland had a higher share of sailing ship tonnage than Norway at the start of the century. While steamships made up almost 64 per cent of the world fleet, in Norway the share was less than 35 per cent. Less than four decades later, more than 60 per cent of the Norwegian fleet consisted of the most

---

[48] *Motorboating*, December 1949, 31.
[49] Shares in 1900 refer to the end of the year fleets of vessels larger than 50 tons and are calculated on the basis of Statistics Norway (1902, 168), with no adjustment between steam and sail tons. Figures for Russia refer to 1899, and include vessels smaller than 50 tons but not ships in the Caspian Sea and the Pacific ports. Italian figures are estimates. Shares in 1939 refer to the June fleets of steam and motor ships larger than 100 gross tons and sailing ships larger than 100 net tons and are calculated on the basis of Statistics Norway (1939, 324). The share for Great Britain and Ireland is calculated on the basis of data that include the Dominions and colonies, but this is unlikely to change the overall picture much, due to the large share of British tonnage (around 85 per cent).

modern technology—the motorship—compared with less than a quarter for the world fleet.

The underdog is loved by history—or, more precisely, by historians. And the underdog—in the shape of the once-proud sailing shipowners on the South Coast of Norway—has traditionally played an important part in the narrative of Norwegian tanker shipping in the interwar period. These shipowners—left by the wayside (or the seaside?) during the transformation from sail to steam—saw a Phoenix-like return in the interwar period, emerging successfully in the transition to the "new" technology, the oil tankers. The Anglo-Saxon vessels were their tickets in the tanker lottery. As the seller provided financing, the purchase of these vessels was a good deal for cash-strapped companies, and 16 of the 28 ships were eventually sold to companies based on the South Coast.

Closer analysis has revealed that the Anglo-Saxon purchases were but a small part of the Norwegian tanker tale.[50] The main growth occurred among newly established companies, particularly in Oslo, that had close relationships to yards in Denmark and Sweden.[51] The expansion was thus a pan-Scandinavian effort. Ships were built at yards in Sweden (around 35 per cent of the newbuilt tanker tonnage) and Denmark (around 15 per cent), but operated by Norwegian shipping companies, sometimes on long charters to the oil companies, at other times not.[52]

One of the main drivers behind the tanker investments was Hugo Hammar, managing director at Götaverken in Gothenburg, who walked around Oslo like a missionary, selling tanker tonnage as the economically attractive escape route from the depressed shipping markets. Helped by eager Oslo brokers, a substantial pressure was built up from the supply side, where both ships and mortgages were on offer.[53] The authorities in several European countries, eager to ensure employment in their shipyards, contributed by offering generous financing that limited the

---

[50] Tenold (2007).

[51] The Norwegian capital was characterized by a sense of identity crisis around the turn of the century. In the official Norwegian nomenclature, Christiania became Kristiania in 1877, while the city authorities accepted the name change in 1897. The name was formally changed to Oslo in 1925.

[52] Market shares based on the more than 200 diesel tankers built during 1925–1939 and listed in *Det Norske Veritas*, 1939.

[53] See Gunnerud (1992) for a comprehensive analysis.

need for Norwegian equity and enabled the entry—or re-entry—of companies with meagre resources. The credits offered by Hammar and Götaverken were initially 50 per cent over five years, but in the 1920s they were increased to 70 per cent, at the same time as the repayment period was increased.[54]

The equity needed to buy a newbuilt Swedish tanker in the late 1920s was around NOK 650,000—a petty sum when we consider that quite ordinary ships could cost 3–4 million or more during the First World War. Typically, the money was raised from a large number of sources: families, friends, business associates and—in many cases very importantly—brokers eager to get commissions. A very telling example of a small and dynamic entrepreneurial venture is Moltzau's Tankrederi, which began its operations in the corner of the shipping company Ivar An. Christensen's waiting room. Ragnar Moltzau was Christensen's secretary.[55] His first tanker contract, a ship in the UK ordered for delivery in the autumn of 1930, had to be resold as he was unable to secure financing following the stock market collapse. In the summer of 1930 Moltzau managed to raise NOK 750,000 in share capital. One-seventh of this came from two broker companies—one in Norway and one in the UK— in exchange for exclusive brokering rights for the ship.[56]

Figure 4.3 shows the strong increase in the number of Norwegian tanker-owning companies, from 11 in 1919 to 107 in 1939.[57] Regionwise, the East shot forward, led by Oslo, the South recovered and the West struggled to keep up. It is also very clear that the main basis for the tanker expansion was Oslo; while the number of tanker owners in Bergen doubled, the number in Oslo multiplied by a factor of 48. The late, but significant, addition of the South Coast is also clear; Arendal—which got its first tanker-owning company in 1928—had as many companies as Bergen 10 years later.

---

[54] Bohlin (1989, 81).
[55] See Fasting (1955).
[56] Kolltveit (1977, 49).
[57] Figure 4.3: Based on information from various issues of the *Veritas*-registry. The dominant cities in the "Other" category are Tønsberg, with eight companies, Stavanger with six and Sandefjord with five companies in 1939. South Coast includes Arendal (eight companies), Farsund (three), Flekkefjord (one), Grimstad (two), Kristiansand (five), Risør (two) and Tvedestrand (one).

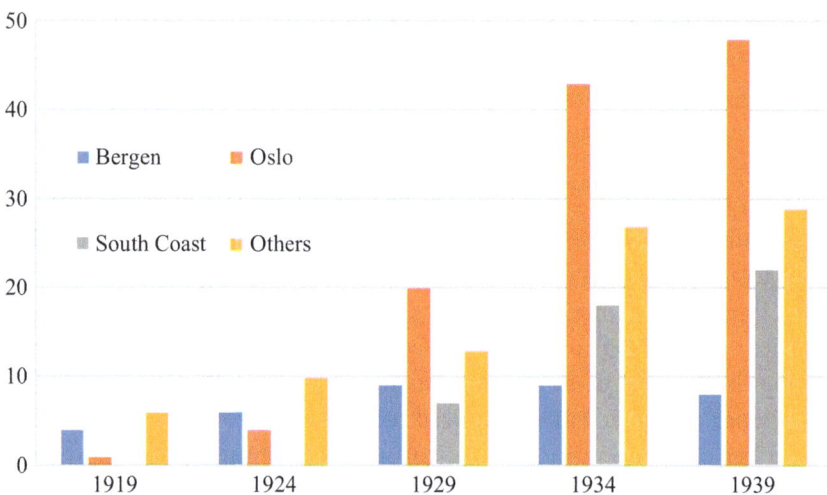

**Fig. 4.3** The number of tanker companies in various Norwegian regions, 1919–1939. (Source: *Veritas*, various issues)

Parallel with the transformation of the Norwegian fleet, the manner in which shipping was conducted in Norway was modernized. With the demise of the sailing ship era, the traditional part ownerships had increasingly been replaced by limited liability companies. However, as many of the first limited liability companies were single-ship companies, the existence of the business was still closely tied to the existence of the vessel.

The interwar period saw a transformation from single-ship companies to multi-ship companies, which implied that the scope for continuity was greatly increased. Capital was raised in the same manner as before—with a relatively wide dispersion of ownership. However, the possibilities of arranging financing through the shipyard, and the improved access to outside capital from ship mortgage institutions, reduced the demand for equity.

The multi-ship companies allowed continuity, but also had advantages with regard to insurance, ship operation, access to credit and preservation of company-specific knowledge. This latter element had been taken care of through managing owners that oversaw the business of several companies, though the First World War showed how easily a hostile takeover could take ships out of the hands of the managers. Another advantage was the multi-ship companies' ability to "smooth out" the effects of business cycles on tax payments, dividends and employment—by definition the fate of the single-ship companies had been tied directly to their one vessel.

The transformation from traditional single-ship to multi-ship companies has been put forward as one explanation of the geographical shifts in Norwegian shipping in the interwar period. From 1920 to 1939 the fleet registered in Oslo increased substantially faster than that of Bergen, and that of Norway in general.[58] Contemporary sources suggest that the reliance on an antiquated ownership structure explains why Bergen "was unable to keep up with the development of technology and business practice."[59]

In his classic book on the decline of Great Britain's maritime hegemony, *British Shipping and World Competition*, Stanley G. Sturmey draws a parallel between the lethargy of British shipowners and the shipowners in Bergen. In both cases, a conservative attitude is used to explain why others took over the advantage.[60] In the case of Oslo, the offensive attitude of the city's own shipping companies also got external help. The capital's growth in the first half of the 20th century was strengthened by the relocation of shipowners from other parts of the country; A.F. Klaveness from Sandefjord in 1907, Wilh. Wilhelmsen from Tønsberg—at the time the country's largest shipping company—in 1916 and Sig. Bergesen d.y. from Stavanger (1939).

The increasing reliance on motor vessels was not only a tanker phenomenon, but also related to another structural change in the operation of the fleet—the gradual reduction of tramp trade at the expense of ships operating on fixed schedules in dedicated lines. Liner companies were the royalty of international shipping, vehicles for transport and national prestige in the case of the UK, France and Germany.

---

[58] This is the main point in Thowsen (1983), which—though focusing on Bergen shipping—through its comparative perspective is perhaps the best source of information on Norwegian shipping in the interwar period.

[59] Magnus (1942, 101).

[60] Sturmey (1962). Gjermoe (1964, 9–15) suggests that Bergen's problem was the number of older, smaller companies, with limited capital, that were based in the city.

As opposed to the tramp trade, the liner trade was not characterized by free competition and flexible prices. The major liner companies cooperated in "conferences," cartel-like structures that fixed prices and sailing schedules and restricted capacity. The Norwegian companies had neither the financial muscle nor the networks needed to acquire a major position in the Atlantic trade. However, they managed to build up substantial niches in various parts of the world, sometimes on their own initiative and sometimes by initially providing a service for foreign interests, for instance by time-chartering vessels to foreign lines.

The first lines began as a vehicle for Norwegian exports—not the "third country"-shipping that had become characteristic of Norwegian companies. Thoresen's *Den subvenerede Norsk-Spanske Linie* [the Subsidized Norwegian-Spanish Line] relied on a government subvention of 75,000 *kroner* and the transport of timber and fish to Spain and Italy when it was established in 1894, and G.M. Bryde's line to Mexico—the first overseas line, established in 1908—also received some government support. The consortium behind the *Den Norske Afrika og Australia Linie* [the Norwegian Africa and Australia Line], established 1911, entered into "peace agreements"—non-competitive clauses—with lines on the Continent. They were granted a hegemony position in Scandinavia, if they refrained from picking up cargoes to and from Continental Europe.

When plans for a joint Scandinavian line were shelved, *Den Norske Amerikalinje* [the Norwegian America Line] became an almost nationalist and patriotic project. The first vessel, *Kristianiafjord*, was launched in the summer of 1913, with King Haakon VII, the cabinet and a large number of Members of Parliament among the dignitaries that joined on the first leg from Kristiania to Bergen.[61] The line was not big enough to challenge the major conference participants, but small enough to be left alone by the otherwise predatory established lines. Still, before the war, the scale and scope of Norwegian liner shipping was limited.

In the interwar period the activity in the liner sector increased, and in his book on the Norwegian liner trade, Dag Bakka jr. refers to the interwar period as "The great expansion." By 1939 Norwegian shipping companies operated around 30 different lines. However, the number of

---

[61] Sebak (2011, 101–124).

shipping companies involved in this business was not much larger than this, as several of the major companies participated in more than one line—Wilh. Wilhelmsen participated in seven and Fred. Olsen and J.L. Mowinckels Rederi both participated in four different lines.[62]

# Whaling

Shipping was not the only industry that sent Norwegians to distant waters. In the second half of the 19th century a whaling community developed in the Vestfold-cities Sandefjord and Tønsberg, on the western side of the Oslofjord. Expeditions of 20–40 ships travelled to the coast outside Finnmark, in the north of Norway, to catch rorquals, finwhales and blue whales. A central premise for this development was the bomb-tipped "grenade harpoon," developed by Svend Foyn and mounted on small steam vessels—the whale catcher boats. Foyn, who came from a shipowner family, had trained as a captain and moved on from the transport of wood cargoes to sealing and whaling.

The new technology developed by Svend Foyn, "the father of modern whaling," was deadly efficient—a fact that was good for business in the short term, but harmful in a longer perspective. In 1904 a 10-year moratorium was introduced in Norwegian waters due to overexploitation of the resource—the grenade harpoon had increased the takings and threatened the local stocks. Around this time Norwegian whalers started a massive global expansion, venturing into both the Northern and Southern hemispheres and ending up with a leadership position in the Antarctic. There, land-based whaling stations at South Georgia—referred to as "the Island" by whalers—were complemented by floating whale factories around South Shetland.[63]

In the 1920s, the development of whale factory ships took the industry into the high seas, independent of shore facilities—what is usually referred to as "pelagic whaling." This activity was closely related to shipping along several dimensions. The two industries competed for investors

---

[62] Bakka (2008, 19–42).
[63] See Basberg 2006 for an interesting discussion of the economic history of the Antarctic.

and labour, and several individuals—workers, investors and entrepreneurs—were engaged in both sectors. There was also an element of complementarity; the main product from the whaling was oil, and the whale factories could also be used to transport mineral oils.

In the 1920s revenues from whaling were substantial and provided important export revenues in a generally difficult period. However, with the improved technology, prices fell and the monopsony power of the main purchasers created problems. In the 1930–1931 season a total of 41 whaling expeditions, with more than 220 boats, produced more than 3.6 million barrels of oil.[64] The Norwegian market share was more than 60 per cent; Norwegians operated five shore stations and 29 floating factories, supported by a total of 160 catcher boats. The Norwegians caught more than 25,000 whales, producing almost 2.3 million barrels of oil, with a value of almost NOK 150 million.

As share of Norwegian production, whaling reached a peak with slightly less than 5 per cent of GDP in the 1930–1931 season. In the subsequent season the market for fats was saturated, and most of the Antarctic whaling fleet was laid up. Production fell from more than 2.3 million barrels to 29,000 barrels.[65] When activities were resumed, the Norwegians lost market shares to other nations. In 1927–1928 Norwegians had produced more than 70 per cent of the Antarctic whale oil, while 10 years later their share of production had fallen to less than 35 per cent.

In terms of economic importance, whaling was never a challenger for the shipping sector. Employment was relatively limited—less than 6500 persons at the peak in the 1930–1931 season—and the industry had an enclave-like position, with only limited spillovers, primarily to shipyards and mechanical industry. However, the spectacular profits from the industry during the peak—some years return on invested capital was 50 per cent or more—helped lay the foundation for investments in shipping. Several of the leading Norwegian shipping companies in the 20th century, particularly in Vestfold, made a mint in whaling and channelled the profits into traditional shipping. Among those that seamlessly

---

[64] Tønnessen and Johnsen (1982, 385).
[65] Statistisk Sentralbyrå (1968, 184).

navigated the waters between whaling and shipping was Anders Jahre—sometimes referred to as "the Prince of Whales." Anders Jahre represented a new type of Norwegian shipowner, with academic merits rather than a seagoing past. Such a background was common for many of the newcomers in interwar shipping.

## The New Breed

The interwar period saw a marked shift in entrepreneurial activity. Though there were still some captains that went ashore and established their own shipping companies, an increasing share of the new ventures were founded by a different breed of entrepreneur—by men with university degrees. Education in economics and law replaced practical seamanship as the basis for a number of newly established shipping companies. This included many of the shipowners who would dominate Norwegian shipping over the subsequent decades.

The previously mentioned Anders Jahre had a degree in law; in 1922 he started to invest in shipping, and in 1928 many of his shipping interests were gathered under the Kosmos umbrella. Leif Höegh, the most expansive of the interwar newcomers, was an economist. Hilmar Reksten, whose growth after the Second World War became almost as legendary as his subsequent downfall, was educated at the *Handelshochshule* in Cologne. Erling Dekke Næss, who established a shipping empire abroad and played a key role in the early growth of the Flags of Convenience, followed his economics degree from the University of Oslo with work in London, where he was heavily influenced by, among others, John Maynard Keynes.[66]

Although the new breed became important, few could challenge "the old guard," when new generations were ready to take over. In many of the

---

[66] See Næss (1977, 1981) for two fascinating autobiographical accounts of Erling Dekke Næss' colourful life in shipping, though with the flaws common for autobiographies. Næss claims that he started his business career speculating in goat cheese during the First World War. He had good mercantile genes; his father was a merchant-cum-banker who died young, while his grandfather was Annanias Dekke, perhaps the most innovative Norwegian shipbuilder of the 19th century; see Chapter 2.

Table 4.1 The 10 leading Norwegian shipping companies, 1 September 1939, fleet size and structure

| Name | City | Est. | Ships | Grt. | % motor | % tankers | % liners |
|---|---|---|---|---|---|---|---|
| Wilh. Wilhelmsen | Oslo | 1861 | 53 | 324.000 | 89 | 2 | 98 |
| Westfal-Larsen | Bergen | 1905 | 34 | 208.000 | 75 | 50 | 39 |
| Knut Knutsen OAS | Haugesund | 1897 | 25 | 140.000 | 91 | 50 | 50 |
| A.F. Klaveness | Oslo | 1869 | 22 | 118.000 | 96 | 45 | 47 |
| Fred. Olsen | Oslo | 1886 | 53 | 113.000 | 66 | 3 | 71 |
| Leif Höegh | Oslo | 1927 | 13 | 102.000 | 100 | 75 | 25 |
| Den Norske Amerikalinje | Oslo | 1910 | 17 | 101.000 | 30 | 0 | 95 |
| Det Bergenske Dampskipselskap | Bergen | 1851 | 51 | 92.000 | 36 | 0 | 47 |
| J.L. Mowinckels Rederi | Bergen | 1898 | 16 | 86.000 | 77 | 41 | 35 |
| Fearnley & Eger | Oslo | 1869 | 19 | 75.000 | 84 | 23 | 51 |

older family-owned companies, the idea of the *Wanderjahre* at sea for the successors, common before the war, was increasingly replaced by a period working onshore. The shipowners' sons would spend time abroad, gaining experience with other shipping companies or brokers. Another way in which the shipping sector acquired new talent was via marriage—some shipping companies explicitly barred daughters from taking over, but sons-in-law were often welcomed into the family business.[67]

Table 4.1 shows that the majority of the largest companies at the end of the interwar period had their roots in the 19th century, and only one had been established after the First World War.[68]

With the exception of the Bergen companies Westfal-Larsen and Mowinckels, and the tanker-focused newcomer Leif Höegh, the majority of the large shipping companies had 40 per cent or more of their tonnage in the liner segment. The larger Norwegian companies had the financial muscle to secure berths in the minor and remote conferences, sometimes using the provision of tonnage to existing participants as a stepping stone. They also expanded in the US market, where liner conferences were less

---

[67] See for instance the fascinating example of the identical twins that married into two prominent Haugesund shipping families in Hammerborg (2011).
[68] The table is based on the list in Thowsen (1992, 28).

concerned about capacity. Revenues from the tanker sector were in many cases important to finance the new liner ships. Only Fred. Olsen and the two "home-based" lines—Den Norske Amerikalinje and Det Bergenske Dampskipsselskap—expanded without any substantial revenues from tanker shipping.

## Not All Rosy

Although the interwar period can be considered a successful period for Norwegian shipping *per se*, this was an era of rapid transformation, and abrupt changes typically leave victims in their wake. We find these victims both among the companies that did not manage to cope with the changes, and among the seafarers that were unable to find work.

Lay-ups reached their highest proportion of the fleet ever after the freight market collapsed in 1920, but the overcapacity was relatively short-lived. Figure 4.4 shows that the overcapacity in the 1930s was more persistent. Lay-up rates amounted to more than 600,000 dead weight tons from 1931 to 1934.[69]

The ups and downs of the business cycle, and the effect of the lay-up rates above, were partly reflected in unemployment among seafarers. There were substantial differences in the unemployment rates among various branches of industry, and seafarers, as well as workers in cyclical industries such as construction, had particularly high rates. On average, unemployment rates among seafarers were slightly more than 11 per cent during the crisis in the first half of the 1920s, but more than doubled, to 23 per cent, in the first half of the 1930s.[70] As a result of the lack of a social safety net, these abstract percentages hide some very real personal tragedies. Seafarers that were out of work in Norway could often rely on help from family and friends—the situation was more problematic for those who were far away from home.

---

[69] Figure 4.4: Calculated on the basis of data in *Statistics Norway* (1929, 84) and *Statistics Norway* (1948, 276). Biannual data have been interpolated for the period 1920–1926.
[70] Calculated on the basis of data for 1921–1925 and 1930–1934 in Grytten (1994, 177–178). Average unemployment for the total labour force was 4.8 and 9.2 per cent, respectively.

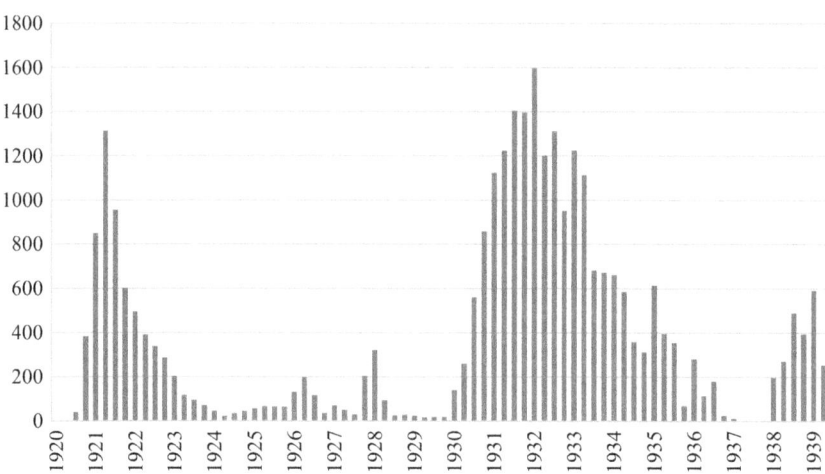

**Fig. 4.4** Norwegian lay-ups, quarterly estimates, 1920–1939, 1000 dead weight tons (dwt). (Source: Calculated on the basis of various statistics from *Statistics Norway*. See footnote for details)

Some of the most tragic fates could be found in the borough of Brooklyn, in New York. *Ørkenen Sur* [the Desert of Shur, a reference to *Exodus*] was a Hooverville where a large number of Norwegian sailors and ex-sailors found temporary shelter in the difficult interwar years.[71] The Norwegian legislation did not provide them with money to get back to Norway and, in the crisis years, jobs in the declining American merchant marine were reserved for the country's own seafarers. A sailor who stayed more than 60 days in the United States without specific permission became an illegal immigrant, and had to watch out for the authorities.

Many of the inhabitants of *Ørkenen* Sur found solace in the Norwegian Seamen's Church in Brooklyn, which had moved into new and larger premises in 1927.[72] They were not alone. By the middle of the 1930s there were more than 600 unemployed sailors in Brooklyn, and the

---

[71] In the Norwegian translation of the Bible, the desert in which Moses and the Israelites wander around is called *"Sur"*. The latter word in the text means "sour" or "bitter", and there is thus a dimension that disappears in the English translation. See the fascinating story of the desert and its inhabitants in Gotaas and Kvarsvik (2010).

[72] See Knudsen, 1936, for a contemporary account of the seamen's churches and the mission among seamen.

church also saw a steady stream of seafarers from ships that still traded.[73] In the church, they would find a reading room, where *Tante Klara* [Aunt Klara] served waffles that reminded them of their childhoods.[74] Some would find a letter from home, others would use the free paper and envelopes to write back to Norway. The church was busier than most Norwegian post offices—more than 100,000 letters arrived there every year—it functioned as a bank for some seafarers, and a safe fixed point for even more.

The seamen's churches are a good example of the substantial network that had been developed abroad to serve the country's shipping industry.[75] The Norwegian Seamen's Church—established in 1864—provided Norwegian seafarers with a link to the home country when they came to foreign ports. In the beginning the churches were located in the seafarers' "home waters in the Atlantic"—the first one was established in Leith in 1864, while the first location in North America, beginning 12 years later, was in Quebec in the summer and Pensacola in the winter. In 1933 the seamen's church in Shanghai became the first establishment in the Far East.[76]

The churches followed the trade of the Norwegian fleet. In 1927 and 1931, respectively, the churches in Newport and Barry, South Wales, were closed after more than 40 years—there were fewer Norwegian ships

---

[73] Gotaas & Kvarsvik, 214.

[74] *Tante Klara*, Klara Brcivik, from Fana near Bergen, began working at the Seamen's Church in Brooklyn in 1926 at the age of 20, and helped and supported "her boys" for the subsequent 37 years. She was a "living legend" among the sailors, known for her ability to remember faces and names, her compassion and her skills at *couronne* [carrom]—the poor man's pool. Another popular "Aunt"—Noel Lowdness in Vancouver—started voluntary work among seamen, before the Scandinavian welfare organizations decided to "employ her" at a fixed fee in the middle of the 1950s. She received the Order of St. Olaf for her work, and after she died in 1977 her ashes were scattered from the *Egda*, owned by Mowinckels in Bergen; see Pettersen and Brundtland (2003, 79–82).

[75] A similar institution was the seamen's homes, operated by *Foreningen for skandinaviske sømandshjem i fremmede havne* [the Association for Scandinavian Seamen's Homes in Foreign Ports], established 1901 and providing safe sleeping facilities for sober seafarers. See Salvesen (1931) for a contemporary presentation of the Norwegian institutions abroad and their most pressing problems.

[76] There had been activity in Hong Kong and Shanghai for a couple of years during the boom around the Russo-Japanese war 1904–1905, but these were closed when "the market" disappeared a few years later—the number of Norwegian ships calling on Asian ports was more than halved from 1905 to 1907; see Brautaset and Tenold (2010, 207).

involved in the declining coal trade from the area. The increasing oil trade, on the other hand, created a basis for new "business" near oil terminals and refineries. Churches were established in Constanta on the Black Sea in 1935, in Stanford-le-Hope in Essex in 1937, and in Willemstad on the island of Curacao in 1939. By 1939 there were more than 25 Norwegian churches in most parts of the world—in Europe, South and North America, Africa and Asia.[77] These provided a holier and healthier alternative to *Sjappa*, the local bar or dive, where alcoholic and corporeal cravings could be satisfied, sometimes at an exorbitant cost in terms of money and health.

The Great Depression affected all types of shipping, even the relatively buoyant tanker market. However, in that sector, the limited number of participants made it possible to arrive at solutions that alleviated individual problems. Effective from the spring of 1934, an international tanker pool ensured that owners with laid-up ships were compensated by those with ships that earned revenues. This solution was the brainchild of Harry T. Schierwater of the United Molasses Company, Ltd., who became the first Chairman of The International Tanker Owners' Association. The pool functioned well due to the participation of the oil companies, which supported the idea in order to ensure orderly conditions in the tanker sector.

While the Norwegian shipping industry regained momentum in the interwar period, helped by yards and finance in Sweden and Denmark, the domestic shipbuilding industry went through a terribly difficult period. In the period 1900–1904 Norway had built more ships than Denmark and Sweden combined, and up until the end of the First World War the production was higher in Norway than in the neighbouring countries. Still, Norwegian shipbuilding peaked in 1915, and then the industry collapsed—in the last five years of the 1930s, production was lower than it had been in the first five years of the century.[78]

---

[77] The churches did not have a presence in Oceania until after the Second World War, and the church in Antarctica (South Georgia) had been closed down after two periods of activity 1912–1914 and 1925–1932; see the overview in Johanson (1989, 113–114). The source confuses "Newport News" and "Newport"; it is quite unlikely that "Newport News" in Virginia, the United States, was operated as a subdivision of the Cardiff branch. On the work of the churches in Belgium and the Netherlands, see Hoel (2016).
[78] Aamundsen (1941, 7–9).

The Danish and Swedish yards managed the transition to motorship building, with a focus on large units, while Norwegian shipyards in the interwar period relied on repair jobs and the increasingly old-fashioned steamship technology.[79] There are many reasons for the relative decline of Norwegian shipbuilding, compared with its neighbours, in this period. Currency developments and tax policy worked unfavourably, the access to finance and credit might have been more limited than in the the rest of Scandinavia and unfortunate conditions in the labour market and the structure of the industry might have played a role.[80]

Mentioning the relative loss of competitiveness in Norwegian shipbuilding is perhaps a typically gloomy, northern European way of considering the development. In reality, the Scandinavian shipping industry (spearheaded by the Norwegians) and shipbuilding industry (led by the other two countries) developed very positively in a period that was extremely difficult for world shipping and shipbuilding.

The Swedish and Danish expansion was clearly atypical in an international perspective. The global shipbuilding industry was strongly affected by the crisis; in the 1920s, on average, 2.8 million gross tons were launched. In the period 1930–1938, the average was less than 1.8 million gross tons.[81] Just like the Norwegian expansion within shipping—based on tankers and diesel engines—went against the international trend, the growing role of Swedish and Danish shipyards—partly based on tankers and diesel engines—stood out internationally.

The interwar period was characterized by economic and political turmoil. International trade stagnated, the monetary system collapsed and the attempts at international political cooperation were famously futile. Against this background, the Scandinavian progress is remarkable.

---

[79] In 1927 only 13 ships, amounting to 4838 gross tons were built—less than a tenth of the tonnage built in 1907; based on steel ships in Aamundsen (1941, 117–123). In contrast, the Swedish production in the early 1930s was more than 10 times larger than it had been before the First World War.

[80] See Basberg (1987) for a comparative analysis. An example of the unfortunate conditions in the labour market is the fact that in the period from 1921 to 1931, more than two years' worth of working days were lost due to strikes; Aamundsen (1941, 28).

[81] In fact, Norwegian tonnage launches actually expanded marginally from the 1920s to 1930–1938, bucking the trend as well. Compared with the growth in Denmark and Sweden, however, the Norwegian increase becomes poor; see the data in Aamundsen (1941, 117).

## The *Sagatind* Aftermath

In March 1938, President Franklin D. Roosevelt recommended to the US Congress that USD5000 be spent to settle a Norwegian claim "arising out of the detention and treatment of the crew" of the *Sagatind* more than 13 years earlier.[82] In May the American Congress accepted the payment, "as an act of grace and without reference to the question of legal liability."[83]

When the *ex gratia* payment was paid out, *Sagatind* was already history. The ship had to be broken up after running aground in October 1931 near Fedje, outside Bergen on the Norwegian West coast. *Sagatind* was carrying timber from Archangel in Russia to London in the UK.[84] Although the loss of the ship marked the end of the shipping company Friis & Lund, the saga continued in the United States.

The *Sagatind* compensation was one of the more mundane matters settled in Congress on 13 May 1938. The subsequent piece of legislation that the American politicians approved that day was to establish a national holiday on 11 November, commemorating the day when the First World War ended. The date was "to be dedicated to the cause of world peace and to be hereafter celebrated and known as Armistice Day."[85]

When the first Armistice Day was celebrated, storm clouds were gathering across the sea. Already Norwegian ships had been involved in dangerous and hostile situations in China—for instance during the Japanese bombing of Shanghai—and in the Mediterranean, where the Spanish Civil War affected shipping. On the second Armistice Day, in November

---

[82] *The New York Times*, 290338, 2.

[83] United States, Parliament, Made into law on 13 May 1938; Public No. 509, Chapter 209; "An act to authorise the payment of an indemnity to the Norwegian Government in full and final satisfaction of all claims based on the detention and treatment of the crew of the Norwegian steamer *Sagatind* subsequent to the seizure of this vessel by the United States Coast Guard cutter *Seneca* on 12 October 1924," *Laws and concurrent resolutions enacted during the third session of the seventy-fifth Congress of the United States of America*, 350.

[84] Thorbjørnsen (1946, 44). The cargo was sought after by the locals, and "some salvaged what others had already salvaged before them…"; see Asphaug (2000, 264–265).

[85] Made into law on 13 May 1938; Public No. 509, Chapter 209; "An act making the 11th day of November each year into a legal holiday," *Laws and concurrent resolutions enacted during the third session of the seventy-fifth Congress of the United States of America*, 351.

1939, things were far more serious. The major powers in Europe were again at war.

In the first months of the war, Norway remained neutral, and the situation was not radically different from the case during the previous world war. The Norwegian fleet was once again vulnerable, and an important asset in the fight among the big powers. This time, however, Norway did not remain neutral for long. After the German invasion on 9 April 1940, Norwegian shipping entered its toughest—and also most heroic—hour.

# Bibliography

L. Albretsen (1942) 'Litt om radio', in O.T. Irgens, *Et lite skippertak* (Bergen: AS John Griegs Boktrykkeri) 64–87

H.W. Andersen (1992) 'Laggards as Leaders: Some Reflections on Technological Diffusion in Norwegian Shipping', in K. Bruland, Kristine (ed) *Technology Transfer and Scandinavian Industrialization* (Oxford: Berg)

A. Asphaug (2000) *Øygarden 1920–1958 – Aktive fiskarbøndar, travle gardskoner*, Vol. 1 (Tjeldstø: Øygarden Kommune)

D. Bakka (1998) *O.H. Meling & Co. Femti år i shipping* (Stavanger: O.H. Meling)

D. Bakka (2008) *Linjer rundt Jorden – Historien om norsk linjefart* (Bergen: Seagull Publishing)

B.L. Basberg (1987) 'Motortankskipenes inntog. En komparasjon av utviklingen i dansk, norsk og svensk skipsbyggingsindustri, ca. 1912 til 1933', *Sjøfartshistorisk Årbok 1986* (Bergen: Bergens Sjøfartsmuseum)

B.L. Basberg (2006) 'Perspectives on the Economic History of the Antarctic Region', *International Journal of Maritime History*, 18:2, 185–304

E. Behr, (1996) *Prohibition: Thirteen Years That Changed America* (New York: Arcade Publishing)

P. Bolle (2006) 'The ILO's New Convention on Maritime Labour: An Innovation Instrument', *International Labour Review*, 145:1–2, 135–142

J. Bohlin (1989) *Svensk varvsindustri 1920–1975: Lönsamhet, finansiering och arbetsmarknad* (Gothenburg: Ekonomisk-historiska institutionen vid Göteborgs Universitet)

C. Brautaset & S. Tenold (2010) 'Lost in Calculation? Norwegian Merchant Shipping in Asia, 1870–1914', in M. Fusaro & A. Polónia (eds) *Maritime History as Global History* (St. Johns: IMEHA) 203–222

J. Bruijn, (2005) 'Seafarers in Early Modern and Modern Times: Change and Continuity', *The International Journal of Maritime History*, 17:1, 1–16

K. Brækhus (1955) *Trampskipsfartens fremtid* (Oslo: Norges Rederforbund)

R. Carlisle (2009) 'Second Registers: Maritime Nations Respond to Flags of Convenience, 1984–1998', *The Northern Mariner/le marin du nord*, 19:3, 319–340

R. Carlisle (2017) *Rough waters: Sovereignty and the American merchant flag* (Annapolis: Naval Institute Press)

R.B. Castelein, (2015) 'The Fairplay freights: compiling a dataset of interwar freight rates', *The International Journal of Maritime History*, 27:2, 302–327

T. Chida & P.N. Davies (1990) *The Japanese Shipping and Shipbuilding Industries: A History of their Modern Growth* (London: Athlone Press)

C. Christensen (1933) *Det hendte i går: En skildring av etterkrigstidens Norge* (Oslo: Johan Grundt Tanum)

H.I. Drevdal (1994) *Fra de hvite seils dager: beretninger og minner om menn og deres skip* (Grimstad: Drevdal)

J.O. Egeland (1930) 'Norges sjøfart. Hvad den var og hvad den er', in G. Stenersen (ed) *Sjømannsboken; sjøfart, hvalfangst, marine: orientering i sjømannskap, veiledning til selvstudium*, (Oslo: Norsk bibliotekforening) 3–37

J.O. Egeland (1973) *Kongeveien*, Volume II (Oslo: H. Aschehoug & Co.)

J. Einarsen (1938) *Reinvestment cycles and their manifestation in the Norwegian shipping industry* (Oslo: J. Chr. Gundersens Boktrykkeri)

K. Fasting (1955) *AS Moltzaus Tankrederi* (Oslo: AS Moltzaus Tankrederi)

L. Fink (2016) 'A Sea of Difference: The ILO and the Search for Common Standards, 1919–45', in J.M. Jensen & N. Lichtenstein (eds) *The ILO from Geneva to the Pacific Rim* (London: Palgrave Macmillan) 15–32

A. Gibson & A. Donovan (2001) *The Abandoned Ocean: A HIstory of the United States Maritime Policy* (Columbia: University of South Carolina Press)

E. Gjermoe (1964) *Kurser og dividender for skipsaksjeselskaper på Bergens børs 1929–1964* (Bergen: Skipsfartsøkonomisk Institutt)

T. Gotaas & R. Kvarsvik (2010) *Ørkenen Sur* (Oslo: Spartacus)

O.H. Grytten (1994) 'En empirisk analyse av det norske arbeidsmarked 1918–1939', PhD-thesis, Bergen: Norges Handelshøyskole

O.H. Grytten (2004) 'A consumer price index for Norway 1516–2003', in Ø. Eitrheim, J.T. Klovland & J.F. Qvigstad (eds) *Historical Monetary Statistics for Norway 1819–2003* (Oslo: Norges Bank) 47–98

J. Gunnerud (1992) 'Tankskipseventyret i Oslo 1925–1939', *Sjøfartshistorisk Årbok 1991* (Bergen: Bergens Sjøfartsmuseum)

M. Hammerborg (2011) 'Inheriting Strategies: Understanding Different Approaches to Shipping During the World War I Boom in Haugesund, Norway', in L.R. Fischer & E. Lange (eds) *New directions in Norwegian maritime history* (St. Johns: IMEHA)

G. Harlaftis (1996) *A History of Greek-Owned Shipping: The Making of an International Tramp Fleet, 1830 to the present day* (Abingdon: Routledge)

G. Harlaftis & I. Theotokas (2004) 'European Family Firms in International Business: British and Greek Tramp-Shipping Firms', *Business History*, 46:2, 219–255

V. Hoel (2016) *Faith, Fatherland and the Norwegian Seaman* (Hilvershum: Verloren Publishers)

C. Haaland (1940) *Norges skipsfart – hva den var og hva den er* (Oslo: Blix Forlag AS)

P.E. Johansen (1994) *Markedet som ikke ville dø: forbudstiden og de illegale alkoholmarkedene i Norge og USA* (Oslo: Rusmiddeldirektoratet)

B. Johanson (1989) *Kirke i verdens hverdag* (Bergen: Den norske sjømannsmisjons forlag)

G. Kåhre (1977) *The Last Tall Ships: Gustaf Erikson and the Åland Sailing Fleets, 1872–1947* (New York: Mayflower Books)

G. Kåhre (1980) *De siste seilskip i handelsfart: Gustaf Erikson og Ålands handelsflåte 1872–1947* (Oslo: Schibsted)

C. Kent (1925) *Under norsk flag* (Oslo: H. Aschehoug & Co.)

K.U. Kloster (1935) *Krigsår og gullflom – Skibsfarten under verdenskrigen* (Oslo: Gyldendal)

R. Kloster (1942) 'Omkring kostholdet til sjøs', in O.T. Irgens, *Et lite skippertak* (Bergen: AS John Griegs Boktrykkeri) 64–87

J.T. Klovland (2016) 'Shipping in dire straits: New evidence on trends and cycles in coal freights from Britain, 1919–1939', *Discussion paper SAM 05/2016* (Bergen: NHH – Norwegian School of Economics)

J.T. Klovland (2017) 'Navigating through torpedo attacks and enemy raiders: Merchant shipping and freight rates during World War I', *Discussion paper SAM 07/2017* (Bergen: NHH – Norwegian School of Economics)

B. Kolltveit (1977) *Skippere Meglere Redere* (Oslo: J.M. Stenersens Forlag AS)

J.A. Langfeldt (1980) *Et liv i shipping* (Kristiansand: J.A. Langfeldt)

E.N. Lawson (2013) *Smugglers, Bootleggers and Scofflaws. Prohibition and New York City* (Albany: State University of New York Press)

N. Livingstone (2016) *The Mistresses of Cliveden: Three Centuries of Scandal, Power, and Intrigue in an English Stately Home* (London: Arrow)

Lombard (1934) *Lombard Shipping and Transport Code* (London: Code Services Ltd.)
K. Magnus (1942) 'Nogen forskyvninger innen norsk skipsfart', in O.T. Irgens *Et lite skippertak* (Bergen: AS John Griegs Boktrykkeri) 88–101
N.L. Middlemiss (1996) *World Tankers* (Newcastle: Shield Publications Ltd.)
G.R. Mohn (1942) 'Navigasjonsundervisningens utvikling i de siste 25 år', in O.T. Irgens, *Et lite skippertak* (Bergen: AS John Griegs Boktrykkeri) 64–87
E. Newby (1956) *The last grain race* (London: Secker & Warburg)
E.D. Næss (1977) *Autobiography of a Shipping Man* (Seatrade, London)
E.D. Næss (1981) *Shipping – mitt liv* (Oslo: AS Hjemmet Fagpresseforlaget)
E. Pettersen & H. Brundtland (2003) *Sjøfolkenes hemmeligheter – opplevelser fra handelsflåten i etterkrigstiden* (Bergen: Edvard'en Forlag)
T. Salvesen (1931) *Havnebyer. Internasjonalt samarbeide til bedring av sjømenns livsvilkår i land* (Oslo: H. Aschehoug & Co.)
J. Schreiner (1963) *Norsk skipsfart under krig og høykonjunktur, 1914–1920* (Oslo: Norges Rederforbund/Cappelen)
P.K. Sebak (2011) 'The Norwegian-American Line: State Incentives and Mediations with Dominant Market Players', in L.R. Fischer & E. Lange (eds) *New directions in Norwegian maritime history* (St. Johns: IMEHA)
J. Seland (1953) *Oversikt over momenter som kan belyse utviklingen i årene fremover av verdenshandelen, verdensflåten og Norges flåte samt over de norske skattereglers virkning for skipsfartsnæringen og andre lands skatteregler* (Oslo: Norges Rederforbund)
J. Seland (1959) *Rederen og skipet. Kristiansand og Mandal fra seil til damp og diesel* (Kristiansand: Christiansands Rederforening)
Statistics Norway (1902) *Statistisk aarbog for kongeriget Norge 1902* (Kristiania: Det Statistiske Centralbureau/H. Aschehoug & Co.)
Statistics Norway (1919) *Statistisk aarbok for kongeriket Norge 1919* (Kristiania: Det Statistiske Centralbyrå/H. Aschehoug & Co.)
Statistics Norway (1929) *Statistisk aarbog for kongeriget Norge 1929* (Kristiania: Det Statistiske Centralbureau/H. Aschehoug & Co.)
Statistics Norway (1939) *Statistisk aarbog for kongeriget Norge 1939* (Kristiania: Det Statistiske Centralbureau/H. Aschehoug & Co.)
Statistics Norway (1948) *Statistiske oversikter 1948* (Oslo: Statistiske Sentralbyrå)
Statistics Norway (1968) *Historisk Statistikk 1968* (Oslo: Statistisk Sentralbyrå)
S.G. Sturmey (1962) *British Shipping and World Competition*, reprint 2010 (St. Johns: IMEHA)
S. Tenold (2006) 'Crisis? What Crisis?', in L.U. Scholl & D.M. Williams (eds) *Crisis and Transition. Maritime Sectors in the North Sea Region 1790–1940* (Bremen: Verlag H.M. Hauschild, GmbH.) 117–134

S. Tenold (2007) 'Norway's Interwar Tanker Expansion – A Reappraisal', *Scandinavian Economic History Review*, 55:3, 244–261

K. Thorbjørnsen (1946) *Av bjergningsvesenets historie – Norsk Bjergningskompani AS, Havarifortegnelser, 1912–1938*, Vol. 3B (Bergen: Norsk Bjergningskompani AS)

A. Thowsen (1983) 'Vekst og strukturendringer i krisetider 1914–1939', *Bergen og Sjøfarten IV* (Bergen: Bergens Rederiforening og Bergens Sjøfartsmuseum)

A. Thowsen (1992) 'Nortraship – Profitt og Patriotisme', *Handelsflåten i krig 1* (Oslo: Grøndahl og Dreyers Forlag AS)

J.N. Tønnessen (1951) 'Fra klipperen til motorskipet', in J.S. Worm-Müller (ed) *Den norske sjøfarts historie: Fra de ældste tider til vore dager*, 2:3 (Oslo: J.W. Cappelens Forlag) 1–222

J.N. Tønnessen & A.O. Johnsen (1982) *The history of modern whaling* (Berkeley and Los Angeles: University of California Press)

N.P. Vigeland (1949) *Norsk seilskipsfart erobrer verdenshavene* (Trondheim: E. Bruns Bokhandels Forlag)

T.R. Aamundsen (1941) *Reisningen av den norske skipsbygginsindustri* (Oslo: Gunnar Stenersens Forlag)

**Open Access** This chapter is licensed under the terms of the Creative Commons Attribution-NonCommercial-NoDerivatives 4.0 International License (http://creativecommons.org/licenses/by-nc-nd/4.0/), which permits any noncommercial use, sharing, distribution and reproduction in any medium or format, as long as you give appropriate credit to the original author(s) and the source, provide a link to the Creative Commons license and indicate if you modified the licensed material. You do not have permission under this license to share adapted material derived from this chapter or parts of it.

The images or other third party material in this chapter are included in the chapter's Creative Commons license, unless indicated otherwise in a credit line to the material. If material is not included in the chapter's Creative Commons license and your intended use is not permitted by statutory regulation or exceeds the permitted use, you will need to obtain permission directly from the copyright holder.

# 5

## The Second World War

The years from 1939 to 1945 were perhaps the most glorious period of Norwegian shipping; the aftermath of the war was not a particularly proud time.

Norway's neutrality policy was scuttled when Nazi Germany invaded the country on 9 April 1940, but the fleet—the majority of which was in neutral or Allied waters and ports—remained outside German control. Instead, the ships were requisitioned by the Norwegian government, paving the way for Nortraship—often referred to as "the world's largest shipping company." The merchant marine played a vital role in the Allied fight against the Axis powers—but at a high cost. More than 700 ships were lost, and around 3700 sailors lost their lives.

In 2012 the thriller-author Jon Michelet's first novel about Halvor Skramstad, *En sjøens helt – Skogsmatrosen* [A hero of the seas – The sailor from the woods], became a surprising best-seller. The initial print run of the first book was 5000 copies; by 2015 the first four volumes in the series had gone on to sell more than 600,000 copies, and the film rights had been picked up by *Norsk Rikskringkasting* [the Norwegian Broadcasting Corporation]. With the series *En sjøens helt*, Michelet and the fate of his fictional hero entered the national psyche. In a poll by the leading newspaper, *Verdens Gang*, in 2014, to commemorate the 200th anniversary of the Norwegian constitution, the anonymous *Krigsseiler* [War sailor] was voted "The most important Norwegian" since 1814.[1]

This was not the first time that Jon Michelet—who had trained and worked as a seaman himself—dealt with the sea, seafarers and shipping in his books. Previously, the author had presented shipowners as unscrupulous capitalist crooks in his crime novels, with some success.[2] This time, however, the angle was more positive—the seafarer as hero, rather than the shipowner as scoundrel. In fact, the series about Halvor Skramstad, Michelet's *magnum opus*, had a specific purpose: Michelet wanted to create a memorial to the Norwegian war sailors.

Michelet's books are thoroughly researched, generally well-written and have a gripping plot. However, their immense success undoubtedly reflects the manner in which the main topic managed to grab the attention of the Norwegian public. There are three main reasons that Norwegian wartime shipping, and the history of the merchant seafarers, appealed to readers.

First, the political situation under which the war sailors rose to prominence was dramatic and provides a proud and powerful backdrop to the novels. Although Norway was occupied by Nazi Germany, the sailors were working on behalf of "Free Norway," aiding the Allied efforts at high risk. The Norwegian military had to rapidly give up their attempts at defending the mainland Norwegian territory, but the ships and seafarers continued the fight. The transport of oil and petroleum products was particularly dangerous and difficult, but crucial to the Allied resistance and eventual victory. The oil tankers were "the artery of the Allied fight for victory."[3] Winston Churchill's alleged claim that the Norwegian seafarers were worth more than a million soldiers is an oft-repeated quote.[4]

---

[1] More than 20,000 people voted in the poll, and the anonymous war sailor got 12 per cent of the votes—more than twice as much as former Prime Minister Einar Gerhardsen in second place; *Verdens Gang*, 030314, 16.

[2] See, for instance, his debut *Den drukner ei som henges skal* (1975) or *Panamaskipet* (1984), as well as the play *Matros Tore Solem og hans skip* (1979), coauthored with Gunnar Bull-Gundersen.

[3] Admiral of the Fleet, Viscount Cunningham of Hyndhope, quoted in Rasmussen (1964, 9).

[4] The origins of the quote are unsure; it was sometimes referenced to an editorial in *The Motor Ship*, and has also been attributed to others rather than Churchill, including the US Admiral Emery Land (see Lindbæk 1948, 17); Anthony Eden (see Steen 1948, 110); President Roosevelt (see Vikøren 1986, 3); and Carl Joachim Hambro (see Hambro 1945, 24).

Second, as maritime employment was still widespread, many Norwegians had a war sailor in their immediate family. Moreover, these seafarers were the Norwegian fighters—both their losses and the tactical results of their struggles exceeded those of the regular armed forces: "For the majority of the Norwegian population in Norway during the German occupation, the war years were a challenge of the more prosaic kind. The aim was human and material survival. [...] Norwegian sailors in the Nortraship fleet had a different wartime experience. They were at war."[5]

Finally, there is an element of shame—maybe a "sin of omission"—related to how the war sailors were treated after the war. Part of this guilt is related to the so-called "Nortraship-fund" and the manner in which the war sailors had to fight for their compensation and rights. Jon Michelet's book series paid respect to the seafarers. The readers gave them the honour that they should have received shortly after the war.

The seafarers and the fleet played a crucial role during the Second World War, as part of the war effort and as a source of funding for the government in exile. Due to the mobility and global reach of Norway's most important export sector, money could be made even though the country was occupied. The massive revenues from the ships that had been requisitioned gave the Norwegian government in London resources that far exceeded those that other countries had.

The funding came at a substantial cost. The seafarers were subject to terrible pressure, stress and trauma, and many found it difficult to return to normal life after the war. For many Norwegian seafarers the war lasted for several decades, as they fought personal battles over and over again. The Second World War also began earlier for the seafarers than for other Norwegians.

## The Forgotten War

In Norwegian history books, the Second World War reaches Norway on 9 April 1940, with the German invasion. For Norwegian seafarers, however, the battle had already lasted more than six months. Almost 60 ships had been sunk and more than 400 Norwegian seafarers had been killed

---
[5] Hjeltnes (1995, 10–11).

by the time the German soldiers started marching on Norwegian soil. The initial months of the war are commonly referred to as "The Phoney War"—or even "The Bore War"—due to the shadow-boxing among the belligerents and the lack of substantial military action. However, for Norwegian seafarers, the Phoney War was very real.

Initially, both the political situation—a mainly German-British conflict with Norwegian neutrality—and the challenges were the same as during the First World War. The war insurance scheme that had been established to ensure that Norwegian ships could sail, was disbanded after the First World War. In 1935 a similar institution, "Den norske Krigsforsikring for Skib – Gjensidig Forening" was established. On the very same day that France and the UK declared war on Germany, the War Insurance Fund, after discussions with the Norwegian Shipowners' Association, *Nordisk Skipsrederforening* [the Nordic Shipowners' Association—which deals primarily with legal issues] and the Norwegian government, ordered vessels in international waters to seek Norwegian or neutral ports as quickly as possible, and to await further orders there. Thus, the charterers lost their right to manage the ship.

A substantial portion of the ships that were redirected were on their way to British ports—the symbiosis between Norwegian shipping and British trade was still strong. However, with the change in propulsion of the Norwegian fleet—from coal-driven steam to diesel-driven motor engines—a British threat of cutting off the coal supply would not harm Norwegian shipping as much as during the previous war. Moreover, the large share of tankers—Norwegians controlled around 40 per cent of the independent tanker fleet—implied that the ships would be particularly important for the provision of fuel for the British war effort. So, a neutral Norway—with a need for provisions—and a UK at war—with a need for transport—clearly echoed the state of affairs from the First World War. However, the relative strength of the two parties had definitely changed.

Nevertheless, the practical solutions were similar. The Norwegian authorities worked behind the scenes, gently pressuring the shipowners to come to a solution with the UK and urging them to send a delegation to London to negotiate; "in the game [to ensure essential imports] Norway could use the Norwegian merchant marine as a trump card."[6]

---

[6] Undersøkelseskommisjonen av 1945 (1945, 55).

This required control of the fleet. A licensing system for the signing or renewal of charters was introduced, ensuring that the authorities had some control. The Board of the Norwegian Shipowners' Association reluctantly introduced measures that gave them the authority to manage the ship on behalf of the owners.[7]

An accord with the British was reached in November 1939 when a delegation—with wide authority—entered into what is referred to as the Scheme Agreement. The agreement was never formally signed. In order to protect Norwegian neutrality, it was only initialled and made to look like a "gentlemen's agreement."[8] Norwegian shipowners put some 150 tankers—around 1.2 million gross register tons (grt)—at British disposal at agreed freight rates, as well as around 150,000 grt of tramp tonnage. This came in addition to tonnage amounting to around 450,000 grt that had already been chartered to the British, and implied that the Allies had access to around 40 per cent of the Norwegian merchant marine.[9]

The access to the Norwegian fleet was important—both the Netherlands and Denmark refused to enter into similar agreements.[10] During the First World War, David Lloyd George, the British Prime Minister, had pointed out that "The road to victory, the guarantee of victory, the absolute assurance of victory is to be found in one word – ships; and a second word – ships; and a third word – ships."[11] As in that war, Norway's substantial merchant marine meant that the country could play a decisive role in the outcome. And during The Phoney War, the situation was very much like it had been some 20 years earlier. Norwegian ships were neutral—but

---

[7] Thowsen (1992, 58).
[8] Nilsen and Thowsen (1990, 24).
[9] The exact figures differ between various sources, as some include subsequent additions to the agreement.
[10] While Norway was concerned with its access to British imports, the Danes primarily cared about access for their exports. Not until the British threatened to close their market for Danish agricultural commodities, did the Danes sign an agreement. Given that the agreement was signed in early April 1940, around a week before the German invasion of Denmark, it had limited practical relevance. When Denmark capitulated, ships available to the Allies were confiscated. Greece (in February 1940) and Sweden (in December 1939) also entered into tonnage agreements with the UK, though the amount of shipping capacity was much lower than in the Norwegian case; see Thowsen (1992, 88–98) for an overview of the neutral fleet.
[11] Address to the American Club in London, 12 April 1917; see Horne (1923, 143) for a transcript.

leaning heavily towards the west. For Norwegian seafarers sailing in British convoys in late 1939 and the first part of 1940, there were no doubts at all about which side they were on.

Another similarity with the 1914–1918 war was the question of naval strength. The German *Kriegsmarine* had clear geographical disadvantages. Control of the sea lanes and other naval concerns were part of the basis for the German decision to invade Norway in April 1940. German submarines, and in particular the surface fleet, could benefit from the long and rugged coastline, and use its shelter to challenge the British domination of the North Sea.[12] The invasion was partly a pre-emptive strike—the Germans feared that if Norway fell into British hands, the North Sea would be completely closed to them. The strategic role of Narvik, as basis for winter shipments of crucial Swedish iron ore, also played an important part in the German decision to invade.

These tactical factors were hardly a secret at the time, but the Norwegian preparations for a potential German invasion were nevertheless famously botched. While the Norwegian merchant marine was for the most part modern, and impressively so in an international perspective, the opposite was the case for the Norwegian navy. Of its 63 vessels, only 19 had been launched after the First World War. The majority—including the four main warships—had been built in the period 1874–1918, and were badly maintained. Still, the antiquity of the fleet had some practical advantages—many of the reservists that would be called up had not been trained for more than two decades, and would have had no knowledge about how to operate more modern vessels.[13]

As a result of the limited military potential of the Norwegian naval defence and the strategic importance of the Norwegian coast, the British had already intervened and infringed upon Norwegian neutrality. In February 1940, British forces entered Norwegian waters and boarded a German vessel, *Altmark*, which was used to transport prisoners of war.

---

[12] While the submarines could perform the kind of hidden and deadly work they had done during the previous war, the German surface navy was not impressive. Admiral Raeder, Commander in Chief and one of the staunchest supporters of the attack on Norway, famously confessed to his diary that the navy was so weak that it could do no more than "show that they know how to die gallantly"; see for instance Bird (2006).

[13] Undersøkelseskommisjonen av 1945 (1945, 42–43).

Given that Norwegian inspections on three separate occasions had failed to discover the around 300 prisoners that were hidden in the hold of the ship, the British double-check was warranted.

The *Altmark* incident provided Norway with a diplomatic dilemma—the case was a clear sign that neither of the belligerents *really* respected Norway's neutrality. Slightly less than two months later this became patently evident. On 8 April British forces placed mines in Norwegian waters, and a Polish submarine, which was part of a Royal Navy flotilla, torpedoed the general cargo carrier *Rio de Janeiro*, a ship full of German soldiers on the South Coast. The approximately 300 German soldiers on the *Rio de Janeiro* were on their way to Bergen. A larger group of around 1000 soldiers were onboard the heavy cruiser *Blücher*, which was sunk in the Oslofjord in the early hours of 9 April. The German invasion was underway.

The *Blücher* sinking "bought time" for the Norwegian authorities, including the government and King Haakon VII. They were able to leave Oslo, and make their way slowly and steadily northwards and then westwards. At the beginning of June the king, the crown prince and most of the government arrived in Scotland. From here, they travelled to London, in order to follow up on their decision of 7 June to move the seat of government abroad.

Although the royal family and the government escaped, the German attack—Operation Weserübung—succeeded in gaining control of much of the crucial infrastructure. Among the first installations targeted by the forces from the Third Reich were the country's two short-wave radio transmitters, Bergen Radio and Oslo Radio. These were the main—and fastest—means of communication between Norway and the valuable merchant marine. The Germans used them to send out messages urging Norwegian vessels to return home or go to neutral ports, preferably in Spain or Italy.[14]

# Nortraship

More than 1000 Norwegian ships were sailing in foreign waters, or anchored in foreign ports, when the Germans invaded. Around 30,000 Norwegian seafarers were suddenly cut off from their home country, with

---

[14] Thowsen (1992, 102–103); see also Rosendahl (2015).

the connections to their homes and families severed.[15] The fact that Norway refused to bow to the Nazi Germans, made the status of Norwegian ships and seafarers complex. In the case of Denmark, which had been attacked at the same time and where the government had capitulated, the British authorities confiscated the vessels and gave them British flag and British terms. A similar solution was likely for the Norwegian fleet, until the country joined the Allies and their fight. Then another dilemma arose: striking the right balance between national and business interests. It is telling that one of the most detailed books about the manner in which the merchant marine was operated during the war has the far from subtle subtitle "Profit and patriotism."[16]

Preparations for a solution occurred along two parallel tracks. In Norway, the government fled north, a few steps ahead of the German forces. Slightly less than two weeks after the invasion, on 22 April, at a cabinet meeting held in an old coaching inn, they decided to requisition the right to use all Norwegian ships larger than 500 grt. The Norwegian merchant marine would be under government control. The shipowner Øivind Lorentzen, who had been appointed head of the Shipping Directorate in 1939, was instructed to go to London as quickly as possible and oversee the practical matters.

Around the same time, in London, preparations were under way to build an infrastructure that could control and manage the fleet. By the time Lorentzen arrived at the end of April, the press had been informed that the Norwegian Shipping and Trade Mission was about to start its business. Four hours before Lorentzen arrived, the offices at 144 Leadenhall Street in the City had opened their doors.[17] The organization's leading managers were Norwegian, but the offices were also staffed with British and American personnel.

The London office quickly grew out of its rented floor in Leadenhall Street, and Nortraship expanded both within and outside the building. Due to lack of space and frequent evacuations during the German air

---

[15] Hauge and Hartmann (1951, iii).
[16] Thowsen (1992, 104–107).
[17] Thowsen (1992, 57–59). The formal name, the Norwegian Shipping and Trade Mission, was seldom used; the organization was known by its telegram address, Nortraship.

raids on central London, in October 1940 parts of the activities were moved to Sunningdale, south-west of the city. The facilities—a former Italian-run convent—were far more agreeable than those in the crowded City. Garden parties with friendly competitions—tug-of-war and football matches between seafarers and office personnel—were held when King Haakon VII arrived for annual inspections. In 1941 he told the participants that when he looked at the huge office staff gathered in Sunningdale, he could "better understand his position as the world's largest shipowner."[18]

The daily operation of Nortraship saw a number of challenges. The lines of command were difficult due to communication problems. On the one hand, information was vital to operate the fleet; on the other hand, it was crucial that this information did not fall into enemy hands. In the end, the solution became a wide network of branches. By the beginning of 1944 the Nortraship operation in London consisted of 17 individual departments, some divided into as many as five sections, while the New York office had one department more. Nortraship had 52 branch offices or representative offices, affiliated with either New York or London, in 26 different countries.[19]

Some shipowners were involved at high levels in the organization, and had to balance their own and Nortraship's interests, while others were stuck in occupied Norway and could not influence what happened to their tonnage. The Germans had been interested in taking control of the Norwegian Shipowners' Association, but the Nazi-friendly owners did not succeed in taking over until the beginning of 1942. Later that same year, the occupants started to round up shipowners with "unclear" loyalties—typically those with vessels in the Nortraship fleet and a limited willingness to cooperate. More than 300 owners withdrew from the association, and a parallel organization was established.[20]

Among the shipowners working for Nortraship, one potential problem was that they could make decisions and transactions that would benefit

---

[18] Woxholth (1965, 50).
[19] Mossige (1989, 283–289).
[20] See Pettersen 1992 for an introduction to the fleet in Norway—"the home fleet"—which made up 45 per cent of the number of ships, but only around 15 per cent of the Norwegian tonnage. For an interesting and personal account by a shipowner left in Norway, see Høegh (1970, 30–42). Given that this book deals with Norwegian shipping in the international market, the home fleet will by and large be ignored here.

their own interests, rather than Nortraship as a whole. Øivind Lorentzen was criticized for appointing his son to a central position, and it was also suggested that the two had led to losses for Nortraship by keeping "their own" Nopal-line in South America going. After long deliberations, a government-appointed committee in 1943 concluded that there were reasons for the criticism of some business decisions, but no basis for any stronger reaction.[21]

Another challenge was the ability to ensure cooperation among strong and powerful individuals who were used to being at the top. Antagonism between Øivind Lorentzen and Ingolf Hysing-Olsen, who built up the London office before Lorentzen's arrival, was partly solved when Lorentzen moved to New York to manage the organization there. Subsequently a number of strong personalities tried to find their positions in the organization. Hilmar Reksten, from Bergen, was an excellent shipping man, but hardly a diplomat, and was involved in a number of controversies both in London and New York. Erling Dekke Næss commenced his work in New York with a handicap: he was viewed with scepticism by many of his colleagues, as he had built up his fleet under foreign flag.

Arne Sunde, the only Liberal member of the London Cabinet, became Minister of Shipping when that post was established on 1 October 1942.[22] That placed him neatly in the line of fire between the politicians, who wanted control of Nortraship, and the Nortraship management, who wanted as little political involvement as possible. He was also a useful lightning rod in the discussions with the British about the allocation of the Norwegian ships.

## Exile on Broad Street

The international orientation of the United States in the interwar period is a debated topic. While some claim that the United States followed a policy inspired by the old British ideas of "splendid isolation," others claim that

---

[21] See Thowsen (1992, 229–240, 243–248 and 281–288).
[22] Sunde had previously been Consultative Councillor of State without portfolio, one of two government members not from the Labour Party, and also headed the Ministry of Provisioning. He arrived in the UK on HMS *Galatea*, together with Øivind Lorentzen and around 200 crates of the gold that had been retrieved from the headquarters of the central bank.

the policy was internationalist, but based on economic involvement—banks not tanks.[23] Regardless of the actual situation before Pearl Harbor, the Japanese attack changed the duration—if not the outcome—of the war. Just as the United States tipped the scales when it entered the First World War, the US entry into the Second World War was a decisive moment. After that, as Winston Churchill famously remarked: "Hitler's fate was sealed. Mussolini's fate was sealed. [The Japanese] would be ground to powder. All the rest was merely the proper application of overwhelming force."[24]

Nortraship had a presence in the United States for a long time before the Americans entered the war, mainly as a result of the substantial shipping activities in and around American waters. It was difficult to control this business from London, and uncertainty about the British ability to withstand the German attacks gave another impetus to establish an office in the United States. When a division of labour between the two offices was determined at the end of 1940, the New York office, located on Manhattan's Broad Street, was given the task to manage around one-third of the Nortraship vessels. However, a relatively large proportion of these ships were "free," in other words not included in the collective agreements with the Allies. Consequently, the shipping activity—management, operation, chartering—was much more differentiated than business conducted from the London office. However, financial responsibility was delegated to the London office, due to its proximity to the Bank of England and the Treasury, and in order to facilitate cooperation with the exiled Norwegian Ministry of Finance.

The operation of the fleet occurred more or less on normal terms. Similar to during the First World War, insurance was an important cost factor. The ships were insured through Lloyd's—conveniently located just around the corner from Nortraship's offices in the City. For a while Nortraship partly functioned as own insurer. Although the idea was that maintenance should take place as usual, this became difficult when the demands of the war dictated otherwise. The strict discipline of the convoys increased wear and tear, and ships sometimes had to take unsuitable cargoes. Most ships were issued with special equipment—additional life boats, armour, guns, protection against mines, and so on.

---

[23] See Braumoeller (2010) for an overview of the debate.
[24] Churchill (1950, 539).

The US entry into the war implied that the question of the Norwegian tonnage became a trilateral problem—British, American and Norwegian interests all had to be taken into account. In late 1942 the remaining "free" ships flying the Norwegian flag were to be included more closely in the Allied operation. During the negotiations, Erling Dekke Næss skilfully played an inexperienced American (David Scoll) against a slightly arrogant British representative (William Weston). The end result was the Hogmanay Agreement, signed on New Year's Eve 1942 and given the Scottish name for a new year's gift. In addition to questions about the chartering and payment of the tonnage, the agreement took into account questions of market access and tonnage availability after the war, in particular with regard to the liner trade.[25] This dichotomy between the short-term, strategic and military goals and the long-term question of Norwegian competitiveness after the return of peace was a crucial element of the Nortraship experience; the country was "Allied and competitor."[26]

One of the most difficult issues in connection with the Nortraship organization was the question of salaries. In October 1942, the Prime Minister and other Cabinet members held a meeting with four members of the Norwegian Seamen's Mission's clergy. Their message to the government was that something was afoot among the seamen. The previous year they had tried to talk to the Minister of Finance about the high salaries in the London administration. Strong words, like "blood money," were used about the salaries that the bureaucrats received.[27] The "administrators" working under relative safe circumstances in the Nortraship offices— even those outside the war zone—were earning more money than the seafarers risking their lives in the middle of the war theatre.

The transfers of funds from Nortraship to the government were initially specified as taxes and tonnage fees. Subsequently, the amounts necessary to balance the budgets were just registered as "Transfer from Nortraship."[28] In total almost £80 million was transferred from Nortraship

---

[25] See Thowsen (1992, 409–423) and Næss (1977, 112–114).
[26] This is the subtitle of Basberg (1993), which succeeds Thowsen (1992) and concentrates on Nortraship in the period from the beginning of 1943 until the 1964 settlement.
[27] Undersøkelseskommisjonen av 1945, Volume I, 1945, 27; pages 118–139 deal specifically with Nortraship.
[28] Undersøkelseskommisjonen av 1945, Volume IV, 1947, 94.

to the Norwegian exile government in the period from 1 July 1940 to 30 June 1945—making up almost 90 per cent of the total government revenues in this period.[29] The revenues from Nortraship were important both during the war and in the reconstruction period. The currency principle—that revenues should preferably be in dollars, but expenses should preferably be paid in pounds sterling—turned out to be very wise, and created some leeway in a period of dollar shortages.

In addition to these pecuniary considerations, Nortraship had another important role—one that affected the long-term development and competitiveness of Norwegian shipping. Nortraship enabled the Norwegian authorities and shipping community to establish or strengthen political and business links to other Allied countries during the war. Moreover, it created a sense of unity among those in exile. Shipowners, shipping company clerks, brokers, lawyers, bankers and bureaucrats shared difficult times and forged friendships and relations that would be very useful in the post-war period.

At the end of the war, it was estimated that Nortraship had an operating profit of approximately NOK550 million. However, this underestimated charter and insurance transfers, as well as profits on the sale of ships that the Norwegian authorities bought from the British during the war. When the books were finally closed, in the early 1960s, they showed a profit of almost NOK819 million, almost three times the value of the gold reserves that were rescued in April 1940.[30] The more than NOK800 million that the authorities received was around 18 per cent of the total Nortraship revenues. The majority of the around NOK4.5 billion Nortraship settlement was distributed to the various shipping companies according to a detailed set of calculations on a ship-by-ship basis. Among the important elements was insurance compensation for ships that had been sunk, which made up around 31 per cent of the "costs."[31]

As Fig. 5.1 shows, the pattern of loss of life and ships during the Second World War echoes the pattern during the previous war. There

---

[29] Undersøkelseskommisjonen av 1945, Volume IV, 1947, 95.
[30] Norway, Parliament, Stortingsmelding 76 (1963–64) 13–15.
[31] See Basberg 1993, 327–345 for a detailed overview of the settlement.

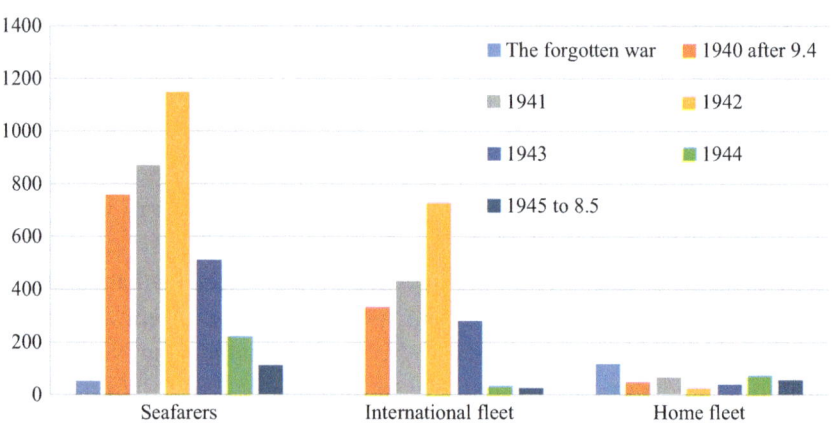

**Fig. 5.1** Losses during the Second World War, persons and 1000 grt, 1939–45. (Source: Statistics Norway (2000, 115). See footnote)

was a gradual increase in losses as a result of increasing hostilities, before a combination of a reduction of the submarine threat and efficient measures, again including convoys, managed to alleviate the situation.[32]

Slightly more than 10,000 Norwegians—9379 men and 883 women—died as a direct result of the war.[33] The losses of the Norwegian military accounted for only one-fifth of this.[34] The highest single group of casualties among Norwegians came from seafarers in the merchant marine. At sea, more than 3600 civilians lost their lives—including 70 women. Consequently, seafarers made up more than a third of all the Norwegian deaths. Their sacrifice was extremely important for the final outcome of the war.

---

[32] Figure 5.1: Based on data from Statistics Norway (2000), Table 116, 115. See the original source for more information on the basis for the original data. The figures differ marginally from those in Statistics Norway (1948), Table 131b, 248, mainly as a result off differences in the periodization. Before the German invasion on 9 April 1940, all ships were registered as belonging to the home fleet.

[33] Based on data from Statistics Norway in Søbye (1999). While around 10,000 Norwegians lost their lives at home and abroad as a direct result of the war, around 13,000 Russian and almost 3000 Yugoslav prisoners of war lost their lives on Norwegian soil; Fure (1999, 37).

[34] In addition to the 2000 deaths in the Norwegian military, almost 700 Norwegians died while fighting for "the other side" on the Eastern Front.

## Peacetime: Rebuilding the Fleet

When the war in Europe was over, the challenges facing the Norwegian shipping industry were substantial. Half of the fleet was gone, and the remaining ships were not in good shape, as maintenance had not been a priority during the difficult period. When the war ended, it had not been decided when the ships would be returned to the owners or how and when the outstanding balances would be settled. While the shipowners were interested in regaining control of their tonnage as soon as the war was over, it was evident that the political desire—at the international level—was to maintain strategic command of the merchant ships. The aim was to ensure rational and efficient management of the world fleet, thus aiding the relief and rebuilding efforts.

According to an agreement from the late summer of 1944, the United Maritime Authority (UMA) would coordinate the merchant marines of important Allied countries for a period of six months after the end of the war. The new intergovernmental organization commenced their operations in May 1945, but for the first months the Norwegian ships remained requisitioned by the authorities. In October, the ships were time chartered on "UMA-terms" to the authorities. Two shipowners that had fled from Norway during the last stages of the war, Fredrik Odfjell and Leif Høegh, represented Norway in the United States and the UK, respectively. The choice of two "industry men" as Norwegian representatives in the executive of this important intergovernmental and bureaucratic organization says something about the Norwegian authorities' experience with and trust of shipowners following the five years of cooperation abroad. This kind of delegation would be quite common throughout the post-war period—even when there was massive discussion and disagreement about domestic matters, the authorities let the shipowners' delegates represent the country in several international institutions.[35]

John Oscar Egeland, one of the most prominent industry "insiders" and Director of *Norges Rederforbund* 1948–1953, sketched two main

---

[35] Egeland (1971, 18).

tasks for the shipowners after the war. The first was to regain control of their tonnage as soon as possible. The second was to obtain new vessels to compensate for the wartime reductions in the fleet.[36]

The main problem was of course the major losses during the war. There had been some minor additions to the fleet. Twelve Liberty-ships, general cargo carriers of around 7000 gross register tons (grt), four smaller C1-A general cargo carriers and eight T2-tankers of around 10,000 grt had been transferred from the United States in the period January 1943– April 1945 as part of the Lend Lease agreement.[37] However, although Norwegian shipowners bought an additional 46 *Liberty* ships from the US after the war, and another eight second-hand from owners in Denmark and Panama, both the relative and absolute position of Norwegian shipping was severely deteriorated.[38]

Still, there was undoubtedly a role for shipping in the Norwegian economy. A 1947 newspaper article points out that shipping "is a dream investment" in a national perspective as it has "a high turnover and high revenues for the country, with only a modest need for labour."[39] The authorities subscribed to this idea. After the war, the rebuilding of the fleet became a national priority. The Labour government—which took over in 1945 supported by an absolute majority in the Parliament—gave precedence to industries that could neutralize the deficit on the Balance of Trade and thus secure valuable foreign currency, in other words US dollars. The mainstay of this policy, in addition to shipping, became export-oriented and energy-intensive manufacturing.

The idea of shipping as a key industry in Norwegian policy-making is a stark contrast to a 1953 paper by the leading shipping lobbyist—chief economist Johan Seland of *Norges Rederforbund*—who painted a really grim picture: shipping's role in the Norwegian economy had declined. Norway's position in world shipping in general, and within tanker transports in particular, was weaker than before the war. Shipping companies

---

[36] Egeland (1971, 17).
[37] Basberg (1993, 176–177). In total, more than 500 ships were transferred from the United States to other Allies. Two countries received more than Norway's 24 ships—341 vessels were transferred to the UK and 93 went to the Soviet Union.
[38] Fon (1995, 73).
[39] *Verdens Gang*, 190347, 6.

had serious financing difficulties and even if markets were good, they would see their capital depleted.[40] Moreover, the Norwegian tax regime was worse than in any other shipping nation, and this forced shipping companies to increase their debts, according to Seland.

What had happened between 1947 and 1953 that gave such different results?

A crucial element of economic policy is striking the right balance between the power of the state and the freedom of individual economic agents. Nortraship and the war experiences had shown that in special circumstances there were reasons to tilt this balance strictly to one side. In the first post-war decades, the authorities in Norway took on a much more active role in economic development than they had done before the war. This was a development that was similar to most European countries. However, in Norway the coalition between interventionist politicians and bureaucrats with a strong belief in planning was more powerful, and lasted longer, than in most countries in Western Europe. One reason for this was the broad support for the Labour Party [*Arbeiderpartiet*] in the post-war elections.

With the gradual rebuilding of Norway, and of the world economy, access to foreign currency became one of the main concerns of the authorities. Export revenues were lower than before the war, while purchases abroad were larger, and the central bank had been forced to reduce its reserves in order to purchase the dollars needed to finance imports. The rebuilding of the merchant fleet was one of the main expenses abroad, but this was initially a desired development. The shipping industry was expected to play a key role as an earner of foreign exchange, and in 1945 and 1946 Norwegian shipowners were allowed to "buy or order all the tonnage that they desired [and] practically all requests for currency to buy ships were granted."[41] In total, around NOK2 billion—more or less equal to the currency reserves earned by the merchant marine during the war—were granted. The authorities were involved as buyers, mediators and distributors, in addition to providing guarantees.

---

[40] Seland (1953, 5–6).
[41] Thowsen (1986, 11–12). Thowsen's article is one of the most comprehensive reviews of the reconstruction of the Norwegian fleet after the war, with a particular emphasis on the political side, including the licensing regime.

By the end of 1946, the fleet was back at the pre-war level, but only when newbuilding contracts are included. However the revenues from shipping failed to live up to expectations. There were two reasons for this. First, the smaller fleet—contracts do not make money—and a high proportion of relatively outdated ships, had a negative effect. Second, the freight rates were controlled for some time after the war, and due to the new tonnage built during the war, there was no post-war boom.

In the minds of the bureaucrats and politicians, the shipping sector's position was one important reason for the reduced foreign exchange reserves. The currency regulations that were used to the benefit of Norwegian shipping immediately after the war were now used to reduce growth. For shipping companies, their access to financing came to be dependent upon a number of features, including war losses, revenues from vessel sales and the markets in which the ships operated—those that ensured freights were paid in dollars were preferred. The restrictions that the authorities introduced clearly favoured the large Norwegian shipping companies, in particular those that were engaged in the liner trade. The Sterling Crisis in 1947—where the premature convertibility of the British pound revealed the extent of Europe's dollar difficulties—made the authorities apprehensive.

In the autumn of 1947 the licensing of new contracts abroad was stopped temporarily. The possibility of ordering ships was resumed after a while if the owner could—through vessel sales abroad or freight revenues—ensure that the contracting did not create a need for foreign exchange. This period of access to "currency neutral" financing lasted until March 1948. Subsequently, there was sporadic granting of licences, before a full contracting ban was introduced in 1949 and 1950—Norwegian shipping companies were simply not allowed to order ships abroad.

The rebuilding of the merchant fleet was at the centre of the debate about the authorities' right—and ability—to direct the economy. Some wanted more control, others less. A Communist Member of Parliament, Emil Løvlien, suggested that the government had given up control of economic policy, and transferred policy design to the shipowners.[42] The

---

[42] Norway, Parliament, *Forhandlinger i Stortinget No. 70*, 15 April 1948, 550–557. Løvlien's speech was so long that the Parliament had to break for lunch. When they returned from the meal, he warned against the "completely dangerous" Marshall Plan, "a morphine injection" that should be

subsequent year, when the restrictions on contracting had been introduced, a member from the Farmers' Party [*Bondepartiet*] was extremely critical about how the authorities dealt with business and the private sector. Probably inspired by Friedrich Hayek's recent writings, he suggested that the ban was the start of a road that would ultimately lead to "a bureaucratic, state-directed dictatorship."[43]

The restrictions that the Labour government had introduced were extremely harmful, according to the shipowners and the Conservatives. Initially their opposition was limited—the state of the market did not encourage new orders anyway. However, when the shipping market boomed in the early 1950s as a result of the Korean War, the criticism was massive: the ban on contracting had enabled Greeks to take over profitable tanker contracts. The focus on liner vessels, with stable rates, had displaced investments in ships for more lucrative markets. The government had destroyed the competitiveness and profitability of Norwegian shipping.

In response to these accusations, the government was quick to point out the privileged access to foreign exchange that shipping had in the immediate post-war years. They saw the restrictions as a necessary measure aimed at averting an acute currency crisis. The end of the ban in 1951 unleashed a rush of new contracts, but by then newbuilding prices had increased dramatically and the waiting time for delivery was long. In the end, the ships were delivered when the boom was over.

## Aftermath: Rehabilitation of the Seafarers

Norwegian soldiers returning from abroad and the members of the *Hjemmefront* [Home resistance] were welcomed as heroes in May 1945—there were parties and public parades, flowers and flags. The war sailors

---

avoided. At the time, Løvlien was one of 11 representatives from *Norges Kommunistiske Parti* [the Norwegian Communist Party], which had received 11.9 per cent of the votes in the 1945 election. *Arbeiderpartiet* [the Labour Party] had an absolute majority, with 76 of the 150 representatives, after receiving 41 per cent of the votes. In 1957 Løvlien became the last Member of Parliament to be elected on the Communist Party ticket.
[43] Gabriel Moseid in Norway, Parliament, *Forhandlinger i Stortinget*, 22 March 1949, 477.

did not receive such a warm welcome—they basically returned unannounced, without a fanfare. Some arrived in the spring or summer of 1945, some arrived that autumn, others in 1946 or even 1947. Most of them arrived according to their ships' schedules. Some stayed abroad, having established relations in Canada, the United States or the UK, while others had to wait until they could find a Norwegian ship to take them home. In the first post-war period, passenger ships were usually reserved for the movement of troops, but one exception was when more than 800 war sailors—all injured or ill—arrived in late July with the steamship *Bergensfjord*.[44]

The vessel *Bergensfjord* is itself an illustration of the action-filled war years; the ship was rebuilt to carry troops and transported some 165,000 passengers—soldiers, prisoners of war and refugees all over the globe. Travelling more than 300,000 nautical miles—equal to 14 times around the Equator—"Lucky *Bergensfjord*" moved in dangerous waters and was on the front line during the invasion of Sicily.[45] The ship's seafarers—both the crew and its injured and ill passengers—had been in the line of fire for more than five years. It was a war experience that was very different from what most Norwegians had been through.

At the start of the war, Norwegian seafarers had been paid for their high-risk work. Before the Nazi invasion, they received a war-risk premium that could be up to 300 per cent of their basic salaries, depending on the zone in which the ship was sailing. In June 1940, after Norway entered the war, the British demanded that the wages of Norwegian and British seafarers should be aligned. As a result, the war-risk bonus was reduced to NOK100 per month. For ordinary seamen this implied a decline of up to NOK500 per month, for captains as much as NOK3000.

Although the war risk did not disappear, the premiums apparently did, to appease the British. Given that the premium reduction was an advantage to the British charterers, one shilling per dead weight ton per month was deposited into a special account, to be used "for the benefit of the seamen after the war."[46] This account is often referred to as "Nortraship's

---

[44] Virkesdal (1991, 17).
[45] Ljone (1982).
[46] Hodne (1992, 174).

secret fund," as it was important that British seafarers did not know that their Norwegian colleagues were paid more. For the Norwegian seafarers, the fund was "a public secret." After the war, the existence and use of this fund was shrouded in controversy. By the end of 1947 the fund, including interest, amounted to almost NOK44 million. Who did the money belong to?

A government committee headed by Arne Sunde and with participation from the four major maritime unions, in 1947 suggested that the money be used for widows and children of seafarers that died during the war, ill and disabled seafarers, older seafarers, and so on. This solution was accepted in Parliament the following year. But parallel with this, a group of war sailors were fighting in the courts, arguing that the money in "the secret fund" belonged to them, and consequently should be divided among those who had participated.

In 1954 the Supreme Court rejected the seafarers' case. However, media pressure in the late 1960s and early 1970s led to a revitalization of the question, and in 1972 Parliament awarded an *ex gratia* payment of some NOK155 million to the war sailors and their surviving relatives. It is very unfortunate that Nortraship—this well-functioning mixture of private ownership and government intervention, of profit and patriotism—is most famous for its "secret fund," which tainted the seafarers' post-war relations with the shipowners and the authorities.

The fund was only one of the many difficult fights that the Nortraship seafarers had to deal with after the war. An everyday example is the fact that some of them had been abroad for so long that they had been removed from the electoral roll. In other words, those who had fought for Norway's freedom were not allowed to participate in the Parliamentary elections. Others were asked to prove their patriotic attitude, or were called up for compulsory military service, after more than five years on the front line.[47]

Some questions were dealt with in a more pragmatic manner. In many instances, families in Norway had been paid while the breadwinner was abroad. This implied that the seafarer could owe money to his employer

---

[47] See Virkesdal (1991, 15).

when he returned, if he had not "sailed enough" to cover the advances. Shipowners would often quietly "forget about" this, and redeem the debts.

The Norwegian authorities were less forthcoming. War sailors received lower pensions than soldiers and those that had been prisoners in Norway—a Parliamentary minority suggested that seafarers should not receive war pensions at all. The term "war sailor syndrome" was coined, a variety of the "KZ syndrome" that affected those surviving the concentration camps.[48] Symptoms included difficulties in adapting to normal life, nightmares, angst, depression, lack of concentration and insomnia. The journalist, Oddvar Schjølberg, refers to this as "the eternal war of the war sailors."[49]

Norwegian seafarers and bereaved families had to fight Norwegian bureaucrats for their rights, and years and even decades passed before they were given recognition and compensation. Up until the late 1960s, they had to prove that their problems were a direct result of the war, in order to receive war pensions. In 1968, the burden of proof was reversed: the authorities had to prove that there was no causality between the war and the health problems.[50] As Jon Michelet phrased it: after the war, "we rebuilt the country, but not the people."[51]

When Norway was invaded in April 1940, around 3200 foreign seafarers worked on the ships that were about to become the Nortraship fleet, and during the first years of the war the proportion of foreigners increased from 12 to 25 per cent. Almost 1000 foreigners lost their lives while working on Norwegian ships. They came from 36 different nations, and the largest losses of lives were among British (323) and Chinese (252) seafarers.[52] The compensation that was paid out was arbitrary, if paid at all. Many received *ex gratia* payments—money given based on goodwill, rather than legal claims—others received nothing.

---

[48] See Askevold et al. (1976), Hartvig (1977) and Hansson (1967).
[49] Schjølberg (2014).
[50] On the struggle to get the right to receive war pensions, see Hjeltnes (1997, 458–474).
[51] *Aftenposten*, 05102013, 2–3.
[52] The information on foreign war sailors is mainly from Rosendahl (2017). In addition to people from 36 different nations, one stateless person lost his life; Jan Alexis Molotov died when *MS Fernhill* was sunk by a submarine in August 1942.

The manner in which Norway treated the war sailors was not particularly appreciative. But the neglect gradually became evident, and an apology from the Minister of Defence was made in public: "The story of our war sailors is a shocking narrative. About a society that was not properly prepared to take care of some of the biggest war heroes. About rejection and denial. You, the war sailors, should not be blamed – you expected that society would appreciate your efforts. But you were disappointed. As a society, we let you down. Today I therefore apologise, on behalf of the Norwegian authorities, for the treatment that war sailors were subject to after the war."[53]

The Minister of Defense was Anne Grethe Strøm-Erichsen from the Labour Party. The year was 2013. For the vast majority of the war sailors, the apology came too late.

The Hall of Remembrance for Sailors [*Minnehallen*] outside Stavern was unveiled in 1926 to commemorate the Norwegian sailors that died during the First World War. The names of fallen sailors are inscribed on a series of copper plates, and after the Second World War almost 3500 names were added to the 1748 from the First World War. The last addition came on 8 May 2017, when 956 names of foreigners were added. Among those that financed the new plates were the Norwegian Shipowners' Association and other companies and foundations in the Norwegian shipping industry. Another important financial contributor was the author Jon Michelet, who has shown how powerful literature can be in shaping our knowledge and ideas about the world in which we live and die.

# Bibliography

F. Askevold, E.A. Løchen, & O. Sjaastad (1976) 'Krigsseilersyndromet', *Tidsskrift for Den Norske Lægeforening*, 96, 868–872

B.L. Basberg (1993) 'Nortraship – Alliert og konkurrent', *Handelsflåten i krig 2* (Oslo: Grøndahl og Dreyers Forlag AS)

---

[53] Minister of Defense, Anne Grete Strøm-Erichsen's speech given when the monument honouring the war sailors was unveiled, 030813. [regjeringen.no/no/aktuelt/mote-med-krigseilere-og-parorende-risor/id733139/] [Read 051017].

K.W. Bird (2006) *Erich Raeder – Admiral of the Third Reich* (Annapolis: Naval Institute Press)
B.F. Braumoeller (2010) 'The Myth of American Isolationism', *Foreign Policy Analysis*, 6:4, 349–371
W. Churchill (1950) *The Second World War*, Volume III, "The Grand Alliance", 6th edition 1985 (New York: Houghton Mifflin Company)
J.O. Egeland (1971) *Vi skal videre: Norsk skipsfart etter den annen verdenskrig, perioden 1945–1970* (Oslo: H. Aschehoug & Co.)
A.M. Fon (1995) 'En stormakt i tørrbulk. En økonomisk-historisk analyse av norsk tørrbulkfart 1950–1973', *PhD-thesis* (Bergen: Norges Handelshøyskole)
O.B. Fure (1999) 'Norsk okkupasjonshistorie. Konsensus, berøringsangst og tabuisering', in S.U. Larsen (ed) *I krigens kjølvann: Nye sider ved norsk krigshistorie og etterkrigstid* (Oslo: Universitetsforlaget)
C.J. Hambro (1945) *Taler i krig* (Oslo: Gyldendal)
P. Hansson (1967) *Hver tiende mann måtte dø: fra konvoifarten under siste krig* (Oslo: Gyldendal)
P. Hartvig (1977) 'Krigsseilersyndromet. En undersøkelse og en diskusjon av begrepets innhold', *Nordisk psykiatrisk tidsskrift*, 31, 302–313
E.O. Hauge & V. Hartmann (1951) *Flukten fra Dakar* (Bergen: J.W. Eides Forlag)
G. Hjeltnes (1995) 'Sjømann – Lang vakt', *Handelsflåten i krig 3* (Oslo: Grøndahl og Dreyers Forlag AS)
G. Hjeltnes (1997) 'Krigsseiler: krig, hjemkomst, oppgjør', *Handelsflåten i krig 4* (Oslo: Grøndahl og Dreyers Forlag AS)
F. Hodne (1992) *Norsk økonomi 1900–1990* (Oslo: TANO)
C.F. Horne (1923) *Source Records of The Great War* (New York: National Alumni)
L. Høegh (1970) *I skipsfartens tjeneste* (Oslo: Gyldendal)
L. Lindbæk (1948) *Tusen norske skip* (Oslo: Gyldendal Norsk Forlag)
O. Ljone (1982) *Bergensfjord – skipet som overlevde alt* (Oslo: Gyldendal Norsk Forlag)
E. Mossige (1989) *Storrederiet Nortraship – Handelsflåten i krig* (Oslo: Grøndahl)
E.D. Næss (1977) *Autobiography of a Shipping Man* (Seatrade, London)
T.L. Nilsen & A. Thowsen (1990) *Handelsflåten i krig 1939–45* (Bergen: Bergens Sjøfartsmuseum)
L. Pettersen (1992) *Hjemmeflåten. Mellom venn og fiende* (Oslo: Grøndahl Dreyer)
A.H. Rasmussen (1964) *Menn uten medaljer: En saga om og av norske sjøfolk* (Oslo: J.W. Cappelens forlag)

B.T. Rosendahl (2015) 'Patriotism, money and control – Mobilization of Norwegian merchant seamen during the Second World War', *Scandinavian Journal of History*, 40:2, 159–194

B.T. Rosendahl (ed) (2017) *De var også krigsseilere* (Kristiansand: Stiftelsen Arkivet)

O. Schjølberg (2014) *Krigsseilernes evige krig* (Larvik: Liv Forlag)

J. Seland (1953) *Oversikt over momenter som kan belyse utviklingen i årene fremover av verdenshandelen, verdensflåten og Norges flåte samt over de norske skattereglers virkning for skipsfartsnæringen og andre lands skatteregler* (Oslo: Norges Rederforbund)

Statistics Norway (1948) *Statistiske oversikter 1948* (Oslo: Statistiske Sentralbyrå)

Statistics Norway (2000) *Statistisk Årbok 2000* (Oslo: Statistics Norway)

S. Steen (1948) *Norges krig, 1940–1945*, Vol. II (Oslo: Gyldendal Norsk Forlag)

E. Søbye (1999) *Statistikk mot år 2000. Krigsdødsfallene under andre verdenskrig.* http://www.ssb.no/befolkning/artikler-og-publikasjoner/krigsdodsfallene-under-2-verdenskrig (15.03.16)

A. Thowsen (1986) 'Skipsfart og planøkonomi. Kontraherings- og lisensieringspolitikken overfor norsk skipsfart i den første etterkrigstiden (1945–1953)', *Sjøfartshistorisk Årbok 1985* (Bergen: Bergens Rederiforening og Bergens Sjøfartsmuseum)

A. Thowsen (1992) 'Nortraship – Profitt og Patriotisme', *Handelsflåten i krig 1* (Oslo: Grøndahl og Dreyers Forlag AS)

Undersøkelseskommisjonen av 1945 (1945) *Undersøkelseskommisjonen av 1945*, Volumes I–III (Oslo: Arbeidernes Aktietrykkeri)

Undersøkelseskommisjonen av 1945 (1947) *Undersøkelseskommisjonen av 1945*, Volume IV (Oslo: Arbeidernes Aktietrykkeri)

D. Vikøren (1986) *Norsk skipsfart i sterk omstilling. Svekkes vår forsvarsberedskap?* (Oslo: Den Norske Atlanterhavskomite)

E. Virkesdal (1991) *Handelsflåten i krig* (Bergen: Bergens Sjøfartsmuseum)

H. Woxholth (1965) *"Kjære landsmenn", Kong Haakon VIIs taler under krigen 1940–1945* (Oslo: Hjemmenes Forlag)

**Open Access** This chapter is licensed under the terms of the Creative Commons Attribution-NonCommercial-NoDerivatives 4.0 International License (http://creativecommons.org/licenses/by-nc-nd/4.0/), which permits any noncommercial use, sharing, distribution and reproduction in any medium or format, as long as you give appropriate credit to the original author(s) and the source, provide a link to the Creative Commons license and indicate if you modified the licensed material. You do not have permission under this license to share adapted material derived from this chapter or parts of it.

The images or other third party material in this chapter are included in the chapter's Creative Commons license, unless indicated otherwise in a credit line to the material. If material is not included in the chapter's Creative Commons license and your intended use is not permitted by statutory regulation or exceeds the permitted use, you will need to obtain permission directly from the copyright holder.

# 6

# Bigger and Bigger: Shipping During the Golden Age, 1950–73

*Hvor seiler vi?* [Where are we sailing?] was a series of four programmes aired in late 1969 by *Norsk Rikskringkasting*. The TV series was not what we would consider classic Friday night entertainment, but rather the kind of programme that could only be broadcast in a country with a single state-owned television channel. In a curious mix of entertainment and public education, the programme presented some of the main European ports frequented by Norwegian sailors. The programme-makers—including Gunnar Bull-Gundersen, who had a background as welfare officer in the merchant marine—visited the main European port cities, Antwerp, Amsterdam, Rotterdam and London, sending home very vivid portrayals of the sailors' lives there.

Norwegian sailors, and employees in the local "entertainment industry" that had been set up to serve them, were interviewed in bars that could at best be considered dives. Both the interview subjects and the interviewer were frequently filmed with a beer and a cigarette in hand. Among the highlights of the programmes was a five-minute story, in broken Norwegian, where a Dutch bar hostess in Antwerp explained that she knew what to do with drunken sailors—she would beat them up whenever they were slow to pay their debts.[1]

In the ports were parallel Norwegian societies, made up of *uteseilere* [sailors based abroad]—seafarers that for various reasons seldom or never visited their home country.[2] Rather than going back to Norway, they frequented bars—often offering accommodation as well—with local names such as Bergen Bar, Tønsberg Bar, Telemarken, Café Måneskinn [Moonshine], Café Solskinn [Sunshine] and Café Håpløs [Hopeless].

*Uteseilere* were sometimes portrayed as a romantic group, with "saltwater in their veins" and a carefree life from port to port, with a drink in one hand and a local girlfriend in the other. However, the sailors interviewed in the TV series—both those based abroad and those still living in Norway—lamented the manner in which the shipping sector had developed. Specifically, the effects of the technological development on seafaring life were presented as problematic. Due to the improved efficiency of shipping, in particular with regard to loading and unloading, long stays in exciting port cities had been replaced by very brief stopovers at isolated and uninteresting terminals: "Those who dreamt of experiences in foreign ports, did not meet anything but the dreary reality of the eternally long oil pipes."[3]

Rather than a lively port city, the sailors frequently found themselves in places such as Europoort, "30 kilometres from Rotterdam and seven kilometres from the closest neighbour."[4] The Norwegian seamen's church even constructed a chapel there, functioning as an annex to the main church in Rotterdam, because the mobility of the seamen was

---

[1] The Dutch bar hostess, married to a Norwegian and working in a seamen's bar in a Belgian port city, is an illustration of the truly international environment that seafarers were exposed to, in a period where travels abroad, whether for business or pleasure, were far less common than today.

[2] A somewhat caricatured presentation of an *uteseiler* was someone who signed off in foreign ports, and stayed there—drinking heavily—until money issues or other problems forced them to sign on a new vessel. The TV series aimed at nuancing this picture, but was criticized for the decision to interview and portray sailors in typical red light district bars, rather than in the local seamen's church. One critic suggested that every one of the 32 Norwegian seamen's churches abroad should have been visited, in order to give the programme the right balance; Gundersen (1970, 10).

[3] Gundersen (1970, 77).

[4] NRK, "Hvor seiler vi," 271169.

increasingly limited. Rationalization and new technologies also implied that life on-board had become more isolated, with fewer colleagues and more solitary work. For the modern seafarer, the physical hardship in the masts or the engine room had been replaced by the mental strain of a lonely life.

In the first post-war decades, two technological trends worked together, and both had a numbing effect on seafaring life. First, vessels became larger and larger, which explains why they had to anchor up in more remote areas. Second, the ships became more specialized, purpose-built to transport a relatively small variety of goods. By designing vessels that were specialized for specific cargoes, the loading and unloading became much more efficient. The time spent in port declined from weeks to days, and as port time was reduced, the monotonous days at sea became more plentiful.

Both of these technological trends were possible as a result of the growing volumes of seaborne transport. The first post-war decades saw a strong increase in world trade. The world economy had clearly rediscovered the growth momentum that had been lost in Sarajevo more than three decades earlier.

## The Golden Age

With two devastating wars and The Great Depression, Europe had squandered much of the potential for income growth in the first half of the 20th century. Figure 6.1 provides a visual representation of economic growth in the 20th century, which reveals the manner in which decades of potential growth were lost to fighting and crisis.[5] The dotted line represents the average long-term growth rate of Gross Domestic Product (GDP) *per capita* in Western Europe. This growth—1.87 per cent annu-

---

[5] Figure 6.1: author's calculations based on data from The Maddison Project, http://www.ggdc.net/maddison/maddison-project/home.htm, 2013 version. The long-term average growth rate is the compound growth-rate found when interpolating the development from 1900 to 2000. The data refer to GDP per capita in 1900 International Geary-Khamis dollars, implying that they are adjusted for inflation and based on purchasing power parity. The 12 Western European countries included in the sample are Austria, Belgium, Denmark, Finland, France, Germany, Italy, the Netherlands, Norway, Sweden, Switzerland and the UK.

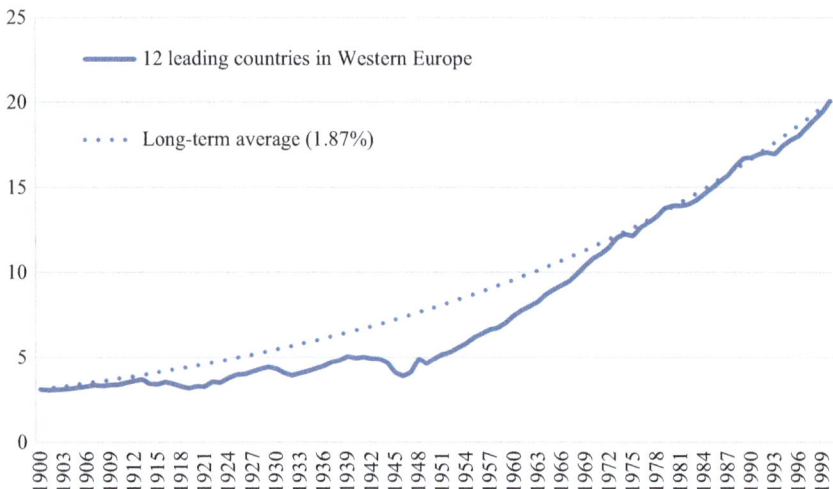

**Fig. 6.1** GDP per capita, long-term trend and actual development (1000 1990 Int.$), 1900–2000. (Source: The Maddison Project, see footnote for details)

ally—is the rate at which the economy would increase if there were no fluctuations and the values for 1900 and 2000 were fixed. The solid line shows the actual growth of GDP *per capita*. The difference between the two lines at a given point in time shows the degree to which the development thus far had deviated from the long-term trend.

At the start of the First World War, the income level in Western Europe was around 6.6 per cent lower than "predicted," but when the war ended this gap had increased to more than 28 per cent. After large fluctuations in the interwar period, the gap was reduced slightly by the outbreak of the Second World War, before plummeting to almost 47 per cent in 1946. In other words—GDP *per capita* after the end of the Second World War was only slightly more than half of what we "would expect" based on the long-term growth rates.

The destruction of two wars and the economic turbulence of the interwar period left Western Europe with an enormous "catching-up" potential. During the period in which this potential was fulfilled, the countries went through a period where living standards and production grew at an unprecedented pace. By 1973 the income level was more or less back on track, having grown almost 4.25 per cent annually. After 1973 the economic growth fluctuated around the long-term trend; a return to normal conditions implied that it would be difficult to repeat the spectacular growth spurt seen in the first post-war decades.

The first decades after the end of the Second World War are frequently referred to as "the Golden Age" in Western Europe and Japan; the Germans had their *Wirtschaftswunder*, the French had their *Les Trente Glorieuses*, and the Japanese their "economic miracle." Only the British remained in the quagmire of low economic growth. What can account for the exceptionally high economic growth in Western Europe in the first decades after the war?

The production possibilities in the middle of the 1940s were severely affected by the war damage. As seen in Fig. 6.1 the European GDP per capita was substantially below its "potential." The destruction of buildings and production capital and the fact that markets for labour, capital goods and services did not function well, meant that production was inefficient. From the late 1940s onwards, Western Europe was like a talented athlete coming back from a long-term injury—so progress was likely to be swift and sustained. As new technologies and organizational methods were introduced and markets were revitalized, higher efficiency followed. In most Western European countries productivity improvements were the main driver behind the high growth.[6]

These productivity improvements were also related to the rebuilding of the international economy. Governments in the leading industrialized countries were willing to go far to avoid a repetition of the dangerous economic nationalism and "beggar-thy-neighbour" policies that had created problems in the 1920s and 1930s and ultimately paved the way for the Second World War. The means to avoid such problems was an institutionalized world economy. With the United States in the lead, a liberal economic world order was established, built around policies and institutions that fostered collaboration and joint support.[7] Multilateral

---

[6] See for instance the analyses in Temin (1997) or van der Wee (1986).
[7] This is of course only one side of the story; the Western one. An important element is the Communist counterpart—The Warzaw Pact, The Council for Mutual Economic Assistance, and so on. The policies in the Soviet Union and its Eastern European satellites turned out to be an unsuccessful—even disastrous—experiment in the long term. However, the Eastern Bloc and its Cold War threats were an extremely important catalyst for the integration in Western Europe and the capitalist world.

institutions such as the International Monetary Fund (macro-economic policies), the International Bank for Reconstruction and Development (aid) and the General Agreement on Tariffs and Trade (trade policy liberalization) were established to oversee the smooth functioning of the international economy. Moreover, the European Recovery Program, usually referred to as Marshall Aid, kick-started a period of rapid and sustained improvement of incomes and living standards in Europe.

The period from 1950 to 1973 was characterized by high—and extremely stable—economic growth rates. In a situation with controlled inflation and low unemployment, Western Europe was one centre of growth in the world economy; the other was East and Southeast Asia, where the Japanese economic miracle of the 1950s and 1960s was followed by a handful of other "miracles" that focused on export-led growth and managed to mobilize resources on an impressive scale.

The strong growth of Japanese manufacturing affected shipping in two ways. First, Japan influenced transport demand: it imported the majority of raw materials used in manufacturing, which was then exported as finished goods—all the while needing shipping space. Estimates suggest that in the late 1960s Japanese demand made up 75 per cent of world coal transport, 60 per cent of iron ore transport and 20 per cent of grain transport.[8] Second, the expansion of shipbuilding was an important ingredient in Japanese industrialization. In 1956 Japan surpassed the UK as the world's leading shipbuilder, and by the early 1970s more than half of the world's ships were built in Japan.[9] The Japanese expansion within manufacturing pushed up the demand for shipping, and at the same time the Japanese built the ships needed to satisfy this demand.

In the first post-war decades world trade increased substantially. Trade liberalization was complemented by productivity-induced reductions in seaborne transport costs. Trade growth is of course extremely positive for shipowners. However, in addition to the volume of trade, the means of

---

[8] Alderton (1973, 78) quoted in Fon (1995a, 134).
[9] See Murphy (2013) for an introduction to the spectacular British decline. Shipbuilders in the UK were closely related to the domestic shipping industry. Among their foreign customers, the Norwegians stood out, but the ships provided by British yards were increasingly mismatched with the demands of the Norwegian owners. The British loss of the Norwegian market is discussed in Johnman and Murphy (1998).

transport and the development of average distances is important—and both developed positively from a shipping point of view. Another important shift was the increasing reliance on oil as a source of energy and as an input in manufacturing. The strong growth in the transport of oil—the vast majority of which was seaborne—resulted in a transformation of the world fleet, where tankers became much more important.

In the second half of the 1960s the increasing demand for seaborne trade was further amplified by the longer average sailing distances after the 1967 closure of the Suez Canal. When the oil tankers to and from the Persian Gulf were forced to go around the Cape of Good Hope, average distances increased. Rather than a 6000 mile, 36-day roundtrip via Suez, tankers going between the Persian Gulf and Europe were subject to a 12,000 mile, 60-day roundtrip. From 1966 to 1973, the length of the average voyage undertaken by crude oil tankers, increased by 40 per cent.[10]

There was a positive feedback loop between the development of shipping demand and supply. Trade liberalization and growing trade volumes lowered unit transport costs as they enabled the utilization of economies of scale. At the same time, the lower unit costs led to a reduction of freight rates, thus reducing transaction costs and encouraging further growth in exports and imports. This development had implications for shipping, and also for the manner in which shipping services were produced.

Once again, Norwegian shipping could grow on the back of a rapidly expanding international economy, just like it had done in the second half of the 19th century. The adaptation to the international market was, however, diametrically opposite of the profitable strategy in the previous century. Then, low-paid sailors operated relatively cheap, old-fashioned and inferior ships financed by a limited Norwegian capital base. In the 1950s, and particularly in the 1960s, high-cost Norwegian seafarers operated one of the most modern and expensive fleets, where the labour-cost disadvantage had been neutralized by means of economies of scale and costly technological solutions.

---

[10] Average distance growth calculated on the basis of Tables 1 and 2 in Fearnley & Eger Chartering Co.'s *Review*, various issues. For a discussion of the geography of maritime trade, see Stopford (2009), Chapter 9 and Knowles (2006).

## Technological Development After the Second World War

Before we look more closely at the Norwegian experience, we should say something about the basis for the dramatic changes in the world fleet in the first post-war decades. The 1950s and 1960s were two decades of great innovative activity and rapid technological development. Shippers, shipowners, naval architects and shipyards worked together to revolutionize seaborne transport. The old "jacks of all trades"—the general cargo carriers—became increasingly unfashionable and were replaced by ships dedicated to the carriage of identical containers, or purpose-built vessels that carried large volumes of the major cargoes.

Innovations are often introduced as a response to bottlenecks in the production process, but usually end up creating new bottlenecks at other stages—the see-saw process between spinning and weaving in the 19th century textile industry is a typical example. In shipping, technological improvements have taken place within a complex framework, where at least four dimensions have to be considered before innovations can be introduced; the trade, the ship, the port and the inland infrastructure.

The basis for practically all international seaborne transport is trade. Countries trade because of price differences, arising as a result of resource endowments or variations in production costs or demand. Large price differences imply that trade leads to substantial benefits. Consider the value of spices in 15th century Europe relative to their price in the East Indies: the potential profits were so enormous that even the highly dangerous sea voyage—with the loss of the ship a very likely outcome—made economic sense.

Tariff reductions and the spread of manufacturing production provided a substantial increase in the benefits from international trade. From a shipping point of view, an important aspect of the development was the fact that the fastest-growing segment was commodities with a high volume or weight relative to their value—oil, iron ore, coal and grain.

Shipping demand is not only determined by the type of cargo, but also by the volumes that are traded. A crucial concept in the development of seaborne transport is the idea of "parcel size"—the typical size of the individual quantities that are transported. The parcel size depends both on the type of cargo and the destination; the need for iron ore at a giant Japanese steel factory is for instance much larger than the demand for sugar in a mid-size village. This difference will be reflected in the parcel size, which affects the choice of the "optimal" ship for a specific trade—or whether sea transport is suitable at all.

If there is potential for seaborne transport, the next question will be related to the ship itself. What are the restrictions with regard to size, storage, cargo handling, and so on? A bigger ship usually has lower unit costs, but one that is too large relative to the parcel size becomes uneconomical. The shift from sail to steam was hailed as revolutionary, as it enabled scheduled services and improved safety. However, in a long-term perspective, the shift from wood to iron and then steel as a building material was extremely important as well. The productivity improvement in world shipping has not been driven by faster ships, but primarily by larger vessels—physical size has been more important than speed.[11] A simple thought experiment might illustrate the enormous size increases. Today, there are container ships with a length of around 400 metres. It takes around four minutes to walk from bow to stern. Picture a ship this size made out of wood, sailing in rough seas. The term "floating coffins"—favoured by both Samuel Plimsoll and Henrik Ibsen to describe the unseaworthy ships of the late 19th century—would take on new dimensions.[12]

---

[11] See Kaukiainen (2006, 2012). The improvements in carrying capacity have been spectacular: the largest bulk carriers today may hold more than 200 times as much cargo as the typical sailing ship of the late 19th century. Speed-wise, however, the improvement is more meagre; with 14 relative to 4 knots, the modern vessel is around four times faster (on days where there is decent wind).

[12] The size limit of wooden ships is partly related to limits in their building material, but surprisingly large wooden vessels have been constructed. In the first part of the 19th century sailing ships of around 90 metres were built, and the motivation for the design was one of the ever-recurring themes of human nature: tax avoidance. The *Columbus* and the *Baron of Renfrew* were so-called "disposable ships," built for one-off journeys from North America to the UK, where they would be dismantled and the timber sold—thus avoiding timber duties. Built in the middle of the 1820s and around 10 times larger than the regular timber vessels at the time, the aim was not "sailing efficiency, but merely [...] getting the largest amount of timber across the Atlantic with the smallest possible expenditure," according to Williams (1968, 378). The *Columbus* became something of an attraction when berthed in London, while the *Baron of Renfrew* broke up into three main pieces outside France and provided a lot of free timber for beachcombers over the following years. A decline in freight rates and timber prices, as well as subsequent relaxation of timber duties, implied

The post-war decades saw a technological improvement that some have claimed had the same far-reaching effects as the transition from sail to steam.[13] While such comparisons are difficult, there is no doubt that the world fleet in the early 1970s was dramatically different from what it had been just a couple of decades earlier. One difference was size: improvements in ship construction—in particular the introduction of welding and new steel types—enabled the building of bigger ships. The average ship in the world fleet in 1948 was around 2700 tons, while it was more than 5000 gross register tons (grt) in 1973.[14] Given that the number of ships almost doubled, and their capacity, speed and turnaround time increased as well, the carrying capacity of the world fleet increased by a factor of more than four.

The average size of the ships increased, but for specific types of vessels, the largest ships became much, much larger. The use of economies of scale was particularly strong in certain trades, for instance in the tanker market. In the early 1920s Esso built 22,000 dead weight ton (dwt) tankers, which remained the world's largest for the next 25 years. The biggest tanker in 1950, the *SS Velutina*, was slightly less than 30,000 dwt. Ten years later, the *Universe Apollo* was four times larger, and the *Universe Ireland*, delivered in 1968, was more than 10 times larger.[15]

The increasing ship sizes posed some challenges, not only in port, but also at sea. Large ships are more difficult to navigate and control. Changing the course takes more time, and the "braking distance" for a 200,000 dwt ship at full speed is 4 kilometres, even after reversing to "full astern." The distance needed to stop would increase to an amazing 10 kilometres if the wind, currents, and so on were unfavourable.[16] Moreover, if there is an accident, the environmental impact of a large ship—with a giant cargo and a huge store of bunkers—would be worse than for a

---

that no more disposable ships were built for this trade. The largest wooden ship built—the six-masted, 3700 gross ton *Wyoming*, built in 1909—illustrates the problems of using "live" wood as a building material on giant vessels. Even though the ship—which at 329.5 feet just pipped the 100-metre line—had been stiffened with steel, the *Wyoming* bent and twisted in bad seas and in 1924 sank with 13 lives lost.

[13] Mayer (1973, 145).
[14] Calculated on the basis of *Lloyds Register of Shipping Statistical Tables*, 1980, 75.
[15] See the overview of the growth in average and maximum sizes in Stopford (2009, 40).
[16] Dahl (1970, 31).

smaller ship. When the *Sinclair Petrolore* exploded in 1960, the oil spill—60 million litres—was more than twice as large as anything seen before.[17] Still, the benefits related to economies of scale, and improvements in shipbuilding, navigation and safety, led to a strong increase in average and maximum sizes.

Size increases were important, but there were also fundamental changes in the composition of the fleet. A number of new ship types were introduced. The 1950s and 1960s saw a massive decline in the proportion of general cargo carriers, and a substantial increase in the share of tankers, bulk carriers and specialized ships. Innovations made the transport of traditional commodities cheaper and more efficient, and also enabled the large-scale transport of cargoes that had previously been too difficult or dangerous to carry on a ship.

The new vessel types—combination carriers, container ships, gas tankers, chemical parcel tankers and car carriers among others—ensured a much greater variety in the types of vessels that made up the world merchant marine. A rapidly growing number and volume of commodities were carried "in bulk"—directly in the hold of the ship, rather than in any kind of packaging. In the first post-war decades, the world fleet became far more specialized—a process that the maritime economist, Martin Stopford, has referred to as "shipping's industrial revolution."[18]

If the first two elements—the trade and the ship—are in place, the next bottleneck will be the port. At some point economies of scale turn into diseconomies of scale. Increasing the ship might reduce the unit costs at sea substantially, but if the vessel spends five weeks in port to be loaded and another five weeks to be emptied, the net benefit might be negative. Bigger is not always better. Consequently, efficiency improvements at sea are futile, if they are not followed up by new solutions in port.

---

[17] Devanney (2006, 23–27). The *Sinclair Petrolore* had been the world's largest ship when delivered in 1955. Just like size records were broken, the oil spill record did not last long. In 1967 the *Torrey Canyon* was grounded after a navigational error, when the captain tried to take a shortcut in order to reach the tide at the Milford Haven terminal in Wales. The *Torrey Canyon* accident paved the way for stricter regulation, including the introduction of the International Convention for the Prevention of Pollution from Ships. The ship also entered pop culture, through an eponymous song by French crooner Serge Gainsbourg, with the catchy refrain "cent vingt mille tonnes de pétrole brut"—120 thousand tons of crude oil.

[18] Stopford (2009, 39–46).

Shipping innovations must be matched by improvements on land to make them profitable. The *Vaderland*, built in the UK in 1872 for the Belgian Red Star Line, was the first steamer designed for the international transport of petroleum in bulk. However, neither the United States nor the Belgian authorities liked the idea of combining flammable petroleum and passengers, even on different legs, and the quayside facilities were inadequate. Consequently, on its first return trip from the United States, *Vaderland* carried general cargo in its tanks, and there is no record of the ship actually performing the bulk petroleum transport for which it was designed.[19]

The technological transformations—from sail to steam to diesel before the war, and improvements in vessel size and specifications after the war—have all reduced the labour intensity of the "shipping" leg of seaborne transport. The sailors have climbed down from the crow's nest and the rigging and the firemen and stokers have left the boiler room. However, even in the first post-war decades, what happened in port—the interface between the sea and the land—was relatively labour intensive, particularly for general cargoes. The large European ports, for instance Antwerp and Rotterdam, relied on large pools of casual labour, dockworkers who cherished the freedom to decide how much they would work and for whom.[20]

The new ships required changes. Although the first super-tankers were loaded at special offshore terminals and had to discharge part of their cargoes to smaller ships in outer bays before they could proceed to the port, the economies of scale involved when the ship was at sea were so large that transhipment still made sense.[21] In time, the ports developed in a manner that made it possible to accommodate the new ship technologies. There was a constant focus on improving the speed of loading and unloading, and the construction of dedicated onshore terminals proved to be a solution for many commodities.

Finally, in order to fully utilize the new advances, it is necessary to be able to transport the cargoes efficiently to their final inland destination.

---

[19] Dunn (1956, 20–21).
[20] Vanfraechem (2012, 150).
[21] Young (1971, 20).

This infrastructure—that stretches the ocean into *the Hinterland*—is sometimes forgotten. However, efficient transfer to subsequent means of transport—pipelines, barges, feeder ships, trains or trucks—is necessary in order to fully utilize the advantages of innovations in ships and ports.

## Three Technological Revolutions: Containerization, Bulkification and Specialization

In the post-war period, three technological concepts have managed to combine all the four critical features above—the trade, the ship, the port and the inland infrastructure. The result has been three related technological development traits—containerization, bulkification and specialization—that have all been bolstered by the more general utilization of "economies of scale" in ship construction and in transport. Together, these developments revolutionized seaborne transport in the decades after the Second World War.

The most visible of these trends, at least in daily life, is *containerization*. In many ways, the ubiquitous containers—usually emblazoned with the logo of one of the large liner companies— Maersk, Evergreen, Hanjin, CMA CGM—have become one of the foremost symbols of globalization. While the average liner had spent only one day at sea for every four days in port, this changed to only one day in port for every day at sea for the container vessels.[22] As ships make money when they transport goods, not when they are in port, the effects on prices, profits and productivity were overwhelming.

The theoretical basis for containerization was standardization—the fact that identical units make storage, movement and planning much easier. Before containerization, managing the consignments on general

---

[22] Vanfraechem (2012, 152). Compared with previous centuries, the transport revolution is even more striking. Efficient container terminals can move around 300 containers from a vessel in one hour—amounting to a conservative 3000 net register tons. These containers would fill one of the large sailing ships of the late 19th century—ships that typically had a turn-around time in port of around a month or more; see for instance Sager and Panting (1990, 141). A couple of hours versus one month makes a lot of difference in an industry where time is money.

cargo carriers often provided the deck officers with a logistical nightmare, where legal, safety and practical issues posed a lot of challenges. A classic example was the US ship *SS Warrior*, which in the middle of the 1950s was subject to one of the first detailed productivity studies within shipping. On a voyage from New York to Bremerhaven, the vessel carried a total of 74,903 cases, 71,276 cartons, 24,036 bags, 53 wheeled vehicles, 22,339 individual pieces in 10 other categories (barrels, reels, etc.), in addition to 1525 units simply identified as "undetermined."[23] All of this had to be stowed securely and accessibly, and the complexity of course spilled over onto the land side.

Ports were characterized by "intense activity dockside. Sacks, boxes, crates – goods of all shapes and sizes – would be laid out in a seemingly disordered fashion, among which dozens of men swarmed carrying out different tasks."[24] The shipping container brought order into this chaos.

The box also brought other benefits. Containerization reduced cargo claims due to damage and pilferage (the proportion of goods that "fell off the back of a lorry" was reduced significantly with containerization). It also enhanced safety. In the mid-1950s half of all longshoremen were injured on the job annually, and one out of six suffered a disabling injury, according to one US study.[25] Containerization reduced accidents and made the dock workers' jobs safer, on a daily basis. In the longer term, the mechanization of course made the job itself insecure—the technology needed fewer, but more skilled workers.

Like most innovations, containerization had a relatively slow start. The US trucker Malcom McLean is credited with the "invention" of the concept, and the inception is dated to 1956 and a trip from New Jersey to Puerto Rico by the ship *Ideal X*, but container sizes and transport

---

[23] The study of the *SS Warrior*'s 10-day trip in March 1954 is frequently used as an example of the complexity; Levinson (2006a). While most sources refer to the Tayloresque productivity studies, the aim was to optimize aspects such as navigation as well; see Allen (1954).

[24] Vigarié (1999, 4); see also Donovan (1999).

[25] National Research Council (1956, 1), from a study of more than 7000 work accidents on the US Pacific Coast in 1954. Among longshoremen there were 92 disabling injuries per million man hours worked—almost eight times as much as in manufacturing in general. The worst place to work was in the hold, where more than half of all the accidents took place, with another 15 per cent occurring on the deck of the ship; National Research Council (1956, 71).

concepts varied for decades after this.[26] As the use of containers increased, up to the point where it had become the dominant technology, work on the docks changed tremendously. Moreover, in many countries the port infrastructure was also transformed, with liberalization, privatization and deregulation complementing the new technological possibilities.

Containerization had a particularly large effect on the transport of finished goods.[27] However, efficiency improvements in shipping also led to a drastic reduction in the cost of moving inputs. The transport of commodities was revolutionized by the utilization of the bulk concept and the introduction of specialized ships that either enabled the transport of new products, or drastically reduced the cost of transporting commodities that had previously been moved by general cargo carriers. Although they are largely absent from the container sector, within bulk and specialized shipping, Norwegian companies were among the pioneers.

The term "liquid bulk" is used to characterize tanker shipping. The dry bulk concept—referring to the manner in which loose commodities were carried directly in the hold of the ship, rather than being individually packaged—actually pre-dated tanker shipping, though at the start of the 1950s it was much less important. The collier (coal ship) *John Bowes*, a hybrid steam/sailing ship built in 1852, is often credited with being the first modern bulk ship. In North America "whalebacks," bulk carriers that have been likened "to a floating cigar with ends upturned," were common on the Great Lakes from the 1890s and well into the post-war period.[28]

In the 1950s and the 1960s, dry bulk shipping became an important activity in the intercontinental market. The combination of longer distances between source and destination for some of the most important commodities, as well as increased volumes, made the bulk concept much more attractive than conventional general cargo ships with several

---

[26] See Levinson (2006b), which gives a good presentation of the history of container shipping or the more condensed Levinson (2006a), which focuses on the port of New York. See Poulsen (2007, 2010) for a presentation of the Scandinavian response to containerization, and Bakka (2008), for a discussion of the impact on Norwegian liner shipping.

[27] When the major South Korean container operator Hanjin Shipping filed for bankruptcy in the autumn of 2016, the company was accused of "spoiling Christmas"; Cooper (2016).

[28] Dunphy (1979, 351).

individual decks in the hold. *Bulkification* was a key ingredient in the spread of manufacturing production. The major market for the dry bulk ships was intercontinental trade of coal, iron ore and grain.[29]

Minor dry bulk goods—steel and forest products, bauxite, alumina and a number of agricultural goods—were transported in specialized ships, reflecting the smaller parcel sizes in these trades. But bulk-like concepts are also behind, for instance, LNG- and LPG-tankers, ships carrying liquid natural gas and liquid petroleum gas, respectively. While such gases had previously been carried in small, individually pressurized tanks, in the 1950s and 1960s purpose-built ships with large tanks, combining pressure and refrigeration, were introduced.

A similar innovation was chemical carriers, often referred to as "parcel tankers." Here, the combination of different parcels on the same ship enabled the use of bulk storage and transport even for smaller volumes. The parcels could be different chemicals, consignments owned by different customers, or cargoes that were coming to or going from different ports. The parcels would typically be too small to justify the chartering of a full ship, but sufficiently large to make individual packaging inconvenient and inefficient. Dedicated ro-ro (roll on-roll off) ships were also built to transport cars and other vehicles, and ships were purpose-built for the carrying of livestock or heavy and bulky cargoes.

The development of the specialized ships implied that there was a large number of new efficient competitors that challenged the position of the old general cargo carriers—the traditional ships that were suitable for almost all cargoes, but well-suited for almost none. *Specialization* had dramatic effects on the cost of transport; freight rates fell by 50 per cent or more, at the same time as the shipping companies' managed to increase their own profits substantially.[30]

In some market segments, the main competition was not new ship types, but other means of transport. The airline industry more or less killed off intercontinental passenger transport in the 1960s. Norwegian

---

[29] With regard to grain, the dry bulk ships also competed with tankers. Properly cleaned oil tankers were used for grain transport if the crude oil market was poor, and even for grain storage if the crude oil market was terrible.

[30] See the example of transport costs for chemicals between the United States and Japan in Murphy and Tenold (2008, 294).

shipping companies had never played a big role in that market—with the exception of the domestically based *Den Norske Amerikalinje*, whose home market was protected. The company's trans-Atlantic activity peaked in 1956, with some 25,000 passengers.[31] Gradually, the company entered the cruise market, one of the many markets that became a "Norwegian specialty" in one of the most expansive periods of Norwegian shipping.

## Norwegian Fleet Expansion

As mentioned in Chap. 2, the expansion of the Norwegian fleet in the 1950s and 1960s was tremendous—the size of the fleet doubled in the 1950s and doubled again in the 1960s. Moreover, the growth was very well adapted to the structural changes in shipping demand. Norwegian owners were at the forefront of the technological development, focusing on two of the three main technological breakthroughs—bulkification and specialization.

The Norwegian owners already had a flying start with regard to bulkification, as a result of their position as the world's largest independent tanker owners. The strong involvement in tanker shipping continued in this period, but the Norwegians were also among the pioneers in the transport of dry bulk goods, with an average market share of 18.7 per cent of the world fleet during the 1960s. The market was dominated by ships registered in Japan, Norway, the UK and (by proxy) Liberia.[32]

Anders Martin Fon, who has written the most authoritative history of Norwegian post-war dry bulk shipping, points out that Norway's leading position in the 1950s and 1960s was the result of the shipowners' openness towards new ideas. An entrepreneurial and creative spirit characterized the owners, both in the early days of dry bulk vessels in the 1950s, and when the trade was increasingly supplemented by combination

---

[31] See Vea, Seland and Schreiner (1960) and Bakka (2008).
[32] Market share calculated on the basis of Fon (1995a, 293). The ownership of the Liberian fleet was divided among several countries; in the beginning of the 1970s around half the fleet was owned by Greek interests, a third by Americans and the rest by shipping companies from various other countries.

carriers—ships that could transport both wet and dry bulk cargoes—in the 1960s.[33]

Regardless of the leading Norwegian position within dry and liquid bulk shipping, the real Norwegian "specialty" was specialized ships. Developments during the 1950s and, in particular, the 1960s, had an impressive effect on the Norwegian share of a handful of specialized shipping segments. In many of the new market segments, Norwegian shipping companies, brokers, ship equipment producers and naval architects played key roles in the development of the new technology. They were instrumental in the introduction or improvement of new ship types, and they also introduced novel ways in which ships could be owned, operated and managed. New types of charter contracts, joint ownership of vessels and pool operation enabled Norwegian shipping companies to build up a substantial presence in many of the new segments, in particular the intercontinental transport of chemicals, gases and forest products.

By the beginning of the 1970s, three of the four largest companies in the chemical tanker market had their roots in Norway. More than 30 Norwegian companies were involved in gas transport, owning around 17 per cent of the world fleet. In Bergen, two competing shipping pools were building up the world's largest fleets of open hatch bulk carriers—ships that were especially suited for the transport of forest products—controlling almost two-thirds of the market by the middle of the decade.[34]

Why did Norwegian shipping companies succeed so well in the development of specialized shipping niches? At least three factors were at play. First, the Norwegians had excellent market knowledge. Their long history and close relationship to major customers implied that they were able to spot opportunities and gather the information necessary to implement new technologies. Many of the new specialized segments could be put in the bracket "industrial shipping," where new contract types and close cooperation between customers and shipowners characterized the business. Long-term contracts of affreightment, where the shipper promised cargo volumes and the shipping company promised transport capacity, often formed the basis for investments in new tonnage.

---

[33] Fon (1995a, 195–235); see also Fon (1995b).
[34] Tenold (2015a, 105–108).

Second, in the period where the Norwegian shipping companies introduced their new technological solutions, shipbuilding was still an important Norwegian industry, and several of the new or refined ship types were designed by Norwegian naval architects and built at Norwegian shipyards. An example is LNG-shipping, where the research arm of the classification society Det norske Veritas was engaged to refine a concept that Hans Ludvig Lorentzen, the oldest son of the shipowner Øivind Lorentzen, had developed. The first ship based on Lorentzen's patented sphere design, *Mundogas Brasilia*, was delivered in 1961—built in Norway and owned by a Lorentzen company.[35] In the longer term, other auxiliary entities—naval architects, consultants, brokers, equipment manufacturers—provided important input into the design of the technology and the development of the service.

Finally, there was room for trial and error in Norwegian shipping. The tax system made investments in new shipping capacity very profitable. The specialized ships carried some risk, but potentially large benefits as well. In a number of cases, innovative entrepreneurs worked together with older, wealthy companies to invest in the new technology. This implied that resourceful individuals with limited means could benefit from the existence of older companies with available funds—and vice versa.

In the 1950s and 1960s the Norwegian shipping industry was propelled forwards by a two-pronged strategy, utilizing two of the technological concepts. On the one hand, there was *bulkification*. The massive investments in crude oil tankers, dry bulk ships and combination carriers weighed heavily in tonnage terms, and are the main explanation of the fact that Norway's share of the world fleet increased from around 6 per cent in the late 1940s to a record-breaking 10 per cent two decades later. On the other hand, there was *specialization*: investments in smaller, specialized ships, often innovative vessels that created their own new markets. Both of these strategic paths depended upon developments abroad, but were forcefully shaped by conditions at home. The Norwegian strategies were determined by the domestic access to labour and capital, influenced by economic policies in general, and shipping policies in particular.

---

[35] Bakka (2017, 97–99).

## Shipping Policy and Factor Costs

In 1967, David Vikøren, Director of the Norwegian Shipowners' Association, gave a presentation called "Merchant Marine Policy of Norway" at a Canadian conference. His presentation suggested that the Norwegian shipping policy at the time was one of minimal interference and preferences—at least of the positive, subsidizing kind. Instead, he claimed that "Norwegian shipping is taxed harder than in most other countries, is subject to stricter manning rules" and was at a disadvantage with regard to technical standards, safety requirements, education and research. Quoting Sturmey's classic book about the decline of British shipping, he concluded that "Norwegian shipping expanded in spite of, not because of, the actions of the government."[36]

Given these alleged internal restrictions, the fact that Norwegian shipping managed to remain competitive and increase its share of the world fleet in the first post-war decades may seem surprising. However, as any airport strategy book will tell you, business is all about adapting to the circumstances, rising to the occasion and laughing in the face of adversity. Thus, Vikøren's negative spin on the authorities' influence should not be accepted unconditionally. The authorities did indeed influence the industry, but for much of the 1950s and 1960s the influence consisted of "nudging" the strategies of the shipping companies. And inadvertently, most shipowners were nudged in the right direction.[37] With the exception of the contracting ban at the very start of the period, the policies did not hold back their business activities, they just shaped the decisions that shipping companies made. And up until 1973, the shipping and economic policies in Norway encouraged shipping companies to make some very wise moves.[38]

---

[36] Vikøren (1967, 8–9).

[37] Here it is important to point out that we are not talking about conscious industrial policy, in the sense that the authorities had the ability to pick winners or forced shipowners to follow a pre-determined strategic pattern. Rather, the main priority of the policies was to fulfil other goals, in particular regarding employment, tax revenue and balance in Norway's external economic relations. The beneficial strategies became an accidental by-product of the regulations.

[38] Two good analyses of the Norwegian shipping policies in the 1950s and early 1960s are Svendsen (1957, 1964).

A case in point is the manner in which the policies influenced the expansion of the fleet. In his analysis of the effects of the tax regime in the interwar period, Eivind Merok has pointed out that the political economy of Norwegian shipping was "highly beneficial for entrepreneurs willing to make bold investments in larger, more expensive vessels, leveraging their investments heavily and betting on future asset prices to generate extraordinary profits."[39] This description fits the situation after the Second World War perfectly, as well.

The Norwegian shipping companies expanded at an impressive rate in the 1950s and 1960s, on average increasing their fleet by almost 7 per cent annually. At the international level, the situation may appear similar to that of the interwar period, when Norway gained market share at the expense of other countries. However, at that time, the Norwegian fleet grew while the world fleet stagnated or declined. In the first post-war decades, Norway gained substantial market share in a market that was growing rapidly.

## Sources of Capital

The Norwegian fleet expansion was based on large, expensive vessels and novel technological solutions. Two questions are particularly interesting in this respect. First, how was it possible to finance this extreme growth? Second, how were the investment decisions, including decisions about the level of total investment and the choice of investment objects, affected by the government's policies?

In general, Norwegian shipping companies had three main sources of capital; retained earnings, domestic equity and loans from domestic and foreign sources. All three were affected by the authorities' policies.

With regard to retained earnings, the authorities encouraged companies to keep profits within the company, rather than paying it out to the owners. From 1953 onwards, domestic regulations limited dividends to a

---

[39] See Merok (2011).

maximum of 5 per cent of the share capital.[40] This restriction had two aims. The first was to keep funds within the company in order to enable investments in new production capacity—in the case of shipping companies: new tonnage. Second, the limitation of the dividends was intended to "regulate the income" available to capitalists, a feature that was also seen in limitations on the salaries of management and the remuneration of company directors.[41] In the ever-present discourse between the market and the authorities—between the invisible hand and the visible hand—the Norwegian system was leaning quite heavily towards state intervention in the first post-war decades.

The design of the Norwegian tax regime also encouraged the reinvestment of profits. Indeed, the tax system almost made the limitations on dividends superfluous; the manner in which dividend payments were taxed—first with respect to the company, then with respect to the shareholder—made them almost prohibitive.[42] The shipping companies' tax rate was high—in the period 1946–1958 income and wealth taxes amounted to almost two-thirds of their taxable income. Furthermore, as the marginal tax rate on dividends could exceed 100 per cent for some individuals, it is evident that it would be better to reinvest profits in new tonnage that gave substantial tax deductions.[43]

The tax system led to a pro-cyclical pattern in the contracting of new-buildings—in years when the market was good, and profits were high, the pecuniary benefits of investing in ships, rather than paying tax, were particularly high. Finally, the double taxation implied that money remained in existing companies, rather than being made available for new investment projects. The tax system consequently had a preserving effect on the industrial structure—policy-induced path dependence. As a lot of money

---

[40] Søilen (1998, 111). It was possible to apply for a dispensation from this rule, and some companies were allowed to pay out more when the market was particularly beneficial. There was also a tendency for the rules to be interpreted more leniently towards the end of the 1950s; see Gjermoe (1968, 50–52; 1972, 49–54).

[41] From a speech by Minister of Finance, Erik Brofoss; Norway, Parliament, *Stortingstidende* (1945–1946), 233–246.

[42] Aars-Nicolaysen (1959, 27). By 1959 the maximum limit had increased to 6 per cent; see also Damman (1958).

[43] Seland (1960, 10–11); typically, the marginal tax rate for wealthy share owners would be in the region 60–80 per cent.

was invested in shipping, a lot of money would remain invested in shipping.

The second source that financed the fleet expansion was equity raised in the Norwegian market. It is very important to keep in mind that the 1950s and 1960 were a period with very limited possibilities for cross-border investment. Due to restrictions on capital movements—mainly introduced in order to keep exchange rates stable—Norwegian funds were to a large extent "locked in" within the country. Again, the "traditional Norwegian predicament"—that alternative investments did not provide particularly large profits—helped the shipping sector.[44]

The part ownership had managed to raise investment capital from quite a large proportion of society in the 19th century, partly as a result of the ability to contribute in kind, partly as a result of limited alternative placements. To which extent was this replicated in the second half of the 20th century—how common were ship investments?

In the early 1960s, the economist Eilif Gjermoe analysed the accounts of Norwegian shipping companies. Around 300 companies owned ships larger than 500 grt in 1963. The main source on limited liability companies, *Kierulfs Håndbok*, gave information on 225 such companies within shipping and whaling, of which 119 were listed on the stock exchanges. In total, the stock exchange listed companies had more than 50,000 shareholders and an ordinary share capital of marginally more than NOK300 million.[45] Only four of the companies had an ordinary share capital of more than NOK10 million, and another 14 had a share capital of between NOK5 million and NOK10 million.[46]

Despite the quite substantial number of shipping companies listed on the stock exchanges at this time, the role of the stock exchange as a source

---

[44] The basis for this low alternative return—limited resources and a thin market—continued to be relevant. However, in the post-war period energy-intensive manufacturing, utilizing Norwegian hydro power, became a profitable alternative that would compete with shipping for funds.

[45] There is some overlap between share owners. It is also likely that investments in the stock exchange-listed companies, which were relatively liquid and easy to buy and sell, was more widespread than for the remaining shipping companies.

[46] Gjermoe (1968, i–ii). Some shipping companies (*rederier*) were affiliated with more than one limited liability company (*aksjeselskap*), while others had different forms of incorporation. The companies included in the analysis on average made up more than one-third of the Norwegian fleet in the period 1946–1964; Gjermoe (1968, 11).

of capital was quite limited. In the period 1965–1970, for instance, only NOK6.4 million worth of new capital was raised for shipping companies at *Oslo Børs*. These emissions—one in 1966 and one in 1970—amounted to less than 1 per cent of fresh capital raised at the stock exchange. Typically, shipping company shares were "not recommended" as investment objects; their development in the 1960s had been "very meagre" and the liquidity of the shares was far from satisfactory.[47]

Finally, the Norwegian shipping companies had access to loan finance at home and abroad. In the first post-war decades the Norwegian authorities sanctioned a low interest rate policy in order to encourage investments. With such a policy, access to capital is not only determined by the borrowers' willingness to pay, but also by political preferences about how the queue for funding is organized and ordered. At the same time, there was an element of competition. In the words of Norway's Central Bank Director, Erik Brofoss, in 1959: "An important aspect of our investments is that 25–30% of the total gross investments are within shipping. It is evident that this industry is willing to pay a far higher interest rate than it would be possible to charge for instance agriculture."[48]

There were several domestic sources. In 1906 a consortium of four banks had established *Norsk Skibs Hypothekbank AS*, which aimed at providing first priority mortgages, but the terms were initially relatively strict. The war insurance arrangement introduced during the First World War was discontinued in 1923 with a NOK48 million profit. This was distributed to the Fund for Seamen (NOK20 million) and compensation for losses on maximum freights (NOK10 million), with most of the remainder going to establish a financing institution, *Norsk Skipshypothek AS*, in 1928, with headquarters at Minde, near Bergen.[49]

---

[47] Nyquist and Wiik (1972, 56–65). The 1 per cent of the new funds raised can be compared with the fact that shipping companies made up 45 per cent of the number of companies listed on *Oslo Børs* in 1971.

[48] Brofoss (1959, 32). This is the same Brofoss that was referred to earlier as Minister of Finance in the immediate post-war years. He also became the first head of Norway's Department of Trade and Shipping (1947–1954), a position he left to become Director of the Central Bank.

[49] Two smaller, differently organized, institutions also provided first priority mortgages. In 1916 *Norges Skipshypotek Forening* was established in Oslo, while *Redernes Skibskreditforening* was established by 14 shipowners on the South Coast in 1929; see Petersen (1979).

A new source of finance, characteristic of the manner in which Norwegian economic development in the first post-war decades was determined at the crossroads of public policy and private institutions, was *Låneinstituttet for skipsbyggeriene* [the Mortgage Institute for the Shipyards]. Established in 1959, it was owned by the leading banks, shipyards and the Norwegian Shipowners' Association, but was provided with a loan from the Ministry of Finance and also given government guarantees. *Låneinstituttet* would only fund vessels built at Norwegian shipyards, and was aimed at helping Norwegian shipbuilding, rather than shipowners.[50] However, given that Norwegian shipowners, partly as a result of the restrictions on their foreign activities, were by far the most important customers at Norwegian yards, there was a beneficial effect for shipping as well.

The Norwegian banks participated in the financing of Norwegian shipping through the cooperative institutions at home and abroad, but also on their own books. They cooperated to establish consortia in Zurich (1958) and Amsterdam (1968) to raise capital abroad for ship investment in Norway. Several banks had shipping as a specific strategic priority, and there were sometimes "revolving doors" between the banks, shipping companies and shipping institutions.[51] The sheer amount of capital involved, and a desire to spread risk, implied that loans to shipping were often organized as syndicates, with the participation of both domestic and foreign banks.

Foreign banks and, in particular, foreign yards and their associated financing institutions, were eager to lend money to Norwegian shipping companies. According to a contemporary report, the shipping sector was responsible for between two-thirds and four-fifths of the private capital imported into Norway in the period 1958–1967.[52] As such, the shipping companies were in a somewhat strange position, finance-wise.

---

[50] See Sejersted (1982) or Knutsen, Lange and Nordvik (1998) for an introduction to the banking side of this, and Platou and Stokke (1980), for a more general introduction. The cunning manner in which the Norwegian authorities managed to raise capital abroad—by depositing the country's currency reserves at terms that were below the market terms in banks that were willing to lend money for ship purchases—is discussed in Knutsen (1997).
[51] Sejersted (1982, 228).
[52] Boldt-Christmas, Fagerland Jacobsen and Tschoegl (2001, 82).

For much of the first two post-war decades, government regulations stipulated that shipowners had to fully finance abroad newbuildings that they ordered from foreign yards, so as not to deplete the limited Norwegian reserves of foreign exchange. This implied that shipowners borrowed money abroad to invest, while at the same time were forced to keep their deposits in Norwegian banks at low interest rates.[53] Although the demand for "currency neutrality" for ship investments implied that Norway formally flouted the rules of the Organization for European Economic Co-operation (OEEC), it was "understood and silently accepted" by the organization.[54]

The main reason for the shipping companies' easy access to financing abroad was expanding capacity in the shipbuilding industry. The Japanese shipyards were formidable challengers to the European hegemony, and the solution to ensuring orders was to provide easy—and often state-subsidized—financing. As a result of a race-to-the-bottom in shipbuilding subsidization, the Organization for Economic Co-operation and Development (OECD) in 1969 introduced an Understanding on Export Credits that stipulated the maximum indirect or direct support.[55] According to the terms of the agreement, interest rates could not be lower than 6 per cent, the repayment period could not be longer than eight years, and financing could not exceed 80 per cent. The aim of the agreement was to increase real competition in the shipbuilding industry and neutralize support measures that had a distorting effect on competition among shipyards and among shipbuilding nations. At the time, the OECD-countries were responsible for around 90 per cent of new deliveries.

The analysis above has shown the many ways in which the authorities influenced the financing of shipping—both the type of investment, as well as the level and timing of investment. A similar influence was seen in connection with labour regulations. The legal framework played a

---

[53] Seland (1959, 43). This regulation was in force from 1947 to 1952 for general cargo carriers, but lasted until the early 1960s for tankers and most other specialized vessels. See also Nossum (1960).
[54] Statistics Norway (1965, 393).
[55] The OECD was the successor of the OEEC, established by the OECD declaration in 1960, between the OEEC countries (in practice "Western Europe" minus Finland), the United States and Canada. Japan joined in 1964 and Finland five years later.

particularly important role for the choice of ship types. While there was relatively good access to capital, the labour situation was more difficult.

## Manning the Fleet

Immediately after the war the question of manning the ships became problematic.[56] Demand for workers onshore was substantial, and many of the seafarers that had kept the Norwegian merchant marine going during the war were still fighting their own battles, which made them ill-equipped to sail. The deficit of Norwegian seafarers could be supplemented by foreigners, but only up to a point, when Norwegian regulations would kick in. By 1967 around a quarter of the seamen on Norwegian ships were foreigners, mainly other Europeans that were employed on Norwegian terms.[57] However, in the longer term the solution to the recruitment problem became rationalization and economies of scale.

One of the most fascinating transformations in shipping in the first post-war decades is the manner in which seaborne trade went from being a labour-intensive activity to becoming a high-technology, capital-intensive business. The Norwegian ships did become more technologically advanced and more expensive throughout the century, but in the first half of the 20th century there were no revolutions in the manner in which cargoes were handled and ships were operated. The number of seafarers per ship was relatively constant (although the ships became bigger) before the Second World War.

After the war, the number of seafarers per ship increased, before levelling out around 1960. The average tonnage per seafarer increased only marginally. During the 1960s, however, there was a break in the development. The amount of tonnage per seafarer accelerated as the average size

---

[56] Egeland (1971, 23–24). Norwegian seafarers sailing on foreign ships were even urged to sign on Norwegian vessels for patriotic reasons; *Verdens Gang*, 190347, 6.

[57] Seafarers' lives and organization have been documented in a series of recent publications. See Olstad (2006) for the period up to 1960, Halvorsen (2007) for seafarers in general, Halvorsen (2010) for the question of foreigners, and Koren (2017) for an overview of the welfare aspect. See also Tenold (2015b) for a broad overview, as well as the discussion of the "uncounted" foreigners in Chap. 8.

of the Norwegian ships increased enormously. From the middle of the 1960s there was also a decline in the number of seafarers per ship—even though the ships got bigger—as rationalizing measures were introduced. This trend towards economies of scale was much stronger in Norway than in other countries.

In 1955 the average Norwegian ship was marginally smaller than the average ship in the world fleet—the difference was 0.4 per cent. Five years later, the average Norwegian ship was 15 per cent larger than the average ship in the world fleet, by 1965 the difference was 49 per cent and by 1970 it was 59 per cent. At the peak, in the middle of the 1970s, the average Norwegian ship was more than 80 per cent larger than the average ship in the world fleet.[58]

This focus on large ships can be explained by the high and increasing labour costs. There were three main reasons that Norwegian labour costs increased more than those in other countries after the Second World War. The first is an above-average increase in Norwegian wage levels, as the Norwegian economy developed. The second is the relatively high manning requirements—the cabin conditions, the turn system and restrictions on working hours contributed to pushing up costs. In 1951 new manning regulations were introduced, which were particularly strict for smaller ships. The small Bergen tanker *Rogn* illustrates the effects of the law. The compulsory manning of the ship increased from 15 to 21 when the new regulations entered into force—a problem, given that the ship only had berths for 17 people. The vessel was sold to Germany, where it could be operated with a crew of 14.[59]

The third reason was that social costs were higher than in many of the competing countries. Gradually, Norwegian seafarers managed to win rights that made their working lives more agreeable, but at the same time they became less attractive from a competition point of view. In 1939 seafarers were given partial compensation for the cost of returning to Norway after three years at sea—a moot point, given that the war made such a return impossible or undesirable. A new Seaman's Act in 1953

---

[58] Calculated on the basis of gross tonnage data from *Lloyd's Statistical Tables 1980*, Table 17, based on all vessels larger than 100 gross tons. Given the properties of the Norwegian fleet, a comparison based on dead weight tonnage would give an even larger increase in the size difference.
[59] Thowsen and Tenold (2006, 256–265).

granted a paid-for return to Norway after 24 months of service.[60] This was reduced to 18 months five years later, to 12 months in the middle of the 1960s, nine months in 1971 and six months in 1973.[61] Given that the Norwegian fleet still operated all over the world, the cost of sending home seafarers was substantial.

Norwegian shipping companies acted rationally and according to economic theory. The relative price of the factors of production in Norway—the fact that capital was relatively cheap and accessible, and labour relatively expensive—should be reflected in investment behaviour. To remain competitive, shipping companies should invest in ships that used the relatively inexpensive factor (capital) intensively, and try to avoid using the expensive factor (labour). The solution—for most—was large and expensive ships.

## Survival of the Fittest

Economies of scale at the ship level—large vessels with limited need for seafarers—enabled the Norwegian shipping industry to compete internationally. However, if we take a closer look at the fabric of the Norwegian shipping industry, we see that not all shipping companies had the same ability to compete. In particular, there was a tendency for the larger shipping companies to grow faster. The proportion of the fleet owned by the 30 largest shipping companies increased from slightly more than 50 per cent in 1950, to almost 60 per cent by 1970.[62] It is evident that many smaller shipping companies were unable to stay in business.

In 1960 a total of 174 Norwegian shipping companies owned vessels larger than 5000 grt, spread across 26 different home ports. During the

---

[60] The 1953 Act also stated that boys had to be at least 15 years old and girls at least 20 years old to be lawfully employed onboard.

[61] The 1939 arrangement was financed one-third each by the authorities, the shipping companies and the seafarers, and came into force after three years, or two years for ships trading in European waters. The service time could be extended by two to three months if the ship would be approaching ports that were closer to home and from which the cost of returning the seafarer would be significantly lower. The 1953 Act and subsequent improvements stipulated that the shipping company and the authorities would split the bill fifty-fifty. From 1975 the regulation also included Norwegians living abroad.

[62] Bakka (2017, 121).

"good times" in the 1960s and early 1970s more than half of the companies that only owned one or two ships disappeared. However, they tended to be replaced by newly established enterprises—by 1973 there had been a net reduction of only three companies.[63]

In comparison, only 11 per cent of the companies that owned from three to nine ships disappeared, and there were no exits at all among the companies that owned more than 10 ships.[64] This suggests that the smaller shipping companies had a clear handicap during the boom period. One explanation for this handicap might be that in a period of rapid technological change, where it was necessary to invest in more expensive ships to remain competitive, smaller companies had insufficient funds to replace their ageing capital. Consequently, they became victims of the improved productivity of their competitors.

Some smaller shipping companies chose cooperation as a survival strategy. One possibility—for companies that could not buy a large and expensive vessel on their own—was to enter into partnerships with other owners, for instance by providing part of the equity for new bulk ship investments. Another possibility was to piggyback on the companies that chose a specialization strategy. Within these segments, the economies of scale were often related to the size of the fleet, rather than the size of the ship.[65]

The specialized segments were particularly well-suited for investments by shipping companies that were unable to keep up with the rapidly escalating newbuilding prices in the bulk market. Very often one of the "larger" shipping companies would be in the driving seat, with the knowledge and the strength needed to be competitive. However, there would sometimes be a symbiotic relationship with smaller shipping companies. An example from the chemical parcel tanker market illustrates this mechanism.

---

[63] The data set used for this calculation is presented in Tenold and Aarbu (2011), where the reinvestment problems that smaller shipping companies faced are analysed in detail.

[64] The rate of the decline for the smallest companies was relatively uniform throughout the period, with a small acceleration after 1970. The medium-sized companies all disappeared in the second half of the 1960s and the first part of the 1970s.

[65] In other words, within specialized segments, it was beneficial to have a fleet of many smaller ships in order to reap the benefits of economies of scale, as one large ship would be incompatible with the trade pattern and parcel sizes. In the bulk segments, the economies of scale were primarily at the ship level; a large ship was more beneficial than many small ships.

The transport of chemicals was a Norwegian speciality, and in the early 1970s the three dominant groups in this market all had their roots in Norway; Stolt-Nielsen, Odfjell and Anco. By 1973 the three companies owned almost 80 per cent of the tonnage in the market for parcel tankers larger than 6000 dwt.[66] The substantial market share that the Bergen company Odfjell had acquired was partly based on its pool partnership with one of Bergen's largest companies, Westfal-Larsen & Co. However, there was an element of segmentation within the chemical tanker market, and Odfjell also participated with a number of smaller shipping companies in the operation of smaller chemical tankers.

Such cooperation enabled Odfjell to expand—and reap the benefits of a diversified and larger fleet—without committing too much of its own resources. The company could offer an improved service to its customers, and there were also commissions involved from the chartering of the ships. In the period 1965–1973, Odfjell bought 10 vessels together with smaller shipping companies, and only one of these companies owned any tonnage when they entered the partnership. The others had all disposed of their last vessels shortly before. One reason for their cooperation with Odfjell might be nostalgia, a desire to maintain their link to shipping. Another reason could be the aforementioned beneficial tax advantages of investing in new tonnage.[67]

## The Heyday of Norwegian Shipping

The TV series *Hvor seiler vi?*, with its unvarnished presentation of Norwegian sailors abroad, created a very heated debate in Norway. Many people were offended by the suggestion that sailors in foreign ports had an above-average interest in alcoholic drinks and the local nightlife. A future Prime Minister, Jan Peder Syse, asked questions about the programme in Parliament, urging the national broadcaster to correct the "fake picture" that had been presented.[68] A radio debate about *Hvor seiler*

---

[66] Thowsen and Tenold (2006, 301); see also Murphy and Tenold (2008) for a more concise introduction to the market.
[67] Thowsen and Tenold (2006, 335–350).
[68] Norway, Parliament, *Forhandlinger i Stortinget nr. 207*, 270170, 1649–1651. Syse, who had previously worked for the shipping company Wilh. Wilhelmsen, referred to the "dismay and sorrow" that the programme had brought to many homes.

*vi?* and its portrayal of Norwegian seafarers pushed "a suite for cello and piano and a programme on archaeology and ghosts at Østre Toten" off the broadcasting schedule on the country's only radio channel.[69]

The TV series, and a subsequent book by a radical publisher, had a clear political agenda. The interviewer, Gunnar Bull-Gundersen, had five years earlier initiated a campaign that raised the minimum age for rookie sailors from 15 to 16 years. In *Hvor seiler vi?* he presented seafarers' lives in a manner that was meant to stir debate: "If you don't remember the programmes, the subsequent debate in the newspapers is not easy to forget."[70]

The widespread debate illustrates the central role that shipping played in the Norwegian economy and society. In 1960 sailors were based in all but two of the 734 municipalities in Norway—so Bull-Gundersen managed to stir up practically the whole country.[71] And shipping was extremely important. According to the most comprehensive report on the Norwegian economy, published by Statistics Norway in 1965, "shipping plays the same role [in Norway] as large-scale manufacturing does in other countries – it is export-oriented, demands very much capital and it attracts labour and initiatives that in other countries and in different circumstances perhaps would have gone towards manufacturing."[72]

In 1965 this was a good description of the Norwegian economy. Ten years later, the picture was changing. Twenty years later, Norwegian shipping had been dethroned from its hegemonic position.

## Bibliography

P.F. Alderton (1973) *Sea Transport. Operation and Economics* (London/Sunderland: Thomas Reed Publications Ltd.)

L. Allen (1954) *A meteorologic and oceanographic analysis of the passage of the* SS Warrior (Washington, DC: National Academy of Sciences – National Research Council)

---

[69] *Arbeiderbladet*, 221269, 18.
[70] *Bok og Bibliotek*, 1970, Vol. 37, NO. 4/5, 294.
[71] Brun (1960, 10).
[72] Statistics Norway (1965, 47–48).

D. Bakka (2008) *Linjer rundt Jorden – Historien om norsk linjefart* (Bergen: Seagull Publishing)
D. Bakka (2017) *Nasjonens ære – Norsk rederinæring mellom marked og politikk* (Bergen: Bodoni Forlag)
M. Boldt-Christmas, S. Fagerland Jacobsen & A.E. Tschoegl (2001) 'The International Expansion of the Norwegian Banks', *Business History*, 43:3, 79–104
E. Brofoss (1959) 'Pengepolitisk lovgivning og frivillig samarbeid med kredittinstitusjonene', *Sosialøkonomen*, 13:1–2: 1, 30–33
F. Brun (1960) 'Handelsflåten og beskjeftigelsen', *Sosialøkonomen*, 14:5, 9–10
C. Cooper (2016) 'The Ghost Ships of Hanjin and Why They're Spoiling Christmas', *Bloomberg*, 9 September 2016
P. Dahl (1970) *Skipsfart og Skipsbygning. Perspektivanalyse utarbeidet på vegne av NTNF's Komite for Skipsteknisk Forskning* (Oslo: Norges Teknisk-Naturvitenskaplige Forskningsråd)
A. Damman (1958) *Investeringspolitikk i Norge etter krigen* (Oslo: Næringsøkonomisk Forskningsinstitutt)
J. Devanney (2006) *The Tankship Tromedy. The Impending Disasters in Tankers*, Second Edition (Tavernier: CTX Press)
A. Donovan (1999) 'Longshoremen and Mechanization', *Journal for Maritime Research*, 1:1, 66–75
L. Dunn (1956) *The World's Tankers* (London: Adlard Coles Limited)
W.P. Dunphy (1979) 'Whalebacks,' *The Mariner's Mirror*, 65:4, 351–355
J.O. Egeland (1971) *Vi skal videre: Norsk skipsfart etter den annen verdenskrig, perioden 1945–1970* (Oslo: H. Aschehoug & Co.)
A.M. Fon (1995a) 'En stormakt i tørrbulk. En økonomisk-historisk analyse av norsk tørrbulkfart 1950–1973', *PhD-thesis* (Bergen: Norges Handelshøyskole)
A.M. Fon (1995b) 'Two Markets or One? – An Historical Study of Price. Behaviour in the Tanker and Dry Bulk Shipping Markets, 1955–1973', *International Journal of Maritime History*, 7:2, 115–134
E. Gjermoe (1968) *Norske skipsaksjeselskaper etter krigen* (Bergen: Skipsfartsøkonomisk Institutt)
E. Gjermoe (1972) *Inntekten m.v. i norske skipsaksjeselskaper* (Bergen: Skipsfartsøkonomisk Institutt)
G.B. Gundersen (1970) *Hvor seiler vi?* (Oslo: Pax Forlag)
T. Halvorsen (2007) *Vi seiler for velstand og lykke* (Oslo: Pax)
T. Halvorsen (2010) 'Vi var "degos, svartinger eller skjevøyde". Utlendinger i den norske handelsflåten 1950–75', *Arbeiderhistorie*, 24, 203–223

L. Johnman & H. Murphy (1998) 'The Norwegian Market for British Shipbuilding, 1945–1967', *Scandinavian Economic History Review*, XLVI, No. 2, 55–78

Y. Kaukiainen (2006) 'Journey Costs, Terminal Costs and Ocean Tramp Freights: How the Price of Distance Declined from the 1870s to the 2000s', *International Journal of Maritime History*, 18:2, 26–43

Y. Kaukiainen (2012) 'The Advantages of Water Carriage: Scale Economies and Shipping Technology, c. 1870–2000', in G. Harlaftis, S. Tenold & J.M. Valdaliso (2012) *The World's Key Industry; History and Economics of International Shipping* (Basingstoke: Palgrave Macmillan)

R.D. Knowles (2006) 'Transport shaping space: differential collapse in time–space', *Journal of Transport Geography*, 14, 407–425

S. Knutsen (1997) 'Staten og norsk skipsfinansiering 1955–1975', in B.L. Basberg, H.W. Nordvik & G. Stang (eds) *det lange løp. Essays i økonomisk historie tilegnet Fritz Hodne* (Bergen: Fagbokforlaget)

S. Knutsen, E. Lange & H.W. Nordvik (1998) *Mellom næringsliv og politikk. Kredittkassen i vekst og kriser, 1918–1998* (Oslo: Universitetsforlaget)

E. Koren (2017) 'Sjøfolk og velferdsstaten', *Arbeiderhistorie*, 31, 107–123

M. Levinson (2006a) 'Container Shipping and the Decline of New York, 1955–1975', *Business History Review*, 80, 49–80

M. Levinson (2006b) *The Box: How the Shipping Container Made the World Smaller and the World Economy Bigger* (Princeton: Princeton University Press)

H. Mayer (1973) 'Some Aspects of Technological Change in Maritime Transportation', *Economic Geography*, 49:2, 145–155

E. Merok (2011) 'After the Boom: The Political Economy of Shipping in Norway in the Interwar Period,' in L.R. Fischer & E. Lange (eds) *New directions in Norwegian maritime history* (St. Johns: IMEHA) 125–150

H. Murphy (2013) '"No Longer Competitive with Continental Shipbuilders": British Shipbuilding and International Competition, 1930–1960', *International Journal of Maritime History*, 25:2, 35–60

H. Murphy & S. Tenold (2008) 'Strategies, market concentration and hegemony in chemical parcel tanker shipping, 1960–1985', *Business History*, 51:3, 291–309

National Research Council (1956) *Longshore Safety Survey – A Survey of Occupational Hazards In the Stevedore Industry* (Washington, DC: National Academy of Sciences – National Research Council)

E. Nyquist & W.E. Wiik (1972) *Kapitalplassering* (Oslo: Johan Grundt Tanum Forlag)

F. Olstad (2006) *Vår skjebne i vår hand* (Oslo: Pax Forlag)

K. Petersen (1979) *Skipsfinansiering i medgang og motgang – Redernes Skibskreditforening, 1929–1979* (Kristiansand: Redernes Skibskreditforening)

F. Platou & B. Stokke (1980) *Skip, Verksted og Finansiering – En studie av A/S Låneinstituttet for skipsbyggeriene* (Oslo: Sjørettsfondet)

R.T. Poulsen (2007) 'Liner shipping and technological innovation: Ostasiat and the container revolution, 1963–75', *Scandinavian Economic History Review*, 55:2, 83–100

R.T Poulsen (2010) 'The Emergence of New Organisational Forms in Liner Shipping: Swedish liner shipping and international consortia, 1960–75', *Journal of Transport History*, 31:1, 69–88

G. Sager & E.W. Panting (1990) *Maritime Capital. The Shipping Industry in Atlantic Canada, 1820–1914* (Montreal & Kingston: McGill-Queens University Press)

F. Sejersted (ed) (1982) *En storbank i blandingsøkonomien. Den norske Credibank 1957–1982* (Oslo: Gyldendal Norsk Forlag)

J. Seland (1959) 'Rundebords-konferanseinnlegg', *Sosialøkonomen*, 13:1–2, 43–48

J. Seland (1960) 'Enkelte finansierings- og skatteproblemer i skipsfartsnæringen', *Sosialøkonomen*, 14:5, 11–12

Statistics Norway (1965) *Norges økonomi etter krigen* (Oslo: Statistisk Sentralbyrå)

M. Stopford (2009) *Maritime Economics*, third edition (London: Routledge)

A.S. Svendsen (1957) *Skipsfartspolitikken i Norge etter krigen* (Bergen: Institute for Shipping Research)

A.S. Svendsen (1964) *Skipsfartspolitikken i Norge etter krigen*, Second updated edition (Bergen: Institute for Shipping Research)

E. Søilen (1998) 'Fra frischianisme til keneysianisme? En studie av norsk økonomisk politikk i lys av økonomisk teori', *PhD-thesis* (Bergen: Norges Handelshøyskole)

P. Temin (1997) 'The Golden Age of European Growth: a review essay', *European Review of Economic History*, Vol. 1, No. 1, 127–149

S. Tenold (2015a) *Geared for Growth. Kristian Gerhard Jebsen and His Shipping Companies* (Bergen: Bodoni Forlag)

S. Tenold (2015b) 'Globalisation and maritime labour in Norway after World War II', *The International Journal of Maritime History*, 27:4, 774–792

S. Tenold & K.O. Aarbu (2011) 'Little Man, What Now? Company Deaths in Norwegian Shipping, 1960–1980', in L.R. Fischer & E. Lange (eds) *New directions in Norwegian maritime history* (St. Johns: IMEHA) 233–252

A. Thowsen & S. Tenold (2006) *Odfjell – The history of a shipping company* (Bergen: Odfjell ASA)

H. Van der Wee (1986) *Prosperity and Upheaval: The World Economy, 1945–1980* (London: Viking)
S. Vanfraechem (2012) 'Why they are tall and we are small! Competition between Antwerp and Rotterdam in the twentieth century', in G. Harlaftis, S. Tenold & J.M. Valdaliso (2012) *The World's Key Industry; History and Economics of International Shipping* (Basingstoke: Palgrave Macmillan)
E. Vea, J. Schreiner & J. Seland (1960) *Den Norske Amerikalinje 1910–1960* (Oslo: Grøndahl & Søn)
A. Vigarié (1999) 'From Break-bulk to Containers: The Transformation of General Cargo Handling and Trade,' *GeoJournal*, 48:1, 3–7
D. Vikøren (1967) 'Merchant Marine Policy of Norway', *manuscript* (Oslo: Norwegian Shipowners' Association)
D.M. Williams (1968) 'Bulk carriers and timber imports: the British North-American trade and the shipping boom of 1824–25', *Mariner's Mirror*, 54:4, 373–382
R.T. Young (1971) 'New ships need new ports', *Tidjschrift voor vervoerswetenschap*, 7:1, 19–24
N. Aars-Nicolaysen (1959) 'Bedriftslivets finansieringsproblemer', *Sosialøkonomen*, No. 1–2, 1959, 24–29

**Open Access**  This chapter is licensed under the terms of the Creative Commons Attribution-NonCommercial-NoDerivatives 4.0 International License (http://creativecommons.org/licenses/by-nc-nd/4.0/), which permits any noncommercial use, sharing, distribution and reproduction in any medium or format, as long as you give appropriate credit to the original author(s) and the source, provide a link to the Creative Commons license and indicate if you modified the licensed material. You do not have permission under this license to share adapted material derived from this chapter or parts of it.

The images or other third party material in this chapter are included in the chapter's Creative Commons license, unless indicated otherwise in a credit line to the material. If material is not included in the chapter's Creative Commons license and your intended use is not permitted by statutory regulation or exceeds the permitted use, you will need to obtain permission directly from the copyright holder.

# 7

# The Shipping Crisis

The photograph of "The King taking the tram" has an iconic position in Norway and is important for the population's self-understanding: the Norwegian monarch, King Olav, sitting relaxed and undisturbed on public transport. The King is on his way to a ski trip on the outskirts of Oslo. Presenting an image of Norway as a nation of egalitarians, where even the royal family is down-to-earth, the photo also pays homage to its self-perception as a nation of ski fanatics and outdoor adventurers. The picture was taken a week before Christmas Eve in 1973, when petrol rationing had led to a ban on the use of private cars at weekends. Even the King loyally respected the regulation, which was a short-term response to the upheaval in the oil market, following the Yom Kippur War.[1]

The rationing of petrol reflected the dominant position of oil in the world's energy consumption. An ever-thirstier world economy had come to rely on the Middle East to produce large amounts of low-cost energy. When some of the taps were turned off, the steady stream of cheap oil that had fuelled the post-war Golden Age was turned into a trickle of expensive energy. The price increase had dramatic effects for countries that produced oil (winners) and countries that imported oil

---

[1] Andersen (1993, 3).

(losers), as well as for the industries that used oil (just about every single one). Moreover, the oil market turmoil had a massive effect on the shipping companies that transported oil. A large number of these companies were Norwegian, and now their market collapsed more or less overnight.

## From the Golden Age to Stagnation

There is no doubt that the 1973 oil crisis and the concomitant energy shortage was a watershed in the development of post-war capitalism. As Marc Levinson has pointed out in a recent book, "an economic boom of extraordinary proportions" was replaced by "job loss, slower wage growth, and pockets of seemingly intractable unemployment" in most of the western world.[2] The Golden Age had been characterized by extremely low unemployment and controlled inflation in all Western European countries. Now a new phenomenon, stagflation—high inflation and unemployment, coupled with low economic growth—presented businesses and politicians with new dilemmas. Income and productivity growth was more sluggish than before. Measures intended to reduce inflation were expected to push up unemployment, and vice versa.

Very specific circumstances had created the Golden Age, something that was not obvious at the time. Instead, the sustained production and productivity growth of the 1950s and 1960s had given a renewed belief in the ability to engineer economic development and improve living standards. The only way was up. Consequently, in 1974 and 1975 it was not evident that the declining economic growth rates were permanent. Few observers and decision-makers realized that the world economy was going through a structural development break, rather than just another cyclical downturn, another temporary lull in growth. With the beautiful benefit of hindsight, it is very clear that the international economy was experiencing a negative structural shift, and it was a dramatic one.

---

[2] Levinson (2016, 3 and 8).

Table 7.1 The break in development; output growth, inflation and unemployment, 1965–1985

|  | 1965–1973 | 1974–1979 | 1980–1985 |
|---|---|---|---|
| Real output growth (%) | 4.9 | 2.8 | 2.1 |
| Inflation (%) | 5.1 | 9.0 | 7.7 |
| Unemployment (%) | 3.1* | 4.9* | 6.9* |

Source: OECD (1977, 70; 1999, 45). Confer footnote

As Table 7.1 shows, there was a clear break in economic development after 1973.[3] Economic indicators moved in the wrong direction. Politicians were confused and resorted to a long list of unsuccessful measures. Countries variously introduced import restrictions, deflationary budgeting, interest rate increases, higher value-added taxes, higher taxes in general, export promotion policies, expansive countercyclical policies, contractive austerity programmes, and so on. European governments used all the arrows in their economic policy quiver. They aimed in all directions. They hardly hit anything.

The high economic growth of the Golden Age was replaced by much more sober growth rates. Norway was no exception to the shift, but in the first post-war decades Norway's growth rates had been very much "middle-of-the-road" in a European perspective. Some even referred to "the Norwegian paradox"—despite very high investments, Gross Domestic Product (GDP) growth was decidedly average.[4] However, the country's emergence as an exporter of petroleum in the 1970s implied a softer landing than in most other countries. As Fig. 7.1 illustrates, Norwegian growth rates went from being below the Western European and world averages 1950–1973, to above these averages in the period 1973–2001.[5] While economic growth in Western Europe was more than halved between these two periods, the decline in Norwegian growth rates was around 20 per cent.

---

[3] Calculated by the author based on OECD (1977, 70; 1999, 45). Unemployment figures refer to 1960–1973, 1974–1979 and 1980–1989, respectively, and only refer to the United States, Japan, Germany, France, Italy, the UK and Canada.

[4] Seland (1994, 153).

[5] Figure 7.1: Calculated on the basis of data from Maddison (2003). The charts refer to compound average growth of GDP, measured in fixed prices and based on purchasing power parity (PPP)—see the source for details. The 12 countries included in the category "Western Europe" are Austria, Belgium, Denmark, Finland, France, Germany, Italy, the Netherlands, Norway, Sweden, Switzerland and the UK.

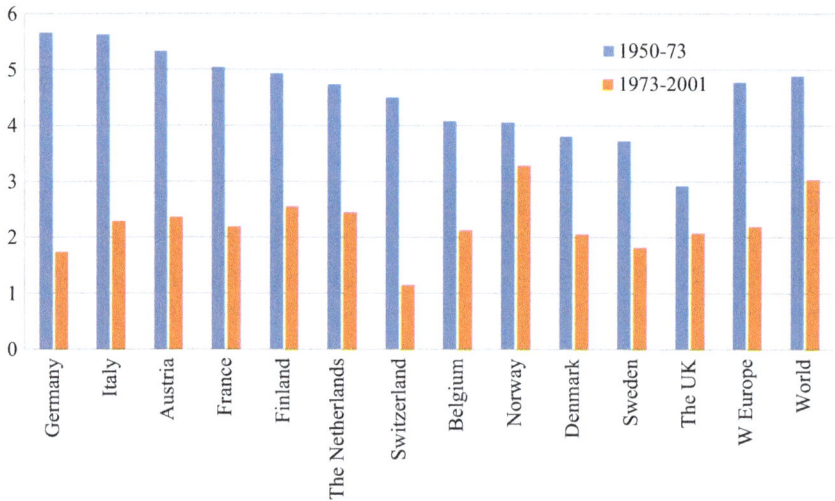

**Fig. 7.1** Average economic growth, based on PPP-adjusted GDP, 1950–73 and 1973–2001. (Source: Maddison (2003), confer footnote)

In the long term the oil price increase had a beneficial effect on the Norwegian economy, paving the way for the country's advance towards the top of the list of the world's wealthiest countries. For the Norwegian shipping sector, however, the effect was disastrous. As a result of the price hike, shipping was dethroned as the leading export sector, while the challenger—offshore oil production—became more powerful than it would otherwise have been.

## The Shipping Crisis

From the middle of the 1970s to the middle of the 1980s, the shipping sector went through a crisis that was longer, deeper and more dramatic than any other previous downturn.[6] The tonnage surplus in the early 1920s was higher, but a profitable market returned relatively quickly, and

---

[6] In Tenold (2000, 332–333) it is suggested that it might be useful to consider the problems as two distinct, but related, crises. The first one was caused by demand stagnation and tonnage growth, the second one by an absolute reduction of tanker demand that aggravated the situation even further. Such a distinction makes sense in a long and detailed analysis of the problems of the 1970s and 1980s, but does not add much to our broader presentation.

the crisis therefore did not have any fundamental long-term effects. The problems during and after the Great Depression lasted longer than those in the 1920s, and the shipping sector had to cope with five years of high lay-up rates. Still, this was a shorter downturn than the one in the 1970s and 1980s. Moreover, the overcapacity during the 1930s was smaller, both in absolute and relative terms.

In the short term, the shipping crisis was characterized by falling freight rates, increasing lay-up rates and vanishing shipping company profits. Freight rates in the tanker market declined almost instantaneously, with rates in the spot market for large tankers falling by more than 75 per cent from October to December 1973.[7] Relatively soon, it became difficult to find employment even at the new depressed rate level—the oil companies reserved the cargoes for their own ships and those they had taken on long-term charters. By the beginning of 1976 more than 100 million dead weight tons (dwt) of tanker tonnage—almost 20 per cent of the fleet—had been laid up. The negative operating results—in many instances coming on top of high financial burdens—seriously depleted the shipping companies' funds.

In the longer term, the crisis led to fundamental changes in vessel ownership and operation, and had severe ramifications for the shipbuilding industry as well. Shipping companies went bankrupt, vessels were reflagged to low-cost registries and the leading shipping nations were forced to change their maritime policies. Some ships were taken over by the creditors, who appointed management companies to oversee their operation. The crisis also sounded the death knell for large-scale shipbuilding in most of Western Europe. After a period of heavy subsidization, European governments realized that it would be impossible to compete with Asian yards in the high-volume segment of the shipbuilding business. Shipyards—often situated in central city locations—became offices, shopping centres, hotels or exclusive apartments.[8]

---

[7] The spot market is the most inelastic part of the shipping market, where ships are hired on a voyage-by-voyage basis. In periods of tonnage shortage, the sky is the limit. Calculated on the basis of the rate from the Persian Gulf to the UK/Continent, monthly figures, from Fearnley & Egers Chartering Co., *Review 1973*, 23.
[8] See Todd (1981, 2011) and Bruno and Tenold (2011). In Chap. 4 we looked at the success of Sweden and Denmark in interwar shipbuilding. When the market collapsed, the trajectory of shipbuilding in these two countries was very different; see Stråth (1987) (for Sweden) and Poulsen and Sornn-Friese (2011), Poulsen (2013) and Olesen (2013) (for Denmark).

Shipowners, desperate to get at least some income, accepted part cargoes and reduced the speed of their ships in order to lower fuel costs. Some ships were used for storage of oil and other cargoes, while a substantial part of the fleet was laid up without any employment at all. These measures soaked up part of the oversupply. In the Norwegian fjords and the bays and inlets of Greece, the large number of mothballed ships made the crisis in the sector evident even for the non-specialists.[9] The tanker overcapacity peaked at more than 100 per cent in the spring of 1983. At that time, the basic demand was around 137 million dwt, while the fleet of tanker and combination carriers amounted to more than 300 million dwt. In other words, there were two ships for every cargo that needed transport.[10] How did the market end up with such an imbalance?

The simple answer to that question is that there was an enormous discrepancy between the expected and the actual development. The oil price increase signalled the end of the era of cheap energy, and consumers and businesses adapted accordingly. The laws of supply and demand worked. When the oil price shot up, demand was reduced. Oil consumption in the Organization for Economic Cooperation and Development (OECD) countries fell by almost 15 per cent, from 37.4 million barrels daily in 1973 to 32.2 million barrels per day in 1982. In 1973, the US Treasury expected that the country's oil consumption in 1980 would amount to around 25 million barrels daily—the actual consumption was 16.5 million. Three years later the actual US imports of oil were less than half of what had been expected a decade earlier.[11]

The oil price increase paved the way for a shock in the tanker market that exceeded the expectations of even the gloomiest pessimists. The consumption decline was in itself problematic. To make matters worse, the demand for tanker transport fell over and above this, in a period where there were expectations of growth. A 1970 report from the Norwegian

---

[9] At one point in the early 1980s, more than 400 ships were laid up in Eleusis Bay, a sheltered basin relatively close to the Greek shipping centre, Piraeus.

[10] Jenkins, Stopford and Tyler (1993), Tables III.12–III.25. Around a quarter of the surplus was neutralized by the acceptance of part cargoes, ships used for storage and waiting time in ports. More than 30 million dwt of tanker tonnage was laid up, while the rest of the surplus was absorbed by slow-steaming ships.

[11] Farrell (1985, 381), Ahrari (1986, 37) and British Petroleum (1984, 7–8 and 16).

Research Council presented a projection of expected tonnage demand in the future. Their base scenario was that a tanker fleet of 450 million dwt would be needed in 1985, with a low projection of 395 million dwt and a high projection of 505 million dwt.[12] In reality, even the low-case scenario suggested three times more tonnage than what was actually needed.

Given the enormity and unpredictability of the change—the term "oil shock" is used for a reason—it is easier to understand why the projections were so spectacularly wrong. We have to remember that the demand for oil transport had grown practically every single peacetime year for more than a century. Over the last 10 years before 1974, the annual demand increase had been around 17 per cent. What would be a likely "worst-case" scenario for development over the next decade? Even the Norwegian report's "worst-case" prediction—where growth fell from 17 to 6.5 per cent annually—turned out to be way too optimistic.

Within oil and shipping, practically everybody believed that the growth would continue. Anyone forecasting the actual development—a reduction in demand of almost 60 per cent from 1974 to 1985—would undoubtedly have been ridiculed and laughed out of the boardroom. Figure 7.2 illustrates the dramatic shift in the development of tanker demand. In particular, the shift in the trend between the periods 1962–1973 and 1974–1985 is spectacular.[13] The demand for tanker transport multiplied by a factor of more than 5.5 in the first of these periods. In the second, the initial stagnation was followed by a strong drop.

Even though demand development, as seen in Fig. 7.2, is extremely dramatic, it tells only half the story. Due to the strong increase in demand before the oil price increase, and periodic shortages of tanker tonnage that had given some spectacular spikes in the rate level, tanker owners had large amounts of newbuildings on order when the demand collapsed. There was clearly no need for these ships when they were delivered—they only added to the already huge amount of superfluous tonnage.

---

[12] Dahl (1970, 18). The source of the chart showing the estimated tonnage demand in the report from the Norwegian Research Council is simply listed as *Det norske Veritas*. Clearly, the researchers were too busy to predict the future to be interested in proper referencing.

[13] Figure 7.2: Calculated on the basis of the demand for the transport of crude oil in Fearnley & Egers Chartering Co., *Review*, various issues, Table 2.

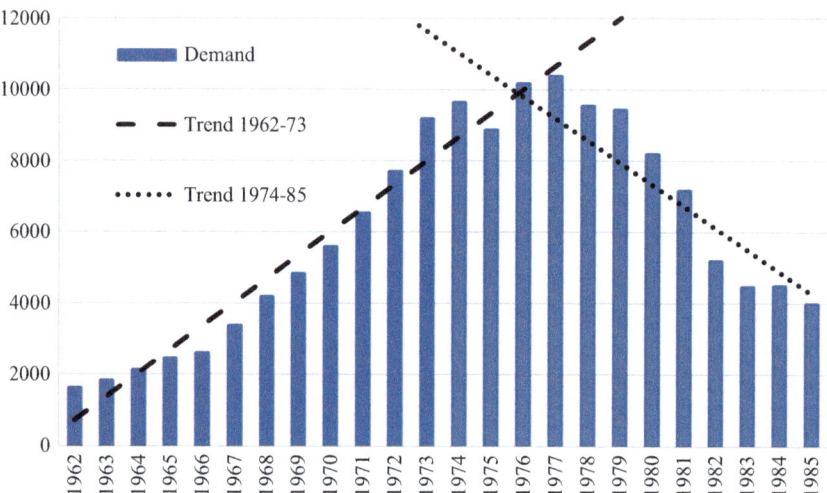

**Fig. 7.2** Seaborne crude oil transport demand, trillion ton-miles, 1962–1973 and 1974–1985. (Source: Authors' calculations based on Fearnley & Eger's *Review*; confer footnote)

Figure 7.3 is an index showing the large and growing imbalance between tanker demand and supply during the crisis.[14] It is evident that the initial problems, from 1973 to 1978, were caused by new deliveries of ships in a stagnating market. In the first half of the 1980s, there was a strong reduction of the demand for tanker transport, which even a gradual pruning of the fleet was unable to neutralize. By the middle of the decade, the demand for tanker transports had fully relapsed, matching the level it had held in 1967, which was more than 20 per cent lower than demand in 1970. The main problem was that there was more than twice as much tanker capacity to do the job.

The problems from the tanker market spilled over to other shipping segments. The dry bulk market had initially developed positively—as oil became more expensive, there was a growth in the transport of relatively low-cost coal. However, the dry bulk market was soon flooded with combination carriers that were unable to find profitable employment within oil

---

[14] Figure 7.3: Calculated on the basis of the demand for the transport of crude oil and oil products measured in ton-miles, as well as the fleet of tankers measured in dead weight tons, in Fearnley & Egers Chartering Co., *Review*, various issues, Tables 2 and 3.

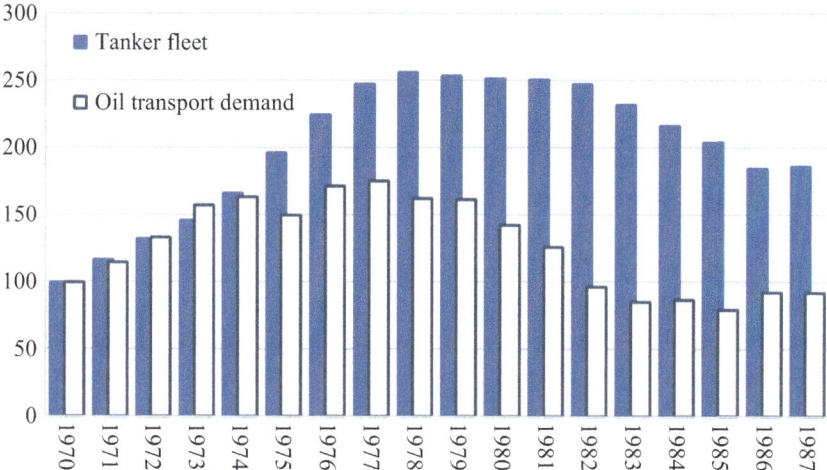

**Fig. 7.3** Supply and demand in the tanker market (1970 = 100), 1970–1987. (Source: Authors' calculations based on Fearnley & Eger's *Review*; confer footnote)

transport. As the 1970s progressed, the conversion of tanker newbuilding orders to other types of vessels added to the problems in other segments. Moreover, the shipbuilding countries' subsidization of newbuildings—selling ships below construction cost in order to maintain activity in the shipyards—contributed to the contagion of the crisis. By the late 1970s not a single segment of the shipping market was untouched by the crisis. However, the problems were particularly strong in the tanker sector—the shipping segment that had been something of a Norwegian specialty for almost half a century.

## The Tables Turned: Too Many Tankers

According to an old Norwegian proverb, "The sea gives and the sea takes." This was what happened in the 1970s. When the international oil cartel, the Organization of Petroleum Exporting Countries (OPEC), raised oil prices in 1973–1974 and then again in 1978–1979, the effects on the Norwegian economy were ambiguous. First, the oil price increase implied a strong growth in the revenues from Norway's nascent production of offshore oil. The price hike made North Sea oil vastly more profitable. Second, the sudden price increase signalled the start of a more than 15-year-long crisis in the main shipping markets. This depression hit Norwegian owners particularly hard.

As a result of the OPEC-orchestrated oil price increase, the strategy that Norwegian shipping companies had successfully followed over the preceding decades became toxic. The Norwegian shipping industry had a particularly unfortunate fate due to its disproportionately high investments in tankers, and other strategic parameters amplified the problems. The compnaies had relatively new ships, relatively large ships and had refrained from ensuring employment through long-term charters. These were exactly the strategic choices that were punished most severely as tanker demand shifted from boom to stagnation, before completely collapsing.

By following an expansive "economies of scale" strategy, with frequent replacement of tonnage by newer and larger ships, Norwegian tanker owners had been very successful in the growth period of the first post-war decades. During the Golden Age the demand for tanker transport had expanded rapidly. As oil consumption increased, oil fields far away from the consumption centres became more important and the 1967 closure of the Suez Canal added to the increase in average distances. When ships had to go around the Cape of Good Hope to carry oil from the Arabian Gulf to Europe, the existing fleet was unable to keep up with demand. As freight rates soared, vessel values increased rapidly as well.

It is important to remember that second-hand values in shipping do not automatically follow the downward trend seen for most investment objects—machinery, buildings and cars. Instead, the value of shipping tonnage follows the freight rate cycle relatively closely, and might go up as well as down. The long-term decline in the value of a ship is typically portioned out over a period of 20–30 years, and variations from one year to the next might be much stronger than this trend—adding to the value or exacerbating the reduction. Consequently, if the timing is right, it is possible to buy tonnage, operate it profitably, and then sell it after several years at additional profit.

The cyclicality had implications both for shipping companies and their sources of capital. In the period before the tanker market collapsed, ships were considered "floating real estate"—there were few instances of problematic loans to the shipping sector.[15] Such price movements should make the shipping market particularly interesting for speculators and gamblers, but the majority of the participants at the time invested in ships with a long-term, operational focus. There were few instances of purely speculative newbuilding activity. This does not mean that shipping companies did not take risks. However, this risk was more related to the rate of expansion and the companies' gearing (the proportion of loan finance, in other words the size of the debt relative to the equity), rather than to "speculative" investments aimed at taking advantage of variations in the value of the ship—so-called asset play.

A fundamental feature of the oil tanker market is the combination of long periods of relatively depressed freight rates with short-lived boom periods. This discovery goes back to the very first research on the market, and continues to be valid.[16] During such peaks, freight rates may exceed operating costs by a factor of five, 10 or more, giving massive profits. Owners may recover their investment very quickly, needing only a handful of voyages, if they are lucky. In the period before the oil price increase there was a latent demand surplus in the tanker market, with frequent cyclical peaks. Tanker owners were making large amounts of money in 1967, in 1971 and again in 1973. The positive sentiment spilled over from freight rates to ship prices. An 80,000 dwt oil tanker, built in 1966–1967, could be sold for more than the original purchase price in every single year from 1969 to 1973. Someone buying this ship second-hand in 1968 would be able to sell it with a profit of almost 150 per cent two years later.[17]

After the market collapsed, ship prices followed suit—and the flexibility of vessel values implies high speed on the way down as well as on the way up. A modern turbine tanker of 220,000 dwt, which was valued at more

---

[15] See Stokes (1992, 25)—and keep in mind that Peter Stokes wrote this in a period when a decline in the value of real estate appeared far-fetched. Today, the metaphor is less convincing. Based on their experiences in the middle of the 1990s and during the 2008 financial crisis, owners and banks in Europe and the United States are fully aware that there are risks involved in real estate investments. They have learned the hard way.

[16] See Koopmans (1939) and Zannetos (1966) for the theoretical and historical view, and any chart of the tanker market showing the development over the last five, 10, 15 or 20 years to confirm that the old ideas are still valid.

[17] Based on price information in Fearnley & Egers Chartering Co., *Review*, various issues.

than USD50 million in 1973, was only worth USD23 million the following year. By 1975 the value had fallen to USD10 million—a reduction of more than 80 per cent relative to the peak two years earlier. The depressed market kept vessel values low. At the same time, the newbuildings that eager shipping companies had ordered during the heyday were delivered. The combination of falling demand and increasing supply created an imbalance that threatened the shipping sector's existence in Norway.

The Norwegian predicament can be seen as a negative reflection of the success in the preceding decades. Broadly speaking, the choices that made many Norwegian tanker companies successful during the Golden Age, came back to haunt them after the oil price increase. Table 7.2 compares the situation in Norwegian shipping with the international situation around the start of the shipping crisis. The second and third columns of the table provide what we today know were the "ideal" strategic parameters during the Golden Age and the shipping crisis, respectively.

As Table 7.2 shows, with regard to eight of the nine fundamental parameters, the Norwegian shipping sector was favourably positioned

Table 7.2 From good to bad—a comparison of strategic indicators at the start of the shipping crisis

|  | Best strategy in the Golden Age | Best strategy during crisis | Norway | World fleet |
|---|---|---|---|---|
| Tanker share (%) | High | Low | 60.1 | 46.5 |
| Average tanker size (1000 dwt) | High | Low | 96 | 63 |
| Orderbook as share of fleet (%) | High | Low | 126 | 88 |
| Average size orders (1000 dwt) | High | Low | 194 | 171 |
| Supertanker share (%) | High | Low | 19.7 | 12.2 |
| Turbine tanker share (%) | High | Low | 30.8 | 35.5 |
| Average age (years) | Low | High | 5.7 | 8.1 |
| Spot market share (%) | High | Low | 26.1 | 13.1 |
| Unfixed newbuildings (%) | High | Low | 80 | 31 |

Sources: See footnote

## The Shipping Crisis 207

in the years before 1973 and adversely placed once the oil price increased and the tanker market broke down.[18] To make matters worse, even the single "positive parameter" was negative if we consider it more broadly.[19]

How can we explain the dominant Norwegian strategy, which was so eminently adapted to the Golden Age and failed so spectacularly when the market collapsed? In a macro-perspective, business strategies are determined at the point where the skills, resources and culture of a company meet and respond to constraints and incentives imposed from the outside. There might thus be both internal and external explanations for Norwegian choices.

---

[18] Table 7.2: Compiled on the basis of a variety of sources from the first part of the 1970s. See the comments to the individual series for details. Tanker share refers to gross tonnage of oil tankers and combination carriers above 100 gross tons from *Lloyd's Register of Shipping Statistical Tables 1973*, Table 2 and is therefore a conservative measure.

Average tanker size (1000 dwt): data for vessels above 10,000 dwt in 1973 from *Review* 1973. World fleet figures include the Norwegian fleet. Again, this is a conservative measure. Based on the data from *Lloyd's Register of Shipping Statistical Tables 1973*, Table 2 the average size of the Norwegian tankers and combination carriers (37,754 gross tons) is more than twice the average size of the non-Norwegian tankers and combination carriers (18,345).

Orderbook as share of the fleet (%): Data for 1974, from *Review* 1974. This year was chosen in order to neutralize the effect of newbuildings cancelled after the freight market broke down. World fleet figures include the Norwegian fleet.

Average size orders (1000 dwt): data for 1973 for tankers above 10,000 dwt in 1973 from *Review* 1973.

Supertanker share (%) based on *Lloyds Statistical Tables 1973*, Tables 3 and 8, calculated on the basis of gross register tonnage. The share refers to the tonnage of tankers larger than 100,000 gross register tons as a proportion of the total fleet.

Turbine tanker share (%): data for 1975 calculated on the basis of Statistics Norway (1984, 45 and 102).

Average age (years): data for 1974 from *Lloyd's Register of Shipping Statistical Tables 1974*, Table 8. The average of the age groups is used when the data are weighted on the basis of tonnage.

Spot market share (%): data from 1973 from Jenkins, Stopford and Tyler (1993, 82–95). World fleet does not include Norwegian fleet.

Unfixed newbuildings (%): data from January 1974 from the Norwegian shipbroker Johan G. Olsen; see Tenold (2000, 185–191).

[19] When we look more closely at propulsion—the share of turbine tankers, which is the only factor where Norway did relatively well—the situation was less positive than it appears from the table. If we include the propulsion of the ships on order, even this last indicator becomes unfavourable from a Norwegian perspective. The proportion of turbine-driven vessels in the Norwegian fleet increased from 30.8 per cent in 1975 to 38.2 per cent three years later. Over the same period, the proportion for the world fleet fell from 35.5 to 33.3 per cent; see Tenold (2000, 165).

There are several internal candidates: perhaps Norwegian owners were more optimistic (or perhaps more naïve) than their foreign competitors? Maybe they were more willing to take risks, or evaluated risk differently, than shipping companies in other countries? Did their long legacy of tanker shipping make it difficult to see the alternatives, or did it make them consider the alternatives differently? Had their success made them speed-blind? Maybe they all looked at their neighbours, following each other—like sheep or lemmings—to the edge of the cliff and beyond?

The questions above all hint at failures at the micro-business level. However, the basis for the Norwegian problems could be structural. There might be external explanations pertaining to Norwegian shipping in general that can explain the groupthink. In the previous chapter we saw that the Norwegian setting advocated investment in large tankers. Maybe the operating conditions—the political framework—limited the alternatives that Norwegian shipowners could consider? Did they just adapt rationally to a tax system that strongly encouraged reinvestment? Perhaps Norwegian owners were lured by cheap money, generous yard credits and unrealistic projections of transport demand?

As is often the case, both explanatory angles are relevant.

The focus on tankers clearly had a long pedigree. As we have seen, the pioneering tanker investments in the interwar period made the Norwegians stand out in an otherwise difficult market. In 1960—before the strong upsurge in tanker demand, and a decade-and-a-half before the market collapsed—132 of the 164 large Norwegian shipping companies (80 per cent) had invested in tanker tonnage. For 37 of these companies, there was no diversification at all—tankers were their only investment. In fact, though the Norwegian companies were "overexposed" to the tanker market in 1973, they had been even more so in 1960.

In 1973 tankers made up more than 60 per cent of the Norwegian tonnage, compared with less than half of the world fleet.[20] The only countries with more tanker tonnage were Liberia, the UK and Japan—but a substantial portion of the ships in these countries were owned by oil

---

[20] The Liberian share was marginally more than 70 per cent, but much of this was owned by oil companies and ensured employment. Liberian lay-up rates in the second half of the 1970s were less than half of the Norwegian ones; Tenold (2000, 153–155).

companies or trading houses that also owned the cargo. These ships were less affected by the tonnage surplus.

Norway had since the early days of tanker shipping controlled the world's largest *independent* tanker fleet, and this had been a profitable strategy. Long traditions can make it difficult for companies to consider alternatives, and changing strategies may be time-consuming—this is what business historians refer to as path dependence. Furthermore, long *successful* traditions can lead to *hubris,* the short-sighted—even blind— belief that the next boom is just around the corner and a failure to appreciate that this time it is different.

Research has indicated that there was an idiosyncratic optimism and a willingness to take risks among Norwegian tanker owners. In 1970 two economists presented a group of Scandinavian tanker owners with a series of hypothetical investment alternatives in order to uncover their attitudes towards risk. The results were astonishing. All but one of the shipowners preferred the risky alternatives to the safe alternatives, even when expected return was the same. In fact, the article was rejected by the editor of the *Journal of Political Economy* because he did not believe that company directors with such a willingness to take risk existed.[21]

This attitude was not confined to those involved in the study. At an overall level, Norwegian shipping executives were clearly optimistic about the tanker sector and willing to channel much of their resources into that market segment. The tanker strategy had served them well for decades: it was expected to serve them well in the future. Still, it would be wrong to blame only the shipping companies for the malaise. There was a structural basis for the crisis as well; an institutional setting that made the unfortunate strategic choices particularly attractive.

Norwegian shipping companies had been eminently placed to reap the benefits of the expansion of seaborne oil transport. Cost increases had pressed the margins in the 1950s and the 1960s, but many tanker owners had experienced shorter bursts of spectacular revenues that made them

---

[21] The analyses were subsequently published elsewhere; Lorange and Norman (1972, 1973). Interestingly, the two academics behind the survey later became involved in the shipping industry, at the Board and ownership level. They had considerably more success than the majority of their research objects, more than half of whom had gone out of business 10 years after the study—see Norman (2012, 207).

forget the periods of low activity. Typically, the profits were reinvested in even more tankers, larger and more expensive than before.

As we have seen, the main alternative for the shipping companies would be to pay dividends, which were heavily taxed. It was better to obtain even more profitable tonnage. As one shipbroker put it: "instead of letting the company pay more than 50 per cent tax on the profit from the sale of a ship, [many shipowners] prefer to build a new ship and use the profits for depreciation. In other words – to put it a bit bluntly – the taxman's money is used for reinvestment."[22] The taxation of profits was high in an international perspective.[23] If the company continuously reinvested its profits, however, the actual tax rate was close to zero.

The institutional setting—where relative costs and the effects of the tax system encouraged frequent reinvestment in larger and larger ships—does not exonerate Norwegian shipping companies. Still, it explains why they had made the "wrong" choices, why supertankers were the favoured investment object. Moreover, just like these supertankers, the response time was very long if the companies wanted to change course. An ultra large crude carrier (ULCC) would need almost a minute to turn 20 degrees, and would move two ships' lengths in the process.[24] Norwegian shipping companies, with resources and competences vested in the tanker segment, could not jump from one strategy to another when the market collapsed. Due to existing ships and contracts, the course was set. And they were going in the wrong direction.

Although the tanker market changed more or less overnight, the impact was not felt immediately by the shipping companies. The solid market in the first part of the year meant that many had record profits in 1973, and quite a large portion of the fleet was committed to charters that ensured revenues, at least for the next year or so.

By 1975 it was evident that the crisis was dragging on. Any hope that the downturn in the shipping market was short-lived—like it had been in

---

[22] Gram (1979, 110). Access to depreciation exceeding 100 per cent of the value of the contract or accelerated depreciation made reinvestment extremely favourable and ensured a strong link between policy and strategy.
[23] A comparison from the early 1960s suggests that Norwegian taxes were 40 times higher than those shipping companies using the Liberian or Panamanian flag would pay; Seland (1960, 11).
[24] Dahl (1970, 31).

the late 1960s and in the early 1970s—was too optimistic. The most unfortunately positioned shipping companies had already been forced to have "the difficult chat" with the banks—their cashflows had dried up, and the drop in ship values had hit the balance sheets hard.

The first major Norwegian owner to encounter serious problems was Hilmar Reksten. His enormous success in the period when the market was going up was overshadowed by his spectacular crash when the market collapsed. In the international press he was presented as a maverick, a shy and reserved tycoon, and a sober Nordic counterpart to the Greek playboys Onassis and Niarchos, whose flamboyant lifestyles filled the pages of the gossip magazines on both sides of the Atlantic.

With a strategy focused on the spot market, Reksten's ships rapidly became surplus to requirements. Moreover, Reksten had an extremely expansive newbuilding programme—ships that would come on stream in a market where there was absolutely no need for them. In May 1975, in a secret session, the Norwegian Parliament bought Hilmar Reksten's shares in a large number of Norwegian and foreign companies to alleviate his financial problems.

The secret decision to help Hilmar Reksten's companies provided only short-term relief, though. His outstanding loans and newbuilding obligations were too high. From 1975 onwards, many tanker owners found themselves in a similar situation. Even a more far-reaching government solution was insufficient.

## Government Involvement: The Guarantee Institute

For more than a century, the shipping industry in Norway had developed within the framework of a neutral or benign political regime that only in shorter periods had negative effects. The important role of shipping in the Norwegian economy and exports had given the industry political clout and influence, and the rebuilding of the fleet in the first years after the Second World War is an example that the industry was given political priority when necessary.[25]

---

[25] Still, the ban on contracting from 1949 onwards indicates that this political priority was not an absolute right—the policy sometimes changed at short notice.

By 1975 the crisis in the shipping sector had become so serious that the authorities saw the need for more far-reaching involvement. The expansive Norwegian newbuilding strategy had, to a large extent, been financed by means of retained equity and foreign loans. Many companies found it difficult to comply with the loan terms when revenues vanished, and therefore ended up in breach of their covenants. A particularly difficult element was the "minimum value clause"—a staple of ship financing contracts—where the lender could demand forced instalments, extra collateral or the sale of the vessel if the value dropped below a certain amount. As a result of the 80 per cent drop in the value of new ships, most expanding shipping companies were in trouble. Moreover, as a number of vessels had been ordered by partnerships—where two or more companies shared liability—the financial problems of one owner could quickly spread to others.

Officially, the Guarantee Institute for Ships and Drilling Vessels Ltd. (GI) was established to alleviate this problem. When the government provided guarantees for the ships' financing, the creditors no longer had any incentive to force the owners to sell. The premise for the GI was the idea that the crisis was a temporary phenomenon and that some sort of market failure for second-hand ships justified government intervention. The aim of the GI was to ensure that tonnage was kept under Norwegian ownership, rather than sold abroad at prices that did not reflect the long-term value. Assets were to be kept on Norwegian hands until their fair value could be recouped.

With vessel values in free fall, very few of the modern, mortgage-financed ships did not violate the minimum value clause. Some shipping companies were in a financial situation where they were able to negotiate with the banks, using lucrative long-term charters or alternative assets as collateral. For other shipping companies, typically those with a large share of tonnage laid up and high financial exposure, the GI provided the financing institutions with guarantees that the mortgages would be honoured. The authorities thus bought time for the shipping companies until values recovered.

However, the politicians clearly had ulterior motives. Among those that would benefit from the arrangement were Norwegian shipyards, and in particular the Aker group. The Aker group had expanded massively, and a large share of its orders were related to three shipowners—Bjørn Bjørnstad & Co., Hagbart Waage and Hilmar Reksten—who had taken the Norwegian large-tanker, spot-market operation strategy to an extreme level. If these shipowners failed, it was likely that the Aker group, Norway's largest manufacturing employer, would be caught in the slipstream.

Throughout the post-war period, ship financing had been one of the most important links between the Norwegian and international financial markets. A wave of shipping bankruptcies would undoubtedly harm Norway's reputation internationally, something that would be very problematic for a country that depended upon foreign funding to build up petroleum production in the North Sea. Again, government guarantees bought time and solved the immediate problem.

In the end, however, the Guarantee Institute was a band aid on an open wound. The shipping market did not recover as expected. Consequently, the ships that the guarantees covered never regained their fair value—this was a concept that only existed in the heads of politicians and bureaucrats, and certainly not in the market place. In the early 1980s the arrangement was largely disbanded, at a significant loss to the Norwegian tax payers, though the GI lived on in the Norwegian court system well into the new millennium.

The GI, the most far-reaching government involvement in shipping in peacetime, was not a success, but an expensive lesson. The unfortunate end result can be explained by the depth and, in particular, the longevity of the tanker crisis.[26] In fact, for the drilling rigs, which had been included in the arrangement due to challenges that were identical to those in the tanker market, the scheme was an unconditional success. Demand picked up, the rates recovered—and the vessels regained their value. For shipping, a brief market upturn around the turn of the decade turned out to provide only very temporary relief. In the 1980s the crisis broadened, affecting new market segments and new companies. By the middle of the decade there was hardly a single company that had a solid financial situation, and many had already been forced to give up.

---

[26] However, given that the Aker group survived, and Norway's international financial standing was unhurt, the question of whether the arrangement was a success or not could be modified.

## The Decline of Norwegian Shipping

The shipping crisis had profound effects on the Norwegian shipping industry and led to several structural changes.[27] The industry became more concentrated in the major shipping centres, Oslo and Bergen. Many smaller ports along the coast saw their last ocean-going ships disappear—scrapped or sold abroad as a result of lost competitiveness. There was also a concentration of ownership in general. Most of the large shipping companies survived the crisis—often at the mercy of their banks, and with original ownership heavily diluted. For smaller companies, it was more difficult to convince the creditors that the best strategy would be to keep the company alive. Many of the banks that entered ship financing in the late 1960s and early 1970s—enticed by the upward trend in asset prices—wanted to withdraw quickly and cut their losses, when their fingers were burnt.

The extreme manner in which the crisis changed the fabric of Norwegian shipping can be illustrated by looking at the population of Norwegian tanker companies. If we take as our point of departure the 105 companies that owned tankers in 1939, almost two-thirds survived the war and the first post-war decades. However, of the 69 companies that survived the 31 years from 1939 to 1970, more than two-thirds disappeared during the period 1970–1987; by 1987 only 21 of the companies had Norwegian-flagged ships. If we add the companies managing ships registered abroad, the number increases to 32, but this still implied that more than half of the "survivors" from 1939 succumbed during the crisis.[28]

Figure 7.4 presents five indices that show the decline of Norwegian shipping along several dimensions—tonnage (tankers and total), the number of shipping companies, employment in foreign-going shipping

---

[27] For an impressively pedestrian walk-through of practically every change in companies and ports from 1970 to 1987, see Tenold (2000, 258–330).

[28] Tenold (2006, 130–132). The starting point here is 105 companies in 1939, whereas Chap. 4 suggests that there were 107 tanker companies that year. The difference is due to the fact that four companies that merged in the period 1939–1970 have been counted as two companies in the 1939 figure.

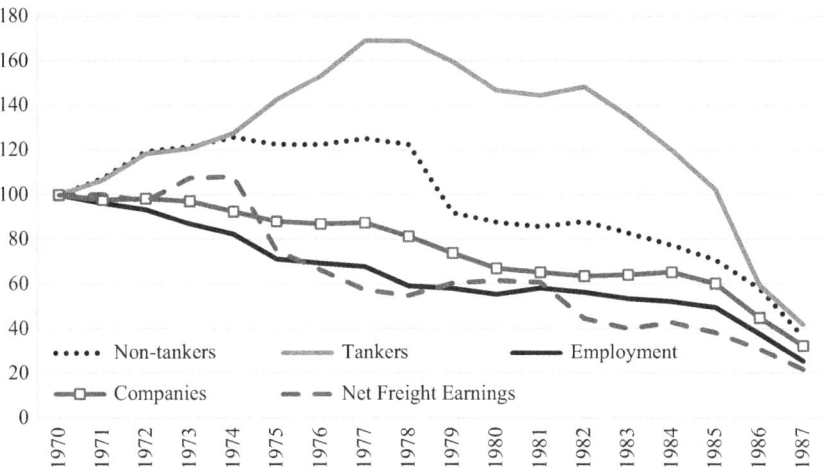

Fig. 7.4 The crisis index. The Norwegian fleet and tankers, number of seafarers and shipping companies and net freight earnings (1970 = 100), 1970–1987

and net freight earnings.[29] The extent of the decline over the period varies—from almost 80 per cent in the case of net freight earnings, to slightly less than 60 per cent in the case of the tanker fleet—but it is evident that all indicators developed very unfavourably.[30] At the same time,

---

[29] Figure 7.4: Calculated by the author on the basis of the following sources:

Tonnage data: Statistics Norway (1994, 481). Based on the gross tonnage of vessels larger than 100 gross register tons.

Number of shipping companies: calculated on the basis of the data set presented in Tenold (2000, 278–308), covering all Norwegian shipping companies that owned vessels larger than 5000 gross register tons. However, relative to the figures presented there, companies that only owned drilling vessels have been deleted.

Employment: crew on board vessels registered in the Norwegian ship register, foreign-going trade only. In 1980 the reporting of employment figures changed, when seafarers on smaller ships and restaurant personnel on crew ships became included in the public statistics, and the data have been adjusted to neutralize the effects of this change.

Net freight earnings: Statistics Norway (1994, 545), deflated by Grytten (2004). Net freight earnings provides a better reflection of the contribution of shipping to the Norwegian economy than gross freight earnings, as it deducts expenses accrued abroad, and thus shows how much money shipping companies "brought home," In the period, the proportion of gross freight earning that was brought home was halved, from around 60 per cent in the early 1970s to around 30 per cent 1982–1987. This partly reflected a structural change, towards shipping segments with a higher proportion of costs abroad, and partly the fact that prices abroad had less downward flexibility than freight rates.

[30] If we compare with the peak, rather than 1970, the decline in the tanker fleet is more than 75 per cent.

the indices show different development patterns. These can be used to explain the unfolding of the crisis and how it manifested itself in Norwegian shipping.

The tonnage data reveal the optimism at the start of the decade. The fleet growth is relatively similar for the tankers and for the fleet as a whole in the period 1970–1973. Subsequently, the tanker fleet starts to grow more rapidly, reflecting the high ordering during the boom. At the peak at the beginning of 1977, the tanker fleet had increased by 69 per cent relative to 1970, while the non-tanker fleet had increased by about a quarter. The fact that the tanker fleet continued to grow for four years after the freight market had broken down, can be explained by the lag between the ordering and delivery of vessels. Such lags are particularly long during boom periods such as in the early 1970s—the amount of tanker tonnage on order more than trebled from 1970 to 1974.

The indices also reveal the strong relationship between the shipping cycles and the fleet development. There was a short reversal of the post-1977 fleet decline in 1982. This atypical growth in a period of practically constant decline was a result of vessels ordered during a brief improvement in freight rates. In 1979 and 1980 lay-up rates declined to around 3 per cent—after having been more than 10 per cent the previous year and more than 20 per cent in 1977—and freight rates increased markedly. The effects are seen both in the levelling out of the freight earnings during 1979–1981 and in the deliveries of new tonnage in 1982—by which time there was already a tonnage surplus again.

Shipping employment and the number of shipping companies did not show any growth, even before the tanker market collapsed. For the employment figures, the decline registered in the early 1970s can be explained by more rational operation of vessels and economies of scale. The number of ships declined every year during 1971–1987, even though the tonnage increased during the first seven years of this period.[31]

The number of companies remained relatively steady during 1971–1973, before a downward trend and two "waves" of liquidation set in; the first from 1977 to 1979 and the second from 1984 to 1987—and the last one was particularly violent. Around 25 per cent of the compa-

---

[31] Statistics Norway (1994, 481).

nies that existed in 1985 had disappeared by 1986, and the rate was even higher from 1986 to 1987. Again, the optimism caused by the freight rate increase around the turn of the decade explains the temporary break in the declining trend. The crisis itself reduced the number of shipping companies with vessels flying the Norwegian flag from 176 to 56—or 64 if we add the ones that had invested in drilling rigs and large vessels for the offshore oil industry.[32] When companies that operated ships under foreign flags are included, the number increases to 91, but even that implies that the number of Norwegian shipping companies had been almost halved.

We have previously suggested that there has always been a substantial turnover in Norwegian shipping—that the industry's longevity occurred against a backdrop of frequently changing participants. The difference between the crisis and other periods is, however, that the number of new ventures was far too small to replace the companies that disappeared. More than 150 new shipping companies were registered in these turbulent years—so there was no dearth of newcomers—but more than 260 companies gave up during 1971–1987.[33]

It was shipping itself that killed off the Norwegian shipping companies. There was little or no tradition of diversification outside the shipping sector. Such conglomerates were far more common in, for instance, the UK. Some of the larger Norwegian owners had separate investments in other industries, and quite a few had ventured capital into the offshore oil business, but in general the companies stuck to their main activity—shipping. Of course, this was unfortunate when that market was in trouble. However, in other countries, large conglomerates—with shipping as one of their many activities—were no guarantee of success. In fact, the activities in other sectors might have exacerbated the difficulties.

---

[32] The analysis of companies is based solely on those companies that have ships larger than 5000 gross register tons; see Tenold (2000, 258–267) for a presentation of the databases that are used. Companies that owned smaller vessels, engaged in local trades or the offshore industry, have not been included in the analysis.

[33] These figures are likely to be somewhat inflated due to temporary exits, temporary establishments by existing companies and companies established by creditors. Among the "shipowners" in the data set are several banks.

One example is the Court Line, a British shipping company with roots at the beginning of the 20th century, which folded in 1974, at the very start of the tanker crisis. Court Line operated six tankers on long-term charters, which at least in principle should buy the company some time after the freight rate declined. However, the main problem was its interests in aviation and charter holidays, which led to acute financial problems due to the oil price increase and the recession in the UK.[34] The Court Line case shows that "too much diversification from core activity could result in problems." In fact, the company went into liquidation way before its more exposed Norwegian competitors, who "only" had to deal with the shipping crisis.[35]

## Specialization as a Survival Strategy

Most Norwegian shipping companies had few investments outside shipping, and even within shipping there was limited diversification. Of the largest 171 shipping companies in 1973, more than half had invested in only one type of ship.[36] Naturally, the degree of diversification was higher for larger companies than for smaller ones—if you only have one ship, it is difficult to have a diversified fleet.[37]

Diversification strategies enable shipping companies to spread risk, as revenues from relatively well-functioning markets could neutralize, or alleviate, the negative effects from the depressed ones. Among the markets that were less affected by the crisis, at least at the outset, were those involving specialized ships such as car carriers, gas tankers, chemical

---

[34] In fact, the company's shipping business contributed positively to its accounts, and the Court Line also sold two newbuilding contracts at a substantial profit before the market crashed; Court Line Limited, *Report of the directors & accounts for the year ended 20 September 1973*, 7. See also Craggs, Murphy and Vaughan (2018, 117–119).

[35] Goss (2013, 247–248). See also Simons (1997).

[36] Calculated on the basis of the database mentioned above. Around 15 per cent of the shipping companies only owned crude oil tankers, and were thus particularly badly placed when the oil price increased. In total, 53 per cent of the companies had invested in oil tankers—as previously mentioned this was down from more than 80 per cent in 1960; see Tenold and Aarbu (2011, 241).

[37] There is one exception to this intuitive claim: companies that own combination carriers, ships that can be used both in the tanker and dry bulk markets. In the analysis, companies with such vessels are considered to follow a diversification strategy.

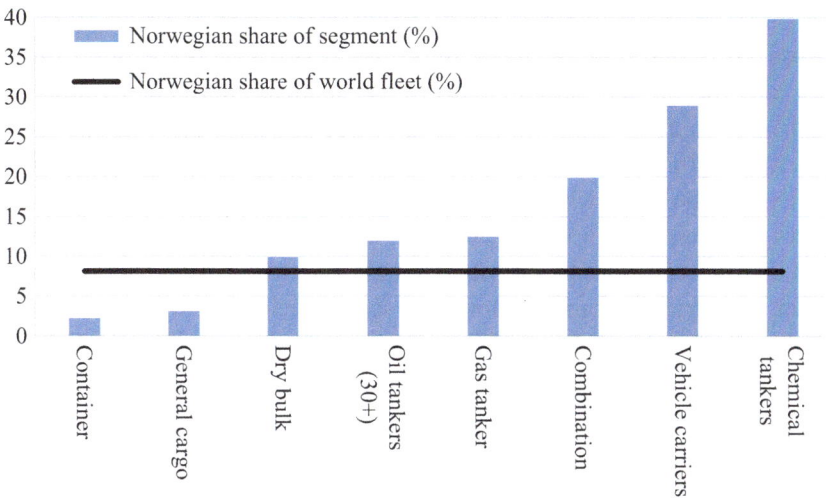

**Fig. 7.5** Norwegian market shares, world fleet and major segments, 1973. (Source: Lloyds, *Statistical Tables 1973*, Table 2 and Norway, Parliament, 1983, 103–108. Confer footnote)

tankers, cruise vessels and so on. Figure 7.5 compares the Norwegian share of the world fleet with the share of some of the main segments.[38] The low shares of containerships and general cargo carriers, as well as the previously presented overrepresentation within the tanker market, are clearly visible. However, it is evident that the Norwegians had an extremely strong position in some of the niche segments.

When the tanker market collapsed, the companies that had invested in specialized tonnage were much better equipped to deal with the new paradigm. In the period 1977–1987, the survival rate among the shipping companies that had invested in ships for specialized markets was more than 75 per cent. Among those that had not invested in such tonnage, less than a quarter survived.[39]

The introduction of specialized vessel types had been one of the dominant technological trends in the first post-war decades. When the crisis

---

[38] Calculated by the author on the basis of Lloyds, *Statistical Tables 1973*, Table 2 and Norway, Parliament, 1983, 103–108. Refers to tankers larger than 30,000 gross tons; for all other vessel types, it refers to all ships larger than 100 tons.
[39] Calculated on the basis of the companies' fleets in 1977; see Tenold (2010, 75).

hit shipping markets hard, specialization turned out to be a relatively safe haven. Although the markets were thinner, there were profit opportunities and the number of competitors was relatively limited. Compared with more mature markets, there were substantial barriers to entry—it was more difficult to acquire the technology and gain market share. This gave the shipowners with special vessels some breathing space. The cashflows were less volatile and typically more predictable, as the companies had usually secured some activity through long-term contracts with their main industrial customers. Moreover, specialized ships were often operated in pools, where revenues were distributed among participating ships according to a fixed set of "pool keys," another mechanism that evened out fluctuations in shipping incomes.

The increasing importance of specialized shipping has two—quite related—explanations. First, the role of the specialized ships, and the shipping companies owning them, automatically increased as major tanker and dry bulk owners folded and other ship types disappeared from the fleet. By default, what remains increases in relative importance. Second, it is evident that the specialized market segments were well-suited to two of the main competitive parameters of Norwegian shipping companies—competence about markets and customers, and access to relatively cheap capital. Shipping companies that invested in these segments were thus able to expand in absolute, as well as relative, terms.

As there were economies of scale at the fleet level—sometimes a fleet of 10 or more ships was necessary to provide an efficient service—the specialized segments frequently saw various types of cooperative strategies; partnerships, joint ownership, pools and so on. One common combination was cooperation between innovative entrepreneurs and established companies. Perhaps the best example of this is the open-hatch bulk market, where ships with completely box-shaped holds, extra-wide hatches and special cranes offered transport of tricky products such as pulp, paper, wood products and so on. In the 1960s, two cash-strapped entrepreneurs—Per Waaler and Kristian Gerhard Jebsen—established the Star and Gearbulk pools together with far wealthier compatriots, including some of the companies that were among Norway's 20 largest companies in the interwar period (Westfal-Larsen and AS J.L. Mowinckels Rederi).

The specialized segments were characterized by innovative solutions. One of Odfjell's selling points in the chemical tanker market was the use of stainless steel tanks, which increased the number of cargoes that could be transported, including highly corrosive products such as sulphuric acid. The ships that performed industrial shipping services were expensive—in the late 1960s a 10,000 dwt chemical tanker was twice as expensive per ton as a conventional tanker of the same size. Compared with a 200,000 dwt tanker, the chemical tanker was six times more expensive per ton.[40] The companies that invested in specialized shipping often had a "value-chain" approach, where the aim was to provide a first-class, integrated service to their main customers. As a result, both Odfjell and Stolt-Nielsen invested in tank terminals that would improve their competitive position—and make it difficult for new competitors to enter the market for the transport of chemicals.

In several of the specialized segments, Norwegian shipping companies and yards came to play a decisive role in the early development of the technology and the market. The first open-hatch bulk carrier—*Besseggen*—was developed by US naval architects, but built by a Norwegian yard, owned by a Norwegian shipowner, equipped with purpose-built Norwegian cranes and chartered long-term to a US industrial conglomerate. Within liquid natural gas, the technological development was a process that took place "in an interplay among shipping companies, research institutions, shipyards and subcontractors."[41] Table 7.3 presents some of the niches in which the Norwegians played an important part in the technological development, and also managed to gain substantial market shares.

As previously mentioned, specialized shipping was the viable alternative to bulkification for Norwegian companies. But the ability to invest was not equally distributed; the specialized segments were expensive, involved trial-and-error and initially entailed substantial risks. The shipping companies that built up a presence had to have a strong position *vis-à-vis* customers and shipbuilders. Again, the ones best suited were the large shipping companies, or the entrepreneurs that managed to get a

---

[40] Tenold (2010, 66).
[41] Bakka (2017, 103).

Table 7.3 Leading Norwegian niches and niche companies

| Market | Pioneers |
| --- | --- |
| Liquid petroleum gas | Øivind Lorentzen, Sigval Bergesen, Einar Bakkevig, Gas Traders Pool |
| Liquid natural gas | Øivind Lorentzen, Leif Høegh, Gotaas-Larsen, Kværner |
| Chemical tankers | Odfjell, Stolt-Nielsen, Panocean Anco [N&GB] |
| Cruise shipping | Norwegian Cruise Line (Kloster) |
| | Royal Caribbean Cruise Line (Skaugen, A Wilhelmsen, Gotaas-Larsen) |
| | Royal Viking Line (Bergenske, Nordenfjeldske, AF Klaveness) |
| Open-hatch bulk | Star (Waaler, Grieg, Westfal-Larsen) |
| | Gearbulk (Kristian Gerhard Jebsen, Mowinckels, Dreyfus [F&GB]) |
| Vehicle carriers | Jan-Erik Dyvi, Leif Høegh, Ugland, Jahre |

financial contribution from the large shipping companies. If we take company size in 1960 as the starting point, more than a quarter of the companies in the top half of the distribution invested in specialized tonnage in the period 1960–1977, compared with less than 10 per cent in the lower half of the size distribution.[42] The fact that specialized markets were relatively well-functioning thus increased the degree of concentration in Norwegian shipping.

Specialization also brought about new regional differences. A century earlier, Bergen had been ahead in the transformation from sail to steam, but had been outgrown by shipowners in other parts of Norway—in particular Oslo—after the First World War. The Bergen shipowners regained their pioneering position as a result of specialization; by the middle of the 1970s, they owned 13 per cent of the Norwegian fleet, but more than 40 per cent of the specialized tonnage. The position was particularly strong within chemical shipping and open-hatch bulk shipping.

A larger proportion of the Bergen shipping companies had invested in specialized ships, and such ships on average made up a larger share of the various companies fleets. The strong position can be explained by cooperation between the companies, vertical integration (into terminals and

---

[42] Tenold (2010, 72). However, as we saw in the last chapter, smaller companies had an inroad into the niche markets by means of minority investments in ships owned by the larger companies.

brokering) and technological innovation. The latter element illustrates the local linkages; the leading international producer of pumps for chemical tankers and one of the leading manufacturers of cranes for open-hatch bulk carriers, were based in the city.[43]

The investment in specialized tonnage gave the Norwegian shipping industry some breathing space during the crisis. In the specialized segments, there was still room for innovation—so investment did not dry up. Moreover, the fact that the technology was quite advanced, meant that shipping companies could justify paying more for the competence that Norwegian seafarers brought to the table—or to bridge and deck. In a period when the Norwegian shipping industry had serious financial problems, the specialized shipping segments performed relatively well. However, as the crisis dragged on into the 1980s, many of these segments became plagued by overcapacity as well. After a century of success, Norwegian shipping reached a low point during the shipping crisis—in terms of profitability and in terms of public perception.

## By the Death Bed

The Norwegian public's image of shipping changed during the crisis, and drastically so. In 1976, the national broadcaster could still fill half an hour eight Friday evenings in a row by following the oil tanker *Vanessa* on a voyage around the world. But the tone had changed compared with the celebratory programmes that were aired in the 1950s and 1960s. The backdrop was no longer our diligent and hard-working heroes at sea, who brought much-needed dollars back to Norway. Now the difficulties had come to the fore; the long hours, the isolation, the dangers, and the difficulties of combining a seafaring career with family life. The sailor's song was no longer an homage to distant ports, interspersed with some melancholic memories of home. From the middle of the 1970s, the Norwegian sailor was pining for the fjords. Would it not be better for him to return to Norwegian waters? Would it not be more profitable to use his mari-

---

[43] See Tenold (2009) for a more thorough analysis.

time competence in the offshore oil industry, than in a loss-making business far from home?[44]

Norwegians had eagerly embraced the country's new-found role as a petroleum producer, and the country's wealth and welfare soon became identified with the export of oil, not with shipping services. On the West Coast, in particular in and around Stavanger and Haugesund, "sheikhs and Arabs" were the new royalty.

The growing offshore oil production presented new opportunities for seafarers, as it had done for shipping companies. Parallel with the declining employment of Norwegian seafarers in deep-sea shipping, there was an increase in the number employed in the North Sea—on rigs and supply vessels. The transfer undoubtedly eased the employment effects of the shipping crisis, and for seafarers there were evident advantages of working closer to home.[45]

Shipping was rapidly eclipsed by the oil sector in the public's impression of where Norwegian wealth came from. This idea was strengthened by the notion that even in the period when shipping was important, shipowners had been shirking their responsibilities. In the second half of the 1970s, tax-evasion charges related to two of the leading shipping personalities—Anders Jahre and Hilmar Reksten—had a negative effect on the public's attitude towards shipowners and shipping. Jahre and Reksten had previously been portrayed as philanthropists and entrepreneurs, who had contributed to building the nation with their work ethic and risky investments, before sharing the profits for the common good. Jahre financed half of the town hall in his native Sandefjord, and donated substantial amounts of money to research and humanitarian purposes. Reksten ensured that the sailing vessel *Statsraad Lehmkuhl*, which was used as a school ship, remained in Bergen, and gave large amounts of money to cultural events and buildings, as well as several other causes.[46]

---

[44] The choice of a masculine pronoun here is a result of reality, not misogyny. In the first half of the 1970s women made up less than 10 per cent of Norwegian seafarers in ocean transport. Among foreigners on Norwegian ships, the female share was less than 5 per cent.

[45] See the discussion in Tenold (2015a).

[46] Given their important roles as entrepreneurs, businessmen and donors, as well as their spectacular falls from grace, Jahre and Reksten have been the subject of a number of books, some emphasizing their former successes, others their downfall. See for instance Jacobsen (1982) and Tjomsland

Their generosity was tainted by the fact that they had been quite tight-fisted in connection with their tax payments.

After their deaths, when government investigations uncovered that both Reksten and Jahre had amassed untaxed funds abroad, the two shipping entrepreneurs were suddenly portrayed as free-riders rather than philanthropists. In a social-democratic, egalitarian society such as Norway, the idea that some of the wealthiest people were not contributing fully to the public good, was frowned upon. When these flames were fanned by the left-wing ideologists that became increasingly vociferous in the 1970s, the result was a decimation of the public image of shipping and shipowners. During the shipping crisis, shipowners saw both their affluence and their influence challenged.[47]

In the 1980s, controversial business decisions continued to put the country's shipping companies in a bad light. Dangerous voyages in the Persian Gulf, where oil tankers were common targets in the Iran-Iraq war, made the shipowners involved seem cynical and ruthless. Moreover, "amoral" transport of cargo to and from South Africa made it easy for a critical press to paint a picture of shipowners as profit-hungry and heartless.[48] There is, however, another adjective that would have been more appropriate: they were desperate. This desperation was evident throughout the shipping industry. Only a relatively limited number of shipping companies traded on ports in the Persian Gulf or South Africa, but the problems were felt everywhere.

The crisis affected the industry so broadly that practically all shipping companies were looking for a way out. Shipping had become "an industry with high risks and low profits" and this put pressure on the limited

---

(2013) (for Jahre), Ilner (2006), Hjellum (1983), and Reksten (1979, 1983) (for Reksten), and Gram (2017) (for both).

[47] For an early and extremely good analysis of the industry's image problem, see Svendsen (1976).

[48] The transport of oil to South Africa was not illegal, but such voyages "were considered morally and politically unacceptable"; Eriksen and Krokan (2000, 199). In 1985, Parliament suggested a system of registration of all Norwegian-owned ships trading on South Africa, and a watered-down version of this procedure was introduced. Although relatively few companies participated in the transport—23 crude oil voyages to South Africa were registered in 1986–1987, but only six different shipping companies were involved—the whole industry was tainted by the actions of the few. Moreover, "the shipowners were a visible target and an 'enemy' [that was] easy to identify and attack," a fact that was used strategically by anti-apartheid activists; see Eriksen and Krokan (2000, 213–214).

equity that remained.⁴⁹ The downturn in the market had forced the authorities to gradually increase access to register ships abroad, in order to reduce costs. Some shipping companies reflagged their vessels and replaced their Norwegian sailors with foreigners, but that was not the dominant strategy. The most common response to the shipping crisis was simply to give up.

By 1986 the outflow of tonnage from Norway had turned into a veritable flood. The liberalization of the flag regime had improved access to registry abroad, but there was still substantial paperwork involved. In the autumn of 1986 the bureaucrats had their hands and desks full. So many shipping companies applied for licence to move their ships from the Norwegian flag that the licensing system had "broken down" and there was a "long backlog" of applications.⁵⁰ Just before Christmas in 1986 *Norges Bank*, which had taken over the licensing procedures from an overworked Ministry of Trade and Shipping, was processing 58 different applications for flagging out, concerning a total of almost 90 vessels.⁵¹

The fleet flying the Norwegian flag declined by more than 5.7 million dwt in 1986—the reduction was more or less the same as the total size of the Norwegian merchant marine 50 years earlier. A symptomatic and poignant incidence took place in February 1987. The red, white and blue flag of the *SS Norway*—at one time the world's largest cruise ship and the pride of the Norwegian fleet—was swapped for the red, white, yellow, black and blue of the Bahamas.⁵²

Norwegian shipping was on its knees—its position was weaker than it had been at any time over the past 100 years. A large portion of the fleet had been sold abroad, despite the expensive GI, the governments' attempt to give emergency relief to struggling shipowners. International shipping under the Norwegian flag was slowly and surely dying out, as companies gave up or fled abroad. However, in the darkest hour, help came from the most unlikely of quarters.

---

⁴⁹*Aftenposten*. 030586, 5.
⁵⁰Tenold (2015a, 162).
⁵¹Jørgensen (1988, 210).
⁵² The Bahamian merchant marine ensign has red fields with a white cross, like a symmetric version of the Danish flag, but the flag of the Bahamas in the upper left quadrant.

# Bibliography

M.E. Ahrari (1986) *OPEC – The Falling Giant* (Lexington: The University Press of Kentucky)

B. Andersen (1993) *Holmenkollbanen: kort historikk fra 1898 til 1993* (Oslo: Lokaltrafikkhistorisk forening)

D. Bakka (2017) *Nasjonens ære – Norsk rederinæring mellom marked og politikk* (Bergen: Bodoni Forlag)

British Petroleum (1984) *BP Statistical Review of World Energy 1984* (London: British Petroleum)

L.C. Bruno & S. Tenold (2011) 'The Basis for South Korea's Ascent in the Shipbulding Industry, 1970–1990', *Mariner's Mirror*, 97:3, 201–217

J. Craggs, H. Murphy & R. Vaughan (2018) 'A shipbuilding consultancy is born: The birth, growth and subsequent takeovers of A&P Appledore (International) and the A&P Group, 1971–2017', *International Journal of Maritime History*, 30:1, 106–130

P. Dahl (1970) *Skipsfart og Skipsbygning. Perspektivanalyse utarbeidet på vegne av NTNF's Komite for Skipsteknisk Forskning* (Oslo: Norges Teknisk-Naturvitenskaplige Forskningsråd)

T.L. Eriksen & A.K. Krokan (2000) '"Fuelling the Apartheid War Machine": A Case Study of Shipowners, Sanctions and Solidarity Movements', in T.L. Eriksen (ed) *Norway and National Liberation in Southern Africa* (Stockholm: Nordiska Afrikainstitutet) 197–215

T.M.A. Farrell (1985) 'The world oil market 1973–1983, and the future of oil prices', *OPEC Review*, 9:4, 1985, 389–416

R.O. Goss (2013) 'Strategies in British Shipping 1945–1970', *Mariner's Mirror*, 97:1, 243–258

H.T. Gram (1979) 'Meklerens rolle som kontaktmann mellom reder og verft', in H.W. Andersen, B. Stråth & T Svensson (eds) *Olje, verft og redere* (Trondheim: Universitetet i Trondheim)

T. Gram (2017) *Penger i paradis: historien om Anders Jahre og Hilmar Rekstens skjulte formuer* (Oslo: Pax)

O.H. Grytten (2004) 'A consumer price index for Norway 1516–2003', in Ø. Eitrheim, J.T. Klovland & J.F. Qvigstad (eds) *Historical Monetary Statistics for Norway 1819–2003* (Oslo: Norges Bank) 47–98

T. Hjellum (1983) *Reksten-saka: ei historie om folkevalgt avmakt og borgarleg herredøme* (Bergen: Institutt for Sammenlignende Politikk)

K. Ilner (2006) *Reksten* (Bergen: Vigmostad & Bjørke)

A.R. Jacobsen (1982) *Eventyret Anders Jahre* (Oslo: Oktober)
G. Jenkins, M. Stopford & C. Tyler (1993) *The Clarkson Oil Tanker Databook* (London: Clarkson Research Studies)
B. Jørgensen (ed.) (1988) *Med Finanskomiteen i arbeid* (Oslo: Stortinget)
T.C. Koopmans (1939) *Tanker Freight Rates and Tankship Building; an analysis of cyclical fluctuations* (London: P. S. King & Co. Ltd.)
P. Lorange & V.D. Norman (1972) 'How attitudes towards risk influence investment decisions', *European Business*, No. 33, 71–84
P. Lorange & V.D. Norman (1973) 'Risk preference in Scandinavian Shipping', *Applied Economics*, 5, 49–59
M. Levinson (2016) *An Extraordinary Time – The End of the Postwar Boom and the Return of the Ordinary Economy* (New York: Basic Books)
A. Maddison (2003) *The World Economy: Historical Statistics* (Paris: OECD)
V.D. Norman (2012) 'A Future for Nordic Shipping?' in S. Tenold, M.J. Iversen & E. Lange (eds) *Global Shipping in Small Nations: Nordic Experiences after 1960* (Basingstoke: Palgrave Macmillan) 202–214
OECD (1977) *Towards Full Employment and Price Stability* (Paris: OECD)
OECD (1999) *Historical Statistics* (Paris: OECD)
T.R. Olesen (2013) 'From shipbuilding to alternative maritime industry – The closure of Danyard Frederikshavn in 1999', *Erhvervshistorisk Årbog*, 62:2, 78–96
R.T. Poulsen (2013) 'Diverting developments – the Danish shipbuilding and marine equipment industries, 1970–2010', *Erhvervshistorisk Årbog*, 62:2, 57–77
R.T. Poulsen & H. Sornn-Friese (2011) 'Downfall delayed: Danish shipbuilding and industrial dislocation', *Business History*, 53:4, 557–582
A. Reksten (1983) *Slik var det* (Oslo: Gyldendal)
H. Reksten (1979) *Opplevelser* (Oslo: Aschehoug)
J. Seland (1960) 'Enkelte finansierings- og skatteproblemer i skipsfartsnæringen', *Sosialøkonomen*, 14:5, 11–12
J. Seland (1994) *Norsk skipsfart år for år 1946–1976* (Bergen: Fagbokforlaget)
G.M. Simons (1997) *Colours in the sky. The story of Autair International Airways and Court Line Aviation* (Peterborough: GMS Enterprises)
Statistics Norway (1984) *Sjøtransport 1983* (Oslo: Statistisk Sentralbyrå)
Statistics Norway (1994) *Historisk Statistikk 1994* (Oslo: Statistisk Sentralbyrå)
P. Stokes (1992) *Ship Finance – Credit Expansion and the Boom-Bust Cycle* (London: Lloyd's of London Press Ltd.)
B. Stråth (1987) *The politics of de-industrialisation: The contraction of the West European Shipbuilding Industry* (London: Croom Helm)

A.S. Svendsen (1976) *Skipsfartskrisen* (Bergen: Institute for Shipping Research)
S. Tenold (2000) 'The Shipping Crisis of the 1970s: Causes, Effects and Implications for Norwegian Shipping', *PhD-thesis* (Bergen: Norwegian School of Economics and Business Administration)
S. Tenold (2006) 'Crisis? What Crisis?', in L.U. Scholl & D.M. Williams (eds) *Crisis and Transition. Maritime Sectors in the North Sea Region 1790–1940* (Bremen: Verlag H.M. Hauschild, GmbH.) 117–134
S. Tenold (2009) 'Vernon's product life cycle and maritime innovation: Specialised shipping in Bergen, Norway, 1970–1987', *Business History*, 51:5, 770–786
S. Tenold (2010) 'So nice in niches: Specialisation strategies in Norwegian shipping, 1960–1977', *International Journal of Maritime History*, 22:1, 63–82
S. Tenold (2015a) *Geared for Growth. Kristian Gerhard Jebsen and His Shipping Companies* (Bergen: Bodoni Forlag)
S. Tenold (2015b) 'Globalisation and maritime labour in Norway after World War II', *The International Journal of Maritime History*, 27:4, 774–792
S. Tenold & K.O. Aarbu (2011) 'Little Man, What Now? Company Deaths in Norwegian Shipping, 1960–1980', in L.R. Fischer & E. Lange (eds) *New directions in Norwegian maritime history*, St. Johns: IMEHA, 26–60
A. Tjomsland (2013) *Anders Jahre – hans liv og virksomhet* (Sandefjord: Tjomsland Media)
D. Todd (1981) *Industrial Dislocation: The Case of Global Shipbuilding* (New York: Routledge)
D. Todd (2011) 'Going East: Was the shift in volume shipbuilding capacity from Britain and continental Europe to the Far East and elsewhere during the latter half of the twentieth century inevitable?' *The Mariner's Mirror*, 97:1, 259–271
Z.S. Zannetos (1966) *The Theory of Oil Tankship Rates* (Cambridge: The MIT Press)

**Open Access** This chapter is licensed under the terms of the Creative Commons Attribution-NonCommercial-NoDerivatives 4.0 International License (http://creativecommons.org/licenses/by-nc-nd/4.0/), which permits any noncommercial use, sharing, distribution and reproduction in any medium or format, as long as you give appropriate credit to the original author(s) and the source, provide a link to the Creative Commons license and indicate if you modified the licensed material. You do not have permission under this license to share adapted material derived from this chapter or parts of it.

The images or other third party material in this chapter are included in the chapter's Creative Commons license, unless indicated otherwise in a credit line to the material. If material is not included in the chapter's Creative Commons license and your intended use is not permitted by statutory regulation or exceeds the permitted use, you will need to obtain permission directly from the copyright holder.

# 8

# Rebound: The Return of Norwegian Shipping

How do you accept the disappearance of an industry that for more than a century has been the most important source of foreign exchange, neutralizing the balance of trade deficit and enabling crucial imports? You don't. You take up the fight, look for solutions and try to adapt. And you accept that help may come from the most surprising quarters.

The old man was something of a legend in both Norwegian and international shipping. Born in Bergen at the start of the century, he left his native country at an early age to work and study in London in the interwar period. During the Second World War, Erling Dekke Næss had worked for Nortraship. In the first post-war decades, from a base in the United States, he built up one of the leading international shipping empires, operating his own and chartered vessels. As leader of the American Committee for Flags of Necessity, he was one of the most vocal supporters of Flags of Convenience, the low-cost institutional arrangement that primarily American and Greek shipowners used.[1]

Although he was based abroad, Dekke Næss had been a frequent visitor to his home town, and he had donated large sums of money to an

---

[1] The autobiographies Næss (1977) (in English) and Næss (1981) (in Norwegian) are among the best insider accounts of modern shipping; confer also Chap. 4.

© The Author(s) 2019
S. Tenold, *Norwegian Shipping in the 20th Century*, Palgrave Studies in Maritime Economics, https://doi.org/10.1007/978-3-319-95639-8_8

Institute for Shipping Research and to a first-class museum in Bergen, telling the history of the city's medieval roots.[2] Now he had come back to his native country to offer his solution to the extreme crisis that haunted Norwegian shipping. The forum was a meeting of shipowners in Oslo—the date was 11 January 1984.

The fundamental premise for the plan that Erling Dekke Næss presented, was a feature that had been characteristic of Norwegian shipping for more than a century: the fact that the ships served the world market, not Norwegian exporters and importers. This implied that the majority of the Norwegian-owned tonnage never visited ports in the home country. Consequently, given that Norwegian shipping was an *international* industry, its scope should be international.

The basis for Norway's competitiveness had changed during the 20th century. A starting position based on low-cost shipping, with old ships and superior seamanship, was replaced by a combination of economies of scale, automated ship operation and innovative specialized tonnage. Technology gave the Norwegians a competitive edge, and neutralized what had now become a labour cost disadvantage. When the shipping crisis struck, and the market became characterized by massive overcapacity, there was little reason to invest in new tonnage. When it was no longer possible to invest in labour-saving technologies, the Norwegian companies' ability to create competitive advantages was reduced. The country still had a well-functioning maritime infrastructure, high competence onshore and offshore, an affinity for the sea and long maritime traditions. However, in a cut-throat competitive situation, this was insufficient to remain afloat.

## The Low Point

In the period from 1970 to 1987 the number of shipping companies operating in the international market fell by more than two-thirds and the newly established businesses were too few and far between to alleviate

---

[2] The author of this book was for a number of years affiliated with the shipping research institute that had been established by Næss' donation.

Rebound: The Return of Norwegian Shipping 233

Table 8.1 The development of important OECD fleets, 1973–1987

|  | Fleet 1973 (million dwt) | Fleet 1980 (million dwt) | Fleet 1987 (million dwt) | Decline 1973–1987 (per cent) |
|---|---|---|---|---|
| Denmark | 6.51 | 8.70 | 6.96 | 6.9 |
| The Netherlands | 7.26 | 9.00 | 5.12 | −29.5 |
| Sweden | 8.8 | 13.52 | 2.40 | −72.7 |
| Germany | 12.15 | 13.33 | 5.66 | −53.4 |
| Italy | 13.19 | 17.95 | 12.18 | −7.6 |
| France | 13.29 | 20.86 | 8.41 | −36.7 |
| Greece | 31.44 | 67.05 | 42.78 | 36.1 |
| Norway | 40.09 | 38.89 | 9.66 | −75.9 |
| The UK | 47.16 | 43.18 | 11.68 | −75.2 |
| Japan | 58.59 | 67.32 | 54.67 | −6.7 |
| Ten country total | 238.48 | 299.80 | 159.52 | −33.11 |

Sources: OECD, *Maritime Transport*, various issues. Confer footnote

the losses to any great extent. From 1970 to 1987 there were only three years when the number of companies increased. On average 15 companies disappeared every year, while only nine new companies were established. There was also a marked acceleration towards the end of the period; in both 1985 and 1986 more than 30 companies sold or transferred their last ships under the Norwegian flag.

Table 8.1 illustrates the massive decline in the fleets of the most important Organization for Economic Cooperation and Development (OECD) nations, and also shows that Norway was harder hit by the crisis than other European countries.[3] Only Denmark and Greece saw their fleets increase from 1973 to 1987, but even these "relative winners" experienced tonnage flight in the first part of the 1980s.

The UK continued the relative decline that had characterized the country for most of the 20th century and saw the largest tonnage loss in absolute terms. In fact, the amount of shipping tonnage that disappeared from the British flag in the period 1980–1987 was larger than the whole UK tonnage in 1900, when the UK controlled around half of the world fleet. This says something about how much the world fleet had increased in those eight decades, but also indicates the extent of the flight from the

---

[3] Based on various issues of OECD, *Maritime Transport*; confer Tenold (2000, 156–158).

flag. In relative terms, the Norwegian experience was even more dramatic, but only barely so—in both the UK and in Norway the merchant marine fell by more than three-quarters. The decline also started earlier—in contrast to other countries, the UK and Norway had less tonnage in 1980 than in 1973.

In May 1987, less than 100 ships larger than 15,000 dwt remained, and half of these were already in the process of being transferred to Flags of Convenience—only bureaucratic slowness kept them on the Norwegian register. As a point of comparison, in 1973 there were more than 600 such vessels in the fleet, and Norwegian owners also had more than 200 such ships on order.[4] From more than 800 to less than 100 is a massive reduction, and the press reported that the Norwegian merchant marine had gone "from being a giant to being a dwarf."[5]

Norwegian shipping was on its death bed and awaiting the last rites. But, instead of the four horsemen of the apocalypse, the combination of a clever political manoeuvre and a rapidly improving market appeared on the horizon.

## The Kiss of Life: The Norwegian International Ship Register

The idea of an international register, which Erling Dekke Næss in 1984 presented as the solution to the problems, was first received with little enthusiasm. Large-scale sales to foreign owners and the illusion of "temporary" flagging out to low-cost registries clearly showed that shipping companies could no longer be competitive when flying the Norwegian flag. However, this new reality was difficult to accept. Most shipping industry associations, the authorities and, in particular, the seafarers' unions, were negative about the idea of a "second" or "open" register where foreign labour could be used. Even the Norwegian Shipowners' Association was lukewarm. Its main concern was access to register ships

---

[4] Estimated on the basis of the Veritas-database, see Tenold (2001) for a presentation, and the list of Norwegian newbuilding contracts in *Norwegian Shipping News*, 2A, 1974, 41–63.
[5] NTB, 200587.

abroad, and it probably feared that an inferior Norwegian solution might lead to the reintroduction of restrictions on the use of foreign flags.

Nobody took responsibility for the Norwegian predicament. The seafarers and the government blamed the shipowners, who had been greedy and had taken on too much risk. The shipowners blamed the government for its tax and labour policies, and the trade unions for their wage demands and expensive social requirements. At first, everybody blamed the markets. Then, everybody blamed foreign competitors. Still, with the massive outflow of tonnage in 1985 and 1986, it was evident that the old template was no longer sustainable. World shipping had gone through massive changes, both in technological and organizational terms. Norway had only participated in the first of these transformations.

In 1967, when the Norwegian Shipowners' Association's Managing Director, David Vikøren, presented Norwegian maritime policy at an international conference, he emphasized the fact that Norwegian shipping had "maximum freedom to combine the factors of production as efficiently as possible, regardless of national considerations."[6] The term "maximum freedom" is revealing. At the time, the "factors of production" appeared to be mainly the ship itself, and the important elements in this respect were access to ships, finance, insurance and markets abroad. The restrictions on the nationality of the seafarers were not taken into account. The ban on the use of Flags of Convenience was not even mentioned.

This perception of reality was gradually challenged—by the shipping crisis, by strong relative growth in Norwegian labour costs, and by the changes in the organization of world shipping, including the increasing use of Flags of Convenience. From 1980 to 1987 more than 15,000 jobs for Norwegian seafarers disappeared as a result of sales and flagging out; "the 1980s turned into a painful blood-letting that threatened to wipe out the Norwegian seafarers."[7] The old ideas of what "Norwegian shipping" should and could be had to be reformulated. Gradually, the shipping organizations, the authorities and the seamen's associations were forced to acknowledge the need for change.

---

[6] Vikøren (1967, 8).
[7] Bakka (1999, 8).

In 1981 a Parliamentary committee on shipping unanimously supported the idea that Norwegian shipping should be based on Norwegian ships, displaying the Norwegian flag and employing Norwegian seafarers.[8] Gradually the crisis forced a relaxation of the requirements. The ban, with minor exceptions, turned into temporary permissions. The temporary permissions turned into permanent access, with minor exceptions.

Free access to register ships abroad had been one of the main strategies of the Norwegian Shipowners' Association. There was initially a reluctance to accept the ideas about the Norwegian International Ship Register (NIS). However, as the crisis became broader and more intense, a working party, established in late 1985 and led by Egil Abrahamsen from the classification society *Det Norske Veritas*, reformulated the goals and the policy. At this point, shipping policy became maritime policy. By considering the fate of the whole maritime community—not only the shipping companies, but auxiliary service industries, shipbuilders and so on—the effects became more visible and weightier. Political clout improved.

*Norges Rederforbund* [the Norwegian Shipowners' Association] had good political connections, in particular in *Høyre* [the Conservative Party]. The Prime Minister, Kåre Willoch, had worked for the association in the 1950s, and he still received a salary from *Norges Rederforbund* when he was a Member of Parliament.[9] The association was known as one of Norway's most efficient lobbying organizations, and now it was fighting for its life. When the shipowners changed their minds, the politicians followed suit. In April 1986 the Conservative government referred to the current problems in shipping when it announced its aim to establish an international register. However, a change of government led to a postponement, as the new Labour government wanted to confer more closely with the unions.

That consultation took around a year, and led to a deterioration in the relationship between the Labour Party and the main trade union, and in particular among the various trade unions representing seafarers. The Act

---

[8] See Tenold (2001, 117–123) for a detailed presentation of the political process leading up to the establishment of the NIS.
[9] *Verdens Gang*, 150282, 12; formally, another lobby organization paid Willoch, but half of this salary was reimbursed from the shipowners; see Espeli (1999, 46). He did not receive such a salary during the period in question, when he was Prime Minister.

establishing the NIS had a long and cumbersome journey through the Norwegian political system. The Socialist Left Party (and two dissenting Labour Party members) voted against the establishment, while the Progress Party wanted fewer restrictions, and suggested that NIS vessels should be exempt from Norway's economic boycott of Namibia and South Africa.[10]

The seamen's organizations were extremely negative to what they referred to as "wage-based apartheid" on Norwegian ships—for a long time they were against any system in which Norwegian and foreigners would receive different wages.[11] They denounced the "racism, slavery conditions, starvation wages and lawlessness" that the NIS would introduce.[12] This was a two-faced stance, however: internationalization had already reached the seamen's organizations. *Norsk Sjømannsforbund* had since 1983 operated a hiring office in Manila, where sailors—if they paid fees to the Norwegian union—could be employed on Norwegian vessels without triggering the boycott threat. This was a pragmatic approach with long traditions—in the 1950s Norwegian seafarers were urged not to sign on Panama-registered vessels, unless they were given a contract in which the seamen's organizations in the United States had accepted the salary and the working conditions.

At a conference in Oslo in 1948, the International Transport Workers' Federation decided to introduce a boycott of Flags of Convenience and throughout the post-war period the Norwegian seafarers' organizations had a more hard-line approach to such registers than similar unions in other countries. The Greek shipping organization in London went so far as to claim that the motivation for the Norwegian fight against Flags of Convenience was to stop the expansion of Greek-owned shipping.[13] Gradually, the stigma associated with such flags disappeared. By the middle of the 1980s the Norwegians had not only embraced Flags of Convenience—they had come up with an alternative arrangement.

---

[10] Norway, Parliament (1986–87) Stortingsforhandlinger 3. juni 1987, 79.
[11] Peter Myklebust, Norsk Sjømannsforbund, NTB 240186. See also Bakka (1999).
[12] *Aftenposten*, 070487, 46.
[13] Jenssen (1999, 204–213).

The political process was long and winding, but the bureaucratic response was surprisingly swift. During the consultation, the shipowners' association had suggested that the register should be opened in January 1988. The Shipping Directorate, however, promised that the moment the politicians had made the decision, it would act rapidly. Moreover, parallel with the preparations for the new register, the legal regime would go through significant simplification and rationalization.

The aim was to establish a competitive Norwegian alternative to Flags of Convenience. Consequently, the red tape had to be limited and much of the control function was delegated to the leading international classification societies.[14] The new registries, NIS for international vessels and NOR (Norwegian Ordinary Register) for ships operating in Norwegian waters, were organized under the auspices of the town clerk [*Byskriver*] in Bergen. As a result of the impressive bureaucratic swiftness, they opened for business on 1 July 1987. Outside the offices, huge crowds were protesting. Inside the offices, the revitalization of Norwegian shipping had begun.

When NIS was formally opened in the summer of 1987, the Norwegian-registered fleet consisted of slightly less than 500 ships, totalling 8.9 million dead weight tons (dwt), with a similar number owned from Norway but registered abroad. Because there had been a tendency to flag out relatively large ships, the fleet under foreign flags amounted to almost 16 million dwt.[15] After NIS was established there was an influx of ships from the conventional registry, but this reregistration was more or less over by the end of 1988.

One condition for NIS-registry was that the owner had a collective agreement with a Norwegian or foreign union. In the early 1990s four such agreements existed; for Nordic seafarers, for Filipinos and Indians, for Polish seafarers and for Pakistani and Indonesian seafarers.[16] As such, the Register can be seen as a vehicle of international solidarity, and this was one of the reasons that a Labour government was willing to introduce such an arrangement. The NIS enabled employment for seafarers from

---

[14] See Vigtel (1988, 87–90) and Bakka (2017, 180–181).
[15] Norway, Parliament (1988–89) Stortingsmelding nr. 39 (1988–89), 7.
[16] Jenssen (1999, 216).

poor countries, but on acceptable terms. For a country that prided itself on its "foreign aid," this was another means of north-south transfer. However, the establishment of the NIS did not imply that foreigners for the first time were employed on Norwegian ships—it just meant that for new groups of foreigners, certain minimum conditions were met.

Before NIS, there were legal restrictions on the extent to which it was possible to use foreign labour.[17] The most numerous and most well-known group consisted of other European seafarers; in the 1950s particularly from Denmark and Sweden, and in the 1960s and 1970s increasingly from Southern Europe. In the early 1950s around a quarter of the foreigners on Norwegian ships came from Denmark. Ten years later around a third of the foreign seafarers came from Spain, while the proportion of Danes had fallen to less than 10 per cent. There were several reasons that Norway had to "import" foreign seafarers; the strong growth of the fleet, labour-demanding reconstruction, expansion within education and manufacturing employment onshore, as well as the relatively small cohorts from the 1930s coming of age.

The Europeans had functioned as "swing capacity"—ensuring that there were sufficient seamen during the tight labour market in the 1950s and 1960s, but disappearing when the market became difficult in the 1970s and 1980s.[18] The foreign seafarers were particularly hard hit by vessel sales and rationalization. Given that they were given the same terms as Norwegians, there were no financial incentives behind the employment. The practice had two main reasons. First, it was part of the "international" market for seamen—which had its counterpart in Norwegian seafarers working for ships registered in other countries. Second, it reflected the difficulties of recruitment in a Norwegian economy where attractive employment alternatives were no longer scarce.

The second group of foreign seafarers on Norwegian ships was not employed on Norwegian terms, and there were both practical and cost reasons for its recruitment. Ships trading in East and Southeast Asia had been allowed to take on local crews, who were signed on *en bloc* from local

---

[17] See Halvorsen (2010) for a concise analysis of foreigners working on Norwegian ships in the period 1950–1975.
[18] See the analysis in Tenold (2015b).

crewing agencies. This practice went back to the start of the century, and a waiver from the normal nationality and tariff requirements was given to ships where the officers were Norwegian.[19] This scheme, where all or practically all of the crew were Asian, had included as many as 150 ships in the middle of the 1960s. Many of these vessels were typically older and labour intensive, and had lost out in the competition in the world market as a result of rapid technological development. However, there were also shipping companies that had specialized in the requirements of this trade. The "Asian-clause" vessels were gradually phased out. At the end of the 1960s, it was estimated that around 100 ships operated under such terms, but the number declined rapidly in the 1970s. By the middle of the 1970s the number had been halved, and by the early 1980s only 15 such ships were left. Some were flagged out, with continued Norwegian ownership interests, while some of the trade was taken over by local companies—at times helped by increasingly nationalistic policies.[20]

The least-documented use of foreign labour on Norwegian ships was found in African waters, where there was a long-standing tradition of taking on a supplemental "crew" in the shape of "krooboys"—local labour that performed non-nautical tasks such as hull cleaning, washing, painting, rust picking, general maintenance and so on. "Krooboys" are first mentioned in Norwegian newspapers as early as in 1880.[21] The name has nothing to do with the word "crew," although it is similar to its phonetic spelling—the term was originally used for people from the coast of Kroo or Kru around Cape Palmas in Liberia, Western Africa, who were "journeymen […] found on board of every vessel [along the African coast]." However, in the Norwegian context "krooboys" became a generic term for all kinds of African casual labour.[22]

---

[19] Molaug (1977, 89–95).
[20] Norway, Parliament (1975–76) Stortingsmelding 23, 29 and Norway, Parliament (1986–87) Ot. prp. 45, 7.
[21] *Hedemarkens Amtstidende*, 08.12.1880, 2.
[22] Bacon (1842, 205). Kroomen were known as the strongest and best workers along the coast; see Phillips (1889, 463). For Norwegian ships, Madagascar became an important source of temporary casual labour on the other side of the continent. In the 19th century Royal Navy, it was not uncommon to employ Seedies recruited in the Indian Ocean (for instance the Seychelles or Zanzibar) and Kroomen recruited on the West Coast. For an overview of the problem of defining the group, see Tonkin (1974).

By the 1970s the system was still in existence on some ships trading along the African coast—locals, usually led by an overseer or headman, lived on the deck and worked very long hours at extremely low wages.[23] However, free food and the ability to profit from cast-offs from the ship and petty trading and barter along the coast, made the work sought after. The Africans had few alternative means of income, and the inhabitants of the "Kroo-town" in some African cities had a higher standard of living than the population in general.[24] As Norwegian shipping changed, and the liner trade with frequent stops along the African coast was abandoned, the krooboys disappeared as well.

Before the shipping crisis, the idea that Norwegian ships should be mainly or completely manned by foreigners was alien even to the shipowners' organizations. However, by the middle of the 1980s, it was the only workable political reality. This change shows how much Norwegian shipping—and Norway—had developed in the 20th century. A book from the interwar period suggested that "as long as the sea flows outside the door of thousands of homes, as long as it lights the desire to explore and nourishes good seamanship, it is hardly likely that our most traditional industry will stagnate due to lack of suitable labour."[25] By the late 1980s the sea still flowed, but suitable—in terms of suitably inexpensive—labour had to be obtained elsewhere.

## The Timing of Their Life

The introduction of the Norwegian International Ship Register made it possible for Norwegian shipping companies to compete on equal terms with the most cost-efficient foreign competitors. The recipe was rapidly copied by other countries, but NIS was initially far more successful than similar measures elsewhere.[26] A comparison of second registers from the

---

[23] *Arbeiderbladet*, 020872, 4 and Kvam (1971, 45–49).

[24] See the fascinating recollection of a trip with Krooboys on a Norwegian liner in the 1960s in Bjørklund and Kolltveit (1989, 281–284).

[25] Egeland (1930, 4).

[26] In 1984 the Isle of Man became a second register for the UK, and the Dutch introduced the Netherlands Antilles, with an office in Curacao, in 1987. Both of these were "offshore" registers,

early 1990s shows that while NIS consisted of some 40 million dwt, the closest challengers—Germany and Denmark—each amounted to around 7 million dwt.[27]

What can explain this rollercoaster development of the Norwegian fleet, from more than 48 million dwt in the beginning of 1977 to only around 10 million a decade later, before shooting back to almost 38 million dwt in 1991?[28] The basis for the reduction is hopefully clear by now—the combination of a collapsing market and unfortunate strategies. What about the rebound? The 57 million tons of shipping registered in Norway and elsewhere was an all-time high for the Norwegian-owned fleet, though the share of the world fleet—which was now slightly less than 9 per cent—had been larger in the late 1960s. There are three main reasons for the rapid ascent after the 1987 nadir; one general, and two specific to Norway.

One reason for the strong growth was market developments. The tanker market slowly improved from 1985 onwards, as demand picked up and superfluous tonnage was scrapped. The cycle in the bulk market changed relatively abruptly in 1987, with rates and values of some vessel classes more than doubling during the year. The fact that ship prices were extremely low—and that the vessels in many instances were owned by banks or other creditors without a long-term, operational scope—implied that it was relatively easy to enter the market. The market improvement was a tide that lifted all boats. Consequently, we have to look elsewhere to explain why Norway's international market share more than trebled from 1987 to 1990.[29]

The first specifically Norwegian reason was that many of the ships that had been flagged out—while ownership or control remained in Norway—

---

and were followed by Kerguelen, a "French Antarctic" registry in 1989. NIS was the first "domestic" open register, followed by Denmark and Germany in 1989 and Italy in 1998; see Carlisle (2009, 322) and Sorrn-Friese and Iversen (2014).

[27] Sletmo and Holste (1993, 249–250).

[28] Data on the Norwegian fleet in December 1991 from UNCTAD, *Maritime Transport 1991*, 11. In addition to the almost 38 million carrying the Norwegian flag, UNCTAD estimates that there was a fleet of almost 19 million dwt flying foreign flags—in total, a fleet of 56,772,906 dwt. Fearnley & Eger, *Review 1991*, 48, refers to a Norwegian fleet of 41 million dwt.

[29] The idea that all countries and companies are equally affected by a market improvement is a simplification: given the different development of the various shipping segments, not all boats are lifted equally.

returned to the Norwegian flag. Although the register, as a public body, had a limited ability to market itself, the Bergen Shipowners' Association actively promoted the new possibilities. Foreign owners, if they had Norwegian representatives, could register ships in NIS, but the number of foreign-owned vessels entered into the register was very low. By the beginning of 1989 only around 30 foreign-owned ships were included, and by 1992 the foreign-owned share was less than 7 per cent of the total, so this played no important role in the growth. Vastly more important was the fact that Norwegian shipowners saw the register as attractive, both with regard to price and procedures. Moreover, the fact that it had been possible to arrive at a political solution—and one that ensured competitiveness while maintaining the link to Norway—created a sense of optimism.

This brings us to the final reason for the rebound: an impressive ability to mobilize capital and identify opportunities.

The crisis had taken its toll on the equity of Norwegian shipping companies, on the loan portfolios of the shipping banks and on the recruitment of personnel to ships and shipping company offices. The crisis had proved that shipping was a high-risk business. However, high risk also means high potential profits. The dream of these profits encouraged a massive wave of Norwegian investment. Norwegian investors were willing to take the risk—and they were eagerly encouraged by the authorities.

In fact, the latter element—the awakening of dormant Norwegian capital—was the most important factor behind the growth. Estimates from the beginning of the 1990s suggest that ships that had "returned home" made up around 20 per cent of the NIS fleet, while ships that had been bought second-hand abroad amounted to 60 per cent of the tonnage. In the period 1987–1991 more than 900 vessels were bought by Norwegian owners, and the majority would be registered in NIS.[30]

With the establishment of NIS, and the changing cost structure, completely new models of operation and ownership became possible. This led to increased diversification in the Norwegian fleet. Before it was possible to use low-cost foreign seafarers, only the most modern, advanced and specialized ships could afford to fly the Norwegian flag. Now it became

---

[30] Bakka (2017, 186–188).

possible to compete on completely equal terms with foreigners, and there was no need to stick with "typically Norwegian" strategies. Consequently, relatively simple, older, second-hand tonnage was bought from abroad, leading to a high degree of diversification in the Norwegian fleet. By the early 1990s there were even suggestions that some of the ships that had been included in NIS were "substandard" and that the reputation of the register was at stake.[31]

## Old and New Hands on Deck

The maritime historian Dag Bakka jr., who has written a very good account of the revitalization of the shipping industry after the introduction of the NIS, points out that three different types of "shipowners" put their mark on Norwegian shipping in the last part of the 20th century.[32] The expansion was orchestrated by "the next generation,", which took over existing companies, a group of enterprising newcomers, as well as those that had survived the crisis; the old-timers.

The first group was a new generation of owners and managers, who took the helm in a number of traditional shipping companies—Bergesen, Kloster, Smedvig and Staubo. The extent to which their inheritance had any *real* value varied—in many cases the shipping crisis had depleted the value of the companies. However, they had a shipping pedigree, and access to national and international networks. Some of the companies had sailed relatively smoothly through the crisis, others started practically from scratch, with little more than a shipping "name" and a shipping reputation.

The second group consisted of experienced owners in established companies—Westfal-Larsen, Fred. Olsen, Leif Höegh and so on. Many of the older shipping companies had a more risk-adverse strategy than the fastest growers in the 1960s and 1970s—their growth was slower, but that also implied that their financial basis was sounder. As we have seen, they were on average more diversified, and had a larger portfolio of specialized

---

[31] *Lloyd's List*, 010492, 11.
[32] Bakka (2017, 186–187).

ships, than the smaller companies. Some of the established companies collapsed during the crisis, while others were busy restructuring their balance sheets and biding their time until there were new profitable opportunities. In the most fertile instances, the established companies had been divided among different branches of the family, paving the way for expansion along parallel lines, both old and new.

In Bergen we find two very good examples of how competition between companies with a joint tradition could give strong growth. Kristian Gerhard Jebsen started his own business in the late 1960s, after leaving the family company, which was taken over by his younger brother, Atle Jebsen. The two brothers were among the most expansive shipowners in the 1980s and 1990s, investing heavily in the specialized bulk markets. Although they both had financial challenges, their companies were among the largest in Norway in the early 1990s.[33] Similarly, when the second cousins, Dan Odfjell and Abraham Odfjell, divided the leading chemical tanker owner, Odfjell, in the 1970s, they both managed to build up companies that were in the Top Four of the chemical tanker market. This kind of growth—by spin-offs from established enterprises—was not confined to Bergen. Various members of the Ugland family based in and around Grimstad on the South Coast, also made their mark, with investments in car carriers, shuttle tankers, bulk carriers and product tankers.

The final group consisted of a number of entrepreneurs, with various backgrounds, who used their skills and networks to create new business. Some came from shipping companies, others from shipbroking or finance. Among these we find John Fredriksen, who from a base in London would go on to become by far the biggest and most successful Norwegian shipowner in the first part of the new millennium. Another newcomer was Herbjørn Hansson, who had worked for Anders Jahre in the Kosmos-system. He built up a substantial tanker fleet by means of a company incorporated in Bermuda, but with operations in Norway. The strategy has been to raise funds from investors on the New York Stock Exchange, where a large number of shareholders saw shipping as an exotic industry and were seduced by the frequent payment of dividends.

---

[33] See Tenold (2015a) and Harvey (2005).

Hansson's business model was quite unique in a Norwegian setting, but in an international perspective, a handful of Greek shipping companies followed the same strategy.

Sometimes the newcomers built their business on the ruins of older companies. Jens Ulltveit Moe had been appointed by the main creditor, Bergen Bank, to take over the management of the troubled Knutsen OAS in Haugesund, which had made unfortunate investments in large tankers.[34] Together with Trygve Seglem, he built up a fleet of advanced Suezmax shuttle tankers. The phoenix-like Knutsen organization was primarily engaged in the operation and management of the ships—the investments funds very often originated from investors in limited partnerships [*kommandittselskap*] that had actual ownership of the vessels.

The *kommandittselskap* became the "typical" form of incorporation for many of the companies that expanded rapidly in the period around 1990. The financial basis for this type of incorporation was the combination of limited liability with substantial tax deductions for the individual owners. For many investors, the tax advantages were the main motivation for the investments—in the worst cases, projects that had negative expected profits turned out to give a positive return when the tax effect was considered. A number of the projects also had an evident speculative character, where the main aim was "asset play"—a desire to reap the benefits of increasing vessel values—rather than revenue from long-term operation.

The limited partnerships were not only linked to deep-sea shipping—they became a favoured means of finance for offshore involvement as well. There had been a steady stream of shipping companies seeking out opportunities in connection with the expansion of the Norwegian offshore sector. First, during the period of high liquidity at the beginning of the 1970s. Second, as a means of diversification when the shipping market wobbled. Finally, as a viable business in its own right, for companies that had managed to build up knowledge about another maritime venture.

---

[34] See Hammerborg (2003, 386–395). Evidently not a big fan of mono-causal explanations, Hammerborg (2003, 386) explains Knutsen's success by the following factors: "luck, coincidence, personal competence, skill, the restructuring of the company, the creditors' patience, technological development, the oil activity in the North Sea and the access to venture capital through the *kommandittselskap*-scheme."

## Returning Home in Search of Black Gold

The 1970s and 1980s were extremely dramatic, and the haemorrhaging of shipping companies during the crisis was unprecedented. The introduction of the Norwegian International Ship Register, which saved Norwegian shipping but sacrificed Norwegian seafarers, was a timely intervention by the authorities. Still, the new regime could not prevent the shipping industry from losing its previous hegemonic position in the economy in general, and in exports in particular. Net freight earnings—the profits that the shipping companies "brought back home" from abroad—had fallen from more than 23 per cent of total exports in the beginning of the 1970s, to less than 4 per cent by 1987.[35]

The reduced importance of shipping in the Norwegian economy was not only caused by the difficult conditions in the shipping market and the reduction of the Norwegian fleet. The transformation of "Norway—the shipping nation" to "Norway—the oil producer" also played a very important part.[36] The export of crude petroleum and natural gas, which was non-existent in 1970, made up more than a third of Norwegian exports in the first half of the 1980s. During this turbulent period, growth in offshore petroleum exploration and exploitation became another outlet for maritime capital and maritime competence.

The relationship between Norwegian deep-sea shipping and offshore oil production is complex. The activity in the North Sea clearly diverted resources away from the shipping industry—both capital and labour found an attractive alternative. At the same time, with international shipping markets developing the way they did, some kind of constraint on the Norwegian exposure was clearly a good thing. Consequently, while the offshore sector temporarily reduced Norway's involvement in

---

[35] Calculated on the basis of Statistics Norway (1994, 532–533 and 544–545). Although the figures never returned to those of the Golden Age—even when we leave out petroleum exports—1987 was a low point.

[36] Gross freight earnings made up 37 per cent and net freight earnings 23.3 per cent of total exports in 1970. By 1987 the shares had fallen to 13.8 per cent for gross freight earnings and 3.4 per cent for net freight earnings. This was partly a result of Norway's emergence as a major oil exporter but even if we exclude the effects of the petroleum exports, there is a substantial decline, to 18.9 and 4.6 per cent, respectively. Due to a smaller fleet and a lower freight rate level, the revenue from shipping declined in absolute terms as well.

international shipping, the long-term effects were positive, for at least three reasons.

First, a number of shipping companies found another investment object that clearly provided a higher return on capital than the crisis-ridden shipping market. For some it provided revenue in difficult times, for others a completely new business model. Second, activity in the North Sea provided the maritime sector with a new base from which it became possible to build up competence and expand on the international stage. Third, for Norwegian seafarers—who were replaced by low-cost foreigners on the ships in the Norwegian deep-sea fleet—activity in the North Sea provided not only alternative employment, but jobs that were better paid and had more attractive conditions than what they could find working in conventional deep-sea shipping.

Geological surveys off the Norwegian coast began in the early 1960s, and the first well was drilled by Esso in the summer of 1966. The shipping companies became involved in a number of projects and activities related to the new industry; investment in oil companies, in onshore bases, in supply ships and, as a swarm of bees in the first half of the 1970s, in oil rigs.

One reason for the shipping companies' involvement was of course the fact that they represented one of the wealthiest industries in Norway. Although "shipping money" typically was reinvested in new transport capacity, shipping companies and shipowners were among the most important capitalists in the country, and a natural starting point for anyone looking for investment funds. Another reason for the inflow of shipping money into the offshore oil sector was the maritime linkages. The offshore oil sector was not the kind of activity that the shipping companies were used to, but it was not far from it. Shipping companies already had substantial competence and relations within areas such as vessel construction and supervision, classification, financing, insurance, manning and son on. This put them in a particularly advantageous position when the offshore petroleum industry was developed.

One example of this bridge between the old and the new maritime interests was the old whale factory ship, *Thorshøvdi*, which was rebuilt by the Aker Group. A 50-metre drilling tower was added to the almost 20-year-old ship. Renamed *Drillship*, the former Thor Dahl vessel was delivered to British interests in the autumn of 1967. Earlier that year, the first Norwegian-built drilling rig, *Ocean Viking*, had been delivered to the US company Ocean Drilling & Exploration Company (Odeco). The rig was responsible for the first major oil find in Norway—what would become the extremely profitable *Ekofisk* field.

The day before Christmas Eve in 1969, Phillips Petroleum announced that the company had discovered *Ekofisk* and the economic fate of Norway was changed forever.[37] However, even before this, shipping interests had entered the offshore sector on a large scale. When Phillips started its activities in 1966, its operations were based at Dusavik, near Stavanger, one of the main supply bases for the offshore industry, and owned by the Stavanger shipping company Smedvigs Tankrederi AS.[38] However, for most of the Norwegian shipping companies, the first point of entry to the oil sector was investment in oil companies.

Three of Norway's leading shipping companies—Sig. Bergesen d.y. & Co., Anders Jahre and Fearnley & Astrup, as well as the Aker Group, where Fred. Olsen was the major owner—participated in the first Norwegian oil consortium, Noco, which was established in 1964. When a second consortium was established the same year, the majority of the owners came from the shipping industry.[39] The participants in these consortia were mainly the larger Norwegian shipping companies. There was also a handful of other companies that had gained exploration rights, and in the early 1970s more than 30 Norwegian shipping companies had bought shares in such companies. In fact, several of the Norwegian companies with parts in the various oil blocks had only or mainly capital from shipping. KS AS Polaris, AS Pelican Co. KS, AS Syracuse Oils Norge, KS

---

[37] See Kvendseth (1988) for Ekofisk and Hanisch and Nerheim (1992); Nerheim (1996); and Ryggvik and Smith-Solbakken (1997) for a more comprehensive history of the development of the Norwegian offshore oil and gas industry.

[38] See Nerheim and Utne (1990) for the well-written business history of Smedvig, an enterprise that went through the full conversion from a traditional shipping company to an offshore company during the period 1965–1995. Smedvig had also participated, together with a cement company, another shipping company and a shipbroker, in the first Norwegian offshore base.

[39] After the two consortia were merged in 1965, 11 of the 20 participating companies had their background within shipping; see Saga Petroleum (1997). Two of the best introductions to the shipping companies' various engagements in the offshore oil industry by the early 1970s, are Seeberg (1974) and Tveit (1973).

25/4 Norsk AS and Scanpet were among the most serious contenders to the large oil companies, and they were all mainly vehicles for shipping companies' investments.[40] In 1972, Saga Petroleum, the major private Norwegian oil company was established. More than 50 of the 96 companies that participated were shipping companies, and these provided around 60 per cent of the capital.[41]

In addition to their role in establishing and developing the leading private oil companies, shipping interests were important participants when the activity on the Norwegian continental shelf grew rapidly in the early 1970s. One important area was supply shipping. Several of the larger shipping companies invested in supply ships, but this was also a way into the offshore market for new owners with traditions stemming from fisheries or coastal transport. The initial support for the offshore industry came from rebuilt fishing vessels and simple, smaller cargo ships. The first purpose-built vessels were delivered in 1971, and by 1973 there were 24 supply vessels flying the Norwegian flag, with another 46 on order.[42] The herd behaviour again had consequences for the functioning of the market: as the supply of such ships gradually became plagued by overcapacity, shipowners began to cooperate with regard to management and operations.

Norwegian companies and seafarers had certain advantages in the operation of vessels in the North Sea. They were aware of and used to the difficult conditions, and also had an advantage in dealing with the routines and procedures of Norwegian bureaucracy. Gradually they acquired competence that enabled them to take on new tasks—traditional supply and stand-by services were supplemented by pipe laying, seismic surveys, well intervention and so on.

The historian Helge Ryggvik has referred to the Norwegian shipping companies' advantages within the supply sector as "self-evident." He sees the entry into rig ownership as more surprising, as this activity—despite the mobility of the rigs—had an "industrial" rather than a "shipping"

---

[40] Tveit (1973, 18–27).
[41] Calculated on the basis of Tveit (1973, 15–18). The other two major Norwegian companies were Statoil, which was fully state-owned, and Norsk Hydro, where the authorities owned the majority of the shares from the early 1970s onwards. See Ryggvik (2000) for a good introduction to the ownership development.
[42] Hanisch and Nerheim (1992, 228–231).

character. This reflected the manner in which the cooperation with foreign interests was organized. Most of the shipping companies that invested in rig ownership initially relied on foreign operators to take care of the drilling—they were "subcontractors, far down in the offshore hierarchy."[43]

In the late summer of 1971 Smedvig was the first Norwegian company to order a purpose-built drilling rig, unleashing a veritable flood of new orders; "in the course of a few autumn months nine semi-submersible platforms were ordered, to be registered in Norway."[44] This signalled the breakthrough for offshore oil in the shipping industry—or the breakthrough for shipping in the oil industry. Almost half of the 25 largest shipping companies participated in the rush for newbuildings in 1971.[45]

The Aker group, in cooperation with the Bergen shipping company Odfjell, developed Aker H-3, a platform specifically designed to cope with the depth and the harsh conditions in the North Sea. The H-3 platform was the focus when the second contracting boom took place, in late 1973 and early 1974. By the end of 1974, 54 drilling rigs had been ordered with Norwegian participation. The Norwegian shipowners brought a new element to the oil industry—speculation. Enticed by the high rates, they ordered rigs without securing employment in advance.[46] The spot-market strategy that would create enormous problems for Norwegian tanker owners was simply transferred to the rig sector.

The motivation was money. In 1974 the Norwegian rig owners managed to get spectacular rates; two-year contracts at USD32,000 per day for an Aker H-3 platform in January were surpassed by a five-year contract at around USD35,000 per day in May and finally, for Fred. Olsen's Borgny Dolphin, USD41,000 per day for the next two years.[47]

In 1975 the many rigs that Norwegian owners had ordered began to come on stream, and the market deteriorated. The increasing supply took place against a cooling market, as new taxation rules held the oil companies'

---

[43] Ryggvik (2000, 237).
[44] R.S. Platou, *The Platou Report 1971*, 23.
[45] See the overview in Tenold (2000, 356–358).
[46] Hanisch and Nerheim (1992, 233).
[47] Hanisch and Nerheim (1992, 239).

exploration activities back. In 1976 more than 60 new rigs—leading to a 30 per cent increase of the fleet—were delivered. As supply eclipsed demand, rigs were laid up or rebuilt to dwelling and service platforms. Although the financial situation was more positive than in the shipping sector, oil rig owners could apply for support from the Guarantee Institute, and 13 drilling vessels were included. When the market picked up again in the late 1970s, these engagements were settled without losses.

When shipping was replaced by petroleum as Norway's most important export sector, the competence that had been built up in the shipping companies played a crucial role. Sometimes the two maritime industries worked closely together, for instance in the case of shuttle tankers—ships transporting oil from the offshore fields, as an alternative to pipelines. Improvements in technology revolutionized this manner of moving oil. In 1971 it took almost two months for the Greek tanker *Theogennitor* to move 34,000 tons of oil from the Ekofisk field to Stavanger. During 2001, when oil production peaked, a fleet of 28 shuttle tankers moved a total of 86.4 million tons of oil, in more than 883 separate voyages.[48] Compared with *Theogennitor*, the shuttle tankers' productivity had multiplied by a factor of 15 as a result of economies of scale—the ships varied from 87,000 to 150,000 dwt—and improved loading and discharging equipment.

By the end of the 20th century, Norwegian companies—relying on both capital and competence from shipping—had become world leaders within the advanced, deep-water search for and production of oil and gas. There is a clear upwards trajectory in the value chain when it comes to the Norwegian shipping companies' offshore involvement. As skills were acquired, the foreign operators were replaced by Norwegian managers, operators and personnel.

The increasing offshore activity on the Norwegian continental shelf was a lifeline for many shipping companies, providing new business opportunities and a revenue stream in a difficult time for shipping. However, there were also shipping companies that attempted to enter the offshore sector, and failed. Just as in the shipping industry, strong fluctuations in rates and activity meant that deep pockets—or patient creditors—were an advantage, and at times a necessity.

---

[48] Lindøe (2009, 19).

## Working (Almost) from Home

For Norwegian seafarers, the offshore activity was undoubtedly a new and beneficial opportunity. Work was closer to home, with good salaries and shorter periods away from home. Again, the timing was very good. From 1973 to 1981 the number of seafarers employed in the foreign-going Norwegian fleet declined from 45,000 to 34,000—a reduction of 11,000 seafarers. At the same time, the number of unemployed seafarers hardly increased, from 1143 to 1594. This 40 per cent growth was in fact lower than for unemployment in general, which increased by more than 90 per cent.[49]

Some of the seafarers left the business altogether, but many started a new working life "offshore." Former seafarers were in high demand. Engineers and other officers "had an education and experience that proved to be extremely valuable in connection with the construction and operation of petroleum installations in difficult North Sea conditions."[50] It is evident that this was a mutually beneficial arrangement; the seafarers emphasize the "very good" working arrangements offshore, which are "much easier" than in the deep sea fleet.[51]

While the introduction of the NIS saved international shipping under the Norwegian flag in the long term, and many seafarers found attractive employment elsewhere, the 1980s was a tough period for those working at sea. As shipping companies replaced the Norwegians with foreigners, "many sailors suffered mentally and emotionally; they lost their income and standard of living in a very short time."[52] By the start of the 1990s, the more than 6000 seafarers that worked on NOR-vessels in Norwegian waters also saw increased competition. The basis was foreign companies, sometimes subsidized, from other European countries.

From 1965 to 1973, in the growth period before the shipping crisis had started to bite, the number of Norwegian seafarers fell by around a third, as a result of rationalization and economies of scale. From 1973

---

[49] Norway, Parliament, NOU 1983, Skipsfartens konkurranseevne, 76–77.
[50] Hanisch and Nerheim (1992, 365).
[51] Mack (2007, 352).
[52] Mack (2007, 353).

until the introduction of the NIS in 1987, the number was halved, to around 17,000, as ships were sold abroad and flagged out.[53] By the year 2000, employment had increased to almost 15,000 Norwegian seafarers on NOR-vessels and almost 4000—mainly officers—on NIS-vessels, in addition to those that worked on ships flying other flags.[54]

Although the decline in employment halted, and was even reversed, the cultural impact of employment on Norwegian ships has changed dramatically. As late as the 1970s, around a third of the male labour force had spent some time at sea. For many, it was a temporary adventure and a way to see the world in the period before mass travel and cheap airplane tickets. For others, it was a means of escape. Up until the 1970s, a stint at sea was seen as the best way to instil discipline and a sense of responsibility in "unruly boys." Today, there are few acceptable alternatives.

In the old days, those working in the cafes and bars in the main ports had a special trick to deal with drunken sailors: when they threw them out of the establishment, they would put their hats on back-to-front. This would make it very clear for the next bar owner that these sailors had had too much to drink, and should be sent back to their ship, rather than be served.[55]

Today, the hats, the red-light districts and adventure-seeking Norwegian sailors in exotic ports have gone. Bergen Bar, Tønsberg Bar and Café Håpløs have closed their doors. Most Norwegian seafarers have returned home. They are no longer the "heroes who came home" telling "about the world or their life experiences," no longer the explorers that "carried the Chesterfields in their pockets and were naturally tanned in the middle of winter."[56]

Today, all kinds of Norwegians go abroad. But the seafarers have largely returned home. The busiest seamen's church—now rebranded as the "Norwegian Church Abroad"—is the one at Gran Canaria, and around a third of the resources that the seamen's church has is used in Spain. The majority of the European seamen's churches are not in important port

---

[53] Calculated on the basis of Statistics Norway (1994, 487).
[54] Norway, Parliament, *Stortingsmelding 31 (2003–2004)*, 30.
[55] Marthinsen (1998, 61).
[56] Mack (2007, 351).

cities, but in tourist destinations, both on the coast and inland. However, there are also seven chaplains working on the oil platforms on the Norwegian continental shelf, and another three involved with supply vessels.[57]

The plan that Erling Dekke Næss presented in 1984 saved Norwegian deep-sea shipping under the Norwegian flag, but it was too late to save most of the seafarers in the ocean-going Norwegian fleet.

# Bibliography

F. Bacon (1842) 'Cape Palmas and the Mena, or Kroomen', *The Journal of the Royal Geographical Society of London*, 12, 196–206

D. Bakka (1999) *I hardt vær. Skipsfartskrise og samlingsproses – Norsk Sjøoffisersforbund 1995* (Bergen: Norsk Sjøoffisersforbund)

D. Bakka (2017) *Nasjonens ære – Norsk rederinæring mellom marked og politikk* (Bergen: Bodoni Forlag)

J.G. Bjørklund & B. Kolltveit (1989) 'Norsk sjøfart i det 20. århundre', in B. Berggren, A.E. Christensen & B. Kolltveit (eds) *Norsk Sjøfart* (Oslo: Dreyers Forlag AS) 126–311

R. Carlisle (2009) 'Second Registers: Maritime Nations Respond to Flags of Convenience, 1984–1998', *The Northern Mariner/le marin du nord*, 19:3, 319–340

J.O. Egeland (1930) 'Norges sjøfart. Hvad den var og hvad den er', in G. Stenersen (ed) *Sjømannsboken; sjøfart, hvalfangst, marine: orientering i sjømannskap, veiledning til selvstudium*, (Oslo: Norsk bibliotekforening) 3–37

H. Espeli (1999) *Lobbyvirksomhet på Stortinget* (Oslo: TANO Aschehoug)

T. Halvorsen (2010) 'Vi var "degos, svartinger eller skjevøyde". Utlendinger i den norske handelsflåten 1950–75', *Arbeiderhistorie*, 24, 203–223

M. Hammerborg (2003) *Skipsfartsbyen* (Bergen: Eide)

T.J. Hanisch & G. Nerheim (1992) 'Fra vantro til overmot', *Norsk Oljehistorie 1* (Oslo: Norsk Petroleumsforening)

W.J. Harvey (2005) *Kristian Jebsens Rederi AS Bergen – A Group History* (Windsor: The World Ship Society)

L.C. Jenssen (1999) '50 år i stampesjø' – Fagbevegelsens kamp mot bekvemmelighetsflagg', *Arbeiderhistorie*, 13, 203–223

---

[57] Sjømannskirken, *Annual report 2017*.

R. Kvam (1971) *Den billige arbeidskraften* (Oslo: Pax Forlag AS)
S.S. Kvendseth (1988) *Funn! Historien om Ekofisks første tyve år* (Stavanger: Phillips Petroleum)
J.O. Lindøe (2009) *From sea to shore – the shuttle tanker story* (Stavanger: Wigestrand Forlag & Stavanger Maritime Museum)
K. Mack (2007) 'When seafaring is (or was) a calling: Norwegian seafarers' career experiences', *Maritime Policy & Management*, 34:4, 347–358
T.-O. Marthinsen (1998) *Sjømann – vel fortjent i trygg havn* (Stavern: Det nasjonale aldershjem for sjømenn i Stavern)
S. Molaug (1977) *Sjøfolk forteller – Hverdagshistorier fra seilskutetiden* (Oslo: Tanum-Norli)
G. Nerheim (1996) "En gassnasjon blir til," *Norsk Oljehistorie 2* (Oslo: Norsk Petroleumsforening)
G. Nerheim & B.S. Utne (1990) *Under samme stjerne – Rederiet Peder Smedvig 1915–1990* (Stavanger: Peder Smedvig AS)
E.D. Næss (1977) *Autobiography of a Shipping Man* (Seatrade, London)
E.D. Næss (1981) *Shipping – mitt liv* (Oslo: AS Hjemmet Fagpresseforlaget)
H. Phillips (1889) 'An Account of the Congo Independent State', *Proceedings of the American Philosophical Society*, 26:130, 459–476
H. Ryggvik (2000) *Norsk oljevirksomhet mellom det nasjonale og det internasjonale. En studie av selskapsstruktur og internasjonalisering* (Oslo: Senter for Teknologi, Innovasjon og Kultur)
H. Ryggvik & M. Smith-Solbakken (1997) 'Blod, svette og olje', *Norsk Oljehistorie 3* (Oslo: Norsk Petroleumsforening)
Saga Petroleum (1997) *Sagaen om Saga* (Oslo: Saga Petroleum ASA)
B. Seeberg (1974) 'Norsk skipsfart og dens engasjement i petroleumsaktivitetene i Nordsjøen', *unpublished thesis* (Bergen: Norwegian School of Economics and Business Administration)
G.K. Sletmo & S. Holste (1993) 'Shipping and the competitive advantage of nations: The role of international ship registers' *Maritime Policy and Management*, 20:1, 243–255
H. Sornn-Friese & M.J. Iversen (2014) 'The establishment of the Danish International Ship Register (DIS) and its connections to the maritime cluster', *International Journal of Maritime History*, 26:1, 82–103
Statistics Norway (1994) *Historisk Statistikk 1994* (Oslo: Statistisk Sentralbyrå)
S. Tenold (2000) 'The Shipping Crisis of the 1970s: Causes, Effects and Implications for Norwegian Shipping', *PhD-thesis* (Bergen: Norwegian School of Economics and Business Administration)

S. Tenold (2001) *Skipsfartskrisen og utviklingen i norske skipsfart 1970–91* (Bergen: Stiftelsen for samfunns- og næringslivsforskning)
S. Tenold (2015a) *Geared for Growth. Kristian Gerhard Jebsen and His Shipping Companies* (Bergen: Bodoni Forlag)
S. Tenold (2015b) 'Globalisation and maritime labour in Norway after World War II', *The International Journal of Maritime History*, 27:4, 774–792
E. Tonkin (1974) 'Review of The Kru Mariner in the Nineteenth Century: An Historical Compendium', *The Journal of African History*, 15:2, 332–334
O.K. Tveit (1973) *Nordsjøoljen* (Oslo: Grøndahl & Søns Forlag)
P.M. Vigtel (1988) 'Norsk Internasjonalt Skipsregister – årsak og virkninger', *Norsk Utenrikspolitisk Årbok* (Oslo: Norsk Utenrikspolitisk Institutt) 83–93
D. Vikøren (1967) 'Merchant Marine Policy of Norway', *manuscript* (Oslo: Norwegian Shipowners' Association)

**Open Access** This chapter is licensed under the terms of the Creative Commons Attribution-NonCommercial-NoDerivatives 4.0 International License (http://creativecommons.org/licenses/by-nc-nd/4.0/), which permits any noncommercial use, sharing, distribution and reproduction in any medium or format, as long as you give appropriate credit to the original author(s) and the source, provide a link to the Creative Commons license and indicate if you modified the licensed material. You do not have permission under this license to share adapted material derived from this chapter or parts of it.

The images or other third party material in this chapter are included in the chapter's Creative Commons license, unless indicated otherwise in a credit line to the material. If material is not included in the chapter's Creative Commons license and your intended use is not permitted by statutory regulation or exceeds the permitted use, you will need to obtain permission directly from the copyright holder.

# 9

# Onshore and Offshore: The New Maritime Norway

At the beginning of the 20th century, Norwegian shipping had a significant position, both domestically and internationally. Shipping was one of the cornerstones of the Norwegian economy, and no country had put so much of its resources into their merchant marine. Although there was a predilection for relatively outdated sailing tonnage, Norwegian owners had managed to carve out important niches in the world market. However, the strong expansion that had characterized development in most of the second half of the 19th century appeared to be over.

From the late 1870s to 1900 the Norwegian share of the world fleet declined, from around 6 per cent to between 4 and 5 per cent.[1] However, the fleet was in the midst of a structural transformation. The technological shift from sail to steam and wood to steel led to changes in a number of areas: the trades in which the ships operated and the manner in which they were managed, the skills that were needed both at sea and on shore,

---

[1] The Norwegian share of the world fleet depends on how and what we measure. The share of the sailing tonnage was around 10 per cent, while the share of the steamship fleet—as seen in Fig. 1.1—was around 3.6 per cent. The most representative measure is probably "effective tonnage," which takes into account the productivity differences between various technologies. The share of the world fleet then becomes between 4 and 5 per cent, depending on the lower cut off-point for the size of individual vessels.

© The Author(s) 2019
S. Tenold, *Norwegian Shipping in the 20th Century*, Palgrave Studies in Maritime Economics, https://doi.org/10.1007/978-3-319-95639-8_9

the localization of shipping companies, the manner in which vessels were financed, and so on.

At the end of the 20th century Norwegian shipping was going through a similar structural transformation related to the increasing activities within offshore petroleum exploration. Both the "Norwegian" and the "shipping" element had changed significantly over the preceding 100 years. The standard, early 20th century definition of a Norwegian ship—a seagoing vessel with Norwegian flag, Norwegian seafarers and Norwegian owners, but typically operating all over the world—would no longer be relevant. Moreover, "shipping" had become a far more diverse activity than it was at the start of the 20th century, and during the century the geographic basis of the industry had developed. The North Atlantic, which was the main arena at the start of the century, had been supplemented by strong growth in other regions, with the Pacific becoming particularly important.

## The Power Centre in the World Economy Shifts

The increasing role of Japan in the world economy and international shipping in the decades after the Second World War was just a harbinger of what was to come. Two generations of Asian "tigers"—led by the super exporters Hong Kong, Singapore, South Korea and Taiwan—were followed by the enormous resources of China.[2] The end result was a dramatic transformation of world production and trade in the second half of the 20th century.

The strong growth of international trade, investment and income in the second half of the 19th century is often referred to as the birth of the international economy. Resources in Africa, America, Asia and Australia—resources that had previously been left isolated and unused—became important in an intercontinental exchange of goods. The integration of

---

[2] These four countries, often referred to as the "First-generation Asian Tigers," were followed by the "Second-generation Asian Tigers"—Malaysia, Indonesia and Thailand. The "Asian economic miracles" lost some of their shine after Japan's lost decades of low economic growth and the Asian crisis in the late 1990s. However, the resurgence of growth, coupled with the economic might of China, implies that the gravity of the world economy has undoubtedly shifted.

resources from different continents led to a strong increase in both production and productivity. Nowhere was this more evident than on the American continent, particularly the northern part, where the coupling of European labour and capital with domestic land and resources led to "the first era of globalization." It also paved the way for the strongest nation—the world's first superpower—in the 20th century.

The post-war integration of several billion Asian workers and consumers in the international economy has had a similar effect, although the economic importance has been more important than the strategic role. New technological possibilities have encouraged specialization and division of labour; outsourcing and foreign direct investment, from "Made in Hong Kong" in the 1970s to "Made in China" in the 1990s. Gradually, Asian countries have produced and exported more and more advanced products—to the benefit of workers at home and consumers abroad.

For many European companies, the Asian expansion came at a cost, as businesses that were unable to compete had to downscale production or seek subsidies or other types of support. The manufacturing sector was particularly vulnerable, and deindustrialization was a phenomenon that demanded a tough social and economic transformation in many Western countries.[3] However, the imports from Asia were only part of the story. Although low-cost production in Asia was seen as a culprit in much of the rhetoric about the loss of manufacturing jobs in the Western World, increasing wealth (giving a higher relative demand for services), productivity growth and domestic outsourcing were more important than international trade in explaining the loss of jobs within manufacturing.[4]

A case in point is the shipbuilding industry. When the demand for new ships dried up during the shipping crisis of the 1970s and 1980s, European authorities responded first by subsidizing production, then by orchestrating a controlled downsizing—and in some instances total removal—of the industry. The shipbuilding industry moved to Asia—where three countries are now totally dominant, particularly in the high-volume segment of the industry. China, Japan and South Korea produced

---

[3] From 1970 to 1994 manufacturing employment in the 23 most advanced economies fell from 28 to 18 per cent of the workforce; Rowthorn and Ramaswamy (1997, 2).
[4] See Rowthorn and Ramaswamy (1997).

around 90 per cent of the world's tonnage in the first decades of the 21st century

In the last part of the 20th century and the beginning of the 21st, Norway was lucky. The country's industrial structure—primarily exporting raw materials and services rather than manufactured products—meant that this high-income economy got a double benefit from the manner in which globalization unfolded. The demand for petroleum and shipping increased, pushing up the price of the country's exports. At the same time, the spread of low-cost production put a downward pressure on the price of the country's imports—but without any serious adverse effects on Norway's domestic industries.

The result was a massive improvement in the terms of trade—a measure of how much import a given amount of export can buy. From 1995 to 2000, the Norwegian terms of trade, measured relative to its most important trade partners, improved by almost 40 per cent.[5] The only other time Norway had seen a terms of trade improvement as strong as the one around the year 2000 was during the First World War, when shipping earnings, in particular, boosted export prices.

## The Centre Shifts at Home

As conventional shipping declined and the exploitation of oil and gas increased, the power centre of the Norwegian economy gradually shifted from one volatile maritime industry to another.

Norway started the 20th century as one of the world's leading maritime nations, sending ships and sailors all over the world to carry goods across the sea. At the end of the century, Norway was still a major shipping nation—and Norway's welfare was still closely linked to the sea. However, the country's shipping industry was both quantitatively and qualitatively different from what it had been 100 years earlier. Some of

---

[5] Data calculated on the basis of the background files for Norway, Parliament, *Stortingmelding* 29 (2016–17), Figure 5.2.C. The terms of trade continued to improve after the turn of the century, peaking in 2008, just before the financial crisis, when the price ratio was more than double that of 1992. In fact, these beneficial price movements implied that the Norwegians got twice as much foreign products for a given volume of exports as they had done 16 years earlier.

the main features of the last century—the rapidly increasing ship sizes and the reliance on distant markets—had been reversed over the last decades. This reflected the fact that traditional seaborne transport—deep-sea shipping in foreign waters—was supplemented by local activity related to the offshore petroleum industry. In 1992 the offshore fleet—including rigs and ships—made up less than 19 per cent of the value of the Norwegian fleet. By 2006 the share was more than 40 per cent, and this increased to approximately half of the fleet, if the shuttle tankers serving in the North Sea are included.[6]

In the last decades of the 20th century the offshore workers on platforms and vessels had more in common with the fishermen than with the sailors a hundred years earlier. They work in a maritime setting, often near the Norwegian coast, harvesting resources, those of the sea and those below the seabed. There was thus a proximity to Norway and Norwegian society that was very different from that of the old sailors on sailing ships or early steam vessels, whose visits to Norway were short and far between.

Traditional deep-sea shipping saw an increased concentration in the last decades of the 20th century, reflecting the fact that the activity has increasingly been confined to a few major maritime centres, from which large parts of the Norwegian merchant marine were managed and operated. Many of the smaller home ports along the coast relied on a handful—or even fewer—companies, and if these folded and there was no longer a critical mass, the result was often the complete disappearance of shipping. At the beginning of the new millennium almost three-quarters of the Norwegian fleet was controlled by companies in Oslo and Bergen.[7] Several other communities—Grimstad, the Tønsberg area, Haugesund—also retained companies involved in deep-sea shipping, but for many coastal towns and cities the link to the sea was largely lost, as shipping companies gave up or moved elsewhere.[8]

---

[6] Bakka (2017, 215).

[7] Due to geographic specialization, this share varied based on the manner in which it was measured. At the end of 2003, 31 per cent of the ships were Oslo owned and 30 per cent were Bergen owned. However, based on dead weight tonnage, the shares become 50.4 and 22.9 per cent, respectively. Based on gross tonnage, Oslo's share was 53.5 per cent and Bergen's 21.3 per cent; Norway, Parliament, *Stortingsmelding 31* (2003–04), 25.

[8] As shown in Hervik and Jacobsen (2001), shipping companies were still present all along the coast, but in many instances their activity and turnover was very limited or their markets were outside traditional merchant shipping.

While traditional shipping saw regional concentration, the services related to the offshore petroleum exploration resulted in a new distribution of the activity along the coast. The establishment of a petroleum-industrial complex in Stavanger, which was chosen as Norway's "oil capital," implied that much of the oil and gas activities were centred there. The city's shipping companies took advantage of the possibilities. Tellingly, Smedvig, the city's major shipping company, was an early investor in oil rigs and facilities for the offshore sector. Following disastrous investments in supertanker tonnage, the company made the transition to a full-fledged rig company in the middle of the 1990s.

The shipping side of the Norwegian offshore industry around the turn of the millennium exhibited two traits that it shared with the development of foreign-going shipping more than a century earlier; the international component and the local component.

With respect to the international dimension, the industry built up skills and competence in local and regional markets. This was subsequently used to gain market share in foreign waters. The offshore industry is in the process of doing the same, although it still has a stronger home presence that the shipping sector did around 1900.[9]

There is another parallel at the local level, concerning the manner in which the offshore industry is embedded in local communities. The expansion of Norwegian shipping in the 1850s and 1860s was primarily based on ships built, equipped, financed and manned locally, particularly on the South Coast. For the offshore supply vessels, there was a similar local base, though the centre had shifted to a number of smaller villages on the West Coast. The majority of the supply companies are located north of Stavanger, south of Bergen and in Møre og Romsdal, a county previously primarily known for fishing.

The offshore industry was characterized by new and more advanced solutions. Shuttle tankers and floating production/storage vessels revolutionized the production process, and the latter types of vessels became particularly important in connection with the exploitation of marginal

---

[9] This comparison is based on the shipping side of the offshore industry, and the points do not necessarily apply to the rig sector.

oil blocks with limited reserves. Supply shipping saw a similar move towards more advanced vessels. Converted fishing vessels began to be replaced by purpose-built supply ships at the beginning of the 1970s. By the last decade of the 20th century, there had been substantial growth and diversification of the supply fleet.

The new ships were not only larger and more powerful versions of the old platform supply vessels, designed for transport, support or anchor handling. There was substantial investment in ships that could perform advanced underwater (subsea) operations, ships with special equipment for seismic surveys, cable and pipe laying ships, construction vessels and so on. Some of the companies were based in traditional shipping centres such as Oslo, Kristiansand, Stavanger and Bergen. However, many smaller places were also engaged, including Skudesneshavn (with deepsea shipping roots) and Bømlo, Austevoll, Fosnavåg and Ålesund (mainly with a basis in fishing).[10]

As a result of the shift from deep-sea shipping to offshore, the structural composition of the Norwegian fleet changed. The strong growth after the introduction of the Norwegian International Ship Register (NIS) had included a number of large and relatively simple ships. Among those was *Knock Nevis*, the world's largest ship, which had been declared a total loss after having been hit by bombs during the Iran-Iraq war. The ship was bought by Norman International, refloated, repaired and renamed: first *Happy Giant* (1989–1991), then sold and renamed *Jahre Viking* (1991–2004).

Norman International is an example of the new manner in which shipping could be conducted. In the period 1985–1990 the company, primarily via ships bought by limited partnerships [*kommandittselskap*], rapidly built up a fleet of more than 4 million dead weight tons (dwt) and became Norway's second largest shipping company. In 1991 the company decided to wind up operations, and make a quick exit—the fleet of 4.1 million dwt in January 1991 had dwindled to zero in January 1992.[11]

The NIS euphoria in the late 1980s had given rise to a lot of speculative purchases. Even Rolf Sæther, Managing Director of the Norwegian

---

[10] See the overview of Norwegian offshore companies in Bakka (2017, 220).
[11] Isachsen (1992, 9–10).

Shipowners' Association, criticized the companies that followed an "asset-play" strategy, based on an increase in shipping values, substandard tonnage and high gearing—often 80 per cent mortgage financing by the banks.[12] When vessel values collapsed in early 1992, following a strong reduction in freight rates, many of the newcomers were forced to ship their oars.

During the 1990s there was gradually a reduction in the role of large tankers and dry bulk ships, as the trend towards specialized tonnage continued. The competitive situation in the different segments partly explains this development—there was substantial variation in the profitability of the various parts of the shipping market. A survey of stock exchange listed companies in the 1990s suggests that while the average annual return on companies involved in chemical shipping and offshore was around 12 per cent, the corresponding figure for dry bulk companies was minus 7 per cent.[13]

The relative reduction in high-volume shipping in Norway was not unique. In fact, the transformation was far more muted than in other Western countries. In the last decades of the 20th century, two groups of countries, in particular, increased their importance in world shipping. The East Asian tiger economies took over a larger part of the value chain with investments in tonnage, and the Flags of Convenience continued to grow.

## A Two-Faced Industry

As shown in Chap. 4, the shipping industry was a pioneer in the use of companies and registration in "unrelated" foreign domiciles. Until the beginning of the 1970s, Flags of Convenience were primarily used by American and Greek shipping companies, in addition to companies in some countries where special geo-political considerations played a role, such as for instance Israel. In connection with the shipping crisis, both the extent and the geographical spread of the use increased substantially.

---

[12] *Aftenposten*, 051092, 23.
[13] Birkeland and Eide (2000, 4).

The establishment of second registries—such as the NIS—only temporarily halted the move towards Flags of Convenience. In the last decades of the 20th century and the beginning of the 21st, Flags of Convenience have basically become "an industry standard." Like fast-food chains, the leading Flags of Convenience offer miniscule and user-friendly variations of an established menu, with the pricing and the product on offer more or less identical, and speed of service an important competitive parameter. By the end of 2000, Panama had a fleet of almost 163 million dwt, Liberia more than 75 million dwt and the Bahamas almost 45 million dwt. The three leading Flags of Convenience controlled almost 38 per cent of the world fleet.

If we go "behind" the Flags of Convenience, and look at the actual ownership of the world fleet, the increasing role of Asia—and the disappearance of many of the old European shipping nations—becomes evident. A comparison of Table 9.1 and Table 2.1 reveals the massive changes in the ownership of the world fleet during the 20th century. Moreover, these

Table 9.1 The 15 most important maritime countries and territories, January 2001

|  | Ships at home | Ships abroad | 1000 dwt at home | 1000 dwt abroad | Foreign flag (per cent) | Per cent of world fleet |
|---|---|---|---|---|---|---|
| Greece | 785 | 2476 | 43,580 | 99,527 | 69.6 | 19.1 |
| Japan | 781 | 2150 | 15,225 | 83,509 | 84.6 | 13.2 |
| Norway | 907 | 791 | 27,733 | 32,308 | 53.8 | 8.0 |
| United States | 508 | 890 | 9788 | 34,947 | 78.1 | 6.0 |
| China | 1617 | 599 | 22,341 | 18,393 | 45.2 | 5.4 |
| Hong Kong, China | 166 | 385 | 9075 | 26,627 | 74.6 | 4.8 |
| Germany | 467 | 1640 | 7436 | 25,437 | 77.4 | 4.4 |
| Republic of Korea | 473 | 430 | 7605 | 18,060 | 70.4 | 3.4 |
| Singapore | 476 | 280 | 12,842 | 7790 | 37.8 | 2.8 |
| UK | 407 | 432 | 8343 | 10,973 | 56.8 | 2.6 |
| Taiwan, PRC | 162 | 359 | 7205 | 11,662 | 61.8 | 2.5 |
| Denmark | 418 | 318 | 7931 | 10,193 | 56.2 | 2.4 |
| Russian Federation | 2190 | 349 | 8566 | 7500 | 46.7 | 2.1 |
| Italy | 502 | 129 | 8712 | 4504 | 34.1 | 1.8 |
| India | 358 | 52 | 10,328 | 1532 | 12.9 | 1.6 |

Source: UNCTAD, *Maritime Transport 2001*, 30–31

changes reflect even more dramatic changes in world production, international trade and global income levels.

With limitations on cross-border investments disappearing, a process of international consolidation took place in shipping, and there were many Norwegian targets.[14] By joining the resources of the Høegh and Smedvig families, among others, Bona shipholding had become the world's second largest operator of Aframax-tankers, oil tankers in the 60,000–100,000 dwt range, and also controlled a fleet of larger combination carriers. In 1999 the company was bought by the Bahamian company Teekay, based in Vancouver, listed on the New York Stock Exchange and originally established by a Dane. Two years later, Teekay took over Ugland Nordic Shipping's fleet of 16 shuttle tankers, but the shopping spree was not over. In 2003 Navion, owned by the oil company Statoil, with a fleet of 50 vessels, was sold to Teekay for around USD800 million. With Stavanger as base, much of the shuttle tanker fleet had been consolidated under the auspices of this Bahamian-Canadian-Norwegian venture. In shipping, nationalization questions were becoming more and more complex.[15]

The internationalization of ownership was not a one-way street. Just like foreign interests bought Norwegian shares and ships, Norwegians invested abroad. For instance, after the merger of Bona and Teekay, the Høegh family was among the largest shareholders in the latter company. The Rasmussen family of Kristiansand had been Statoil's partner in Navion, but sold its share before the Teekay takeover. Subsequently, the family reduced its exposure in Norway, but became major investors in Norden, one of the leading Danish shipping companies, where they at times owned more than 20 per cent of the shares.

The most well-known, and definitely most international, of all "Norwegian" shipowners, is John Fredriksen. After training and working as a broker in Montreal, New York, Oslo and Singapore, he moved to London in the late 1970s, became a Cypriot citizen in 2006 and used the Swedish company Frontline, listed on the stock exchanges in Oslo and

---

[14] See Klepsland (2011), for an analysis of the ownership structure of shipping company shares listed on the Oslo Stock Exchange, including a good discussion of foreign ownership.
[15] Bakka (2017, 206–211). For the fascinating story of Teekay's impressive expansion, see Ingpen (2013).

New York, to become one of the world's largest tanker owners. The case of Fredriksen illustrates that perhaps the whole idea of using the nation state as a label may become outdated in the case of shipping.[16]

## Redefining the Maritime Nation

Up until the middle of the 1970s, Norwegian shipping had been dealt a very good hand in the card game that is domestic politics. Relevance, importance and money are always convincing arguments. The industry's crucial role in the balance of trade had been one trump card. More than 50,000 seafarers—many of them living in rural areas with few employment alternatives—had been the other. By the late 1980s, these arguments were no longer valid.

The Norwegian Shipowners' Association had to look elsewhere when it wanted to convince the authorities that it was still relevant and important. Its new arguments centred around the idea that it played a crucial role in a broader maritime industry, what it referred to as Norway's "maritime cluster." The relationships and interconnections among companies that were engaged in different parts of the Norwegian maritime industry created competitiveness and value. Internationally leading companies—shipping banks, shipping insurance companies, naval architects and a classification society—depended upon the shipping companies.

Words are important. The shift from "shipping" to "maritime," which was first introduced during the fight for NIS, gained ground. It was reflected in new cooperative organizations such as *Maritimt Forum* [Maritime Forum], established 1990, which promoted the significance of a wider network of maritime activities and businesses. Moreover, the argument was accepted by the authorities, who in the 1990s gradually replaced the notion of a "shipping policy" with the need for a "maritime policy."[17]

In 1984 there had been a similar rebranding, when the Norwegian Shipowners' Association changed its name from *Norges Rederforbund* (the

---

[16] However, calling a book "Norwegian shipping in the first part of the 20th century, then a gradually more nationless shipping industry" would only be confusing.
[17] See the thorough analysis of the political process and discourse in Fougner (2006, 177–201).

Norwegian word *reder* means an individual owning ships) to *Norges Rederiforbund* (where a *rederi* is the Norwegian word for a shipping company). This change was more than semantic. It reflected the new realities and the manner in which the industry had developed; shipping had become a modern industry, where there was often a separation of ownership and management. As such, the name change was overdue. However, it was also a meaningful clarification *vis-à-vis* the general public; "we serve companies, not wealthy individuals."

From the late 1980s onwards there was a shift in the reasoning about economic policy in many countries. Inspired by the Harvard professor Michael Porter, politicians and industry federations embraced the ideas of economic "clusters," where competitiveness was enhanced by interplay between agents in a specific industry.

The Norwegian Shipowners' Association was among the pioneers in the use of such arguments in a Norwegian context. A huge research project on the competitiveness of Norwegian industries emphasized the strong international position of the maritime industry in general and the shipping companies in particular. They were the driving force in "the most complete, the most international and the most knowledge-based" industrial cluster in the country.[18] The very first table in the 1992 report on Norwegian shipping presents "maritime employment." Deep-sea shipping companies—referred to as the "core activity"—employed 22,300 Norwegians, around a quarter on land and more than 17,000 on rigs and on NIS- and NOR-registered ships. However, the central message was the fact that these people were crucial for the wider maritime activities, which added almost 40,000 employees.[19]

For more than 150 years the demand for Norwegian shipping has been quite detached from local markets. Consequently, the driving force in the maritime clusters is not the competition for customers and market shares domestically. Rather, it is the competition for labour and skills, technology, knowledge and ideas in the local market. Moreover, the strength of the cluster allegedly lies in the manner in which the shipping companies interact with companies performing auxiliary functions such as insurance, finance, consulting, classification and research.

---

[18] See Reve, Lensberg and Grønhaug (1992) and Fougner (2006).
[19] Wergeland (1992, 4).

The maritime cluster contained a number of companies that had managed to climb on the shoulders of Norwegian shipping companies and build up leading positions internationally. Det Norske Veritas had developed a substantial consulting and naval architecture business along with its role as one of the leading international classification societies. The company had also followed the shipping companies into the North Sea and beyond, and built up a position as an important technical and business consultant for both shipping and offshore companies.[20]

Another group of companies that had managed to develop strong international market positions were the maritime insurance companies, which in 2000 received premiums amounting to almost USD600 million. Hull and protection and indemnity (P&I) insurance each made up around 40 per cent of the total, with energy and cargo insurance providing the rest of the turnover.[21]

The initial international expansion of Norwegian banking to a large extent followed in the slipstream of Norwegian shipping. They "followed their customers" and the one area in which they had "unique competence" was within shipping.[22] London-based Hambros Bank was the banker *par excellence* for the Norwegian state, and also for Norwegian shipowners. The bank employed a substantial number of Norwegian nationals, and was a typical merchant bank, based on relationship banking. In 1968 three Norwegian Banks, in cooperation with a Dutch bank and Hambros, established Ship Mortgage International in Amsterdam, in order to provide first-priority mortgages.

Gradually, as the domestic markets became liberalized, other banks increased their interest in shipping, often acquiring competence and personnel from within the shipping companies. Kredittkassen in the mid-1980s decided to market itself as a leading shipping bank for European customers, regardless of whether their business was related to Norway.

---

[20] See Paulsen, Andersen, Collett and Stensrud (2014, 147–176).

[21] CEFOR (2000, 10). There are several examples of how "auxiliary industries" become world-leading even without the presence of important local shipowners. On the South Coast, Gard has remained a world-leading provider of P&I (protection and indemnity) insurance services from a base in Arendal, even after most of the city's shipping companies had disappeared. Much of the technical research has been centred around Marintek and the technical university and research environment in Trondheim, a city with an extremely modest maritime heritage.

[22] Knutsen, Lange and Nordvik (1998, 156); see also Gisnås (1995).

The basis was its "considerable expertise in shipping and the long history of dealing with shipping customers." The bank saw this as a competence for which there had to be a market abroad.[23]

Classification, insurance and banking lived side-by-side with the shipping companies for more than a century. However, the manner in which shipping developed—with a separation of seafaring labour and the ownership of the vessel—opened up a number of new business opportunities. One was the sale of manning and ship management services. Several companies with Norwegian connections established themselves in this new market.[24]

With the question of flag and labour costs out of the picture, the main differences between shipping companies in various countries were related to onshore elements such as tax, wage levels for office personnel and the quality of infrastructure. For the Norwegian Shipowners' Association, the tax question became a priority. A tax reform introduced in 1992 made the conditions for Norwegian shipping companies much more difficult. Aiming at "inter-industry" neutrality, shipping lost some of its tax advantages. In addition to strengthening the previously generous depreciation regime, the reform reduced the availability of capital by tightening up the rules regulating limited partnerships.

In 1996 the Norwegian authorities changed their minds. The introduction of a tonnage tax system, where tax is paid on the basis of the tonnage, rather than operating profits, was welcomed by the shipowners.[25] Moreover, the introduction of a system of reimbursement for the use of Norwegian seafarers made it more attractive to use local labour, and increased the competitiveness of ships operating in Norwegian

---

[23] Knutsen, Lange and Nordvik (1998, 286).

[24] Lorange (2009, 100), presents the six leading ship-operating companies: V.Group, Thome, Denholm, Wallem, OSM and the Schulthers Group. Three of these companies were established by Norwegians: Thome from Vestfold in Singapore in the 1970s and OSM on the South Coast of Norway in the late 1980s. Haakon Wallem from Bergen established a shipping company in the Far East at the start of the century, and in the 1970s the company began selling management services from a Hong Kong base. In 2006 the Wallem company was bought back by Haakon Wallem's great grandson, after having been in foreign hands.

[25] The tax on operating profits was formally defined as a credit, which would have to be paid if companies exited the arrangement to be taxed like "normal" companies. This was done in order to avoid shipping companies planning to exit in years with an operating deficit, when they would be liable to pay tax under the tonnage tax system, but not under the regular, non-shipping tax regime.

waters. The special tax arrangement for shipping companies and reimbursement for the use of Norwegian seafarers created optimism. However, towards the end of the century the frequent political challenges to the regime put the sincerity of the "shipping friendly" Norwegian policies in doubt, and the arrangement was considered very unpredictable.

# Bibliography

D. Bakka (2017) *Nasjonens ære – Norsk rederinæring mellom marked og politikk* (Bergen: Bodoni Forlag)
S. Birkeland & T. Eide (2000) *Lønnsomheten i norsk skipsfart* (Bergen: Stiftelsen for samfunns- og næringslivsforskning)
CEFOR (2000) *Annual report* (Oslo: The Central Union of Marine Underwriters)
T. Fougner (2006) 'Economic Nationalism and Maritime Policy in Norway', *Cooperation and Conflict: Journal of the Nordic International Studies Association*, 41:2, 177–201
L. Gisnås (1995) *Jakten på kjempemarkedet – norsk business i Singapore* (Bergen: Fagbokforlaget)
A. Hervik & E. Jacobsen (2001) *Det regionale maritime Norge – En vital nasjonal næring med regionale særpreg* (Oslo: Handelshøyskolen BI)
B. Ingpen (2013) *Teekay – the first 40 years* (Bermuda: Kattegat Limited)
F. Isachsen (1992) *Crude Oil Shipping* (Bergen: Stiftelsen for samfunns- og næringslivsforskning)
J.E. Klepsland (2011) *Utvikling av eierstrukturen i rederier notert på Oslo Børs* (Bergen: Stiftelsen for samfunns- og næringslivsforskning)
S. Knutsen, E. Lange & H.W. Nordvik (1998) *Mellom næringsliv og politikk. Kredittkassen i vekst og kriser, 1918–1998* (Oslo: Universitetsforlaget)
P. Lorange (2009) *Shipping Strategy: Innovating for Success* (Cambridge: Cambridge University Press)
G. Paulsen, H.W. Andersen, J.P. Collettt & I.T. Stensrud (2014) *Building trust – The history of DNV 1864–2014* (Høvik: Dinamo Forlag)
T. Reve, T. Lensberg & K. Grønhaug (1992) *Et konkurransedyktig Norge* (Oslo: Tano AS)
R. Rowthorn & R. Ramaswamy (1997) 'Deindustrialization – Its Causes and Implications', *IMF Economic Issues 10* (Washington DC: International Monetary Fund)
T. Wergeland (1992) *Norsk skipsfarts konkurranseevne* (Bergen: Stiftelsen for samfunns- og næringslivsforskning)

**Open Access** This chapter is licensed under the terms of the Creative Commons Attribution-NonCommercial-NoDerivatives 4.0 International License (http://creativecommons.org/licenses/by-nc-nd/4.0/), which permits any noncommercial use, sharing, distribution and reproduction in any medium or format, as long as you give appropriate credit to the original author(s) and the source, provide a link to the Creative Commons license and indicate if you modified the licensed material. You do not have permission under this license to share adapted material derived from this chapter or parts of it.

The images or other third party material in this chapter are included in the chapter's Creative Commons license, unless indicated otherwise in a credit line to the material. If material is not included in the chapter's Creative Commons license and your intended use is not permitted by statutory regulation or exceeds the permitted use, you will need to obtain permission directly from the copyright holder.

# 10

# Epilogue: A Century of Norwegian Shipping

At the start of this book, I suggested that Norway's strong position in international shipping at the beginning of the 20th century was based on a combination of favourable geographical circumstances, a historical legacy and a strong maritime culture. At the end of the 20th century, these factors still played important roles, though they had changed dramatically over the past 100 years.

The geographical circumstances were originally related to the long coast—"Highway No. 1, the way to the north"—that had given Norway its name. The coast made maritime skills a necessity. However, by the end of the century the geographic dimension included not only the sheltered sea lane and the rich fisheries, which had been so important during previous centuries. Now, as a result of improvements in technology, the favourable geography also included the vast exploitable petroleum resources below the seafloor on the Norwegian continental shelf. These resources have laid the fundament for new maritime activity and for new international expansion. The sea is no longer as present in Norwegian daily life as it was in the sailing ship era, when there was a sailor in most families along the coast in the southern part of Norway and a fisherman in most families in the north. However, the bounties of the sea are more visible in

Norwegian statistics than ever before, and have helped make Norway one of the world's wealthiest countries.

Geography—and our ability to make use of resources—is a dynamic concept. So is history.

Another 100 years have been added to Norway's maritime history. The 20th century was a century of new opportunities, new policies, new lessons, new ideas and new strategies. It was also the century where shipping lost its dominant position in the Norwegian economy and in particular the hegemonial role in Norwegian exports. In the first 75 years of the 20th century, shipping revenue made up more than 43 per cent of Norwegian exports, in the last quarter of the century the share was less than 17 per cent.

At the start of the 20th century, shipping was an extremely important source of personal wealth, and this fact was also reflected in politics. Money was power, and well-off shipowners like Michelsen, Mowinckel and Knudsen played crucial roles in the birth and redefinition of Norway as a fully independent nation: "Shipowners held such an honourable position in the public opinion that they, almost as a matter of course, were expected to guide the national ship and bring the country and the people to a safe harbour."[1] Towards the end of the century, large private fortunes were primarily made in other sectors and statesmanlike Prime Ministers have been found elsewhere. Shipowners no longer make up such a large proportion of "the establishment" as before, and "the establishment" itself has lost part of its privilege and power. During the 20th century, shipping went from being extremely important to being "just" important. Still, a history of relative decline is also a history.

The 20th century brought a set of new heroes from the sea: the war sailors who kept supply lines open and risked—and lost—their lives for the Allied cause. The fact that it took decades for their crucial war efforts to be rewarded and acknowledged echoes the manner in which the sea and seafarers had previously been played down in Norwegian nation-building. There was a similar lack of recognition of the maritime dimension during the national romantic period in the 19th century, when

---

[1] Svendsen (1976, 7).

Norway fought to develop its own national identity and throw off the shadows of Danish and Swedish rule. Inspired by the German traditions of von Herder, the archetypal Norwegian—the one inhabiting the spirit of the nation—was found inland, among peasants, in the forests and on the mountains, rather than along the coast.[2]

For many decades, the typical heroes of the Second World War were the domestic Norwegian resistance movement, often referred to as *Gutta på skauen*—the boys from the woods. The prominence that they were awarded in most stories of the fight against the Nazis overshadowed the crucial role that Norwegian seafarers played in the outcome of the war.[3] It also downplayed the sacrifices that the war sailors made—more than 3600 seafarers died as a result of the war, more than a third of all Norwegian deaths. A detailed academic history of the Norwegian war at sea was not written until the 1990s, while the war sailors had to wait another 20 years until the authorities apologized in public for the lack of recognition in the period after the war.

With the gradual removal of the shipping and seafaring dimension from the lives of most people, maritime history and maritime culture have become increasingly intertwined. Norwegians in the coastal areas continue to have a strong maritime identity, but it is typically related to forefathers that went to sea and old fortunes and artefacts, rather than to their own experiences. This detachment accelerated in the last part of the 20th century. As late as in the 1970s, around a third of all men in the Norwegian labour force had spent some time at sea—a fascinating figure that says something about the extent to which people's lives were influenced by the shipping sector and its opportunities. Then—abruptly—the development changed. The shipping crisis, and the policy shifts that followed in its wake, implied that seafaring became far less important, both as a temporary "rite of passage" and as a full-fledged career.

---

[2] Iversen (2011, 129).

[3] The common version of the war history even put particular emphasis on certain parts of the domestic resistance against the Nazis. Some factions of the resistance movement—for instance those illegal groups that had a Communist bent—were sometimes erased, or at least obscured, from the official history of the war. See Borgersrud and Eriksen (2015, 595), where the term "monopoly of information" is used about the non-Communist resistance.

Norway, the shipping nation, continues to be relevant, although the number of Norwegian seafarers has shrunk and the ships people see and hear about are more likely to be offshore vessels or cruise vessels than cargo ships.[4] The maritime culture changed gradually—first with the transformation from sail to steam, then, as the ships got larger; they became almost invisible, far removed from daily life. At the same time, the nostalgic element has shifted—the memories and the tales of the white sails have now been replaced by stories of young rookie sailors picking rust and experiencing exotic locations around the world.

In 1948, Karin Larsen, Professor of History at St. Olaf College in Minnesota, published a much-lauded book on the history of Norway. She pointed out that "[t]hroughout Norway's history the greatest economic, political, and cultural advance has been achieved when the people have had untrammelled access to the surrounding ocean and have been able to make use of the opportunities this offers."[5] When she wrote this claim, it turned out to have just as much relevance for the future—the second half of the 20th century—as for the past.

In the second half of the 20th century, new knowledge and new technologies enabled Norway to make use of opportunities that had been developing for thousands of years on the Norwegian sea bed. Exploitation of petroleum resources changed the economy, the politics and the culture. The maritime experience was extremely important for the formation of Norway as a petroleum producer. Shipowners, shipyards and seafarers all tried their luck in waters closer to home, then used the capabilities that they acquired there to expand abroad. Consequently, the manner in which these events unfolded was not unlike the expansion of Norwegian shipping in the 19th century: build up competence at home, and then compete in the world market.

---

[4] An exception is along the West Coast of Norway, all the way up to the north, where seaborne transport is still important for the movement of both passengers and cargoes. However, in particular in the densely populated areas in the south-western part of the country, trucks perform a surprisingly large part of the cargo transport. In these areas, the Norwegian authorities have built ridiculously expensive bridges and tunnels in order to get a "Highway number two," more or less parallel with the one that nature had already constructed.

[5] Larsen (1948, 4).

# A Maritime Nation (-ation, -ation, -ation, -ation)

What characterized Norwegian shipping in the 20th century? What were the external and internal forces that shaped its development? Which resources—and which responses—enabled Norwegian shipping companies to keep their position among the most important providers of seaborne transport services?

This book has presented the main development traits, the different breaking points and eras. We have seen how the international economy provided the backdrop—the ups and downs of world trade, affected by business cycles and trade policies, resource endowments and global shifts in production technology. We have seen how the two world wars were states of emergency, where shipping became a crucial, but deadly dangerous, activity, with substantial losses of men and tonnage. At the same time, the wars also ushered in modernization of the fleet, and thus paved the way for long-term growth. We have seen how Norway developed economically, politically and socially—how a maritime career went from being month after month at sea to another "Nice day at the office?" job.

Merchant shipping, "has been, and remains, arguably the world's most international business," according to the leading maritime historian, Skip Fischer.[6] In order to be successful in an industry with global competition, the domestic skill-set and strategies have to be aligned with the requirements of markets far from home. This is extremely difficult, but Norway has managed to do it with impressive consistency.

Initially, we asked the question, "Which factors—specific to Norway, either alone or in combination—can explain the country's leading role in international shipping throughout the 20th century?" Returning to that question, we can now conclude that Norway's successful navigation of the world's most global industry depended on a number of factors: globalization, liberalization, concentration, specialization and innovation. These specific developments can be linked to the four analytical arenas that were presented in Chap. 1: the international, the national, the

---

[6] Fischer (2016, 78).

regional and the company perspective. Naturally, the manner and pace with which these factors have evolved have not been uniform across the century—there have been periods of slow change and periods of rapid change, and even periods of reversal.

## International Development: Globalization

From an *international perspective* it is fairly unproblematic to explain the development of the shipping industry and the relative position of the Norwegian participants. All we need is the most basic instrument in the economists' toolbox—the concepts of demand and supply. By linking demand and supply to economic *globalization*—increased integration in the world economy, seen as growing flows of goods, services and factors of production—the symbiotic relationship between the world economy and Norwegian shipping is easy to identify.

The expansion of world trade—higher volumes, more countries, new commodities—led to a high and increasing demand for the seaborne transport services that Norwegian shipping companies could offer. Although there has not been a one-to-one relationship between the growth of world trade and the development of the shipping market, the correlation between the two is strong. The overall trend has been going in one direction—more trade, and more demand for seaborne transport. But for shipping, the most turbulent periods have been when development has deviated from this trend. The shipping business is especially interesting when demand for transport capacity grows faster or more slowly than the international economy in general.

From a Norwegian perspective, three peacetime periods were particularly important—two with positive, and one with negative connotations. The first period in which the international market developed positively from a Norwegian point of view was the interwar period, when Norway's share of the world fleet doubled—from around 3.3 per cent in 1919 to more than 7 per cent by 1939.[7] The collapse of world trade during the

---

[7] See Fig. 1.1. The data in this chapter primarily refer to figures and tables that have been presented previously, and the footnotes will point to the previously used material, rather than the original source.

Great Depression was partly a monetary phenomenon, appearing much more violent because of falling prices, but in the interwar period trade grew at a slower pace than before the First World War. However, seaborne trade increased faster than trade in general, as a result of longer distances and the fact that ships spent more time sailing "in ballast." In fact, certain segments even grew rapidly. The Norwegian strategy was focused on the main growth segment, oil tanker transport. A combination of outsourcing of transport services, extremely strong volume growth and increased distances made this by far the most positive segment of the shipping market in an otherwise difficult period.

Following the large losses during the Second World War, Norwegian shipping increased its market share in the years after the hostilities ended. Massive growth in manufacturing production and trade led to a strong increase in the transport of raw materials. Consequently, the focus on bulk transport continued to serve Norwegians well in the 1950s and 1960s—the heyday of modern Norwegian shipping. Crude oil transport continued to expand rapidly, and was complemented by strong growth in the seaborne trade of dry bulk goods such as coal and iron ore. The industrialization of Japan, a country with a shortage of natural resources and an abundance cheap labour, was a particularly strong influence on the demand for shipping. Subsequent national industrialization projects in Asia—first in the "tiger economies" and then in China towards the end of the century—have had a similar positive effect on shipping demand.

In the interwar period and the first post-war decades, Norwegian shipping companies performed better than most of their competitors, due to their investments in market segments that grew more rapidly than other parts of the shipping sector. In this period they made a lucky bet on the tanker development, which was followed up by more resources when the benefits of the strategy became evident. In the bulk and specialized markets, Norwegians could supplement their vast market knowledge and international network of contacts by economies of scale and innovations in vessel technology to remain competitive.

This strategy was favourable in a growing market, but became problematic after the demand for shipping collapsed. Following the oil price increases of the 1970s, Norwegians performed relatively badly, in a market where overall development was particularly negative. The trajectory had gone from outperforming a growing market, to underperforming in a market that was going down. The collapse of the crude oil trade was the most important factor behind the adverse Norwegian development. Many owners had put all their eggs in one basket, and that was the basket where the handle broke…

During the shipping depression of the 1970s and the 1980s, it took almost 15 years before the markets recovered.[8] As a result of the severity of the downturn—in particular the fact that there were hardly any profits to be made for more than a decade—Norwegian shipping was not far from being eradicated. The strategies that had made Norwegian owners particularly successful when the market increased—economies of scale, frequent tonnage renewal, a focus on bulk transport—made them particularly vulnerable when the market crashed.

Expensive investments in redundant tonnage led to high capital costs, and Norwegian labour costs were also high in an international perspective. With low freight revenues—or even no income at all, in the case of laid-up ships—the equity of many Norwegian shipping companies was rapidly depleted. Some survived due to the generosity of creditors, who waited patiently until the market recovered. Others were forced to approach the Norwegian authorities for support. By the beginning of 1979 the crisis had been such a drain on resources that more than half of the shipping companies had negative equity.[9] And the crisis was far from over.

As the financial problems dragged on, and the creditors and the authorities ran out of patience, two of the avenues for survival were closed, with dramatic results. Banks forced the sale of ships. The authorities wound up their engagements in the Guarantee Institute, which at its peak had helped the owners of around a quarter of the fleet. The results were dire. The majority of the Norwegian shipping companies that existed in 1973 were out of business by 1987. Despite the most

---

[8] There was a brief recovery—a false dawn—around the turn of the decade. Optimistic shipowners reacted by ordering more tonnage, even before the existing surplus had been absorbed. The bad times consequently came back with a vengeance.
[9] Norway, Parliament (1980), Norges Offentlige Utredninger 45, 35.

far-reaching support to the shipping sector ever, the authorities had only been able to put a plaster over what turned out to be a life-threatening wound.

Most of the shipping companies that survived the crisis were in a precarious financial situation. They were floating aimlessly, in choppy waters, and were about to sink when they were thrown two lifelines at the same time. The first one came from the market itself, where demand picked up and the removal of surplus tonnage ensured that freight rates followed suit. The second lifeline came from the Norwegian authorities. They introduced the Norwegian International Ship Register, thus enabling the use of low-cost foreign seafarers on Norwegian-flagged ships.

This takes us to the complementary, flipside explanation of the manner in which *globalization* influenced the development of Norwegian shipping. Globalization of demand was strong throughout the period after the Second World War, and increasing international trade was the fundamental precondition behind the growth of the world fleet. The last decades of the century also saw the globalization of supply.[10] Increasing international integration has given better access to capital and labour outside Norway's borders. However, the degree to which shipowners have been able to utilize foreign inputs has varied.

With regard to capital, access to foreign funding has in fact been important since before the Second World War. The interwar growth in the tanker market was partly financed by Danish, Swedish and British yard credits, thus enabling an expansion that would have been impossible if it had been drawn from Norwegian sources only. What was originally a cyclical phenomenon—access to finance in order to secure shipyard activity during a downturn—ended up as a permanent phenomenon, a competitive parameter for shipbuilders. In the post-war period 80 per cent credit at generous terms became the norm for shipping companies that wanted to buy new tonnage. The shipyards, helped financially by the authorities, ensured much of the financing. Consequently, the expansion of the fleet could to some extent occur independently of Norway's own

---

[10] Even though the tanker market crashed due to the oil shocks, globalization—in terms of increasing international integration, in particular trade liberalization and growth—remained the order of the day in most other markets.

financial resources. Most of the costs of a new ship could be acquired abroad, often with a long-term charter securing the income and consoling the creditors. Second-priority mortgages could be arranged by government-supported Norwegian institutions.

Due to other governments' desire to build up or maintain capacity in the shipbuilding industry, foreign loans financed much of the expansion of Norwegian shipping. Foreign equity, on the other hand, has been limited by Norwegian law for much of the century. Even in the late 1980s, shipping companies that wanted to increase their funds by opening up share ownership to foreign interests had to issue non-voting B-shares. By then, foreign funds were accepted, but not foreign influence. This was soon to change.

In the last years of the 20th century, and particularly at the beginning of the 21st century, there was a strong inflow of foreign equity into Norwegian shipping. There were two main reasons for this. First, the liberalization of international capital movements made it difficult, or in some instances even illegal, to discriminate against foreign owners. The Norwegian authorities were forced to open up the borders, and could no longer reserve ownership and influence for Norwegians. Second, the strong market position, the international character and the competitive competence of Norwegian shipping companies made them particularly attractive for mergers and takeovers. Foreign equity flowed into Norway in search of profit, and Norwegian equity went abroad in search of the same.[11]

The access to foreign investment capital (as opposed to foreign mortgages) was limited for most of the 20th century, before this regime change. This corresponds very well with the situation for foreign labour. For a long time, Norwegian shipping was based almost exclusively on Norwegian personnel. During the labour shortages in the 1950s and 1960s, seafarers from other European countries played a part, and there were also some foreign-crewed ships operating in local markets in Asia.

---

[11] And sometimes Norwegian investors went abroad, only to return to the Norwegian market under more tax-friendly foreign schemes. Klepsland (2011, 3) points out that before 2003 active foreign ownership in stock exchange listed Norwegian shipping companies was related to acquisitions and delisting, while the foreign ownership from 2003 to 2007 was characterized by "Norwegian tax refugees."

Still, the rule-of-thumb was Norwegian ship, Norwegian flag, Norwegian seafarers—or European seafarers on Norwegian terms—well into the 1980s. The big shift came in 1987, when the establishment of the Norwegian International Ship Register (NIS) lifted restrictions for ships that operated outside Norwegian waters.

## The Domestic Dimension: Liberalization

The establishment of the NIS is perhaps the best example of how the *domestic dimension* has been characterized by significant *liberalization* of the maritime-political regime. The increasing inflow of foreign equity changed Norwegian shipping; access to inexpensive foreign labour saved it. Norway's transition to a high-wage country—where seafarers' working conditions improved immensely during the course of the century—was incompatible with the relentless focus on costs in an industry with international competition. The liberalization of labour requirements was a necessary condition for the "second wind" that pushed Norway's shipping industry forward in the last decades of the 20th century. Without this measure, it is likely that many of the remaining Norwegian shipping companies would have followed their Swedish neighbours into obscurity and oblivion, and the establishment of new companies would have been much lower.[12]

Despite this timely intervention by the Norwegian government, the relationship between the shipping companies and the authorities has been very complex. The design of the economic and political regime has varied across time, and the effects on shipping company strategy and profitability are difficult to disentangle. Many shipowners would claim that the regulation of the industry, in particular in the period around 1950, was a serious encroachment on their free enterprise and had a detrimental effect on the expansion of their shipping activities. The detailed regulation of business decisions such as contracting, operation and financing has been referred to as a "straitjacket."[13]

---

[12] Lennerfors, Lindgren and Poulsen (2012).
[13] Bakka (2017).

At the same time, it is evident that the Norwegian authorities have also given the shipping industry priority, due to its role as the most important earner of foreign exchange. This has been evident with regard to explicitly preferential measures—such as access to investment funds and generous accounting and tax rules. There have also been periods—for instance in the 1950s and 1960s—when the general economic policy favoured shipping investments. Regulations such as double taxation—which made it profitable to maintain capital within the company—and the low interest-rate regime had a preserving character on the industrial structure. Access to funds was easy for established companies, while it was difficult for newcomers. And shipping was clearly an established industry.

The international character of shipping makes regulation, both policy design and policy implementation, particularly difficult. On the one hand, it might be desirable to treat shipping in the same way as other domestic sectors. This ideal of "industrial neutrality" implies that tax rates, investment framework (for instance duties and depreciation rates), access to capital and so on should be identical across all sectors of the economy. The benefit would be that the country's resources—at least in theory—would be utilized efficiently, as they would be allocated to those sectors that give the highest return, without any policy-induced distortions.

Alternatively, it might be claimed that policies should be adapted to the special features and needs of individual sectors, and also take into account policy aims other than just "economic efficiency." The support to the agricultural sector in most industrialized countries—motivated by a desire for self-sufficiency in food production, a heavy dose of nostalgia and some very capable lobbying—is a case in point. When everyone else is subsidizing, why can't we? According to this view, policies towards the shipping sector should, due to shipping's mobile nature, be designed with "competitive neutrality" in mind. How can we keep taxing our shipping companies, when they can easily move their activities to a no-tax location? Following this line of thought, the framework conditions should be identical to those that the shipping industries in other countries are subject to.

Norwegian policy has vacillated between these two aims—between industrial neutrality and competitive neutrality. Moreover, when the shipping industry has been subject to "special treatment" this has been both of the favourable and the unfavourable kind, with the changes often abrupt and unexplained. As such, the influence of shipping policy has been unpredictable. For instance, in the immediate post-war years, shipping was given priority in the access to foreign exchange—the aim was to resurrect the industry and its dominant position as a foreign-exchange earner. When the revenues failed to materialize to the extent that had been hoped for—mainly as a result of inferior tonnage and low freight rates—the authorities introduced a ban on contracting abroad in 1949 and 1950.

Greek owners copied the timecharter-based financing that the Norwegians had pioneered in the interwar period and "exploited the gap created in the tanker market by the hitherto dominant Norwegians."[14] The gap in the market was the direct result of the political restrictions on the ordering of new ships abroad. Norwegians had to say "no" to lucrative tanker contracts and were unable to fully take advantage of the boom during the Korean War. Preference was followed by prohibition. Go was followed by stop.

Political measures such as the contracting ban had an immediate and direct effect on Norwegian shipping companies and their competitiveness. In the longer term, however, the indirect effects have been more important. The overall policy regime, in addition to the specific short-term measures, has influenced the business decisions of shipping companies. One example is how the combination of tax policy and labour regulations, in a pincer-like movement, shaped the "economies of scale"-based investment strategy in the 1960s. As a result of this focus on large ships and the frequent fleet renewal, the Norwegian share of the world fleet peaked around 10 per cent in the late 1960s.

Until the crisis in the 1970s, shipping's important role in the Norwegian economy was sufficient to ensure its position in the Norwegian political landscape. There was a joint understanding that the shipping industry was left to its own devices. When the crisis threatened the viability of the

---

[14] Harlaftis and Theotokas (2009, 20).

sector, the policies changed "from benign neglect to government intervention."[15] Two important political measures were introduced.

- First, the Guarantee Institute for Ships and Drilling Vessels (GI) was established in 1975 to avoid ships being sold abroad due to bankruptcies and creditor demands. It is not evident that the shipping companies were the main beneficiaries of the GI—the authorities had ulterior motives, and the establishment was important both for shipyards and the financial sector. The GI had the desired short-term effects—it succeeded in keeping tonnage in Norway—but in reality it only delayed an inevitable decline in the fleet.
- The second political change had important long-term effects. As mentioned above, the introduction of the NIS ensured that the Norwegian shipping companies could regain their competitiveness. With the increasingly cut-throat competition in the shipping market, and with freight rate levels too low to give investments in labour-saving tonnage, the only viable alternatives were sales to foreigners and transfers to Flags of Convenience. The introduction of the NIS combined the labour cost flexibility of the Flags of Convenience with a continued "genuine link" to Norway. Moreover, by limiting the areas in which the ships could trade, shipping along the coast remained a domain for Norwegian seafarers.

Norway's introduction of a second or open register was followed by similar measures in other countries. It was both a response to and an element in the liberalization of shipping at the international level. It was another step in the constitution of shipping as the most global of industries. The liberalization of the shipping regime was not unique in a domestic context either. Indeed, it should be seen in relation to the liberalization of the Norwegian economy and society in general. The important thing is the end result, though: without deregulation, Norwegian shipping would not have been able to maintain market shares and profitability.

---

[15] Nordvik (1997).

## The Regional Dimension: Concentration and Specialization

The *regional dimension* has seen Norwegian shipping develop from an industry scattered all along the coast, to a higher degree of *concentration*, with Oslo and Bergen as the leading centres. There has also been an evident concentration of other maritime activities in these two major cities, although with some more isolated pockets of activity in other places. The other development trend that has characterized the spatial distribution of Norwegian shipping is *specialization*, the manner in which a functional division of labour has developed among Norway's regions.

Norwegian shipping survived as an economic activity along the coast far longer than in neighbouring countries such as Sweden and Denmark. In Denmark, in particular, the shipping industry in the capital largely overshadowed what was going on in other parts of the country.[16] However, the large reduction in the number of shipping companies as a result of the shipping crisis sounded the death knell for a number of home ports along the coast.

The increased concentration of Norwegian shipping was also reflected in policy-making and political lobbying. Two developments in the 1980s implied that the industry's economic importance was no longer as self-evident as it had previously been. First, shipping's dominant role as a foreign exchange earner had been dethroned by the petroleum sector. Second, Norwegian sailors in the deep-sea fleet were replaced by foreigners. As a result of the industry's reduced standing, the Norwegian Shipowners' Association changed its strategy *vis-à-vis* the authorities. It increasingly emphasized the crucial role that shipping companies played as the hub of a "maritime cluster," where other maritime businesses—within finance, insurance, ship equipment, classification and so on—were involved. The economic health of the shipping companies was important for the strength of the cluster.

---

[16] The development of the offshore oil industry brought some decentralization in Denmark as well, with Esbjerg emerging as the most important harbour for the oil industry, and with offshore wind power emerging as another important business area in the new millennium.

With regard to the regional dimension, there have been two contrasting ownership trends. On the one hand, we have seen an overall development towards concentration: by the end of the 20th century around half the fleet, measured by dead weight tonnage, was owned by shipping companies in Oslo, and almost a quarter by Bergen-based shipping companies. On the other hand, in connection with the expansion of the offshore petroleum industry, the related services have to a large extent been based in the Stavanger region, as well as in a number of relatively small locations along the coast—villages and islands that had not usually featured in the list of home ports for the Norwegian foreign-going fleet. In places such as Austevoll, Bømlo and Fosnavåg—small communities with a fishing, rather than a shipping tradition—resourceful owners entered the supply shipping industry. In some cases they expanded by purchasing second-hand ships from larger shipping companies that had decided to exit the segment. The conditions in the North Sea are extremely rough, and the companies were able to use the competence built up in Norwegian waters to expand internationally.

In 1900 Norwegian shipping could be characterized as a relative uniform industry—with significant regional variations primarily along *one* dimension: the extent to which the transformation from sail to steam had progressed. There have been various degrees of *specialization* in different parts of Norway. Strategies based on new technology, new forms of operation and specific market niches enabled Norwegian shipping companies to carve out profitable niches. The different trajectories that characterized the development of the various regions pay some testament to the idea of maritime clusters. These clusters could be based on beneficial (or dangerous) follow-thy-neighbour groupthink, or on the synergy effects of having a number of competitors within the same market segment.

The specialization was evident in the case of Oslo and Bergen. In Oslo, the activity was based on traditional bulk activities, with substantial players in the dry bulk and crude oil markets, as well as a number of diversified companies. Bergen, on the other hand, became the "industrial shipping capital," where long-term customer relations had built up world-class niche companies. The city housed two of the world's leading chemical tanker operators, Odfjell and JO Tankers. It was also the original home of the two companies that dominated the world market for open-hatch bulk transport, Star Shipping and Gearbulk. They had a joint market share of around 60 per cent, while Saga Forest Carriers, the third largest operator, also had close links to Norway.

Gearbulk and Saga Forest Carriers are good illustrations of the increased internationalization of Norwegian shipping. The entrepreneur behind Gearbulk, Kristian Gerhard Jebsen, sold 40 per cent of the company to the Japanese Mitsui OSK Lines in 1990, and moved the operation of the company to the UK a few years later. He still had much shipping activity in Bergen, and used his hometown as the basis for investments in other segments. Saga Forest Carriers, on the other hand, had originally grown out of a Norwegian pool based in the eastern part of the country, but was in 1995 taken over by the Japanese company Nippon Yushen Kaisha (NYK). The Japanese decided to maintain accounting and management with the company Hesnes Shipping, a specialized shipbroker based near Tønsberg.

The concentration of the shipping industry at the geographical level reflected the success—or lack of such—of shipping companies in various Norwegian regions, as well as the relocation of companies. It might seem paradoxical that parallel with the reduced cost of communication, shipping companies tended to be located more closely together, and closer to auxiliary services such as insurance and banking. In 1900—when communication was difficult—they were spread all along the coast. A century later—when communication was uncomplicated and the whole world was just an e-mail or a phone-call away—they tended to be lumped together in Oslo or Bergen.

# Business Development: Professionalization and Innovation

The location paradox above may perhaps be explained by the manner in which the competitive advantage has changed. As a result of technological and regulatory developments, the amount of information available, and the need for documentation, has become more plentiful. This has led to a *professionalization* of Norwegian shipping. Separation of ownership and management and bureaucratic organizations with a functional division of labour characterize the leading Norwegian shipping companies.

The competitive advantage has changed from local knowledge—in the port—to centralized knowledge—at the company's headquarters. It has changed from personal competence—the captain and crew at sea and the shipowner onshore—to organizational competence—the many divisions of the shipping company, each with a specific role and designated tasks. The days where Ragnar Moltzau could operate his own little tanker shipping company from the corner of the office he shared with his employer are over.[17] Shipping today is characterized by vetting, governance and compliance; by throughput, integrated logistics solutions, documentation and due diligence.

As communications improved, having excellent ship captains became less of a competitive advantage, as more and more of the business decisions were made at the company's headquarters. However, this does not imply that competence on the ship became irrelevant. Captains had to organize work on board and in port as efficiently as possible, they had to strike the right balance between overseer and officer. They still had important knowledge about the crew, the ships and the ports. Moreover, captains often went onshore, temporarily or permanently, to work as building supervisors or port captains, or to perform other important tasks.

Shipowners and shipping companies had to be able to optimize the business model and choose the right strategies. They had to be able to source cost-efficient inputs—ships, capital, labour—and to identify and target the markets where they could make a profit. Again, we have to remember that there was not *one* Norwegian strategy or policy, and many shipping companies failed on both counts—high costs led to uncompetitive production, and a focus on wrong markets led to low, or non-existent, revenues.

One feature that ensured the competitiveness of Norwegian shipping was *innovation*. This took place at two levels—technological and organizational. The technological dimension refers to the manner in which shipping companies managed to strengthen their competitive position by means of investments that alleviated their comparative disadvantages.

---

[17] See Fasting (1955).

Sometimes the owners played a key role in the development of the new technologies, other times they imitated, and sometimes they failed to invest—or refrained from investing—in the "winning" technologies.

In the post-war period, in particular, technological innovation enabled Norwegian shipping companies to gain market shares and operate profitably. The establishment and expansion of specialized shipping niches—gas and chemical tankers, cruise ships, vehicle carriers, open-hatch bulk ships—provided periods of substantial market power and large profits. Moreover, when the dry and liquid bulk markets were characterized by a structural crisis in the 1970s and 1980s, the niches were relatively well-functioning.

Organizational innovation is an umbrella that covers various new ways of "doing shipping"; operational innovation, institutional innovation, financial innovation and so on It includes new ways of organizing the companies—from regional part ownerships to stock exchange listed entities with owners from all over the world. It includes new types of business relations—the long-term charters with the oil companies in the interwar period naturally spring to mind. It includes new ways of raising capital—the use of shipyard credits, limited partnerships and incomprehensible financial instruments. It includes new ways of operation and management—outsourcing of parts of the business, joint partnerships and cooperation in pools. And, importantly, organizational innovation includes new ways of relating to the rest of the world—foreign seafarers, foreign flags, foreign investors, foreign partners. One of the defining development trends in shipping is the manner in which resources can be sourced where they are most cost-efficient. This implies that the Norwegian dimension becomes obscured, as more and more transactions have a foreign base and large parts of the business can be outsourced.

The manner in which shipping companies managed to deal with these two parameters—professionalization and innovation—was important in determining whether they became successes or failures. The transformation of Norwegian shipping in the 20th century saw a massive turnover in the agents of the industry. At the company level, survival was the exception, not the rule. At the same time, when we look at Norwegian shipping in general, the industry has shown exceptional resilience. Even today, we find a two-digit number of companies that have been involved in shipping for a century or more. However, the majority of the companies have a much shorter history. Some have been established on the ruins of failed companies, others have seen new opportunities. Some will remain competitive, others will fail.

## Still a Shipping Nation?

Norwegian shipping companies gained their leading position in shipping by chasing international demand all over the world in the second half of the 19th century. They have maintained their leading position by utilizing international supply—global factors of production—in the last part of the 20th century. With most of the employment and parts of the ownership and management located elsewhere, is Norway still a shipping nation? Are Norwegians still shipowners?

In order to answer this question, it may be useful to draw a parallel to another old industry—farming. Previously, the farmer and his family often did "everything" themselves; worked in the field, tended the animals in the barn and sold their produce at the local market. Gradually, as technology and infrastructure improved, farm sizes increased, farmers specialized and machines and hired hands took over much of the manual work. Many of the farmers today are managers and administrators—some do not even have dirt on their boots. They may spend most of the day indoors, shifting papers around. But they still own and develop their main asset—the farm—and make the decisions that ultimately decide whether this business is viable or not. It is very clear, that "the old way" would not be a viable manner in which to conduct farming business.[18]

The business of Norwegian shipping companies is much the same. More than a century ago, time ran out for the old part ownership, with a strong community foundation and a base of local labour and capital.

---

[18] Some farmers might today receive a higher price for growing in an old-fashioned manner, selling the produce with a "bio-dynamic" or "organic" premium, while others supplement their incomes by farm visits. Although such ventures might be profitable on an individual basis, for the sector as a whole, this is not a viable strategy. The shipping equivalent would be the larger sailing ships offering shorter voyages to a moneyed clientele that wants to experience a pleasurable and sugar-coated version of the days of the windjammers.

Gradually, more and more of the inputs were acquired further and further away from home. The local inputs became national, then the national inputs became international. Still, the core of the business—the decisions that give profits or losses—and a substantial part of the ownership remains within Norway. There is also an infrastructure—for financing, insurance, broking and so on—which supports these decisions, and which also has a strong local component.

In the 20th century the Norwegian shipping industry—seafarers, investors, managers—experienced enormous amounts of drama and change. Both world wars presented challenges, even though the status of the fleet was very different. Norwegian shipping companies grasped new opportunities in the interwar period and during the post-war boom. They had to fight to remain floating during the shipping crisis of the 1970s and 1980s. The introduction of the NIS, fortuitously coinciding with the rebound of the market, gave them a fresh start. Throughout the century, everyone working for Norwegian shipping has been tested again and again.

Consequently, the actual development provides us with a real-world evaluation of how well they succeeded. The grade transcript clearly shows that Norwegian shipping passed, and passed with honours. For the shipping industry as a whole, there must have been more successes than failures. Without a steady influx of successful newcomers that could replace the ones that were punished by the market forces for their bad decisions, the industry would have disappeared—like it did in so many other European countries. Norway started and finished the 20th century as one of the world's leading shipping nations, though the basis for the position had changed tremendously.

# Early 21st Century Blues: Taxing Times

Norwegian shipping companies owned between 4 and 5 per cent of the world fleet at the start of the 20th century and more than 8 per cent at the end of it. Along the way, the share varied substantially: it was particularly low after the two world wars, and peaked at around 10 per cent in the late 1960s. In the first half of the 1980s, the fleet appeared to be disappearing, before an improving market and domestic institutional innovation enabled an impressive rebound.

The fleet's development during the 20th century was far more positive than what its most important competitors experienced. The dominant shipping nation in 1900—the UK—fell from around half of the world fleet to less than 3 per cent, Germany saw its 9 per cent share more than halved, while the United States fell from more than 8 to less than 6 per cent.[19] Norway had apparently escaped the loss of competitiveness that had befallen its main competitors.

However, if we update the end point, the picture is not as clear. If we terminate the analysis in 2017, rather than at the end of the 20th century, the Norwegian success story becomes less convincing, it is less of a success story. By 2017 Norway had fallen from third to ninth place on the list of the world's leading ship-owning nations. The proportion of the world fleet had fallen from more than 8 to around 2.8 per cent. In other words, over this brief period—less than two decades—the Norwegian market share declined more than Germany's had done throughout the 20th century.

One of the reasons for the decline was the fact that some of the largest and most successful shipping companies were taken over by foreigners. The national consolidation processes in the 1990s were just the first step. These were then engulfed by an international wave of mergers and acquisitions. In many instances the Norwegian shipping companies were attractive targets. Sig. Bergesen dy had taken over the fleets of two other companies to become one of the leading international companies in the gas carrier market, and also had a substantial tanker fleet. In 2003 the company—whose fleet amounted to more than 10 million dead weight tons, making up slightly more than 20 per cent of the Norwegian fleet—was sold to Hong Kong interests. Although some parts of the operation continued from Norway, the jewel in the crown was gone.

The first years of the new millennium were characterized by sales of tonnage abroad. In contrast to the sales in the 1980s, the ships were not sold because the companies had problems. The ships and the companies

---

[19] Confer Tables 2.1 and 9.1 for details on the data. Percentages measured as share of effective tonnage in 1900 and dead weight tonnage in 2001.

were sold because they were attractive to foreign investors. This period was also marked by substantial turbulence among the companies that remained, in particular in their relationship with the authorities. The basis for the animosity was a well-known topic: tax.

The dogfight about tax marked a low point in the relationship between the authorities and the shipping companies—mistrust of a kind that had not been seen since the restrictions on foreign contracting in the late 1940s and early 1950s. The basis was the transfer to a tonnage tax regime in line with most European Union countries. In principle, the introduction of a beneficial tax system should have been welcomed by Norwegian shipowners. However, they believed that they already operated in a benign tax regime, and had done so since the last major reform, in 1996.

They were wrong. The small print revealed that the 1996 system only deferred tax payments, it did not abolish them. In 2005 the government revealed how it would "harmonize" the tax system with other European countries; this would be done by introducing a new tonnage tax regime. Somewhat surprisingly, those companies that wanted to be included in the new regime had to pay the accrued (and deferred) taxes for all the years after 1996.

The tax bill was enormous—NOK 21 billion, of which two-thirds should be paid and one-third could be "written off" in exchange for environmentally friendly investments. The retrospective taxation also had some truly bizarre effects. In 2007—one of the best years ever for shipping, when an iron- and coal-hungry China drove up bulk rates—many Norwegian shipping companies reported enormous after-tax losses. Two years later, part of the tax payments was reversed following a Supreme Court decision that ruled out the claim for backdated taxes. In a shipping market that had gone from red hot to decidedly chilly, Norwegian shipping companies could post quite impressive results.[20]

It was not only the relationship with the Norwegian authorities that was strained. In addition to the trouble on the home front, a number of

---

[20] An example is Bergen-based Kristian Gerhard Jebsen Skipsrederi AS, which in 2007, when the latent payment was activated, paid a tax bill of more than USD200 million. When added to financial costs, this turned an operating surplus of USD211 million into a deficit. In 2009, the repatriation of USD120 million, following the Supreme Court ruling, gave the company one of its best results ever in a generally dismal year; see Tenold (2015, 298–299).

shipping companies ended up in trouble abroad. One of the Norwegian success stories of the late 20th century was how companies had managed to build up dominant positions in niche markets. Now some of these companies were targeted by the competition authorities and accused of anticompetitive practices.

In a series of dawn raids in February 2003, the competition authorities, in cooperation with the EFTA Surveillance Authority, visited the offices of the world's leading chemical tanker operators. The Bergen shipping companies Odfjell ASA and JO Tankers were among four companies that were in trouble with the US competition authorities. Accused of colluding to keep freight rates high in the chemical tanker market, the companies agreed to pay substantial settlements to the US authorities and major customers. Stolt-Nielsen, another company with Norwegian roots, was given an amnesty in the case, claiming "whistle-blower" status. Still, for the involved companies the total costs, including legal fees, amounted to hundreds of millions of dollars.

Around 10 years later there were new raids. In September 2012, the European competition authorities, working together with colleagues in Japan and the United States, raided the offices of several car carrier companies. The companies, including Wallenius Wilhelmsen Logistics and EUKOR, subsidiaries of Wilh. Wilhelmsen ASA, were accused of keeping rates in their segment artificially high. So far, the companies have paid penalties for price-fixing, bid-rigging or related practices in, among other countries, Japan, China, the United States, Korea and the European Union.[21]

The two cases above show that Norwegian shipping companies still played an important role in the international market, although the declining Norwegian share of the world fleet in the period 2000–2017 reveals a substantially reduced position in the world fleet *per se*. There are primarily three factors that can explain the decline, and all of these suggest that the notion of a much weakened Norwegian shipping industry should be nuanced.

The first is the aforementioned sales of all or part of Norwegian shipping companies to foreign owners. In many instances important activities

---

[21] Wallenius Wilhelmsen, *Annual Report*, various issues.

remained in Norway, even though the ownership changed. In other cases there were substantial underreported Norwegian ownership interests in companies abroad. Due to the difficulties of determining the "nationality" of ships and shipping companies, the statistics leave a lot to be desired. There is no doubt that there was a reduction in Norwegian ownership as companies were sold out. However, the statistics tend to overestimate the effects. The more than two percentage points decline in the Norwegian share from 2003 to 2005 was to a large extent related to the fact that the Bergesen group and Navion were sold to foreign interests. However, activity at the companies' headquarters in Oslo and Stavanger was practically unchanged in the short term.

The second reason that the decline has to be nuanced is the manner in which the world fleet increased. After 2000 the world fleet has gone through its most rapid growth period ever, while the size of the Norwegian fleet has practically been standing still—hence the reduced share. However, a large proportion of the new tonnage was relatively simple vessels. In particular, in the period 2005–2010 there was a flood of bulk carriers built to satisfy China's almost insatiable appetite for iron ore. Although some Norwegian shipping companies were involved in this expansion, the main investors were found elsewhere.

The difference to the boom at the beginning of the 1970s is striking. In 1974, Norwegian shipping companies owned around 9 per cent of the world fleet, but held almost 13.5 per cent of the newbuilding orders.[22] Thirty years later, they owned around 5 per cent of the world fleet, but were responsible for only 3 per cent of the new orders.[23] This was partly a reflection of the fact that Norwegians refrained from investing in ships that weigh heavy in tonnage terms—the simple large tankers and dry bulk carriers—but continued to buy ships that were technologically advanced and had a high value per ton.

This brings us to the final reason, where the price per ton is taken to the extreme: the Norwegian investments in offshore. In the year 2000, the offshore vessels made up the most valuable part of the Norwegian fleet, and these hardly count at all if the market share is calculated on the

---

[22] Calculated on the basis of Fearnley & Egers Chartering Co, *Review 1974*.
[23] *Aftenposten*, 11012005, 5.

basis of gross tonnage or dead weight tonnage. The declining Norwegian share of the world fleet at the beginning of the 21st century is a continuation of the trend that characterized the last part of the 20th century. As we saw in the last chapter, this echoes the apparent stagnation in the Norwegian fleet at the end of the 19th century. When we take into account the properties of the tonnage—a shift from sail to steam, or from large simple ships to small specialized vessels—the stagnation becomes a statistical artefact, not reflecting the realities.

If we consider the value of the fleet, rather than tonnage figures, Norway was sixth in the world in 2015, even at a time when the value of offshore vessels was depressed. Although there had been little or no growth in tonnage terms, the value of the Norwegian fleet had more than doubled after the year 2000. Still, with the rapid growth of the world fleet, this doubling of the value was insufficient to maintain the international share. However, the relative decline in value was much less dramatic than the decline in tonnage terms.

The transformation of the activities is reflected in the fact that Norway owned 16 per cent of the world offshore fleet, by value, substantially more than for most other segments. In a recent report, the Norwegian Shipowners' Association excludes the three largest tonnage groups—dry bulk vessels, tankers and container ships. By focusing on the advanced part of the world merchant marine, Norway in fact comes out on top, owning the world's most valuable fleet.[24] In 2013–2014 offshore vessels made up almost half of the value of this fleet.

A similar shift towards offshore is evident if we look at employment in the Norwegian maritime sector. From 2004 to 2014, the traditional shipping companies, those involved in deep-sea shipping, had a reduction in the number of employees of more than 4000. This was a result of the movement of companies and functions abroad. Some of the foreign interests that had bought Norwegian companies relocated all or part of their activities. Moreover, many Norwegian-owned companies also began a process where operations, management, technical services and so on were outsourced internationally. The offshore shipping companies, on

---

[24] Norges Rederiforbund (2015, 8). Creative ways of counting are something of a Norwegian specialty.

the other hand, increased the number of employees by more than 8000, giving a net increase in the number of persons employed in shipping companies.[25]

The development in the first decades of the 21st century has also seen regional displacement. Activities in the two main shipping centres have developed very differently; "while traditional shipping has gradually been built down, moved out or changed in a financial direction in Oslo, Bergen has been able to maintain its position as a shipping city." By 2015 the tonnage registered in Bergen made up more than 40 per cent of the Norwegian fleet, and the city's fleet was more than one-third larger than the Oslo fleet. Expansion in old companies and a set of active newcomers in Bergen, combined with a decline in the fleet registered in the capital, can explain why the two have traded places at the top of Norwegian shipping in the first decades of the 20th century.[26] Moreover, overinvestment in the offshore sector, followed by a rate drop and a dramatic decline in the value of the vessels, created a need for restructuring. This consolidation process has increased the concentration in that part of the shipping industry, both company- and location-wise.

## Is There a Future for Norwegian Shipping in the 21st Century?

People in northern Europe are known for having a relatively worried attitude to life; the glass is usually half empty, seldom half full. In Norway, the question of "How can we make a living when the oil in the North Sea runs out?" has preoccupied the population and the authorities for decades. Two insights from the analysis in this book might provide some help in answering this question.

First, by adapting strategies and policies, it is possible to remain competitive in an international market, even for a country with a high income level. Shipping did this for most of the 20th century, changing investment

---

[25] Menon (2017, 11).
[26] Menon (2017, 86).

strategies and the regulatory framework to be able to utilize competitive advantages.

The offshore oil exploration in the North Sea has enabled the accumulation of a vast body of competence, and this can be employed elsewhere. The export of offshore services has already begun on a large scale. Norwegian companies operating offshore vessels get around 60 per cent of their revenue from ships working outside the Norwegian sector, and 40 per cent from Norwegian waters.[27]

The manner in which the offshore industry became internationalized had much in common with the manner in which Norwegian shipping grabbed global market share in the 19th century. It built up skills in a relatively protected home market, before venturing out to compete on the world stage. Norwegian shipping showed that it was possible to become a leading maritime nation without a big home market. Consequently, Norwegian oil industry participants—including the many companies involved in maritime activities—can do the same when activity in the North Sea is reduced.[28]

Moreover, there is another similarity between the current offshore expansion and the shipping expansion after 1850. To a large extent, the activities are embedded in local communities, where the ship is built at local yards and much of the technology is provided by local producers. At the end of the 19th century, the shipbuilding industry in Norway encountered severe problems, as it was "stuck" in an old technological paradigm—wooden sailing ships—when steam and steel took over. Today, the Norwegian offshore yards are at the technological frontier. They have a leading position, both when it comes to the vessels that are manufactured and the manner in which they are built.

The second insight from the analysis is also related to the competitiveness of Norwegian shipping. Even before oil was found, Norway had a high standard of living and relatively balanced external economic relations. More than any other sector, shipping played a crucial role in this respect, neutralizing the deficit on the balance of trade. At the same time,

---

[27] Norges Rederiforbund (2015, 4).
[28] Of course, given what we know about climate and the environment, the long-term viability of a business model centred around petroleum exploration, even when freed from the limited Norwegian resources, can be debated.

the manner in which Norway remained competitive, gradually eroded the country's advantages. Norwegian shipping maintained a large share of the international market for seaborne transport by becoming *less Norwegian*.

Foreign demand had been the main basis of Norwegian shipping ever since the late 19th century. Financing from abroad was important for much of the 20th century, but in the last decades two additional "international" elements were added. First, Norwegian deep-sea seafarers were replaced by foreigners. Second, foreign companies bought up Norwegian companies, both the hardware—the ships—and the software—the knowledge.

Due to the international character of shipping, Norwegian companies argue that they need "a level playing field"—that the rules of the game should be identical to their competitors. The result has been a beneficial tax regime, an international ship register, competitive labour conditions and so on. However, as the conditions become more equal, it becomes much more difficult to build national distinction, much more difficult to stand out. Current shipping industry buzzwords such as "digitalization" and "big data" will most likely contribute further to this trend.

When every shipping company has access to the same information, which competitive parameters can the Norwegian shipping industry rely on? When labour and capital is drawn from a global pool, why should it choose Norwegian ships and Norwegian companies? When registration costs and tax conditions are practically identical in most countries, why choose Norway?

We can go back to the beginning of this chapter, where we repeated the question about Norwegian shipping, about its role and about its basis. We can then "fast forward" the question 100 years. The reformulated problem is then: "Which factors—specific to Norway, either alone or in combination—can ensure that the country maintains a leading role in international shipping in the 21st century?"

Although it is impossible to answer this question, it might be worth trying to identify some of the critical issues. Three factors make Norway stand out in an international perspective, even in the "practically all things equal" world of shipping. First, the country has a broad and high-skilled maritime milieu, and sea-related activities make up a very large share of the economy. Second, Norway has long maritime traditions, and there is still a maritime identity and awareness that is lacking in many other countries. Third, Norway is a high-income economy, but one with an egalitarian culture and a compressed wage structure.

The first Norwegian advantage is the broad maritime milieu. The shipping companies have been at the centre of a business cluster that included shipbuilders and manufacturers of maritime equipment, in addition to a wide range of service industries—shipbrokers, classification agencies, naval architects, insurance companies and banks. Gradually, the frontiers of this cluster have become fuzzier.

Just like when the term "shipping policy" was replaced by "maritime policy" in the 1990s, the maritime dimension keeps growing. The Ministry of Trade, Industry and Fisheries in 2015 launched a comprehensive maritime strategy, where it uses the term "the ocean-based industries."[29] In the government's new strategy, the term refers to the oil and gas industry, the maritime industry (including ships and other floating units), as well as the seafood industry. In 2017, the Ministry of Trade, Industry and Fisheries and the Ministry of Petroleum and Energy jointly launched an "ocean strategy" [*havstrategi*], an initiative given the heading "New growth, proud history."[30]

Government policies can lay the foundation for success or failure, but they cannot determine the result. Luckily, the Norwegian maritime milieu is much more than political decisions. Norway's coastline is still among the longest in the world, and around 80 per cent of the Norwegian population lives less than 10 kilometres from the sea. The Norwegian area at sea is six times larger than the country itself. Norwegian businesses continue to look for ways to profit from the sea, and the ocean-based industries make up more than 70 per cent of Norwegian export revenues,

---

[29] Norway, Ministry of Trade, Industry and Fisheries, 2015, *Maritime muligheter – blå vekst for grønn fremtid*.

[30] A report published in 2016—"Norway – the ocean nation"—starts off with an bold claim: "Norway is the leading ocean nation in the world"; Norges Rederiforbund et al. (2016, 3). The government's new maritime strategy is more modest; "Norway is one of the leading ocean nations in the world"; Norway, Ministry of Trade, Industry and Fisheries/Ministry of Petroleum and Energy, 2017, *Ny vekst. Stolt historie*, 6. It is worth noting that the report "Norway – the ocean nation" is a joint publication by the Norwegian Shipowners' Association and four other industry associations, covering manufacturing, petroleum, fish farming and fishing.

37 per cent of the private sector's Gross Domestic Product and 14 per cent of private sector employment.[31]

In other words, the sea has a larger presence—in daily life and in the economy—than in most other countries. This geographic advantage is unlikely to change in the 21st century.

The second advantage is the maritime traditions and heritage, and the manner in which the long history of Norwegian shipping shapes self-perception and occupational and investment choices. It was this tradition that created the maritime cluster, and it was this tradition that enabled the building up of capital and competence. As suggested above, maritime history is nowadays getting more intertwined with "maritime culture."

Norway is the home of world-leading shipping companies and associated businesses. These are seen as interesting places to work, and thus manage to attract qualified people that in other countries would have preferred other sectors. Moreover, the existence of a maritime infrastructure—practical and theoretical education, research, networks and so on—facilitates recruitment to the shipping sector.

The maritime heritage and culture is not static. So far, the critical mass of the shipping companies and their partners has been sufficient for the shipping sector to regenerate itself.[32] Moreover, the manner in which the various "ocean industries" have started to cooperate can be seen as a means to ensuring that a critical mass is maintained. It is also a way of increasing the value added. Given the development of traditional deep-sea shipping, where countries have competed to attract activity, many of the mechanisms that gave economic benefits in the 20th century have disappeared or been reduced. Among these are both the ability to extract large tax revenues from shipping companies and the employment effect of seafarers in the deep-sea fleet. The land-based activities are therefore increasingly important, and it would be beneficial if these could be linked to other ocean-based industries to ensure critical mass.

However, one part of maritime culture is eroding: the number of people with actual experience of the sea is declining rapidly. The shipping

---

[31] Norway, Ministry of Trade, Industry and Fisheries/Ministry of Petroleum and Energy, 2017, *Ny vekst. Stolt historie*, 6.
[32] This is one of the main points in Norman (2012).

companies and the authorities have tried to introduce measures that can alleviate this—recruitment drives, cadet positions, compensation for the use of Norwegian seafarers and tax breaks. Norway prides itself on its maritime competence, and this competence has traditionally been transferred from the sea to the shore. When Norwegian shipping built up its international position, the captains that went ashore and started their own companies were crucial. In the post-war period, seafarers came ashore with skills and knowledge that made them valuable assets in the daily operation of the business. They became managers, port captains, supervisors, surveyors and consultants.

Today, the on-board competence—in a purely Norwegian setting—is disappearing. By far the highest proportion of those working on the NIS vessels are foreigners. Most shipping companies have outsourced the employment of seafarers to management companies abroad. We do not know how this will affect the future of the industry, but it is unlikely to have a positive impact. Employment in Norwegian waters goes some way towards alleviating the negative development, but even this part of the business is "threatened" by foreign labour.

As a result of the rich maritime history, Norwegian companies and individuals have a maritime identity and awareness that stands out in an international perspective. This maritime culture is, however, the most volatile and vulnerable of the three advantages.

In Chap. 2, we divided the cultural dimension into a "maritime culture" element and a "Norwegian culture" element. While the first of these has changed quite a lot, in particular during the past decades, there are still aspects of the "Norwegian culture" that differ from other countries. Consequently, the third and final element that might make the country competitive within shipping and other maritime industries is therefore the specific "Norwegian culture." Important aspects are egalitarianism, gender equality and governance.

Norway continues to be relatively egalitarian, despite its strong wealth and income growth. Egalitarianism is reflected in, among other things, a compressed wage structure. Unskilled labour is relatively expensive and highly educated labour is relatively cheap. The compressed wage structure implies that Norwegian shipping, despite a high overall wage level, might in fact have a competitive advantage when it comes to the price of competence. When we adjust for productivity, the costs of using Norwegian engineers, for instance, is not necessarily higher than in countries with a much lower *general* wage level.

The relatively low price of high-quality skills can be a competitive advantage, not only for shipping companies, but also for many of the auxiliary industries that are related to shipping. Banking, insurance, marine equipment production and so on are all high competence and high value-added industries. Moreover, Norway is at the international forefront with regard to maritime research, with technological and operational innovations that spill over into business.

The egalitarian attitude is also reflected in questions of gender. Norway and the other Nordic countries rank among the top three in the world on indices that measure differences between men and women, such as the Gender Inequality Index and the Global Gender Gap Index.[33] Gender equality can be an advantage for economic and business development—it makes little sense to choose skills and competence from only half of the population. Moreover, diversity is more likely to reduce groupthink.[34] At the same time, with regard to gender, Norwegian business is not as progressive as, for example, politics and education, despite policies such as quotas at Board level in stock exchange listed companies. While 45 per cent of the ministers in the Norwegian government are women—including all of the three most important posts—only 5 per cent of the 100 largest companies listed on the *Oslo Børs* have female chief executive officers.

The shipping sector is known for being particularly conservative—at the international level it is 20 years behind other businesses, according to one female insider.[35] Still, this implies that there is scope for improvement, and Norway has a shorter way to go than many other countries. In 2008 the Bergen shipowner Elisabeth Grieg became the first female President of

---

[33] Nordic Council of Ministers (2017, 12).
[34] Although most studies find no statistically significant effects of female participation on profits, a recent analysis of more than 22,000 companies from more than 90 countries suggest that "the presence of women in corporate leadership positions may improve firm performance"; Noland, Moran and Kotschwar (2016, 3).
[35] *Tradewinds*, 14032018. Of the Fortune 500 companies, only 6 per cent are headed by women, and "the inequality is even higher in shipping"; *Tradewinds*, 25012018.

the Norwegian Shipowners' Association, and she has taken an active stand in promoting women in business. Today, there are several initiatives that aim to encourage and support women who work in shipping, including female-focused organizations and mentoring programmes.

The final cultural element that might make Norwegian maritime industries competitive is governance and social capital. Efficient and accountable politicians and bureaucrats, as well as the (relative) absence of corruption, characterize Norwegian economy and business. The combination of high social capital—trust, norms and networks—and good governance has been used to explain the economic success of Norway and the other Nordic countries.[36] It can be used as a competitive advantage in shipping and other maritime industries.

## Finally: Summing Up

What are the lessons from the 20th century development? How can a small country such as Norway remain competitive in the world's most global industry?

Norwegian shipping *was competitive* at the beginning of the 20th century due to a favourable starting point. The combination of geography, history and culture enabled the Norwegians to take advantage of the strong growth of seaborne trade in the second half of the 19th century. In other words, when the 20th century began, the Norwegian shipping community had a head start.

Norwegian shipping *remained competitive* by becoming less Norwegian. By embracing markets abroad, by attracting foreign capital, and by combining domestic competence and technology with labour from low-cost countries, the country's shipping companies managed to hold on to market shares and ensure profitability.

In a shipping world where the playing field has been levelled, and national differences have almost been wiped out, perhaps Norwegian shipping can *maintain competitiveness* by embracing the distinctively

---

[36] Nordic Council of Ministers (2017, 14–17).

Norwegian elements again: a vast maritime sector, where shipping is complemented by industries that harvest the resources of the ocean; a national bias towards shipping and the sea; a compressed wage structure; and an egalitarian society, with gender equality, good governance and high social capital. Geography, history and culture.

# Bibliography

D. Bakka (2017) *Nasjonens ære – Norsk rederinæring mellom marked og politikk* (Bergen: Bodoni Forlag)

L. Borgersrud & I.B. Eriksen (2015) *Sabotører i vest – Sabotasjeorganisasjonen på Vestlandet 1940–1945* (Bergen: Bodoni Forlag)

K. Fasting (1955) *AS Moltzaus Tankrederi* (Oslo: AS Moltzaus Tankrederi)

L.R. Fischer (2016) 'The International Merchant Marine in Comparative Perspective: An Analysis of Canada and Norway, 1870–1900', in *Schifffahrt und Handel/Shipping and Trade: Vorträge, gehalten anlässlich der Verabschiedung von Lars U. Scholl in den Ruhestand im März 2012* (Bremen: Edition Falkenberg) 77–99

G. Harlaftis & I. Theotokas (2009) *Leadership in World Shipping: Greek Family Firms in International Business* (Basingstoke: Palgrave Macmillan)

G. Iversen (2011) 'Inventing the nation: Diorama in Norway 1888–1894', *Early Popular Visual Culture*, 9:2, 123–129

J.E. Klepsland (2011) *Utvikling av eierstrukturen i rederier notert på Oslo Børs* (Bergen: Stiftelsen for samfunns- og næringslivsforskning)

K. Larsen (1948) *A History of Norway* (Princeton: Princeton University Press)

T. Lennerfors, H. Lindgren & R.T. Poulsen (2012) 'The Two Declines of Swedish Shipping', in S. Tenold, M.J. Iversen & E. Lange (eds) *Global Shipping in Small Nations: Nordic Experiences after 1960* (Basingstoke: Palgrave Macmillan) 100–128

Menon (2017) *Maritim verdiskapningsbok 2017* (Oslo: Menon Business Economics)

M. Noland, T. Moran & B. Kotschwar (2016) 'Is Gender Diversity Profitable? Evidence from a Global Survey', *Working Paper 16-3* (Washington DC: Peterson Institute for International Economics)

Nordic Council of Ministers (2017) *Is the Nordic region best in the world?* (Copenhagen: Nordic Council of Ministers)

Norges Rederiforbund (2015) *Norske offshorerederier – i krevende farvann* (Oslo: Norges Rederiforbund)

Norges Rederiforbund et al. (2016) *Havnasjonen Norge* (Oslo: Norges Rederiforbund, Norsk Industri, Norsk olje og gass, Sjømat Norge, Norges Fiskarlag)

V.D. Norman (2012) 'A Future for Nordic Shipping?' in S. Tenold, M.J. Iversen & E. Lange (eds) *Global Shipping in Small Nations: Nordic Experiences after 1960* (Basingstoke: Palgrave Macmillan) 202–214

H.W. Nordvik (1997) 'From Benign Neglect to Active Intervention: Norwegian Government Shipping Policies from the 1970s Shipping Crisis to the Present', *unpublished manuscript* (Bergen: Norwegian School of Economics and Business Administration)

A.S. Svendsen (1976) *Skipsfartskrisen* (Bergen: Institute for Shipping Research)

S. Tenold (2015) *Geared for Growth. Kristian Gerhard Jebsen and His Shipping Companies* (Bergen: Bodoni Forlag)

**Open Access** This chapter is licensed under the terms of the Creative Commons Attribution-NonCommercial-NoDerivatives 4.0 International License (http://creativecommons.org/licenses/by-nc-nd/4.0/), which permits any noncommercial use, sharing, distribution and reproduction in any medium or format, as long as you give appropriate credit to the original author(s) and the source, provide a link to the Creative Commons license and indicate if you modified the licensed material. You do not have permission under this license to share adapted material derived from this chapter or parts of it.

The images or other third party material in this chapter are included in the chapter's Creative Commons license, unless indicated otherwise in a credit line to the material. If material is not included in the chapter's Creative Commons license and your intended use is not permitted by statutory regulation or exceeds the permitted use, you will need to obtain permission directly from the copyright holder.

# Index

## A

Aalborg, 32, 32n23
Aasgaardstrand, 83
Abrahamsen, Egil, 236
Admiral Raeder, 138n12
Aframax, 268
Africa/African, 28, 116, 124, 240, 241, 260
Agder, 11, 12
Aker group, 212, 213, 213n26, 248, 249, 251
Aker H-3, 251
Akershus, 13n13
Allied supply lines, 64
*Altmark*, 138, 139
The American Committee for Flags of Necessity, 231
Americas, 24n5, 25, 27, 27n14, 27n16, 28, 67n14
Amsterdam, 159, 183, 271
Amundsen, Roald, 75n46, 125n79–81
Andersen, Håkon With, 109
Anglo-Saxon Petroleum Co., 101
Antarctica, 124n77
Antwerp, 159, 170
Apartheid, 237
Arabian Gulf, 204
Archangel, 126
Arctic Ocean, 72
Arendal, 14, 35, 38n37, 113, 113n57
Argentina, 23, 32n23, 94n5
Armistice Day, 126

---

[1] Note: Page numbers followed by 'n' refer to notes.

Asia/Asian, 3, 123n76, 124, 199, 240, 260, 260n2, 261, 267, 281, 284
"Asian-clause" ships, 240
Asian crews, 240
AS Pelican Co. KS, 249
*Asra*, 64
AS Reidar, 92
Association of Cotton Factories, 71
AS Syracuse Oils Norge, 249
Athens, 104
Atlantic, 5, 92, 116, 211
Austevoll, 265, 290
Australia/Australian, 23, 24n5, 24n6, 25, 28, 66, 66n12, 72n27, 84, 110, 116, 161n5, 197n5, 260
Average age, 102, 108, 108n40, 206
Average tanker size, 206, 207n18
Azores, 110

B

Bahamas, 226, 267
Bahia, 31
Bakka, Dag, Jr., vii, 116, 244
Bakkevig, Einar, 222
Balance of trade, 148, 231, 269, 302
Balholm, 66
Bang, Johan, 110
Bank of England, 143
Barry, 123
*Belen Quezada*, 104
Belgium/Belgian, 23, 27n14, 65, 65n7, 66, 94n5, 124n77, 161n5, 197n5
Belize, 31
Bergen, 12–14, 13n13, 25, 34, 34n26, 35, 37n32, 38n37, 49n73, 55, 56, 66, 76, 76n48, 78, 82, 83, 107, 108n37, 113, 115, 115n58, 115n60, 116, 120, 123n74, 126, 139, 142, 176, 182, 186, 189, 214, 222, 224, 231, 232, 238, 243, 245, 251, 263–265, 263n7, 272n24, 289–291, 301, 307
Bergen Bank, 246
Bergen Bar, 160, 254
Bergen Radio, 139
*Bergensfjord*, 152
Bergens Stuertforening, 106
Bergesen, Sigval, 222, 299
Bermuda, 245
*Besseggen*, 221
Biørn Biørnstad & Co., 213
Bjørnstad and Brækhus, 83, 84
Black Sea, 104n27, 124
*Blücher*, 139
*Blue Riband*, 5
Bolsheviks, 97n15
Bona shipholding, 268
Boom, 15, 57, 68, 80–86, 95, 97, 123n76, 150, 151, 188, 196, 204, 205, 209, 216, 251, 287, 295, 299
Bordeaux, 64
The Bore War, 136
Borgny Dolphin, 251
Bratsberg, 13n13
Brazil/Brazilian, 23, 51n82
Bremerhaven, 172
British America, 22n3, 32, 144
British Asia, 23
British Australia, 22n3
British blockade, 70
British Isles, 78
Broad Street, 83, 142–146
Brofoss, Erik, 180n41, 182, 182n48

Brooklyn, 91, 122, 123n74
Buenos Aires, 31
Bulkification, 171–175, 177, 221
Bull-Gundersen, Gunnar, 134n2, 159, 160n2, 190
Business cycles, 57, 115, 121, 279
Buskerud, 13n13
Bygder, 17, 35
Bømlo, 265, 290
Bør Børson Jr., 79n58

C
C1-A general cargo ships, 148
Cadiz, 31
Café Håpløs, 160, 254
Café Måneskinn, 160
Café Solskinn, 160
Cape of Good Hope, 165, 204
Cape Palmas, 240
Capital mobilization, 243
Capital sources, 182
Captains' Associations, 106n32
Captain shipowners, 55
Car carriers, 169, 218, 245, 298
Cardiff, 31, 124n77
Central America, 27n14
Centralization, 289n16
Charters, 27, 27n15, 29, 47, 75, 101, 112, 137, 145, 176, 199, 204, 210, 212, 218, 284, 293
Chemical tankers, 176, 189, 218, 221–223, 245, 290, 298
Chile, 23, 110
China, 27n16, 32n23, 34n25, 126, 260, 260n2, 261, 267, 281, 297–299
Christensen, Ivar An, 113
Christiania, *see* Oslo

Churchill, Winston, 134, 134n4, 143
Clyde, 31, 110
CMA CGM, 171
Coastline, 34, 34n25, 65, 103, 104, 138, 304
The Cold War, 163n7
Communications technology, 16
Compensated tonnage, 41n47, 42, 94n5
Competence, 15, 16, 40, 210, 220, 223, 224, 232, 246n34, 247, 248, 250, 252, 264, 271, 272, 278, 284, 290, 292, 302, 305–308
Competitive advantages, 47, 49, 232, 291, 292, 302, 306–308
Competitive neutrality, 286
Concentration of ownership, 214
Concrete ships, 95
Congress (US), 25, 45, 126
Constanta, 124
Consuls, 36n31, 56, 69, 69n18
Containerization, 171–175
Continental, 27n14, 32, 47, 252, 255, 275
Continental Europe, 28, 34, 116
Contracts of affreightment, 176
Cooperation, 46, 55, 73, 77, 125, 142, 143, 147, 176, 188, 189, 220, 222, 251, 293, 298
Copenhagen, 34n26, 38
Corresponding owner, 11n10, 54
Council for Mutual Economic Assistance, 163n7
Court Line, 218, 218n34
Covenants, 212
Crude oil transports, 202, 281
Cruise shipping, 105, 222, 226, 293

Cruise vessels, 219, 278
Culture, 33–49, 51, 93, 169n17,
 207, 278, 304, 305, 308
Curacao, 124, 241n26
Currency regulation, 150
Cyclicality, 204
Cyprus, 268

D

Danzig, 105n29
Dead weight tonnage (dwt), 55n93,
 75, 121, 122, 152, 168,
 186n58, 199, 202n14, 238,
 263n7, 265, 290, 296,
 296n19, 300
Dekke, Annanias, 42, 119n66
Denmark/Danish, 15, 22, 23, 26,
 27n14, 32n23, 33, 38, 39,
 39n42, 47, 64, 70n21, 72, 75,
 77, 80, 83n71, 84, 93, 112,
 124, 125, 125n81, 137,
 137n10, 140, 148, 161n5,
 197n5, 199n8, 233, 239, 242,
 242n26, 267, 268, 277, 283,
 289, 289n16
Den Norske Afrika og Australia
 Linie, 116
Den Norske Amerikalinje, 116, 120,
 121, 175
Den norske Krigsforsikring for Skib,
 136
Den norske sjøfarts historie, 18
Den oversjøiske eksportforening, 69
Den subvenerede Norsk-Spanske
 Linje, 116
Depreciation, 96, 210, 210n22, 272,
 286
The Desert Shur, *see* Ørkenen Sur

Det Bergenske Dampskipselskap,
 120
Det norske Veritas, 112n52, 177,
 201n12, 236, 271
*Deutschland*, 5
Ditlev-Simonsen, Olav, 54, 55,
 55n93
Diversification, 208, 217, 218,
 218n37, 243, 244, 246, 265
Donations, 232n2
Dreyfus, 222
Drilling rigs, 213, 217, 249, 251
Dry bulk goods, 174, 175, 281
Dry bulk market, 202, 218n37, 293
DS AS Vestlandet, 64, 79, 84
Dusavik, 249
Dutch Republic, 34
Dyvi, Jan-Erik, 222

E

East Asia, 25, 164, 239
East Asian Tigers, 266
The Eastern Bloc, 163n7
Eastern Mediterranean, 78
The East Indies, 51, 166
Economies of scale, 165, 168–171,
 185–188, 188n65, 204, 216,
 220, 232, 252, 253, 281, 282,
 287
Eden, Anthony, 134n4
EFTA Surveillance Authority, 298
Egalitarianism, 52, 306
Egeland, John Oscar, 14, 94n5,
 96n10, 103n24, 147, 185n56
Ekofisk, 249, 249n37, 252
Empire, 24, 27, 102, 103, 119, 231
Energy transports, 100
Engineers, 196, 253, 307

*En Sjøens Helt*, 133
Equality, 17, 52, 306, 307, 309
Equity, 45, 84, 97, 113, 114, 179, 181, 188, 205, 212, 226, 243, 282, 284, 285
Eriksson, Gustaf, 110n47
Established companies, 15, 112, 220, 244, 245, 286
EUKOR, 298
European Recovery Program, 164
Europoort, 160
Evergreen, 171
Export revenues, 2, 70, 99, 118, 149, 304

F

Factors of production, 15, 187, 235, 280, 294
Farmers Party (Bondepartiet or Senterpartiet), 151
Fearnley & Astrup, 249
Fearnley & Eger, 120, 165n10, 199n7, 201n13, 202, 202n14, 203, 205n17, 242n28, 299n22
Fedje, 126
Fine art, 85
Finland/Finnish, 23, 26, 27n14, 76, 111, 161n5, 184n55, 197n5
Finnmark, 117
Finnmarken, *see* Finnmark
First era of globalization, 68, 86, 96, 261
First World War, 7, 36n31, 37n33, 42, 63–86, 94, 97, 99, 102, 113, 114, 119n66, 120, 124, 125n79, 126, 136–138, 143, 155, 162, 182, 222, 262, 281

Fischer, Skip, vii, 279
Fish exports, 70n21, 71, 76n47
Fjords, 33, 34n25, 35, 66, 200, 223
Flag of Convenience, 38, 105, 105n29, 119, 231, 234, 235, 237, 238, 266, 267, 288
Flagging out, 226, 234, 235
Fleet value, 29n17, 37, 204, 263, 300
Foreign currency, 148, 149
Foreign ownership, 268n14, 284n11
Foreningen for skandinaviske sømandshjem i fremede havne, 123n75
Fosnavåg, 265, 290
Foundations, 36, 36n31, 45, 48, 49, 68, 103, 118, 155, 294, 304
Foyn, Svend, 117
France/French, 22, 23, 25, 27n14, 36, 65n5, 78, 92, 99, 115, 136, 161n5, 163, 169n17, 197n3, 197n5, 233
Francia, 33
Fred. Olsen, 80n60, 117, 120, 121, 244, 249, 251
Fredriksen, John, 245, 268, 269
Fredrikshald, 110
Freight rates, 56, 57, 68, 80, 81, 97, 98, 137, 150, 165, 174, 199, 204, 205, 215n29, 216–218, 247n36, 266, 283, 287, 288, 298
Friis, Finn, 92
Friis & Lund, 97n15, 126
Frimann & Pedersen, 64
Fruit trade, 25, 25n8, 103, 103n24
Furness Withy & Co., 74
Furuseth, Andrew, 104

## G

G.M. Bryde, 116
Gainsbourg, Serge, 169n17
Gas tankers, 169, 218
Gas Traders Pool, 222
Gearbulk, 220, 222, 291
Gender balance, 17
General Agreement on Tariffs and Trade, 164
General Consul Storm, 69
Gentlemen's agreement, 137
Geography, 33–48, 165n10, 275, 276, 308, 309
George, David Lloyd, 137
Gerhardsen, Einar, 134n1
Germany/German, 5, 21, 23, 24n6, 25, 26, 27n14, 34, 44, 63–80, 65n5, 66n10, 67n14, 70n21, 71n22, 77n52, 84, 94n5, 99, 102–104, 103n25, 115, 127, 133, 135, 136, 137n10, 138–141, 138n12, 143, 146n32, 161n5, 163, 186, 197n3, 197n5, 233, 242, 242n26, 267, 277, 296
Globalization, 4, 4n4, 9, 171, 262, 279–285, 283n10
The Golden Age, 107, 159–190, 195–198, 204, 206, 207, 247n35
Goole, 31
Gotaas-Larsen, 222
Gothenburg, 112
Governance, 292, 306, 308, 309
Gran Canaria, 254
Great Britain/British, 8, 12, 21, 22, 22n4, 24, 26, 27, 27n14, 27n16, 29, 32, 37, 38, 40, 44, 47, 65n5, 66n10, 67–71, 71n22, 72n27, 73–75, 74n37, 76n48, 78, 80, 82n70, 100, 101n19, 102, 103n25, 108, 108n38, 111n49, 115, 136–140, 137n10, 142–145, 150, 152–154, 163, 164n9, 178, 200n11, 218, 233, 249, 283
The Great Depression, 93, 99, 124, 161, 199, 281
The great espionage affair (Bergen), 76
Great Lakes, 173
The Great Northern War, 37n32
Greece/Greek, 9–11, 9n8, 22, 23, 24n6, 27n14, 34n25, 36n30, 94n5, 103, 103n25, 104, 104n27, 137n10, 151, 175n32, 200, 200n9, 211, 231, 233, 237, 246, 252, 266, 267, 287
Grieg, Elisabeth, 21n1, 222, 307
Grieg, Nordahl, 21, 80
Grimstad, 14n16, 110, 113n57, 245, 263
Gross Domestic Product (GDP), 1, 118, 161–163, 161n5, 197, 197n5, 198, 305
Gross freight earnings, 27–29, 27n15, 29n17, 66n10, 80, 97, 97n16, 98, 215n29, 247n36
Gross register tonnage (grt), 7n6, 29n17, 78, 137, 148, 168, 207n18, 215n29, 217n32, 300
The Guarantee Institute, 211–213, 252, 282, 288
Gutta på skauen, 277
Götaverken, 112, 113

Index     317

H
Haakon VII, 116, 139, 141
Hague, 96
Ha Ha Bay, 32, 32n23
Halden, 110
Halifax, 31
Hambro, Carl Joachim, 134n4
Hambros Bank, 271
Hamburg, 31, 51
Hammar, Hugo, 112, 113
Hanjin, 171, 173n27
Hannevig, Christoffer, Jr., 82–85, 83n73, 96
*Hans Broge*, 64
Hanse, 34
Hansson, Herbjørn, 245, 246
*Happy Giant*, 265
Hayek, Friedrich, 151
Hesnes Shipping, 291
Highway No. 1, 275
Hinterland, 171
History, 173n26, 175, 176, 232, 249n37, 249n38, 272, 276–278, 277n3, 294, 304–306, 308, 309
Hodne, Fritz, 2n2, 44, 44n56
Hogmanay Agreement, 144
*Hohenzollern*, 66, 66n11, 67
Honduras, 105
Hong Kong, 123n76, 260, 261, 267, 272n24, 296
Hooverville, 122
*Hubris*, 209
Human Development Index, 1, 1n1
Hungary/Hungarian, 23
*Hvor seiler vi?*, 159, 189, 190
Hysing-Olsen, Ingolf, 142

Høegh, Leif, 141n20, 147, 222, 268
*Høyre* (The Conservative Party), 236

I
Ibsen, Henrik, 14, 14n16
*Ideal X*, 172
Ilboe, Fredrik W., 63, 63n1
India, 267
Indian Ocean, 240n22
Indonesia, 260n2
Industrial cluster, 270
Industrial neutrality, 286
Inflation, 70, 75, 80, 82, 98, 161n5, 164, 196, 197
Innovation, 16, 95, 166, 169–172, 174, 223, 279, 281, 291–294, 296
Institute for Shipping Research, 232
Insurance, 12n10, 16, 36, 46, 47, 53, 77–81, 81n67, 84, 96, 114, 136, 143, 145, 235, 248, 270–272, 289, 291, 295, 307
Insurance companies, 53, 269, 271, 304
International Bank for Reconstruction and Development, 164
Internationalization, 237, 268, 291
International Labour Organization (ILO), 105
International Monetary Fund, 164
International solidarity, 238
The International Tanker Owners' Association (Interntanko), 124

International trade, 5, 27, 34, 35, 39, 50, 68, 93, 94, 99, 104, 125, 166, 260, 261, 268, 283
The International Transport Workers' Federation, 237
Italy/Italian, 6, 22n3, 23, 24n5, 27n14, 78, 94n5, 111n49, 116, 139, 161n5, 197n3, 197n5, 233, 242n26, 267

J

Jahre, Anders, 119, 224, 245, 249
*Jahre Viking*, 265
Japan/Japanese, 3, 23, 24n6, 27n16, 102–104, 103n22, 103n25, 123n76, 126, 143, 163, 164, 167, 174n30, 175, 184, 184n55, 197n3, 208, 233, 260, 260n2, 261, 267, 281, 291, 298
Jarlsberg and Larvik, 13n13
Jebsen, Atle, 245
Jebsen, Kristian Gerhard, 220, 222, 245, 291, 297n20
Jobbetid, 80–86, 82n70
Johannessen, Peder, 110
*John Bowes*, 173
JO Tankers, 290, 298
*Journal of Political Economy*, 8, 50n77, 209

K

Kalmar Union, 39n42
Keilhau, Wilhelm, 76n48, 79, 79n57, 81n67
Kent, 111

Kerguelen, 242n26
Keynes, John Maynard, 119
Kiær, Anders Nikolai, 8, 22, 26, 29, 50, 50n77
King Midas, 83
King Olav V, 195
Klaveness, A.F., 115, 120, 222
Kloster, K.U., 81n65
Kloster, R., 106n33
Klovland, Jan Tore, vii, viii, 32n20
Knowledge, 16, 25, 40, 54–56, 93, 102, 114, 138, 155, 176, 188, 246, 270, 278, 281, 292, 303, 306
Knudsen, Gunnar, 14, 57, 57n98, 66, 276
Knut Knutsen OAS, 120, 246
Knutsen OAS
*Kommandittselskap*, 246, 265
Korean War, 151, 287
Kosmos, 119
*Kriegsmarine*, 138
Krigsseiler, *see* War sailor
Kristiania, *see* Oslo
*Kristianiafjord*, 116
Kristiansand, 109, 110, 113n57, 265, 268
*Kronprinz Wilhelm*, 5
Krooboys, 240, 241
Krupp, Count Gustav, 84
KS AS Polaris, 249
KS 25/4 Norsk AS, 249–250
Kværner, 222

L

Labour Party (*Arbeiderpartiet*), 149
Labour-saving technologies, 232

Laguna, 31
Land, Emery, 134n4
Larsen, Karin, 278
Larvik, 13n13
Lay up rates, 97, 121, 199, 208n20, 216
Lay-ups, 97, 121, 122
Lea, Erik Grant, 83, 85
Leadenhall Street, 140
Legal infrastructure, 49
Leith, 123
Les Trente Glorieuses, 163
Levinson, Marc, 172n23, 173n26, 196
Liberalism, 56
Liberalization, 40, 41, 164, 165, 173, 226, 279, 283n10, 284–288
Liberia, 10, 175, 208, 240, 267
Liberty-ships, 148
Licensing, 137, 149n41, 150, 226
Lillesand, 14
Limited liability companies, 53, 54, 114, 181, 181n46, 246
Limited partnerships, 246, 265, 272, 293
Liner conferences, 32, 120
Liquid Natural Gas (LNG), 174, 221, 222
Liquid Petroleum Gas (LPG), 174, 222
Lister, 13n13
Liverpool, 31
Llanelly, 32
*Lloyd's*, 7n6, 31, 31n19, 103n23, 143, 186n58, 207n18
*Lloyd's List*, 26, 29, 31n19, 32, 32n20, 51n82

Local networks, 49
London, 29, 31, 32, 32n20, 49n73, 83, 104, 110, 119, 126, 135, 136, 137n11, 139–144, 159, 231, 237, 245, 268
London Cabinet, 142
Longevity, 213, 217
Lorentzen, Hans Ludvig, 177
Lorentzen, Øyvind, 140, 142, 142n22, 177, 222
Losses of lives, 65, 78, 133, 146, 146n33, 154, 276
Losses of ships, 73n32
Lowdness, Noel, 123n74
Lund, Carl Otto, 92
*Lusitania*, 5
Luxembourg, 65, 66
Læst, 34n26
Løvlien, Emil, 150, 150–151n42
*Låneinstituttet for skipsbyggeriene*, 183


M

Madagascar, 240n22
Maddison, Angus, 161n5, 162, 197n5, 198
Maersk, 171
Major dry bulk goods, 174
Malaysia, 260n2
Mandal, 13n13
Manhattan, 143
Manufacturing, 3, 44, 56, 81n67, 85, 99, 102, 148, 164–166, 172n25, 174, 181n44, 190, 213, 239, 261, 261n3, 281, 304n30
Maranham, 31
Margate, 111
Mariehamn, 110n47

Maritime centres, 263
Maritime cluster, 11, 269–271, 289, 290, 305
Maritime culture, 48–55, 275, 277, 278, 305, 306
Maritimt Forum, 269
Marseilles, 31, 110
Marshall Aid, 164
Marshall Islands, 10
McLean, Macolm, 172
Mellanrikslagen, 39
Mexico, 27n14, 116
Michelet, Jon, 133–135, 154, 155
Michelsen, Christian, 14, 56, 276
The Middle East, 195
Miller, Michael, 67
Minde, 182
Minimum value clause, 212
Minister of Defense, 79n57, 155, 155n53
Minister of Shipping, 142
The Ministry of Finance, 143, 183
The Ministry of Petroleum and Energy, 304, 304n30
The Ministry of Provisioning, 74, 142n22
The Ministry of Trade, Industry and Fisheries, 304, 304n30
Minor dry bulk goods, 174
Mister Angus, 84
Mitsui OSK, 291
Moltzau, Ragnar, 113, 292
Moltzau's Tankrederi, 113
Montreal, 268
Moorsom measuring system, 34n26
Mortgages, 54, 112, 114, 182, 182n49, 183, 212, 266, 271, 284

Mowinckel, Johan Ludwig, 14, 78, 86, 276
Multinational, 11, 16
Multi-ship companies, 114, 115
*Mundogas Brasilia*, 177
Museums, 36, 51, 52, 110n47, 232
Møre og Romsdal, 264

N

Namibia, 237
Nansen, Fridtjof, 75
Napoleonic Wars, 37
Nash Creek, 32, 32n21
National gallery, 85
Naturalization levy, 43
Navigation Laws, 40
Navion, 268
Nazi Germany, 133, 134
Nedenes, 13n13
Net freight earnings, 215, 215n29, 247, 247n36
The Netherlands Antilles, 241n26
The Netherlands/Dutch, 11, 27n14, 36, 64, 72, 73, 75, 101, 124n77, 137, 159, 160n1, 161n5, 197n5, 233, 241n26, 271
Neutrality, 38, 64, 65, 65n7, 74, 75, 77, 79n57, 133, 136–139, 272
New Brunswick, 32, 32n21
Newbuildings, 68, 72, 150, 151
Newport, 31, 123, 124n77
Newport News, 124n77
New York, 31, 32, 51, 64, 83, 91, 104, 110, 122, 141–143, 172, 173n26, 268, 269
New York Stock Exchange, 245, 268
Niarchos, Stavros, 211

Niches, 5, 10, 25, 116, 176, 219, 221, 222, 222n42, 259, 290, 293, 298
Nippon Yushen Kaisha (NYK), 291
Noco, 249
Nopal, 142
Norden (company), 268
Nordenfjeldske, 222
Nordisk Skipsrederforening, 136
Nordland, 13n13
Nordre Bergenhus, 13n13
Nordre Trondhjem, 13n13
Norðvegr, 33
Norges Bank, 226
Norges Handels og Sjøfartstidende, 69, 69n18
Norges Rederiforbund, 36n31, 147, 148, 236, 269, 270, 304n30
Norsk Rikskringkasting, 133, 159
Norsk Sjømannsforbund, 237
Norsk Skibshypothek AS, 182
Norsk Skibs Hypothekbank AS, 182
North America, 3, 27n14, 123, 124, 173
North Atlantic, 5, 78, 260
The North Sea, 40, 64, 65, 67, 70–77, 138, 213, 224, 246n34, 247, 248, 250, 251, 253, 263, 271, 290, 301, 302
North Sea Declaration, 65, 65n5
North Sea oil, 204
Nortraship, 133, 135, 139–145, 144n26, 149, 153, 154, 231
The Nortraship-fund, 135
Nortraship's secret fund, 152
Norwegian Cruise Line, 222
Norwegian culture, 49, 52, 306
Norwegian government, 65, 126n83, 133, 135, 136, 285, 307

The Norwegian International Ship Register (NIS), 7n6, 8, 234–244, 242n26, 247, 253, 254, 265, 267, 269, 285, 288, 295, 306
Norwegian Navy, 138
The Norwegian Ordinary Register (NOR), 7n6, 238
Norwegian Research Council, 200, 201n12
Norwegian Seamen's Church, 122, 123, 160, 160n2
Norwegian Shipowner's Association, 36n31
The Norwegian Shipping and Trade Mission, *see* Nortraship
*Nydal*, 79, 84
Næss, Erling Dekke, 119, 119n66, 142, 144, 231, 232, 234, 255

O

Ocean Drilling & Exploration (Odeco), 249
Oceania, 124n77
*Ocean Viking*, 249
Odfjell, 189, 221, 222, 245, 251, 290, 298
Odfjell, Abraham, 245
Odfjell, Dan, 245
Odfjell, Fredrik, 147
Offshore oil production, 198, 224, 247
Oil consumption, 200, 204
Oil price increase, 198, 200, 201, 203, 204, 206, 207, 218, 218n36, 281
Oil products, 202n14

Oil tankers, 10, 100, 101, 103, 112, 134, 165, 174n29, 177, 205, 207n18, 218n36, 223, 225, 268, 281
Onassis, Aristotle, 211
OPEC, *see* Organization of Petroleum Exporting Countries
Open hatch bulk, 176, 220–223, 291, 293
Operating costs, 28, 37, 205
Operation Weserübung, 139
Orderbook, 206, 207n18
Organization for Economic Cooperation and Development (OECD), 7n6, 184, 184n55, 197, 197n3, 200, 233
Organization for European Economic Cooperation (OEEC), 184, 184n55
Organization of Petroleum Exporting Countries (OPEC), 203
Oslo, 12, 74, 79n57, 112, 112n51, 113, 115, 119, 120, 139, 182n49, 195, 214, 222, 232, 237, 263, 263n7, 265, 268, 268n14, 289–291, 299, 301
Oslofjord, 12, 13n13, 110, 117, 139
Oslo Radio, 139
OSM, 272n24
Ottoman Empire, 103
Outflow of tonnage, 226, 235
Outsourcing, 101, 261, 281, 293
Overcapacity, 97, 98, 121, 199, 200, 232, 250

P
Pacific, 22n3, 25, 111n49, 172n25, 260
Panama, 10, 104, 105, 148, 267
Panocean Anco, 222
Parcels, 167, 169, 174, 188, 188n65, 189
Part ownerships, 11, 11–12n10, 45, 46, 53, 114, 181, 293, 294
Partsrederi, 52
Paspébiac, 32
Path dependence, 42, 180, 209
Pearl Harbor, 143
Pensacola, 31, 51, 123
Pernambuco, 31, 51n82
Persian Gulf, 165, 225
Philadelphia, 31
Phillips Petroleum, 249
The Phoney War, 136, 137
*The Pillars of Society*, 14
Piraeus, 36n30, 104, 200n9
Poland/Polish, 139, 238
Politics, 5, 14, 70, 85, 269, 276, 278, 307
*Pommern*, 110n47
Pools, 16, 53, 123n74, 124, 170, 176, 189, 220, 291, 293, 303
Porter, Michael, 270
Port Glasgow, 110, 110n47
Portugal/Portuguese, 23–25, 27n14, 111
Prime Ministers, 14, 56, 57, 66, 86, 134n1, 137, 144, 189, 236, 236n9, 276
"The Prince of Whales," 119
Privateering, 38
Pro-British bias, 66
Procyclicality, 180

Produktplakatet, 39
Professionalization, 291–294
Profits, 15, 28, 29n18, 46, 53, 77,
　79–81, 82n70, 84, 85n81, 96,
　98, 105, 118, 145, 153, 166,
　171, 174, 179–182, 199, 204,
　205, 210, 218n34, 220, 224,
　241, 243, 246, 247, 272,
　272n25, 282, 284, 292, 293,
　295, 304, 307n34
Progress Party (Fremskrittspartiet),
　237
Protection & Indemnity (P&I)
　insurance, 271
Protectionism, 39, 94, 99
Puerto Rico, 172

Q

Quebec, 31, 123

R

Rasmussen, A. H., 49n76, 268
Rationalization, 161, 185, 238, 239,
　253
Rederi, J.L. Mowinckels, 117, 120,
　220
Regional concentration, 264
Regional differences, 10–14, 222
Reksten, Hilmar, 119, 142, 211,
　213, 224, 224–225n46, 225
Republic of Korea, *see* South Korea
Requisition, 140
Rig ownership, 250, 251
*Rio de Janeiro* (Ship), 139
Rio Grande, 31
Rio Janeiro, 31

Risk, 46, 73, 77–80, 93, 134, 152,
　177, 183, 205, 205n15, 208,
　209, 218, 221, 235, 243
Romsdal, 13n13
Roosevelt, Franklin D., 126, 134n4
Rotterdam, 159, 160, 170
Royal Caribbean Cruise Line, 222
Royal Navy (British), 139, 240n22
Royal Viking Line, 222
Rule, Britannia, 102n21
Rumania, 23, 27n14
Rum Row, 92
Russia/Russian, 11, 11n9, 22n3, 23,
　26, 27n14, 34n25, 65n5,
　67n14, 85, 99, 111n49, 126,
　146n33, 267
The Russo-Japanese War, 57, 123n76
Ryggvik Helge, 249n37, 250,
　250n41

S

Saga Forest Carriers, 291
Saga Petroleum, 249n39, 250
*Sagatind*, 91–93, 92n3, 97, 97n15,
　126–127
Sagen, Tryggve, 83
Sailing ships, 7n6, 11–14, 11n9,
　22n3, 25, 28–30, 29n18, 35,
　43, 43n54, 48, 50, 54, 78n56,
　82, 94, 101, 109–111,
　110n46, 111n49, 114,
　167n11, 171n22, 173, 263,
　275, 294n18, 302
Sailing vessels, 7n6, 10, 16, 17,
　25, 31n19, 47, 64, 108, 109,
　224
Sailors' gifts, 51

Salaries, 144, 152, 180, 236, 236n9, 237, 253
Sandefjord, 113n57, 115, 117, 224
Savannah, 31
Scandinavia, 27, 27n14, 39n43, 64, 73, 83n71, 116, 125
Scanpet, 250
Scheme Agreement, 137
Schierwater, Harry T., 124
Schjølberg, Oddvar, 154
Schreiner, Johan, 18n22, 18n23, 74n39, 86, 86n83
The Schulters Group, 272n24
Scoll, David, 144
Scotland, 33, 139
Seafarers, 2, 35, 64, 92, 134, 151–155, 160, 232, 235, 260, 276
Seafarer's unions, 234
The Second Boer War, 56
Second-hand prices, 81
Second World War, 7, 55, 97, 104n27, 105, 108, 111, 119, 124n77, 133–155, 162, 163, 166–171, 179, 185, 186, 211, 231, 260, 277, 281, 283
Seglem, Trygve, 246
Segments, 10, 12, 25, 100, 120, 166, 174, 176, 188, 188n65, 199, 202, 203, 209, 210, 213, 215n29, 219–221, 223, 242n29, 261, 266, 281, 290, 291, 298, 300
Seismic surveys, 250, 265
Sekula, Alan, 9, 9n8
Seland, Johan, 110n46, 148, 210n23
*Seneca*, 91, 126n83
Serbia, 66
Seychelles, 240n22

Shanghai, 123, 123n76, 126
Ship brokers, 36, 82, 207n18, 210, 249n38, 291, 304
Shipbuilding, 14, 38n37, 44, 94, 95, 102, 124, 125, 164, 169, 177, 183, 184, 199, 199n8, 203, 261, 284, 302
Ship financing, 212–214
Ship Mortgage International, 271
Shipping banks, 36, 243, 269, 271
Shipping companies, 2, 32, 64, 93, 145, 174, 196, 232, 260, 279
Shipping cycles, 96, 216
Shipping Directorate, 140, 238
Shipping industry associations, 234
Shipping policy, 177–179, 178n38, 236, 269, 287, 304
Shipping shares, 54, 81
Shuttle tankers, 245, 246, 252, 263, 264, 268
Sig. Bergesen d.y., 115, 249, 296
*Sinclair Petrolore*, 169, 169n17
Singapore, 260, 267, 268, 272n24
Single vessel partnerships, 15
Single-ship companies, 114, 115
Sing Sally Oh, 51n82
Sjappa, 124
Sjøloven av 1860, 46
*Skaregrøm*, 110, 110n47
Skaugen, 222
Skudeneshavn, 265
Smålenene, 13n13
Smedvig, 244, 249, 249n38, 251, 264, 268
Smith-Petersen, Morten, 14n16
Smuggling, 92, 92n3, 93, 93n4, 105
Social-democratic, 225
Socialist Left Party (Sosialistisk Venstreparti), 237

Sognefjord, 66
S.O. Stray, 110, 110n46
South Africa, 225, 225n48, 237
South America, 25, 27, 27n14, 69n18, 142
South coast, 11–14, 38, 42, 45, 95, 101, 109, 110, 112, 113, 113n57, 139, 182n49, 245, 264, 272n24
Southeast Asia, 25, 164, 239
Southern Europe, 239
South Georgia, 117, 124n77
South Korea, 260, 261
South Shetland, 117
Spanish Civil War, 126
Spain/Spanish, 23, 27n14, 36, 103n24, 116, 139, 239, 254
Specialization, 2, 32, 94, 100, 171–175, 177, 188, 218–223, 261, 279, 289–291
Specialized markets, 219, 220, 222, 281
Speculators/speculation, 69, 80, 82, 84–86, 205, 251
Spot market, 199, 199n7, 206, 207n18, 211, 213, 251
*SS Norway*, 226
*SS Warrior*, 172, 172n23
Stagflation, 196
Stanford-le-Hope, 124
Staubo, 244
Stavanger, 13n13, 25, 31, 35, 113n57, 115, 224, 249, 252, 264, 265, 268, 290, 299
Steamships, 7n6, 11n9, 13, 14, 21, 22, 22n3, 25, 28–30, 29n18, 31n19, 35, 41n47, 42, 54, 64, 94, 102, 109, 111, 125, 152, 259n1

Sterling Crisis, 150
Stettin, 31
Stock exchange, 82, 84, 181, 182, 266, 268, 268n14, 284n11, 293, 307
Stolt-Nielsen, 189, 221, 222, 298
Stopford, Martin, vii, 169, 200n10, 207n18
Strategic parameters, 204, 206
Strøm-Erichsen, Anne Grethe, 155, 155n53
Sturmey, Stanley G., 115, 178
Submarines, 63, 64, 67, 72–76, 72n28, 138, 138n12, 139, 146, 154n52
Subsea, 265
Subsidies, 45, 261
Subsidization, 184, 203
Suez Canal, 165, 204
Sunde, Arne, 142, 142n22, 153
Sunningdale, 141
Supertankers, 206, 207n18, 210, 264
Supply shipping, 250, 265, 290
Supply vessels, 224, 250, 255, 264, 265
Supreme Court, 153, 297, 297n20
Sweden-Norway, 39, 40
Sweden/Swedish, 6, 11, 11n9, 23, 26, 27n14, 39, 39n42, 40, 47, 56, 72n28, 75, 77, 84, 93, 112, 113, 124, 125, 125n79, 125n81, 137n10, 138, 161n5, 197n5, 199n8, 233, 239, 268, 277, 283, 285, 289
Switzerland, 161n5, 197n5
Syse, Jan Peder, 189
Sæther, Rolf, 265
Søndre Bergenhus, 13n13
Søndre Trondhjem, 13n13

## T

Table Bay, 31
Taiwan, 260, 267
Tanker fleet, 100, 101, 136, 201, 209, 215, 216, 245, 268, 296
Tanker share, 206, 207n18
Tanker shipping, 100, 112, 121, 173, 175, 208, 209, 292
Tante Klara (Klara Breivik), 123, 123n74
Tax reform, 272
Tax system, 177, 180, 208, 210, 272, 272n25, 297
Technological improvement, 16, 106, 166, 168
Technological innovation, 223, 293
Technological revolution, 171–175
Teekay, 268
Telegram, 16, 66, 79n58, 108n37, 140n17
Terminals, 124, 160, 169n17, 170, 171n22, 221, 222
Thailand, 260n2
*Theogennitor*, 252
Third-country shipping, 37
Thome, 272n24
Thor Dahl, 248
Thoresen, 97n14, 116
*Thorshøvdi*, 248
*Titanic*, 5
Tonnage agreement (1917), 74, 78, 137n10
Tonnage *per capita*, 8, 22n3
*Torrey Canyon*, 169n17
Traditions, 5, 15, 42, 46, 48, 209, 217, 232, 237, 240, 245, 250, 277, 290, 304, 305
Tramp trade, 5, 115, 116

Trapani, 31
Treasury, 143, 200
Tromsø, 13n13
T2-tankers, 148
Turbine tankers, 205, 206, 207n18, 207n19
Tønsberg, 25, 35, 113n57, 115, 117, 263
Tønsberg Bar, 160, 254

## U

Ugland, 222, 245
Ugland Nordic Shiping, 268
Ulltveit Moe, Jens, 246
Ultra Large Crude Carriers (ULCC), 210
Understanding on Export Credits, 184
Unemployment, 105, 106, 121, 164, 196, 197, 253
Union with Denmark, 39n42
Union with Sweden, 39
United Fruit Company, 105
United Maritime Authority (UMA), 147
United Nations Development Programme (UNDP), 1, 1n1
The United States/American, 9, 21, 22, 22n3, 25, 27, 28, 32, 34n25, 40, 45, 63, 66, 67, 67n14, 72, 75, 78, 83, 91, 92, 94–96, 94n5, 99, 100, 102, 103n25, 104, 105, 107, 107n33, 120, 122, 124n77, 126, 126n83, 140, 142–144, 147, 148, 148n37, 152, 163, 170, 172, 200, 205n15, 221,

231, 237, 249, 261, 266, 267, 296, 298
Unrestricted submarine warfare, 64, 74, 78
Urbanization, 17
US Coast Guard, 91, 92
US Congress, 25, 45, 126
Uteseilere, 160

V
*Vaderland*, 170
Vancouver, 123n74, 268
*Vaterland*, 5
Vera Cruz, 31
*Verdens Gang*, 134, 134n1, 236n9
Vertical integration, 222
Vestfold, 118, 272n24
V.Group, 272n24
*Vikingen*, 105
Vikings, 33, 49, 50n77
Vikøren, David, 178, 235
Virginia, 124n77
von Gerich, Walter Harald, 76
von Rautenfels, Baron, 76, 77

W
Waage, Hagbart, 213
Waaler, Per, 220, 222
Wallem, 272n24
Wallenius Wilhelmsen Logistics, 298
*Wanderjahre*, 50, 120
War insurance, 77, 136, 182
The War Insurance Fund, 136
War losses, 77–80, 109, 146n33, 150

Wars, 36, 63–89, 93–100, 133, 161, 214, 265, 276
War sailor, 134, 134n1, 135, 151–155, 154n52, 155n53, 276, 277
The Warzaw Pact, 163n7
Westfal-Larsen, 120, 189, 220, 222, 244
West Indies, 27n14
West of Norway, 13
Weston, William, 144
Whale oil, 118
Whaling, 13n13, 48, 81n67, 117–119, 181
Wilh, Wilhelmsen, 115, 117, 120, 298
Wilhelm II, Kaiser, 66
Wilhelmsen, Anders, 222, 298
Wilhelmshafen, 67
Willoch, Kåre, 236, 236n9
*Wirtschaftswunder*, 163
"Worst case" scenario, 201
Wuhu, 32, 32n23

Z
Zanzibar, 240n22
Zarate, 32, 32n23
Zurich, 183

Ø
*Ørkenen Sur*, 122
Østre Toten, 190

Å
Åland, 110, 110n47
Ålesund, 265

The manufacturer's authorised representative in the EU is Springer Nature Customer Service Centre GmbH, Europaplatz 3, 69115 Heidelberg, Germany. If you have any concerns regarding our products, please contact ProductSafety@springernature.com

Printed and bound by CPI Group (UK) Ltd, Croydon, CR0 4YY
23/03/2026
02076667-0008